COMMON CORE MATHEMATICS

A Story of Functions

Algebra I, Module 3: Linear and Exponential Functions

COMMON CORE™ *consider the source*

JB JOSSEY-BASS™
A Wiley Brand

Cover design by Chris Clary

Published by Jossey-Bass
A Wiley Brand
One Montgomery Street, Suite 1200, San Francisco, CA 94104-4594—www.josseybass.com

ISBN: 978-1-118-81114-6

Printed in the United States of America
FIRST EDITION
PB Printing   10 9 8 7 6 5 4 3 2 1

WELCOME

Dear Teacher,

Thank you for your interest in Common Core's curriculum in mathematics. Common Core is a non-profit organization based in Washington, DC dedicated to helping K-12 public schoolteachers use the power of high-quality content to improve instruction.[1] We are led by a board of master teachers, scholars, and current and former school, district, and state education leaders. Common Core has responded to the Common Core State Standards' (CCSS) call for "content-rich curriculum"[2] by creating new, CCSS-based curriculum materials in mathematics, English Language Arts, history, and (soon) the arts. All of our materials are written by teachers who are among the nation's foremost experts on the new standards.

In 2012 Common Core won three contracts from the New York State Education Department to create a PreKindergarten–12th grade mathematics curriculum for the teachers of that state, and to conduct associated professional development. The book you hold contains a portion of that work. In order to respond to demand in New York and elsewhere, modules of the curriculum will continue to be published, on a rolling basis, as they are completed. This curriculum is based on New York's version of the CCSS (the CCLS, or Common Core Learning Standards). Common Core will be releasing an enhanced version of the curriculum this summer on our website, commoncore.org. That version also will be published by Jossey-Bass, a Wiley brand.

Common Core's curriculum materials are not merely aligned to the new standards, they take the CCSS as their very foundation. Our work in math takes its shape from the expectations embedded in the new standards— including the instructional shifts and mathematical progressions, and the new expectations for student fluency, deep conceptual understanding, and application to real-life context. Similarly, our ELA and history curricula are deeply informed by the CCSS's new emphasis on close reading, increased use of informational text, and evidence-based writing.

Our curriculum is distinguished not only by its adherence to the CCSS. The math curriculum is based on a theory of teaching math that is proven to work. That theory posits that mathematical knowledge is most coherently and

---

1. Despite the coincidence of name, Common Core and the Common Core State Standards are not affiliated. Common Core was established in 2007, prior to the start of the Common Core State Standards Initiative, which was led by the National Governors Association and the Council for Chief State School Officers.
2. *Common Core State Standards for English Language Arts & Literacy in History/Social Studies, Science, and Technical Subjects* (Washington, DC: Common Core State Standards Initiative), 6.

effectively conveyed when it is taught in a sequence that follows the "story" of mathematics itself. This is why we call the elementary portion of this curriculum "A Story of Units," to be followed by "A Story of Ratios" in middle school, and "A Story of Functions" in high school. Mathematical concepts flow logically, from one to the next, in this curriculum. The sequencing has been joined with methods of instruction that have been proven to work, in this nation and abroad. These methods drive student understanding beyond process, to deep mastery of mathematical concepts. The goal of the curriculum is to produce students who are not merely literate, but fluent, in mathematics.

It is important to note that, as extensive as these curriculum materials are, they are not meant to be prescriptive. Rather, they are intended to provide a basis for teachers to hone their own craft through study, collaboration, training, and the application of their own expertise as professionals. At Common Core we believe deeply in the ability of teachers and in their central and irreplaceable role in shaping the classroom experience. We strive only to support and facilitate their important work.

The teachers and scholars who wrote these materials are listed beginning on the next page. Their deep knowledge of mathematics, of the CCSS, and of what works in classrooms defined this work in every respect. I would like to thank Louisiana State University professor of mathematics Scott Baldridge for the intellectual leadership he provides to this project. Teacher and trainer Jill Diniz, who is the lead writer for grades 6–12, has brought extraordinary intelligence and judgment to this work. Jill's ability to thrive in situations in which others would be lucky just to persevere, is uncommon.

Finally, this work owes a debt to project director Nell McAnelly that is so deep I'm confident it never can be repaid. Nell, who leads LSU's Gordon A. Cain Center for STEM Literacy, oversees all aspects of our work for NYSED. She has spent days, nights, weekends, and many cancelled vacations toiling in her efforts to make it possible for this talented group of teacher-writers to produce their best work against impossible deadlines. I'm confident that in the years to come Scott, Robin, and Nell will be among those who will deserve to be credited with putting math instruction in our nation back on track.

Thank you for taking an interest in our work. Please join us at www.commoncore.org.

Lynne Munson
President and Executive Director
Common Core
Washington, DC
October 25, 2013

Common Core's 6-12 Math Staff

Scott Baldridge, Lead Mathematician and Writer
Robin Ramos, Lead Writer, PreKindergarten–5
Ben McCarty, Mathematician

Nell McAnelly, Project Director
Tiah Alphonso, Associate Director
Jennifer Loftin, Associate Director
Catriona Anderson, Curriculum Manager,
    PreKindergarten–5
Jill Diniz, Lead Writer, 9-11 and Curriculum
    Manager

Sixth Grade

Erika Silva, Lead
Debby Grawn
Glenn Gebhard
Krysta Gibbs

Sixth and Seventh Grade

Anne Netter, Lead
Beau Bailey
Saki Milton
Hester Sutton
David Wright
Korinna Sanchez

Seventh Grade

Julie Wortmann, Lead
Joanne Choi
Lori Fanning
Bonnie Hart

Eighth Grade

Stefanie Hassan, Lead
Winnie Gilbert
Sunil Koswatta, Mathematician

Ninth Grade

Miki Alkire
Chris Bejar
Carlos Carrera
Melvin Damaolao
Joe Ferrantelli
Jenny Kim
Athena Leonardo

Rob Michelin
Noam Pillischer
Alex Sczesnak

Tenth Grade

Pia Mohsen, Lead
Bonnie Bergstresser
Ellen Fort
Terrie Poehl

Ninth, Tenth, and Eleventh Grade

Kevin Bluount
Wendy DenBesten
Abe Frankel
Thomas Gaffey
Kay Gleenblatt
Sheri Goings
Pam Goodner
Selena Oswalt
William Rorison
Chris Murcko
Surinder Sandhu
Pam Walker
Darrick Wood

Statistics

Henry Kranendonk, Lead
Michael Allwood
Gail Burrill
Beth Chance
Brian Kotz
Kathy Kritz
Patrick Hopsfensperger
Jerry Moren
Shannon Vinson

Document Management Team

Kristen Zimmerman

Advisors

Richard Askey
Roger Howe
James Madden
Roxy Peck
James Tanton

Mathematics Curriculum

Table of Contents[1]

Linear and Exponential Functions

---

[1] Each lesson is ONE day, and ONE day is considered a 45 minute period.

	Module 3:	Linear and Exponential Functions	1
	Date:	9/12/13	

Algebra I • Module 3

Linear and Exponential Functions

OVERVIEW

In earlier grades, students define, evaluate, and compare functions and use them to model relationships between quantities (**8.F.A.1**, **8.F.A.2**, **8.F.A.3**, **8.F.B.4**, **8.F.B.5**). In this module, students extend their study of functions to include function notation and the concepts of domain and range. They explore many examples of functions and their graphs, focusing on the contrast between linear and exponential functions. They interpret functions given graphically, numerically, symbolically, and verbally; translate between representations; and understand the limitations of various representations.

In Topic A, students explore arithmetic and geometric sequences as an introduction to the formal notation of functions (**F-IF.A.1**, **F-IF.A.2**). They interpret arithmetic sequences as linear functions with integer domains and geometric sequences as exponential functions with integer domains (**F-IF.A.3**, **F-BF.A.1a**). Students compare and contrast the rates of change of linear and exponential functions, looking for structure in each and distinguishing between additive and multiplicative change (**F-IF.B.6**, **F-LE.A.1**, **F-LE.A.2**, **F-LE.A.3**).

In Topic B, students connect their understanding of functions to their knowledge of graphing from Grade 8. They learn the formal definition of a function and how to recognize, evaluate, and interpret functions in abstract and contextual situations (**F-IF.A.1**, **F-IF.A.2**). Students examine the graphs of a variety of functions and learn to interpret those graphs using precise terminology to describe such key features as domain and range, intercepts, intervals where function is increasing or decreasing, and intervals where the function is positive or negative. (**F-IF.A.1**, **F-IF.B.4**, **F-IF.B.5**, **F-IF.C.7a**).

In Topic C, students extend their understanding of piecewise functions and their graphs including the absolute value and step functions. They learn a graphical approach to circumventing complex algebraic solutions to equations in one variable, seeing them as $f(x) = g(x)$ and recognizing that the intersection of the graphs of $f(x)$ and $g(x)$ are solutions to the original equation (**A-REI.D.11**). Students use the absolute value function and other piecewise functions to investigate transformations of functions and draw formal conclusions about the effects of a transformation on the function's graph (**F-IF.C.7**, **F-BF.B.3**).

Finally, in Topic D students apply and reinforce the concepts of the module as they examine and compare exponential, piecewise, and step functions in a real-world context (**F-IF.C.9**). They create equations and functions to model situations (**A-CED.A.1**, **F-BF.A.1**, **F-LE.A.2**), rewrite exponential expressions to reveal and relate elements of an expression to the context of the problem (**A-SSE.B.3c**, **F-LE.B.5**), and examine the key features of graphs of functions, relating those features to the context of the problem (**F-IF.B.4**, **F-IF.B.6**).

The Mid-Module Assessment follows Topic B. The End-of-Module Assessment follows Topic D.

Focus Standards

Write expressions in equivalent forms to solve problems.

A-SSE.B.3 Choose and produce an equivalent form of an expression to reveal and explain properties of the quantity represented by the expression.*

    c.   Use the properties of exponents to transform expressions for exponential functions. *For example the expression 1.15^t can be rewritten as $(1.15^{1/12})^{12t} \approx 1.012^{12t}$ to reveal the approximate equivalent monthly interest rate if the annual rate is 15%.*[2]

Create equations that describe numbers or relationships.

A-CED.A.1[3] Create equations and inequalities in one variable and use them to solve problems. *Include equations arising from linear and quadratic functions, and simple rational and exponential functions.**

Represent and solve equations and inequalities graphically.

A-REI.D.11[4] Explain why the *x*-coordinates of the points where the graphs of the equations $y = f(x)$ and $y = g(x)$ intersect are the solutions of the equation $f(x) = g(x)$; find the solutions approximately, e.g., using technology to graph the functions, make tables of values, or find successive approximations. Include cases where $f(x)$ and/or $g(x)$ are linear, polynomial, rational, absolute value, exponential, and logarithmic functions.*

Understand the concept of a function and use function notation.

F-IF.A.1 Understand that a function from one set (called the domain) to another set (called the range) assigns to each element of the domain exactly one element of the range. If *f* is a function and *x* is an element of its domain, then $f(x)$ denotes the output of *f* corresponding to the input *x*. The graph of *f* is the graph of the equation $y = f(x)$.

F-IF.A.2 Use function notation, evaluate functions for inputs in their domains, and interpret statements that use function notation in terms of a context.

F-IF.A.3[5] Recognize that sequences are functions, sometimes defined recursively, whose domain is a subset of the integers. *For example, the Fibonacci sequence is defined recursively by $f(0) = f(1) = 1$, $f(n+1) = f(n) + f(n-1)$ for $n \geq 1$.*

---

[2] Tasks have a real-world context. As described in the standard, there is an interplay between the mathematical structure of the expression and the structure of the situation such that choosing and producing an equivalent form of the expression reveals something about the situation. In Algebra I, tasks are limited to exponential expressions with integer exponents.

[3] In Algebra I, tasks are limited to linear, quadratic, or exponential equations with integer exponents.

[4] In Algebra I, tasks that assess conceptual understanding of the indicated concept may involve any of the function types mentioned in the standard except exponential and logarithmic functions. Finding the solutions approximately is limited to cases where $f(x)$ and $g(x)$ are polynomial functions.

[5] This standard is part of the Major Content in Algebra I and will be assessed accordingly.

	Module 3:	Linear and Exponential Functions
	Date:	9/12/13

4

Interpret functions that arise in applications in terms of the context.

F-IF.B.4[6]   For a function that models a relationship between two quantities, interpret key features of graphs and tables in terms of the quantities, and sketch graphs showing key features given a verbal description of the relationship. *Key features include: intercepts; intervals where the function is increasing, decreasing, positive, or negative; relative maximums and minimums; symmetries; end behavior; and periodicity.*[*]

F-IF.B.5   Relate the domain of a function to its graph and, where applicable, to the quantitative relationship it describes. *For example, if the function h(n) gives the number of person-hours it takes to assemble n engines in a factory, then the positive integers would be an appropriate domain for the function.*[*]

F-IF.B.6[7]   Calculate and interpret the average rate of change of a function (presented symbolically or as a table) over a specified interval. Estimate the rate of change from a graph.[*]

Analyze functions using different representations.

F-IF.C.7   Graph functions expressed symbolically and show key features of the graph, by hand in simple cases and using technology for more complicated cases.[*]

    a.   Graph linear and quadratic functions and show intercepts, maxima, and minima.

F-IF.C.9[8]   Compare properties of two functions each represented in a different way (algebraically, graphically, numerically in tables, or by verbal descriptions). *For example, given a graph of one quadratic function and an algebraic expression for another, say which has the larger maximum.*

Build a function that models a relationship between two quantities.

F-BF.A.1[9]   Write a function that describes a relationship between two quantities.[*]

    a.   Determine an explicit expression, a recursive process, or steps for calculation from a context.

---

[6] Tasks have a real-world context. In Algebra I, tasks are limited to linear functions, quadratic functions, square-root functions, cube-root functions, piecewise functions (including step functions and absolute-value functions), and exponential functions with domains in the integers.

[7] Tasks have a real-world context. In Algebra I, tasks are limited to linear functions, quadratic functions, square-root functions, cube-root functions, piecewise functions (including step functions and absolute-value functions), and exponential functions with domains in the integers.

[8] In Algebra I, tasks are limited to linear functions, quadratic functions, square-root functions, cube-root functions, piecewise functions (including step functions and absolute-value functions), and exponential functions with domains in the integers. The focus in this module is on linear and exponential functions.

[9] Tasks have a real-world context. In Algebra I, tasks are limited to linear functions, quadratic functions, and exponential functions with domains in the integers.

Build new functions from existing functions.

F-BF.B.3[10] Identify the effect on the graph of replacing $f(x)$ by $f(x) + k$, $k\,f(x)$, $f(kx)$, and $f(x + k)$ for specific values of k (both positive and negative); find the value of k given the graphs. Experiment with cases and illustrate an explanation of the effects on the graph using technology. *Include recognizing even and odd functions from their graphs and algebraic expressions for them.*

Construct and compare linear, quadratic, and exponential models and solve problems.

F-LE.A.1 Distinguish between situations that can be modeled with linear functions and with exponential functions.*

    a. Prove that linear functions grow by equal differences over equal intervals, and that exponential functions grow by equal factors over equal intervals.

    b. Recognize situations in which one quantity changes at a constant rate per unit interval relative to another.

    c. Recognize situations in which a quantity grows or decays by a constant percent rate per unit interval relative to another.

F-LE.A.2[11] Construct linear and exponential functions, including arithmetic and geometric sequences, given a graph, a description of a relationship, or two input-output pairs (include reading these from a table).*

F-LE.A.3 Observe using graphs and tables that a quantity increasing exponentially eventually exceeds a quantity increasing linearly, quadratically, or (more generally) as a polynomial function.*

Interpret expressions for functions in terms of the situation they model.

F-LE.B.5[12] Interpret the parameters in a linear or exponential function in terms of a context.*

Foundational Standards

Work with radicals and integer exponents.

8.EE.A.1 Know and apply the properties of integer exponents to generate equivalent numerical expressions. *For example, $3^2 \times 3^{-5} = 3^{-3} = 1/3^3 = 1/27$.*

---

[10] In Algebra I, identifying the effect on the graph of replacing $f(x)$ by $f(x) + k$, $k\,f(x)$, $f(kx)$, and $f(x+k)$ for specific values of k (both positive and negative) is limited to linear and quadratic functions. Experimenting with cases and illustrating an explanation of the effects on the graph using technology is limited to linear functions, quadratic functions, square-root functions, cube-root functions, piecewise functions (including step functions and absolute-value functions), and exponential functions with domains in the integers. Tasks do not involve recognizing even and odd functions. The focus in this module is on linear and exponential functions.
[11] In Algebra I, tasks are limited to constructing linear and exponential functions in simple (e.g., not multi-step) context.
[12] Tasks have a real-world context. In Algebra I, exponential functions are limited to those with domains in the integers.

Module 3:	Linear and Exponential Functions
Date:	9/12/13

8.EE.A.2   Use square root and cube root symbols to represent solutions to equations of the form $x^2 = p$ and $x^3 = p$, where p is a positive rational number. Evaluate square roots of small perfect squares and cube roots of small perfect cubes. Know that $\sqrt{2}$ is irrational.

Define, evaluate, and compare functions.

8.F.A.1   Understand that a function is a rule that assigns to each input exactly one output. The graph of a function is the set of ordered pairs consisting of an input and the corresponding output.[13]

8.F.A.2   Compare properties of two functions each represented in a different way (algebraically, graphically, numerically in tables, or by verbal descriptions). *For example, given a linear function represented by a table of values and a linear function represented by an algebraic expression, determine which function has the greater rate of change.*

8.F.A.3   Interpret the equation $y = mx + b$ as defining a linear function, whose graph is a straight line; give examples of functions that are not linear. *For example, the function $A = s^2$ giving the area of a square as a function of its side length is not linear because its graph contains the points (1,1), (2,4) and (3,9), which are not on a straight line.*

Use functions to model relationships between quantities.

8.F.B.4   Construct a function to model a linear relationship between two quantities. Determine the rate of change and initial value of the function from a description of a relationship or from two *(x, y)* values, including reading these from a table or from a graph. Interpret the rate of change and initial value of a linear function in terms of the situation it models, and in terms of its graph or a table of values.

8.F.B.5   Describe qualitatively the functional relationship between two quantities by analyzing a graph (e.g., where the function is increasing or decreasing, linear or nonlinear). Sketch a graph that exhibits the qualitative features of a function that has been described verbally.

Reason quantitatively and use units to solve problems.

N-Q.A.1   Use units as a way to understand problems and to guide the solution of multi-step problems; choose and interpret units consistently in formulas; choose and interpret the scale and the origin in graphs and data displays.

N-Q.A.2[14]   Define appropriate quantities for the purpose of descriptive modeling.

N-Q.A.3   Choose a level of accuracy appropriate to limitations on measurement when reporting quantities.

---

[13] Function notation is not required in Grade 8.
[14] This standard will be assessed in Algebra I by ensuring that some modeling tasks (involving Algebra I content or securely held content from Grades 6-8) require the student to create a quantity of interest in the situation being described.

	Module 3:	Linear and Exponential Functions	
	Date:	9/12/13	7

Interpret the structure of expressions.

A-SSE.A.1 Interpret expressions that represent a quantity in terms of its context.★

    a. Interpret parts of an expression, such as terms, factors, and coefficients.

    b. Interpret complicated expressions by viewing one or more of their parts as a single entity. *For example, interpret $P(1+r)^n$ as the product of P and a factor not depending on P.*

A-SSE.A.2 Use the structure of an expression to identify ways to rewrite it. *For example, see $x^4 - y^4$ as $(x^2)^2 - (y^2)^2$, thus recognizing it as a difference of squares that can be factored as $(x^2 - y^2)(x^2 + y^2)$.*

Create equations that describe numbers or relationships.

A-CED.A.2 Create equations in two or more variables to represent relationships between quantities; graph equations on coordinate axes with labels and scales.★

A-CED.A.3 Represent constraints by equations or inequalities, and by systems of equations and/or inequalities, and interpret solutions as viable or non-viable options in a modeling context. *For example, represent inequalities describing nutritional and cost constraints on combinations of different foods.*★

A-CED.A.4 Rearrange formulas to highlight a quantity of interest, using the same reasoning as in solving equations. *For example, rearrange Ohm's law V = IR to highlight resistance R.*★

Understand solving equations as a process of reasoning and explain the reasoning.

A-REI.A.1 Explain each step in solving a simple equation as following from the equality of numbers asserted at the previous step, starting from the assumption that the original equation has a solution. Construct a viable argument to justify a solution method.

Solve equations and inequalities in one variable.

A-REI.B.3 Solve linear equations and inequalities in one variable, including equations with coefficients represented by letters.

Solve systems of equations.

A-REI.C.6[15] Solve systems of linear equations exactly and approximately (e.g., with graphs), focusing on pairs of linear equations in two variables.

Represent and solve equations and inequalities graphically.

A-REI.D.10 Understand that the graph of an equation in two variables is the set of all its solutions plotted in the coordinate plane, often forming a curve (which could be a line).

---

[15] Tasks have a real-world context. In Algebra I, tasks have hallmarks of modeling as a mathematical practice (e.gi.e., less-defined tasks, more of the modeling cycle, etc.).

	Module 3:	Linear and Exponential Functions
	Date:	9/12/13

Focus Standards for Mathematical Practice

MP.1 **Make sense of problems and persevere in solving them.** Students are presented with problems that require them to try special cases and simpler forms of the original problem to gain insight into the problem.

MP.2 **Reason abstractly and quantitatively.** Students analyze graphs of non-constant rate measurements and apply reason (from the shape of the graphs) to infer the quantities being displayed and consider possible units to represent those quantities.

MP.4 **Model with mathematics.** Students have numerous opportunities to solve problems that arise in everyday life, society, and the workplace (e.g., modeling bacteria growth, and understanding the federal progressive income tax system).

MP.7 **Look for and make use of structure.** Students reason with and analyze collections of equivalent expressions to see how they are linked through the properties of operations. They discern patterns in sequences of solving equation problems that reveal structures in the equations themselves. (e.g., $2x + 4 = 10$, $2(x - 3) + 4 = 10$, $2(3x - 4) + 4 = 10$)

MP.8 **Look for and express regularity in repeated reasoning.** After solving many linear equations in one variable (e.g., $3x + 5 = 8x - 17$), students look for general methods for solving a generic linear equation in one variable by replacing the numbers with letters ($e.g., ax + b = cx + d$). They pay close attention to calculations involving the properties of operations, properties of equality, and properties of inequalities, to find equivalent expressions and solve equations, while recognizing common ways to solve different types of equations.

Terminology

New or Recently Introduced Terms

- **Function** (A *function* is a correspondence between two sets, X and Y, in which each element of X is matched[16] to one and only one element of Y. The set X is called the *domain*; the set Y is called the *range*.)
- **Domain** (Refer to the definition of *function*.)
- **Range** (Refer to the definition of *function*.)
- **Linear Function** (A *linear function* is a polynomial function of degree 1.)
- **Average Rate of Change** (Given a function f whose domain includes the closed interval of real numbers $[a, b]$ and whose range is a subset of the real numbers, the *average rate of change on the interval* $[a, b]$ is $\frac{f(b)-f(a)}{b-a}$.)
- **Piecewise Linear Function** (Given non-overlapping intervals on the real number line, a (real) *piecewise linear function* is a function from the union of the intervals to the set of real numbers such that the function is defined by (possibly different) linear functions on each interval.)

---

[16] "Matched" can be replaced with "assigned" after students understand that each element of x is matched to exactly one element of y.

Familiar Terms and Symbols[17]

- Numerical Symbol
- Variable Symbol
- Constant
- Numerical Expression
- Algebraic Expression
- Number Sentence
- Truth Values of a Number Sentence
- Equation
- Solution
- Solution Set
- Simple Expression
- Factored Expression
- Equivalent Expressions
- Polynomial Expression
- Equivalent Polynomial Expressions
- Monomial
- Coefficient of a Monomial
- Terms of a Polynomial

Suggested Tools and Representations

- Coordinate Plane
- Equations and Inequalities
- Graphing Calculator

---

[17] These are terms and symbols students have seen previously.

Assessment Summary

Assessment Type	Administered	Format	Standards Addressed
Mid-Module Assessment Task	After Topic B	Constructed response with rubric	F-IF.A.1, F-IF.A.2, F-IF.A.3, F-IF.B.4, F-IF.B.5, F-IF.B.6, F-IF.C.7a, F-BF.A.1a, F-LE.A.1, F-LE.A.2, F-LE.A.3
End-of-Module Assessment Task	After Topic D	Constructed response with rubric	A-CED.A.1, A-REI.D.11, A-SSE.B.3c, F-IF.A.1, F-IF.A.2, F-IF.A.3, F-IF.B.4, F-IF.B.6, F-IF.C.7a, F-IF.C.9, F-BF.A.1a, F-BF.B.3, F-LE.A.1, F-LE.A.2, F-LE.A.3, F-LE.B.5

Mathematics Curriculum

Topic A:

Linear and Exponential Sequences

F-IF.A.1, F-IF.A.2, F-IF.A.3, F-IF.B.6, F-BF.A.1a, F-LE.A.1, F-LE.A.2, F-LE.A.3

Focus Standard:	F-IF.A.1	Understand that a function from one set (called the domain) to another set (called the range) assigns to each element of the domain exactly one element of the range. If f is a function and x is an element of its domain, then $f(x)$ denotes the output of f corresponding to the input x. The graph of f is the graph of the equation $y = f(x)$.
	F-IF.A.2	Use function notation, evaluate functions for inputs in their domains, and interpret statements that use function notation in terms of a context.
	F-IF.A.3	Recognize that sequences are functions, sometimes defined recursively, whose domain is a subset of the integers. *For example, the Fibonacci sequence is defined recursively by* $f(0) = f(1) = 1, f(n + 1) = f(n) + f(n-1)$ *for* $n \geq 1$.
	F-IF.B.6	Calculate and interpret the average rate of change of a function (presented symbolically or as a table) over a specified interval. Estimate the rate of change from a graph.★
	F-BF.A.1a	Write a function that describes a relationship between two quantities.★
		a. Determine an explicit expression, a recursive process, or steps for calculation from a context.
	F-LE.A.1	Distinguish between situations that can be modeled with linear functions and with exponential functions.★
		a. Prove that linear functions grow by equal differences over equal intervals, and that exponential functions grow by equal factors over equal intervals.
		b. Recognize situations in which one quantity changes at a constant rate per unit interval relative to another.
		c. Recognize situations in which a quantity grows or decays by a constant percent rate per unit interval relative to another.
	F-LE.A.2	Construct linear and exponential functions, including arithmetic and geometric sequences, given a graph, a description of a relationship, or two input-output pairs (include reading these from a table).★

	F-LE.A.3	Observe using graphs and tables that a quantity increasing exponentially eventually exceeds a quantity increasing linearly, quadratically, or (more generally) as a polynomial function.*
Instructional Days:	7	
	Lesson 1:	Integer Sequences—Should You Believe in Patterns?
	Lesson 2:	Recursive Formulas for Sequences
	Lesson 3:	Arithmetic and Geometric Sequences
	Lesson 4:	Why Do Banks Pay YOU to Provide Their Services?
	Lesson 5:	The Power of Exponential Growth
	Lesson 6:	Exponential Growth—U.S. Population and World Population
	Lesson 7:	Exponential Decay

In Lesson 1 of Topic A, students challenge the idea that patterns can be defined by merely seeing the first few numbers of the pattern. They learn that a sequence is an ordered list of elements, and that it is sometimes intuitive to number the elements in a sequence beginning with 0 rather than 1. In Lessons 2 and 3, students learn to define sequences explicitly and recursively and begin their study of arithmetic and geometric sequences that continues through Lessons 4–7 as students explore applications of geometric sequences. In the final lesson, students compare arithmetic and geometric sequences as they compare growth rates.

Throughout this topic, students use the notation of functions without naming it as such—they come to understand $f(n)$ as a "formula for the nth term of a sequence," expanding to use other letters such as $A(n)$ for Aliki's sequence and $B(n)$ for Ben's sequence. Their use of this same notation for functions will be developed in Topic B.

Lesson 1: Integer Sequences—Should You Believe in Patterns?

Student Outcomes

- Students examine sequences and are introduced to the notation used to describe them.

Lesson Notes

A sequence in high school is simply a function whose domain is the positive integers. This definition will be given later in the module (after functions have been defined). In this first lesson, we are setting the stage for an in–depth study of sequences by allowing students to become acquainted with the notation. For now, we will use the description: A *sequence* can be thought of as an ordered list of elements. The elements of the list are called the *terms of the sequence.*

For example, (P, O, O, L) is a sequence that is different than (L, O, O, P). Usually the terms are *indexed* (and therefore ordered) by a subscript starting at 1: $a_1, a_2, a_3, a_4, \dots$. The "…" symbol indicates that the pattern described is regular; that is, the next term is a_5, the next is a_6, and so on. In the first example, a_1 = 'P' is the first term, a_2 = 'O' is the second term, and so on. Infinite sequences exist everywhere in mathematics. For example, the infinite decimal expansion of $\frac{1}{3}$ = 0.333333333… can be thought of as being represented by the sequence 0.3, 0.33, 0.333, 0.3333, …. Sequences (and series) are an important part of studying calculus.

In general, a sequence is defined by a function f from a domain of positive integers to a range of numbers that can be either integers or real numbers (depending on the context) or other non-mathematical objects that satisfies the equation $f(n) = a_n$. When that function is expressed as an algebraic function only in terms of numbers and the index variable n, then the function is called the *explicit form of the sequence (or explicit formula)*. For example, the function $f: \mathbb{N} \longrightarrow \mathbb{Z}$, which satisfies $f(n) = 3^n$ for all positive integers n, is the explicit form for the sequence $3, 9, 27, 81, \dots$.

Important: Sequences can be indexed by starting with any integer. For example, the sequence $3, 9, 27, 81, 343, \dots$ can be indexed by $a_4 = 3, a_5 = 9, a_6 = 27, \dots$ by stating the explicit formula as $f(n) = 3^{n-3}$ for $n \geq 4$. This can create real confusion for students about what the "fifth term in the sequence" is: In the list, the 5th term is 343, but by the formula, the 5th term could mean $a_5 = f(5) = 9$. To avoid such confusion, in this module **we adopt the convention that indeces start at 1**. That way the first term in the list is always $f(1)$ or a_1, and there is no confusion about what the 100th term is. Students are, however, exposed to the idea that the index can start at a number other than 1. The lessons in this topic also offer suggestions about when to use $f(n)$ and when to use a_n.

Classwork

Opening Exercise (5 minutes)

After reading through the task, ask students to discuss part (a) with a partner; then share responses as a class. Next, have students answer parts (b) and (c) in pairs before discussing as a class.

- Because the task provides no structure, all of these answers must be considered correct. Without any structure, continuing the pattern is simply speculation—a guessing game.

- Because there are infinitely many ways to continue a sequence, the sequence needs to provide enough structure to define, say, the 5th, 10th, and 100th terms.

- A sequence can be thought of as an ordered list of elements. If you believe a sequence of numbers is following some structure or pattern, then it would be nice to have a formula for it.

> *Scaffolding:*
> Challenge early finishers to come up with other possible patterns for this sequence.

Opening Exercise

Mrs. Rosenblatt gave her students what she thought was a very simple task:

What is the next number in the sequence 2, 4, 6, 8, …?

Cody: I am thinking of a "plus 2 pattern," so it continues 10, 12, 14, 16, ….

Ali: I am thinking a repeating pattern, so it continues 2, 4, 6, 8, 2, 4, 6, 8, ….

Suri: I am thinking of the units digits in the multiples of two, so it continues 2, 4, 6, 8, 0, 2, 4, 6, 8, ….

1. Are each of these valid responses?

   Each response must be considered valid because each one follows a pattern.

2. What is the hundredth number in the sequence in Cody's scenario? Ali's? Suri's?

   Cody: 200   Ali: 8   Suri: 0

3. What is an expression in terms of n for the nth number in the sequence in Cody's scenario?

   $2n$ is one example. Note: Another student response might be $2(n + 1)$ if the student starts with $n = 0$ (see Example 1).

Example 1 (5 minutes)

The focus of this example should be on the discussion of whether to start the sequence with $n = 0$ or $n = 1$, a concept that can be very challenging for students. Allow students a few minutes to consider the example independently before discussing the example as a class.

The main point of this example: Even though there is nothing wrong with starting sequences at $n = 0$ (or any other integer for that matter), *we will agree that during this module we will always start our sequences at $n = 1$.* That way, the nth number in the list is the same as the nth term in the sequence, which corresponds to $f(n)$ or a_n or $A(n)$ or whatever formula name we give the nth term.

Lesson 1:   Integer Sequences—Should You Believe in Patterns?
Date: 9/11/13

15

- Some of you have written 2^n and some have written 2^{n-1}. Which is correct? Allow students to debate which is correct before saying…

- Is there any way that both could be correct?

  - *If we started by filling in 0 for* n, *then* 2^n *is correct. If we started with* n = 1, *then* 2^{n-1} *is correct.*

- Get into a discussion about starting the sequence with an index of one versus an index of zero. Either formula is correct. Thus, a decision must be made when writing a formula for a sequence as to whether to start the term number at 0 or 1. Generally, it feels natural to start with 1, but are there cases where it would feel more natural to start with 0?

  - *Yes! If the sequence is denoting values changing over time, it often makes sense to start at time 0 rather than a time of 1. Computer programmers start with term 0 rather than term 1 when creating Javascript arrays. The terms in a polynomial* $a_0 + a_1 x + a_2 x^2 + \cdots + a_n x^n$ *begin with 0.*

MP.7 & MP.8

Your goal as the teacher in having this discussion is to acknowledge and give validation to students who started with 0 and wrote 2^n. Explain to the class that there is nothing wrong with starting at 0, but to make it easier for us to communicate about sequences during this module, we will adopt the convention that during this module we will always start our sequences at $n = 1$.

- Use the discussion as an opportunity to connect the term number with the term itself as well as the notation by using the following visual:

Start with this table:

Term Number	Term
1	1
2	2
3	4
4	8
5	16
6	32

Then, lead to this table:

Sequence Term	Term	New Notation:
a_1	1	$f(1)$
a_2	2	$f(2)$
a_3	4	$f(3)$
a_4	8	$f(4)$
a_5	16	$f(5)$
a_6	32	$f(6)$

a_n $f(n)$

- Students are already familiar with the a_n notation. Let this lead to the f(n) notation as shown outside of the second table above. Emphasize how each of these is spoken. The third term of a sequence could be called "a sub 3" or "f of 3."

COMMON CORE™ | Lesson 1:   Integer Sequences—Should You Believe in Patterns?
Date: 9/11/13

16

Example 1

Jerry has thought of a pattern that shows powers of two. Here are the first 6 numbers of Jerry's sequence:

$$1, 2, 4, 8, 16, 32, \ldots$$

Write an expression for the nth number of Jerry's sequence.

The expression 2^{n-1} generates the sequence starting with $n = 1$.

Scaffolding:

For students who are struggling, assist them in writing out a few calculations to determine the pattern: $2^0, 2^1, 2^2, 2^3, 2^4, \ldots$

Example 2 (8 minutes)

We are introducing function notation $f(n)$ right away but without naming it as such and without calling attention to it at this stage. The use of the letter f for *formula* seems natural, and the use of parentheses does not cause anxiety or difficulty at this level of discussion. Watch to make sure students are using the $f(n)$ to stand for *formula for the nth term* and not thinking about it as the product $f \cdot n$.

- Should we always clarify which value of n we are assuming the formula starts with?
  - □ *Unless specified otherwise, we are assuming for this module that all formulas generate the sequence by starting with $n = 1$.*

- Are all the points on a number line in the sequence?
  - □ *No, the graph of the sequence consists of only the discrete dots (not all the points in between).*

Example 2

Consider the sequence that follows a "plus 3" pattern: $4, 7, 10, 13, 16, \ldots$.

a. Write a formula for the sequence using both the a_n notation and the $f(n)$ notation.

   $a_n = 3n + 1$ *or* $f(n) = 3n + 1$ *starting with $n = 1$.*

b. Does the formula $f(n) = 3(n - 1) + 4$ generate the same sequence? Why might some people prefer this formula?

   Yes. $3(n - 1) + 4 = 3n - 3 + 4 = 3n + 1$. It is nice that the first term of the sequence is a term in the formula, so one can almost read the formula in plain English: Since there is the "plus 3'" pattern, the nth term is just the first term plus that many more threes.

c. Graph the terms of the sequence as ordered pairs $(n, f(n))$ on the coordinate plane. What do you notice about the graph?

   The points all lie on the same line.

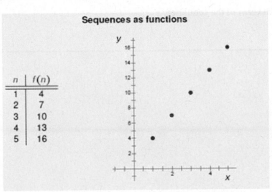

COMMON CORE™

Lesson 1:   Integer Sequences—Should You Believe in Patterns?
Date: 9/11/13

17

Exercises 1–5 (17 minutes)

Allow students time to work on the exercises either individually or in pairs. Circulate the room assisting students when needed, especially with writing the formula. Then, debrief by sharing answers as a class.

After students work individually, ask the following:

- If we had instead used the formula $f(n) = 30 - 5n$ to generate the sequence $30, 25, 20, 15, 10,\ldots$ by starting at $n = 0$, how would we find the 3rd term in the sequence? The 5th term? The nth term?

  □ *$f(2), f(4), f(n - 1)$*

Point out to students that by choosing to start all formulas at $n = 1$, we do not need to worry about how to compute the nth term of a sequence using the formula. For example, by using the formula $f(n) = 35 - 5n$, we can compute the 150th term simply by finding the value $f(150)$.

Make sure the students are making discrete graphs rather than continuous.

- Were any of the graphs linear? How do you know?

  □ *Example 2 was linear because it has a constant rate of change (subtract 5 each time).*

Exercises 1–5

1. Refer back to the sequence from the Opening Exercise. When Dr. T was asked for the next number in the sequence $2, 4, 6, 8, \ldots$, he said 17. 17?

    Yes, using the formula, $f(n) = \frac{7}{24}(n-1)^4 - \frac{7}{4}(n-1)^3 + \frac{77}{24}(n-1)^2 + \frac{1}{4}(n-1) + 2$

    a. Does his formula actually produce the numbers $2, 4, 6$, and 8?

        Yes. $f(1) = 2$, $f(2) = 4$, $f(3) = 6$, $f(4) = 8$

    b. What is the 100th term in the Dr. T's sequence?

        $f(100) = 26,350,832$

2. Consider a sequence that follows a "minus 5" pattern: $30, 25, 20, 15, \ldots$.

    a. Write a formula for the nth term of the sequence. Be sure to specify what value of n your formula starts with.

        $f(n) = 35 - 5n$ *if starting with $n = 1$.*

    b. Using the formula, find the 20th term of the sequence.

        -65

COMMON CORE™

Lesson 1:   Integer Sequences—Should You Believe in Patterns?
Date: 9/11/13

18

c. Graph the terms of the sequence as ordered pairs $(n, f(n))$ on a coordinate plane.

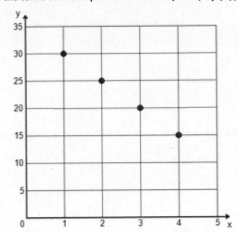

3. Consider a sequence that follows a "times 5" pattern: $1, 5, 25, 125, \dots$.

   a. Write a formula for the nth term of the sequence. Be sure to specify what value of n your formula starts with.

   $f(n) = 5^{n-1}$ *if starting with* $n = 1$.

   b. Using the formula, find the 10th term of the sequence.

   $1,953,125$

   c. Graph the terms of the sequence as ordered pairs $(n, f(n))$ on a coordinate plane.

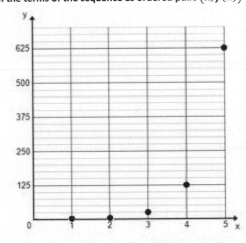

4.   Consider the sequence formed by the square numbers:

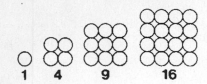

1   4   9   16

a.   Write a formula for the nth term of the sequence. Be sure to specify what value of n your formula starts with.

$f(n) = n^2$ *starting with* $n = 1$.

b.   Using the formula, find the 50th term of the sequence.

$2,500$

c.   Graph the terms of the sequence as ordered pairs $(n, f(n))$ on a coordinate plane.

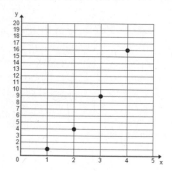

5.   A standard letter-sized piece of paper has a length and width of 8.5 inches by 11 inches.

a.   Find the area of one piece of paper.

93.5 *square inches*

b.   If the paper were folded completely in half, what would be the area of the resulting rectangle?

46.75 *square inches*

c.   Write a formula for a sequence to determine the area of the paper after n folds.

$f(n) = \dfrac{93.5}{2^n}$ *starting with* $n = 1$, *OR* $f(n) = \dfrac{93.5}{2^{n+1}}$ *starting with* $n = 0$.

d.   What would the area be after 7 folds?

0.73046875 *square inches*

MP.4

Lesson 1:   Integer Sequences—Should You Believe in Patterns?
Date: 9/11/13

20

Closing (5 minutes)

- Why is it important to have a formula to represent a sequence?
  - *It is important to have a formula to represent a sequence to demonstrate the specific pattern and to help in finding any term of the sequence (20th term, 50th term, 1000th term, etc.). This is very useful when we need to make predictions based on the formula chosen to model the existing data sequence.*
- Can one sequence have two different formulas?
  - *Yes, depending on what value of n you chose to start with. Some students may point out that two different-looking formulas may be related by equivalent expressions: $5(n + 2)$ is different than $5n + 10$.*
- What does $f(n)$ represent? How is it read aloud?
  - *It represents the nth term of a sequence just like a_n. It is read "f of n."*

Lesson Summary

A sequence can be thought of as an ordered list of elements. To define the pattern of the sequence, an explicit formula is often given, and unless specified otherwise, the first term is found by substituting 1 into the formula.

Exit Ticket (5 minutes)

Lesson 1:   Integer Sequences—Should You Believe in Patterns?
Date: 9/11/13

21

© 2013 Common Core, Inc. All rights reserved. commoncore.org

Name _____   Date_____

Lesson 1: Integer Sequences—Should You Believe in Patterns?

Exit Ticket

1. Consider the sequence given by a "plus 8" pattern: $2, 10, 18, 26, ...$ Shae says that the formula for the sequence is $f(n) = 8n + 2$. Marcus tells Shae that she is wrong because the formula for the sequence is $f(n) = 8n - 6$.

    a.   Which formula generates the sequence by starting at $n = 1$? At $n = 0$?

    b.   Find the 100th term in the sequence.

2. Write a formula for the sequence of cube numbers: $1, 8, 27, 64, ...$

COMMON CORE™

Lesson 1:   Integer Sequences—Should You Believe in Patterns?
Date: 9/11/13

22

Exit Ticket Sample Solutions

1. Consider the sequence given by a "plus 8" pattern: $2, 10, 18, 26, \ldots$.

   Shae says that the formula for the sequence is $f(n) = 8n + 2$. Marcus tells Shae that she is wrong because the formula for the sequence is $f(n) = 8n - 6$.

   a. Which formula generates the sequence by starting at $n = 1$? At $n = 0$?

      Shae's formula generates the sequence by starting with $n = 0$, while Marcus's formula generates the sequence by starting with $n = 1$.

   b. Find $f(100)$ for each formula.

      Marcus's formula: $f(100) = 8(100) - 6 = 794$.

      Shae's formula: $f(100) = 8(100) + 2 = 802$.

2. Write a formula for the sequence of cube numbers: $1, 8, 27, 64, \ldots$.

   $f(n) = n^3$ *starting with $n = 1$.*

Problem Set Sample Solutions

1. Consider a sequence generated by the formula $f(n) = 6n - 4$ starting with $n = 1$. Generate the terms $f(1), f(2), f(3), f(4),$ and $f(5)$.

   $2, 8, 14, 20, 26$

2. Consider a sequence given by the formula $f(n) = \dfrac{1}{3^{n-1}}$ starting with $n = 1$. Generate the first 5 terms of the sequence.

   $1, \dfrac{1}{3}, \dfrac{1}{9}, \dfrac{1}{27}, \dfrac{1}{81}$

3. Consider a sequence given by the formula $f(n) = (-1)^n \times 3$ starting with $n = 1$. Generate the first 5 terms of the sequence.

   $-3, 3, -3, 3, -3$

COMMON CORE™

Lesson 1:   Integer Sequences—Should You Believe in Patterns?
Date: 9/11/13

23

4. Here is the classic puzzle that shows that patterns need not hold true. What are the numbers counting?

The number under each figure is counting the number of (non-overlapping) regions in the circle formed by all the segments connecting all the points on the circle. Each graph contains one more point on the circle than the previous graph.

a. Based on the sequence of numbers, predict the next number.

32

b. Write a formula based on the perceived pattern.

$f(n) = 2^{n-1}$ *starting with* $n = 1$.

c. Find the next number in the sequence by actually counting.

31

d. Based on your answer from (c), is your model from b effective for this puzzle?

No, it works for $n = 1$ *to* $n = 5$ *but not for* $n = 6$. *And we don't know what happens for values of* n *larger than 6.*

In problems 5-8, for each of the following sequences:

a. Write a formula for the nth term of the sequence. Be sure to specify what value of n your formula starts with.

b. Using the formula, find the 15th term of the sequence.

c. Graph the terms of the sequence as ordered pairs $(n, f(n))$ on a coordinate plane.

5. The sequence follows a "plus 2" pattern: $3, 5, 7, 9, \ldots$.

a. $f(n) = 2(n-1) + 3$ *starting with* $n = 1$.

b. $f(15) = 31$

c.

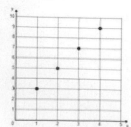

COMMON CORE™

Lesson 1:   Integer Sequences—Should You Believe in Patterns?
Date: 9/11/13

24

6.   The sequence follows a "times 4" pattern: $1, 4, 16, 64, ...$

   a. $f(n) = 4^{n-1}$ stating with $n = 1$.

   b. $f(15) = 268,435,456$

   c.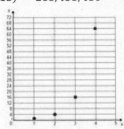

7.   The sequence follows a "times -1" pattern: $6, -6, 6, -6, ...$

   a. $f(n) = (-1)^{n-1} \cdot 6$ starting with $n = 1$.

   b. $f(15) = 6$

   c.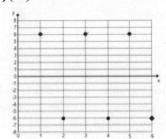

8.   The sequence follows a "minus 3" pattern: $12, 9, 6, 3, ...$

   a. $f(n) = 12 - 3(n - 1)$ starting with $n = 1$.

   b. $f(15) = -30$

   c.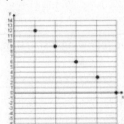

COMMON
CORE™

Lesson 1:   Integer Sequences—Should You Believe in Patterns?
Date: 9/11/13

25

Lesson 2: Recursive Formulas for Sequences

Student Outcomes

- Students write sequences with recursive and explicit formulas.

Lesson Notes

In this lesson, students will work on recursive formulas building on the ideas that were introduced in Module 1, Lessons 26 and 27 (The Double and Add 5 Game).

Classwork

Opening (2 minutes)

Remind students of their previous experiences with sequences.

- In Lesson 1, we worked on writing explicit formulas for sequences. Explicit formulas relate each term in a sequence directly to its placement in the sequence. This type of formula allows us to *jump* to any term of the sequence by simply replacing n with a specific number and evaluating the expression that describes the nth term of the sequence.

- Today, we will be looking at recursive formulas. You saw these at the end of Module 1 when we played The Double and Add 5 Game.

Example 1 (10 minutes)

Allow students a minute to examine the sequence and to answer part (a). Then, lead the following discussion, building on what was learned in Lesson 1.

Example 1

Consider the sequence 5, 8, 11, 14, 17, ….

a. If you believed in patterns, what might you say is the next number in the sequence?

  20 (adding 3 each time)

- She decided to call the sequence the "Akelia" sequence and so chose to use the letter A for naming it.

- When asked to find a formula for this sequence, Akelia wrote the following on a piece of paper:

  (record this on the board for the students)

MP.8

$$5$$
$$8 = 5 + 3$$
$$11 = 5 + 3 + 3 \qquad = 5 + 2 \times 3$$
$$14 = 5 + 3 + 3 + 3 = 5 + 3 \times 3$$

- Can you use her reasoning to help you write a formula for Akelia's sequence?
  - $A(n) = 5 + 3(n - 1)$
- Record the formula in your student materials.

---

b. **Write a formula for Akelia's sequence.**

$A(n) = 5 + 3(n - 1)$

- What does $A(n)$ represent again?
  - *It means the nth term of the sequence.*

Perhaps replace the $A(n)$ of the formula with the words "the nth term of Akelia's sequence." Continue to emphasize the point that $A(n)$ does not mean multiply A and n.

- Can you explain Akelia's formula and why it works?
  - *To find each term in the sequence, you are adding 3 one less time than the term number. To get the 1st term, you add three zero times. To get the 2nd term, you add three one time. To get the 5th term, you add three 4 times. In her formula, she is starting with $n = 1$.*
- Record the explanation in your student materials.

---

c. **Explain how each part of the formula relates to the sequence.**

To find each term in the sequence, you are adding 3 one less time than the term number. To get the 1st term, you add three zero times. To get the 2nd term, you add three one time. To get the 5th term, you add three 4 times.

- Akelia's formula is an explicit formula. You can use the formula to find the value of any term you want without having to know the value of the term before it. For example, if you wanted to know the 88th term, just substitute 88 for n and evaluate.
- When Johnny saw the sequence, he wrote the following: $A(n + 1) = A(n) + 3$ for $n \geq 1$ and $A(1) = 5$. (Display the formula on the board.)
- But what does the $A(n + 1)$ mean? Look back at the sequence. (Write the following on the board.)

  > 5
  > 8 = 5 + 3
  > 11 = 8 + 3
  > 14 = 11 + 3
  > 17 = 14 + 3

  What do we call the 5th term? $A(5)$
  How could we find the 5th term in terms of the 4th term? $A(4) + 3$
  If we want the 6th term in terms of the 5th term? $A(5) + 3$
  If we want the $(n + 1)$th term in terms of the nth term? $A(n) + 3$

- Now explain what Johnny's formula means.
  - *His formula is saying to find any term in the sequence just add 3 to the previous term. For example, to find the 12th term, add 3 to the 11th term: $A(12) = A(11) + 3$. To find the 50th term, add 3 to the 49th term: $A(50) = A(49) + 3$. To find the $(n + 1)$th term, add 3 to the nth term.*

- Record the explanation in your student materials.

> **d. Explain Johnny's formula.**
>
> *His formula is saying to find any term in the sequence just add 3 to the term before it. For example, to find the 12th term, add 3 to the 11th term → $A(12) = A(11) + 3$. To find the 50th term, add 3 to the 49th term. To find the $(n + 1)$th term, add 3 to the nth term. It is critical that the value of the very first term be specified; we need it to get started to find the values of all the other terms.*

- The statement $A(n + 1) = A(n) + 3$ is a recursive formula. A recursive formula relates a term in the sequence to the preceding term or terms of the sequence.

(Note: For students that struggle to understand notation involving $n, n + 1, n - 1$, consider quick exercises of this type: "If we start with 3, what expression would name the next whole number, 4?" $(3 + 1)$. "What expression would name the previous whole number, 2?" $(3 - 1)$.)

- Would it be equivalent to write the sequence as $A(n) = A(n - 1) + 3$? Why or why not?
  - *Yes, $A(n - 1)$ is the term before $A(n)$ just like $A(n)$ is the term before $A(n + 1)$. Both formulas are saying that to find any term in the sequence, add three to the previous term.*

Warn students that they will see recursive formulas written in both of these ways.

Again, caution students that $A(n + 1)$ is not $A \cdot (n + 1)$.

- Why does Akelia's formula have a "times 3" in it, while Johnny's formula has a "plus 3"?
  - *Akelia's formula specifies the nth term directly as an expression in n. Johnny's formula evaluates the $(n + 1)$th term by using the nth term, which means he only as to observe the rule that takes one term to the next consecutive term. In this case, the rule is to add 3 to the previous term.*

- If we wanted the 200th term of the sequence, which formula would be more useful?
  - *Akelia's — just fill in 200 for n.*

- If we wanted to know how the sequence changes from one term to the next, which formula would be more useful?
  - *Johnny's recursive formula would be more useful.*

- Using Johnny's recursive formula, what would we need to know if we wanted to find the 200th term?
  - *We would need to know the 199th term.*

Exercises 1–2 (8 minutes)

As students work through Exercises 1 and 2, circulate the room making sure that students understand the notation. Ask students to read the notation aloud and explain the meaning. Debrief by having students share answers.

- Throughout these exercises, ask students to translate the sequences into words:
  - *$A(n + 1) = A(n) - 3$ is a sequence where each term is three less than the term before it.*

Exercises 1–2

1. Akelia, in a playful mood, asked Johnny: What would happen if we change the "+" sign in your formula to a "−" sign? To a "×" sign? To a "÷" sign?

   a. What sequence does $A(n+1) = A(n) - 3$ for $n \geq 1$ and $A(1) = 5$ generate?

      $5, 2, -1, -4, \ldots$

   b. What sequence does $A(n+1) = A(n) \cdot 3$ for $n \geq 1$ and $A(1) = 5$ generate?

      $5, 15, 45, 135, \ldots$

   c. What sequence does $A(n+1) = A(n) \div 3$ for $n \geq 1$ and $A(1) = 5$ generate?

      $5, \dfrac{5}{3}, \dfrac{5}{9}, \dfrac{5}{27}, \ldots$

2. Ben made up a recursive formula and used it to generate a sequence. He used $B(n)$ to stand for the nth term of his recursive sequence.

   a. What does $B(3)$ mean?

      It is the third term of Ben's sequence.

   b. What does $B(m)$ mean?

      It is the mth term of Ben's sequence.

   c. If $B(n+1) = 33$ and $B(n) = 28$, write a possible recursive formula involving $B(n+1)$ and $B(n)$ that would generate 28 and 33 in the sequence.

      $B(n) = B(n-1) + 5$ *[Note that this is not the only possible answer; it assumes the sequence is arithmetic and is probably the most obvious response students will give. If the sequence were geometric, the answer could be written $B(n+1) = \left(\dfrac{33}{28}\right)B(n)$].*

   d. What does $2B(7) + 6$ mean?

      It is 2 times the 7th term of Ben's sequence plus 6.

   e. What does $B(n) + B(m)$ mean?

      It is the sum of nth term of Ben's sequence plus the mth term of Ben's sequence.

   f. Would it necessarily be the same as $B(n+m)$?

      No, adding two terms of a sequence is not the same as adding two of the term numbers and then finding that term of a sequence. Consider, for example, the sequence $1, 3, 5, 7, 9, 11, 13, \ldots$. Adding the 2nd and 3rd terms does not give you the 5th term.

   g. What does $B(17) - B(16)$ mean?

      It is the 17th term of Ben's sequence minus the 16th term of Ben's sequence.

- When writing a recursive formula, what piece of information is necessary to include along with the formula?
  - *The value of the initial term with which the sequence starts, which is usually identified as the first term and indexed by the term number 1.*

Point out to students that there is no hard-and-fast requirement that all recursive sequences start with index at 1. In some cases, it is convenient to start the index at 0 (as was done in the Double and Add 5 Game). However, in this sequence of lessons, we are mostly concerned with building up to the idea of function, so we will mostly stay with sequences starting at index 1.

- What additional piece of information is needed when writing a recursive formula?
  - *We need to describe what n the formula holds for. For example, Johnny's formula $A(n + 1) = A(n) + 3$ does not hold for $n = -5$.*

Example 2 (5 minutes)

Point out the new notation of using a subscript rather than parentheses. Assure students that the two notations are essentially the same and that they will see both throughout the unit. Give students a few minutes to complete the problem.

Example 2

Consider a sequence given by the formula $a_n = a_{n-1} - 5$, where $a_1 = 12$ and $n \geq 1$.

    a.   List the first five terms of the sequence.

        $12, 7, 2, -3, -8$

    b.   Write an explicit formula.

        $a_n = 12 - 5(n - 1)$ *for* $n \geq 1$.

    c.   Find a_6 and a_{100} of the sequence.

        $a_6 = -13$ $a_{100} = -483$

- What type of formula is given in the question: recursive or explicit?
  - *Recursive because it relates a term in the sequence to the term before it.*
- Which formula did you use to find a_6? a_{100}?
  - *Probably recursive to find the 6th term. Since the 5th term was known, it makes sense to just continue the sequence to find the 6th term. The explicit formula is the easiest to use to find the 100th term. In order to use the recursive formula, we would need to know the 99th term.*

Exercises 3–6 (12 minutes)

Give students time to work through the exercises either individually or in pairs, circulating the room to make sure students are recognizing the differences between the two types of formulas and are using correct notation.

Exercises 3–6

3. One of the most famous sequences is the Fibonacci sequence:

   $1, 1, 2, 3, 5, 8, 13, 21, 34, \ldots$

   $f(n+1) = f(n) + f(n-1)$, where $f(1) = 1$, $f(2) = 1$, and $n \geq 2$.

   How is each term of the sequence generated?

   By adding the two preceding terms

4. For each sequence below, an explicit formula is given. Write the first 5 terms of each sequence. Then, write a recursive formula for the sequence.

   a. $a_n = 2n + 10$ for $n \geq 1$

      $12, 14, 16, 18, 20$

      $a_{n+1} = a_n + 2$, *where* $a_1 = 12$ *and* $n \geq 1$

   b. $a_n = \left(\frac{1}{2}\right)^{n-1}$ for $n \geq 1$

      $1, \frac{1}{2}, \frac{1}{4}, \frac{1}{8}, \frac{1}{16}$

      $a_n + 1 = a_n \div 2$, *where* $a_1 = 1$ *and* $n \geq$

5. For each sequence, write *either* an explicit or recursive formula.

   a. $1, -1, 1, -1, 1, -1, \ldots$

      $a_{n+1} = -a_n$, *where* $a_1 = 1$ *and* $n \geq 1$

   b. $\frac{1}{2}, \frac{2}{3}, \frac{3}{4}, \frac{4}{5}, \ldots$

      $f(n) = \frac{n}{n+1}$ *and* $n \geq 1$

6. Lou opens a bank account. The deal he makes with his mother is that if he doubles the amount that was in the account at the beginning of each month by the end of the month, she will add an additional \$5 to the account at the end of the month.

   a. Let $A(n)$ represent the amount in the account at the beginning of the nth month. Assume that he does, in fact, double the amount every month. Write a recursive formula for the amount of money in his account at the beginning of the nth month.

      $A(n+1) = 2A(n) + 5$, *where* $n \geq 1$ *and* $A(1)$ *is the initial amount.*

   b. What is the least amount he could start with in order to have \$300 by the beginning of the 3rd month?

      \$72

Month	1	2	3
Amount	72	149	303

- Notice that in the Fibonacci sequence, each term depends on the two previous terms. This means we had to know the first two terms in order to start the sequence. Point out that an explicit formula would be much more complicated to come up with in this case.

- For problems 5(a) and 5(b), which type of formula did you write?

  □ *For 5(a), either formula was fairly easy to come up with. For 5(b), an explicit formula is easier to write. The recursive formula would be pretty tough to come up with. If you want to share the recursive formula for 5(b) just for fun, it is* $f(n + 1) = \dfrac{(n+1)^2 f(n)}{n(n+2)}$.

- Does problem 6 seem familiar?

  □ *We are revisiting the Double and Add 5 Game from Module 1!*

Closing (3 minutes)

- What are two types of formulas that can be used to represent a sequence?

  □ *Explicit and recursive*

Go over the definition of each as given in the lesson summary. If time permits, have students put an example next to each definition, and then share a few with the class.

- What information besides the formula would you need in order to write each of these two types of formulas?

  □ *To write an explicit formula, you need to know what integer you are using for the first term number.*

  □ *To write a recursive formula, you need to know what the first term is, or first several terms are, depending on the recursive relation.*

Lesson Summary

RECURSIVE SEQUENCE (description). An example of a *recursive sequence* is a sequence that (1) is defined by specifying the values of one or more initial terms and (2) has the property that the remaining terms satisfy a recursive formula that describes the value of a term based upon an expression in numbers, previous terms, or the index of the term.

An explicit formula specifies the nth term of a sequence as an expression in n.

A recursive formula specifies the nth term of a sequence as an expression in the previous term (or previous couple of terms).

Exit Ticket (5 minutes)

Name _____   Date_____

Lesson 2: Recursive Formulas for Sequences

Exit Ticket

1. Consider the sequence following a "minus 8" pattern: $9, 1, -7, -15, \ldots$.
    a. Write an explicit formula for the sequence.

    b. Write a recursive formula for the sequence.

    c. Find the 38th term of the sequence.

2. Consider the sequence given by the formula $a(n + 1) = 5a(n)$ and $a(1) = 2$ for $n \geq 1$.
    a. Explain what the formula means.

    b. List the first 5 terms of the sequence.

Exit Ticket Sample Solutions

1. Consider the sequence following a "minus 8" pattern: $9, 1, -7, -15, \ldots$.

   a. Write an explicit formula for the sequence.

   $f(n) = 9 - 8(n - 1)$ *for* $n \geq 1$

   b. Write a recursive formula for the sequence.

   $f(n + 1) = f(n) - 8$ *and* $f(1) = 9$ *for* $n \geq 1$

   c. Find the 38th term of the sequence.

   $f(38) = 9 - 8(37) = -287$

2. Consider the sequence given by the formula $a(n + 1) = 5a(n)$ and $a(1) = 2$ for $n \geq 1$.

   a. Explain what the formula means.

   The first term of the sequence is 2. *Each subsequent term of the sequence is found by multiplying the previous term by* 5.

   b. List the first 5 terms of the sequence.

   $2, 10, 50, 250, 1250$

Problem Set Sample Solutions

For problems 1-4, list the first five terms of each sequence.

1. $a_{n+1} = a_n + 6$, where $a_1 = 11$ for $n \geq 1$

   $11, 17, 23, 29, 35$

2. $a_n = a_{n-1} \div 2$, where $a_1 = 50$ for $n \geq 2$

   $50, \ 25, \ 12.5, \ 6.25, \ 3.125$

3. $f(n + 1) = -2f(n) + 8$ and $f(1) = 1$ for $n \geq 1$

   $1, 6, -4, 16, -24$

4. $f(n) = f(n - 1) + n$ and $f(1) = 4$ for $n \geq 2$

   $4, 6, 9, 13, 18$

For problems 5-10, write a recursive formula for each sequence given or described below.

5. It follows a "plus one" pattern: $8, 9, 10, 11, 12, \ldots$.

   $f(n + 1) = f(n) + 1$, *where* $f(1) = 8$ *and* $n \geq 1$

6. It follows a "times 10" pattern: $4, 40, 400, 4000, \ldots$.

   $f(n + 1) = 10f(n)$, *where* $f(1) = 4$ *and* $n \geq 1$

7. It has an explicit formula of $f(n) = -3n + 2$ for $n \geq 1$.

   $f(n + 1) = f(n) - 3$, *where* $f(1) = -1$ *and* $n \geq 1$

8. It has an explicit formula of $f(n) = -1(12)^{n-1}$ for $n \geq 1$.

   $f(n + 1) = 12f(n)$, *where* $f(1) = -1$ *for* $n \geq 1$

9. Doug accepts a job where his starting salary will be $30,000 per year, and each year he will receive a raise of $3,000.

   $D_{n+1} = D_n + 3000$, *where* $D_1 = 30,000$ *and* $n \geq 1$

10. A bacteria culture has an initial population of 10 bacteria, and each hour the population triples in size.

    $B_{n+1} = 3B_n$, *where* $B_1 = 10$ *and* $n \geq 1$

Lesson 3: Arithmetic and Geometric Sequences

Student Outcomes

- Students learn the structure of arithmetic and geometric sequences.

Lesson Notes

In this lesson, students will use their knowledge of sequences developed in Lessons 1 and 2 to differentiate between arithmetic and geometric sequences.

Classwork

Opening (12 minutes)

In Lessons 1 and 2, students wrote formulas for arithmetic sequences and graphed the terms of the sequence as ordered pairs in the Cartesian plane. Continue to emphasize the point that $A(n)$ does not mean multiply A and n. It means the nth term of the sequence defined by the formula (function) A.

Write the following sequences that were discussed last lesson on the board, and allow students to discuss ideas as a class. Scaffold their discussion as needed with the following:

- Yesterday we talked about the sequences created by Akelia.

  What sequence does $A(n + 1) = A(n) - 3$ and $A(1) = 5$ for $n \geq 1$ yield?

  □ $5, 2, -1, -4, -7, \dots$

- What sequence does $A(n + 1) = A(n) + 3$ and $A(1) = 5$ for $n \geq 1$ yield?

  □ $5, 8, 11, 14, 17, \dots$

- Johnny suggests that they plot the sequences to help them understand the patterns. What do they discover?

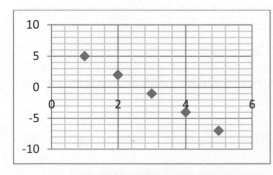
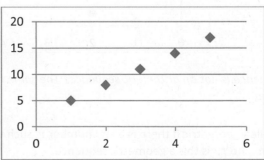

Take time to allow students to discuss the patterns and explain these patterns in words. We want students to notice that the data forms a linear pattern. Ask students what the slope of the line connecting the points would be. Is there a relationship between the slope of that line and the sequence itself? We are trying to get students to see that for both sequences, any two consecutive terms differ by the same number (in the first, its -3, in the second sequence its 3).

Likewise, the line containing a sequence has a constant average rate of change over all equal–length intervals. Students might not use the words "average rate of change"; in this case, introduce the term into the discussion yourself to put that concept in their minds for a later lesson.

Ask students to write a definition of an arithmetic sequence in their own words.

ARITHEMETIC SEQUENCE (description). A sequence is called *arithmetic* if there is a real number d such that each term in the sequence is the sum of the previous term and d.

Arithmetic sequences are often called "linear sequences." Have students explain why.

> *Scaffolding:*
> Is every arithmetic sequence given by a formula of the form $f(n) = mn + b$? Is every formula of the form $f(n) = mn + b$ going to yield an arithmetic sequence?

Example 1 (10 minutes)

Now students will look at a geometric sequence. Have students discuss their findings. Some will try to talk about slope, but we want them to see that we no longer have linear data.

What does this mean about our sequence?

- Now look at the sequence $1, 3, 9, 27, \ldots$. What do you notice? How is the sequence different from the sequences above?

  □ *We are multiplying each term by 3 and not adding or subtracting.*

- Plot this sequence by starting the index of the terms at 1. Is it an arithmetic sequence (i.e., linear sequence)? Is the same number added to each term to get the next?

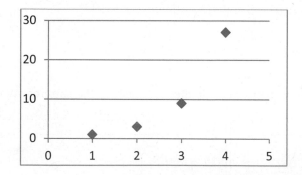

  □ *This sequence is not an arithmetic sequence. The same number is not being added. Each term is being multiplied.*

- A sequence is called geometric if there is a real number r, such that each term in the sequence is a product of the previous term and r. Is this a geometric sequence?

  □ *Yes. Each term in the sequence can be found by multiplying or dividing the previous term by 3.*

Ask students to write the definition of a geometric sequence in their own words.

Exercise 1 (15 minutes)

Have students work in groups to identify the following sequences as arithmetic or geometric. Give each group a set of index cards with one sequence on each (all groups should have the same cards). On the board, create two columns with the headings **Arithmetic** and **Geometric**. Students should classify the sequences as arithmetic or geometric, write the reason on the card, write a formula for the sequence, and then tape each card under the correct type of sequence. Some students may have trouble writing geometric sequence formulas, but let them try. Have a class discussion after all groups have placed their cards. Be sure to look at the formulas and make sure students have identified the term they are starting with. You can even revisit the terms recursive and explicit.

> *Scaffolding:*
>
> Teachers can model sequences either by (1) naming the products/differences between terms to help develop the recursive formula and/or (2) naming/showing the operations that lead from the term number to the term to help develop the explicit formula.

Index Card Sequences

1. $-2, 2, 6, 10, \ldots$ Arithmetic   Add 4 $A(n + 1) = A(n) + 4$ for $n \geq 1$ and $A(1) = -2$, or $A(n) = -6 + 4n$ for $n \geq 1$.

2. $2, 4, 8, 16, \ldots$ Geometric   Multiply by 2 $A(n + 1) = A(n) \cdot 2$ for $n \geq 1$ and $A(1) = 2$, or $A(n) = 2^n$ for $n \geq 1$.

3. $\frac{1}{2}, 1, \frac{3}{2}, 2, \frac{5}{2}, \ldots$ Arithmetic   Add $\frac{1}{2}$ $A(n + 1) = A(n) + \frac{1}{2}$ for $n \geq 1$ and $A(1) = \frac{1}{2}$, or $A(n) = \frac{1}{2}n$ for $n \geq 1$.

4. $1, \frac{1}{3}, \frac{1}{9}, \frac{1}{27}, \ldots$ Geometric   Multiply by $\frac{1}{3}$ $A(n + 1) = A(n) \cdot \frac{1}{3}$ for $n \geq 1$ and $A(1) = 1$, or $A(n) = \left(\frac{1}{3}\right)^{n-1}$ for $n \geq 1$.

5. $10, 1, 0.1, 0.01, 0.001\ldots$ Geometric   Multiply by 0.1 or $\frac{1}{10}$ $A(n + 1) = A(n) \cdot (0.1)$ for $n \geq 1$ and $A(1) = 10$, or $A(n) = 10(0.1)^{n-1}$ for $n \geq 1$.

6. $4, -1, -6, -11, \ldots$ Arithmetic   Add -5 or subtract 5 $A(n + 1) = A(n) - 5$ for $n \geq 1$ and $A(1) = 4$, or $A(n) = 9 - 5n$ for $n \geq 1$.

Exercise 2 (Optionally, if time allows)

> **Exercise 2**
>
> Think of a real–world example of an arithmetic/geometric sequence? Describe it and write its formula.
>
> *Answers will vary.*

Exercise 3 (Optionally, if time allows)

> **Exercise 3**
>
> If we fold a rectangular piece of paper in half multiple times and count the number of rectangles created, what type of sequence are we creating? Can you write the formula?
>
> *We are creating a geometric sequence because each time we fold, we double the number of rectangles. $R(n) = 2^n$, where n is the number of times we have folded the paper.*

Closing (3 minutes)

- Explain the difference between arithmetic and geometric sequences.

Students may say something like, "*Arithmetic sequences grow additively; geometric sequences grow multiplicatively.*" However, such a statement is only partially true. The sequence may be decaying or decreasing instead of growing. Prompt students to get more specific so as to include both increasing and decreasing sequences in their description of the differences.

- Why are arithmetic sequences sometimes called linear sequences?
    - *If we graph an arithmetic sequence as points $(n, A(n))$ on the Cartesian plane, the points lie on a line. That's why we sometimes call arithmetic sequences linear sequences.*

> **Lesson Summary**
>
> Two types of sequences were studied:
>
> **ARITHMETIC SEQUENCE (description).** A sequence is called *arithmetic* if there is a real number d such that each term in the sequence is the sum of the previous term and d.
>
> **GEOMETRIC SEQUENCE (description).** A sequence is called geometric if there is a real number r such that each term in the sequence is a product of the previous term and r.

Exit Ticket (5 minutes)

Name _____   Date_____

Lesson 3: Arithmetic and Geometric Sequences

Exit Ticket

1. Write the first 3 terms in the following sequences. Identify them as arithmetic or geometric.

   a. $A(n + 1) = A(n) - 5$ for $n \geq 1$ and $A(1) = 9$.

   b. $A(n + 1) = \frac{1}{2} A(n)$ for $n \geq 1$ and $A(1) = 4$.

   c. $A(n + 1) = A(n) \div 10$ for $n \geq 1$ and $A(1) = 10$.

2. Identify each sequence as arithmetic or geometric. Explain your answer, and write an explicit formula for the sequence.

   a. $14, 11, 8, 5, \ldots$

   b. $2, 10, 50, 250, \ldots$

   c. $-\frac{1}{2}, -\frac{3}{2}, -\frac{5}{2}, -\frac{7}{2}, \ldots$

Exit Ticket Sample Solutions

1. Write the first 3 terms in the following sequences. Identify them as arithmetic or geometric.

   a. $A(n + 1) = A(n) - 5$ for $n \geq 1$ and $A(1) = 9$.

   $9, 4, -1$ *Arithmetic*

   b. $A(n + 1) = \frac{1}{2}A(n)$ for $n \geq 1$ and $A(1) = 4$.

   $4, 2, 1$ *Geometric*

   c. $A(n + 1) = A(n) \div 10$ for $n \geq 1$ and $A(1) = 10$.

   $10, 1, \frac{1}{10}$ *or* $10, 1, 0.1$ *Geometric*

2. Identify each sequence as arithmetic or geometric and explain your answer. Write an explicit formula for the sequence.

   a. $14, 11, 8, 5, \ldots$ *Arithmetic* -3 *pattern* $17 - 3n$, *where n starts at 1*

   b. $2, 10, 50, 250, \ldots$ *Geometric* $\times 5$ *pattern* $2(5^{n-1})$, *where n starts at 1*

   c. $-\frac{1}{2}, -\frac{3}{2}, -\frac{5}{2}, -\frac{7}{2}, \ldots$ *Arithmetic* -1 *pattern* $-\frac{3}{2} - n$, *where n starts at 1*

Problem Set Sample Solutions

For problems 1–4, list the first five terms of each sequence, and identify them as arithmetic or geometric.

1. $A(n + 1) = A(n) + 4$ for $n \geq 1$ and $A(1) = -2$

   $-2, 2, 6, 10, 14$ *Arithmetic*

2. $A(n + 1) = \frac{1}{4} \cdot A(n)$ for $n \geq 1$ and $A(1) = 8$

   $8, 2, \frac{1}{2}, \frac{1}{8}, \frac{1}{32}$ *Geometric*

3. $A(n + 1) = A(n) - 19$ for $n \geq 1$ and $A(1) = -6$

   $-6, -25, -44, -63, -82$ *Arithmetic*

4. $A(n + 1) = \frac{2}{3}A(n)$ for $n \geq 1$ and $A(1) = 6$

   $6, 4, \frac{8}{3}, \frac{16}{9}, \frac{32}{27}$ *Geometric*

For problems 5–8, identify the sequence as arithmetic or geometric, and write a recursive formula for the sequence. Be sure to identify your starting value.

5. $14, 21, 28, 35, \ldots$

   $f(n + 1) = f(n) + 7$ *for* $n \geq 1$ *and* $f(1) = 14$ *Arithmetic*

6. $4, 40, 400, 4000, \ldots$

   $f(n + 1) = 10f(n)$ *for* $n \geq 1$ *and* $f(1) = 4$ *Geometric*

7. $49, 7, \frac{1}{7}, \frac{1}{49}, \ldots$

    $f(n+1) = \frac{1}{7}f(n)$ *for* $n \geq 1$ *and* $f(1) = 49$ *Geometric*

8. $-101, -91, -81, -71, \ldots$

    $f(n+1) = f(n) + 10$ *for* $n \geq 1$ *and* $f(1) = -101$ *Arithmetic*

9. The local football team won the championship several years ago, and since then, ticket prices have been increasing $20 per year. The year they won the championship, tickets were $50. Write a recursive formula for a sequence that will model ticket prices. Is the sequence arithmetic or geometric?

    $T(n) = 50 + 20n$, *where* n *is the number of years since they won the championship;* $n \geq 1$ *(*$n \geq 0$ *is also acceptable). Arithmetic.*

    Or,

    $T(n+1) = T(n) + 20$, *where* n *is the number of years since the year they won the championship;* $n \geq 1$ *and* $T(1) = 70$ *(*$n \geq 0$ *and* $T(0) = 50$ *is also acceptable). Arithmetic.*

10. A radioactive substance decreases in the amount of grams by one third each year. If the starting amount of the substance in a rock is $1,452$ g, write a recursive formula for a sequence that models the amount of the substance left after the end of each year. Is the sequence arithmetic or geometric?

    $A(n+1) = \frac{2}{3}A(n)$ *or* $A(n+1) = 2A(n) \div 3$, *where* n *is the number of years since the measurement started,* $A(0) = 1,452$

    Geometric

    Since the problem asked how much radioactive substance was left, students must take the original amount, divide by 3 or multiply by $\frac{1}{3}$, *then subtract that portion from the original amount. An easier way to do this is to just multiply by the amount remaining. If* $\frac{1}{3}$ *is eliminated,* $\frac{2}{3}$ *remains.*

11. Find an explicit form $f(n)$ for each of the following arithmetic sequences (assume a is some real number and x is some real number):

    a. $-34, -22, -10, 2, \ldots$

        $f(n) = -34 + 12(n-1) = 12n - 46$, *where* $n \geq 1$

    b. $\frac{1}{5}, \frac{1}{10}, 0, -\frac{1}{10}, \ldots$

        $f(n) = \frac{1}{5} - \frac{1}{10}(n-1) = \frac{3}{10} - \frac{1}{10}n$, *where* $n \geq 1$

    c. $x+4, x+8, x+12, x+16, \ldots$

        $f(n) = x + 4 + 4(n-1) = x + 4n$, *where* $n \geq 1$

    d. $a, 2a+1, 3a+2, 4a+3, \ldots$

        $f(n) = a + (a+1)(n-1) = a + an - a + n - 1 = an + n - 1$, *where* $n \geq 1$

12. Consider the arithmetic sequence $13, 24, 35, \ldots$.

   a. Find an explicit form for the sequence in terms of n.

   $$f(n) = 2 + 11(n-1) = 11n - 9, \text{ where } n \geq 1$$

   b. Find the 40th term.

   $$f(40) = 431$$

   c. If the nth term is 299, find the value of n.

   $$299 = 11n - 9, n = 28$$

13. If $-2, a, b, c, 14$ forms an arithmetic sequence, find the values of $a, b,$ and c.

   $$14 = -2 + (5-1)d \qquad a = -2 + 4 = 2$$
   $$16 = 4d \qquad\qquad b = 2 + 4 = 6$$
   $$d = 4 \qquad\qquad c = 6 + 4 = 10$$

14. $3 + x, 9 + 3x, 13 + 4x, \ldots$ is an arithmetic sequence for some real number x.

   a. Find the value of x.

   $$13 + 4x = 3 + x + (3-1)(6 + 2x)$$
   $$13 + 4x = 15 + 5x$$
   $$-2 = x \qquad \textit{Sequence: } 1, 3, 5, \ldots$$

   b. Find the 10th term of the sequence.

   $$f(n) = 1 + 2(n-1) = 2n - 1, \text{ where } n \geq 1$$
   $$f(10) = 19$$

15. Find an explicit form $f(n)$ of the arithmetic sequence where the 2nd term is 25 and the sum of the 3rd term and 4th term is 86.

   $a, 25, b, c$

   $$25 = a + (2-1)d \qquad b = 25 + d \qquad c = 25 + 2d$$
   $$25 = a + d \qquad\qquad b = a + 2d \qquad c = a + 3d$$

   $$b + c = (a + 2d) + (a + 3d) = 2a + 5d = 86$$
   $$a + d = 25$$

   Solving this system: $d = 12, a = 13, \text{ so } f(n) = 13 + 12(n-1) \text{ where } n \geq 1$

   $$b = 13 + 2(12) = 37 \qquad\qquad c = 13 + 3(12) = 49$$

16. (Challenge) In the right triangle figure below the lengths of the sides a cm, b cm, c cm of the right triangle form a finite arithmetic sequence. If the perimeter of the triangle is 18 cm, find the values of a, b, and c.

    $a + b + c = 18$ $\qquad b = a + d \qquad c = a + 2d$

    $a + (a + d) + (a + 2d) = 18$
    $3a + 3d = 18$
    $a + d = 6$ $\qquad$ *Now do not forget that it is a right triangle, so the Pythagorean Theorem must apply:* $a^2 + b^2 = c^2$, *so* $a^2 + 36 = c^2$.

    If $b = 6$, *equation #1 becomes* $a + c = 12$, *so solving this system of equations gives us the answer:* $a = \dfrac{9}{2}, b = 6, c = \dfrac{15}{2}$.

17. Find the common ratio and an explicit form in each of the following geometric sequences:

    a. $4, 12, 36, 108, \ldots$

    $r = 3 \qquad\qquad f(n) = 4(3^{n-1}),$ *where* $n \geq 1$

    b. $162, 108, 72, 48, \ldots$

    $r = \dfrac{108}{162} = \dfrac{2}{3} \qquad f(n) = 162\left(\dfrac{2}{3}\right)^{n-1},$ *where* $n \geq 1$

    c. $\dfrac{4}{3}, \dfrac{2}{3}, \dfrac{1}{3}, \dfrac{1}{6}, \ldots$

    $r = 2 \qquad\qquad f(n) = \left(\dfrac{4}{3}\right)\left(\dfrac{1}{2}\right)^{n-1} = \left(\dfrac{4}{3}\right)(2)^{1-n},$ *where* $n \geq 1$

    d. $xz, x^2z^3, x^3z^5, x^4z^7, \ldots$

    $r = xz^2 \qquad f(n) = xz(xz^2)^{n-1},$ *where* $n \geq 1$

18. The first term in a geometric sequence is 54, and the 5th term is $\dfrac{2}{3}$. Find an explicit form for the geometric sequence.

    $\dfrac{2}{3} = 54(r^4) \qquad\qquad \dfrac{1}{81} = r^4 \qquad\qquad r = \dfrac{1}{3} \text{ or } -\dfrac{1}{3} \qquad f(n) = 54\left(\dfrac{1}{3}\right)^{n-1}$

19. If $2, a, b, -54$ forms a geometric sequence, find the values of a and b.

    $a = 2r, \qquad b = 2(r)^2 \qquad\quad -54 = 2(r)^3$
    $\qquad\qquad\qquad\qquad\qquad\qquad -27 = r^3$
    $\qquad\qquad\qquad\qquad\qquad\qquad -3 = r \quad$ *so* $a = -6$ *and* $b = 18$

20. Find the explicit form $f(n)$ of a geometric sequence if $f(3) - f(1) = 48$ and $\dfrac{f(3)}{f(1)} = 9$.

    $f(3) = f(1)(r^2) \qquad\qquad f(1)r^2 - f(1) = 48 \qquad f(1)(r^2 - 1) = 48$

    $\dfrac{f(3)}{f(1)} = r^2 = 9 \qquad\qquad r = 3 \text{ or } -3 \qquad\qquad f(1)(8) = 48$

    $\qquad\qquad\qquad\qquad\qquad\qquad\qquad\qquad\qquad\qquad\qquad f(1) = 6$

    $f(n) = 6(3)^{n-1},$ *where* $n \geq 1$ *or* $f(n) = 6(-3)^{n-1},$ *where* $n \geq 1$

Lesson 4: Why do Banks Pay YOU to Provide Their Services?

Student Outcomes

- Students compare the rate of change for simple and compound interest and recognize situations in which a quantity grows by a constant percent rate per unit interval.

Classwork

Opening Exercise (5 minutes)

Begin class with a discussion of why banks pay you interest to provide a service to you. Pose the question first and have students discuss their ideas, and then give them a bit of history on this topic. We will revisit this question at the end of the lesson.

- Have you ever thought it odd that banks pay YOU interest for the honor of looking after your money for you?

Give students time to think about this. Some students may have no concept of this. That is okay. You will give them a little history, and they can become familiar with the concept throughout the lesson. They will have a chance to answer as we move through the lesson.

- Throughout history, people had to PAY BANKS to look after their money. In the Renaissance, with the rise of world exploration, banks realized that looking after people's money was an incredibly good thing for them. They could make money off of the large amounts of money they were keeping for others. They wanted to encourage more people to give them their money to keep, so they started paying customers.

Have students think about how banks could make this work. If they are paying people to keep their money and making money on this money, what are some things that they could be doing?

Example 1 (10 minutes)

Banks originally computed simple interest, and that is the type of interest that we will study in this example. Simple interest is calculated at the end of each year on the original amount either borrowed or invested (the principal). Use the basic example below to make sure that students understand the concept of simple interest. It is critical that students have a good grasp of simple interest before you move to the next example.

Example 1

Kyra has been babysitting since 6th grade. She has saved $1000 and wants to open an account at the bank so that she will earn interest on her savings. Simple Bank pays simple interest at a rate of 10%. How much money will Kyra have after 1 year? After 2 years, if she does not add money to her account? After 5 years?

$1100 after 1 year, $1200 after 2 years, $1500 after 5 years

Lesson 4:	Why do Banks Pay YOU to Provide Their Services?	
Date:	9/11/13	44

The diagram below will help students see how the interest works.

▪ This diagram shows $1000 invested at 10% interest for 1 year.

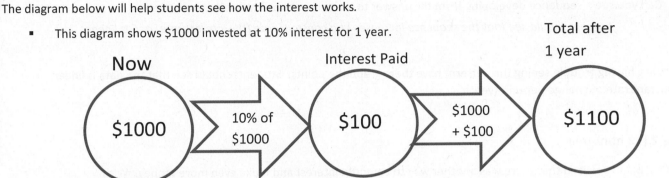

Now — $1000

Interest Paid — 10% of $1000 → $100

$1000 + $100 → **Total after 1 year** — $1100

▪ This diagram shows $1000 invested at 10% interest for 2 years.

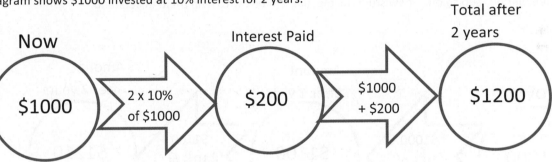

Now — $1000

2 x 10% of $1000 → **Interest Paid** — $200

$1000 + $200 → **Total after 2 years** — $1200

▪ Come up with a formula to calculate simple interest.

Allow students time to struggle with this formula before suggesting variable symbols and/or providing them with a formula.

◻ *I(t) = Prt, where I(t) is the interest earned after t years, P is the principal amount (the amount borrowed or invested), r is the interest rate in decimal form.*

It is important to point out here that this formula calculates only the interest earned, and to find the total amount of money, you must add the interest calculated to the original amount.

> Raoul needs $200 to start a snow cone stand for this hot summer. He borrows the money from a bank that charges 4% simple interest a year.
>
> a. How much will he owe if he waits 1 year to pay back the loan? If he waits two years? 3 years? 4 years? 5 years?
>
> $208, $216, $224, $232, $240
>
> b. Write a formula for the amount he will owe after t years.
>
> $200 + 0.04(200)(t - 1)$

Be sure students understand that you must pay the bank to use their money. You pay banks to use their money, and they pay you to keep your money.

Lesson 4: Why do Banks Pay YOU to Provide Their Services?
Date: 9/11/13

45

- Can you see a sequence developing from the answer to these questions? What do you notice?
  - *Students should see that the sequence increases at a constant rate (the interest rate) and is linear.*

If students are having trouble seeing the pattern, have them graph the points. Students should see that the data is linear with a constant rate of change per unit (year).

Example 2 (12 minutes)

In the 1600s, banks realized that there was another way to compute interest and make even more money. With compound interest, banks calculate the interest for the first period, add it to the total, then calculate the interest on the total for the next period, and so on. Show students the diagram below to help them understand.

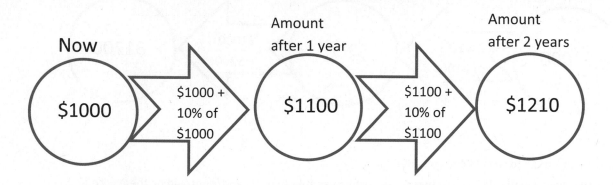

Ask students to try to write the formula. Let them struggle for a while before modeling this process for them. Help students write this as a formula by writing out what would happen each year for 5 years.

Year 1: $1000 + 0.1(1000) = 1000(1.1) = 1100$

Year 2: $1100 + 0.1(1100) = 1100(1.1) = [1000(1.1)](1.1) = 1210$

Year 3: $1210 + 0.1(1210) = 1210(1.1) = [1000(1.1)(1.1)](1.1) = 1331$

Year 4: $1331 + 0.1(1331) = 1331(1.1) = [1000(1.1)(1.1)(1.1)](1.1) = 1464.1$

Year 5: $1464.1 + 0.1(1464.1) = 1464.1(1.1) = [1000(1.1)(1.1)(1.1)(1.1)](1.1) = 1610.51$

We want them to see this pattern: $FV = PV(1 + r)^n$,

where FV = future value, PV = present value, r = interest rate as a decimal, and n = time in years.

Have a class discussion to decide on and choose the variables for this problem. Have students write the defined variables on their papers. You many need to show students how to raise values to an exponent on their calculators.

Ask students if they see a sequence forming, and have them describe it. Have students graph the points $(n, f(n))$ starting with $n = 0$ where n is the number of years that have passed and $f(n)$ is the amount of money after n years.

Lesson 4:   Why do Banks Pay YOU to Provide Their Services?
Date: 9/11/13

46

Example 2

Jack has $500 to invest. The bank offers an interest rate of 6% compounded annually. How much money will Jack have after 1 year? 2 years? 5 years? 10 years?

$530, $561.8, $669.11, $895.42

Add a scaffolding box: Have students write formulas for these sequences.

This is a perfect time to remind students about rounding to hundredths for money. Why?

- *Students should say that money is counted in dollars and cents, and cents are 1/100 of a dollar.*

Example 3 (10 minutes)

Allow students to work in groups or pairs to come up with an answer to Example 3, and then discuss. It is important to allow students to work through this process and do not be tempted to help them too soon. As students are answering the questions, look for students writing formulas, making graphs, making lists, and discussing the patterns.

Example 3

If you have $200 to invest for 10 years, would you rather invest your money in a bank that pays 7% simple interest or 5% interest compounded annually? Is there anything you could change in the problem that would make you change your answer?

7% for 10 years gives $140 *in simple interest or* $340 *total.*

5% compounded for 10 years gives $325.78.

When students present their work, be sure that they have considered changing interest rates, interest types, time invested, and amount invested. If they have not considered all of these, the problems below can aid students in seeing the changes that would take place. Really take time to look at different cases.

- What would happen if we changed both interest rates to 5%?
  - *The simple interest total would be* $300.
- Changed the time for each to 20 years?
  - *The simple interest total would be $480, and the compound interest total would be $530.66.*
- Changed the amount invested to $1000 for 10 years?
  - *The simple interest of 7% would be a total of* $1700, *and the compound interest at 5% would be a total of* $1628.89.

Do more problems like this if necessary. Identify in the room various models, formulae, graphs, tables, or lists that students may have used. Facilitate a discussion about the usefulness of the different models developed by students.

Lesson 4: Why do Banks Pay YOU to Provide Their Services?
Date: 9/11/13

47

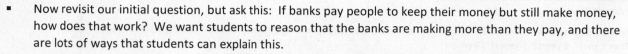
- Now revisit our initial question, but ask this: If banks pay people to keep their money but still make money, how does that work? We want students to reason that the banks are making more than they pay, and there are lots of ways that students can explain this.

    □ *Students could say that the banks invest at higher rates than they pay their customers. Students may say that the banks pay simple interest but invest money at compound interest.*

Closing (3 minutes)

- Explain the difference between simple and compound interest.

    □ *Simple interest is calculated once per year on the original amount borrowed or invested. Compound interest is calculated once per period (in this lesson per year) on the current amount in the account or owed.*

- Are there times when one type of interest is better than the other for the investor or borrower?

    □ *Either type could be better. It depends on the interest rates, the amount of time money is left in the bank or borrowed over, and the amount of money.*

Lesson Summary

Simple Interest – Interest is calculated once per year on the original amount borrowed or invested. The interest does not become part of the amount borrowed or owed (the principal).

Compound Interest – Interest is calculated once per period on the current amount borrowed or invested. Each period, the interest becomes a part of the principal.

Exit Ticket (5 minutes)

Lesson 4:   Why do Banks Pay YOU to Provide Their Services?
Date: 9/11/13

48

Name _____   Date_____

Lesson 4: Why do Banks Pay YOU to Provide Their Services?

Exit Ticket

A youth group has a yard sale to raise money for a charity. The group earns $800 but decided to put its money in the bank for a while. Calculate the amount of money the group will have if:

a. Cool Bank pays simple interest at a rate of 4% and the youth group leaves the money in for 3 years.

b. Hot Bank pays compound interest at a rate of 3% and the youth group leaves the money in for 5 years.

c. If the youth group needs the money quickly, which is the better choice? Why?

COMMON CORE™   Lesson 4:   Why do Banks Pay YOU to Provide Their Services?
Date: 9/11/13

49

Exit Ticket Sample Solutions

A youth group has a yard sale to raise money for a charity. The group earns $800 but decided to put its money in the bank for a while. Calculate the amount of money the group will have if:

a. Cool Bank pays simple interest at a rate of 4% and the youth group leaves the money in for 3 years.

$800(0.04)(3) = \$96$ *interest earned*

$896 *total*

b. Hot Bank pays compound interest at a rate of 3% and the youth group leaves the money in for 5 years.

$800(1.03)^5 = \$927.42$

c. If the youth group needs the money quickly, which is the better choice? Why?

If the youth group needs the money quickly, it should use Cool Bank since that bank pays a higher rate than Hot Bank. The lower rate is better for a longer period of time due to the compounding.

Problem Set Sample Solutions

1. $250 is invested at a bank that pays 7% simple interest. Calculate the amount of money in the account after 1 year; 3 years; 7 years; 20 years.

   $267.50, $302.50, $372.50, $600.00

2. $325 is borrowed from a bank that charges 4% interest compounded annually. How much is owed after 1 year; 3 years; 7 years; 20 years?

   $338.00, $365.58, $427.68, $712.12

3. Joseph has $10,000 to invest. He can go to Yankee Bank that pays 5% simple interest or Met Bank that pays 4% interest compounded annually. After how many years will Met Bank be the better choice?

#Years	Yankee Bank	Met Bank
1	$10,500	$10,400
2	$11,000	$10,816
3	$11,500	$11,248.64
4	$12,000	$11,698.59
5	$12,500	$12,166.53
6	$13,000	$12,653.19
7	$13,500	$13,159.32
8	$14,000	$13,685.69
9	$14,500	$14,233,12
10	$15,000	$14,802.44
11	$15,500	$15,394.54
12	$16,000	$16,010.32

At 12 years, Met Bank is a better choice.

COMMON CORE

Lesson 4:   Why do Banks Pay YOU to Provide Their Services?
Date: 9/11/13

50

Lesson 5: The Power of Exponential Growth

Student Outcomes

- Students are able to model with and solve problems involving exponential formulas.

Lesson Notes

The primary goals of the lesson are to explore the connection between exponential growth and geometric sequences and to compare linear growth to exponential growth in context. In one exercise, students graph both types of sequences on one graph to help visualize the growth in comparison to each other. In the closing, students are challenged to recognize that depending on the value of the base in the exponential expression of a geometric sequence, it can take some time before the geometric sequence will exceed the arithmetic sequence. Students begin to make connections in this lesson between geometric sequences and exponential growth and between arithmetic sequences and linear growth. These connections are formalized in later lessons.

Classwork

Opening Exercise (5 minutes)

Direct students to begin the lesson with the following comparison of two options.

Opening Exercise

Two equipment rental companies have different penalty policies for returning a piece of equipment late:

Company 1: On day 1, the penalty is $5. On day 2, the penalty is $10. On day 3, the penalty is $15. On day 4, the penalty is $20 and so on, increasing by $5 each day the equipment is late.

Company 2: On day 1, the penalty is $0.01. On day 2, the penalty is $0.02. On day 3, the penalty is $0.04. On day 4, the penalty is $0.08 and so on, doubling in amount each additional day late.

Jim rented a digger from Company 2 because he thought it had the better late return policy. The job he was doing with the digger took longer than he expected, but it did not concern him because the late penalty seemed so reasonable. When he returned the digger 15 days late, he was shocked by the penalty fee. What did he pay, and what would he have paid if he had used Company 1 instead?

Company 1		Company 2	
Day	Penalty	Day	Penalty
1	$5	1	$0.01
2	$10	2	$0.02
3	$15	3	$0.04
4	$20	4	$0.08
5	$25	5	$0.16
6	$30	6	$0.32
7	$35	7	$0.64
8	$40	8	$1.28
9	$45	9	$2.56
10	$50	10	$5.12
11	$55	11	$10.24
12	$60	12	$20.48
13	$65	13	$40.96
14	$70	14	$81.92
15	$75	15	$163.84

1. Which company has a greater 15 day late charge?

    Company 2

2. Describe how the amount of the late charge changes from any given day to the next successive day in both companies 1 and 2.

    For Company 1, the change from any given day to the next successive day is an increase by $5. For Company 2, the change from any given day to the next successive day is an increase by a factor of 2.

3. How much would the late charge have been after 20 days under Company 2?

    $5,242.88

Then discuss the following:

- Write a formula for the sequence that models the data in the table for Option 1.
    - $f(n) = 5n$, *where n begins with* 1.
- Is the sequence Arithmetic, Geometric, or neither?
    - *Arithmetic*
- Write a formula for the sequence that models the data in the table for Option 2.
    - $f(n) = 0.01(2)^{n-1}$, *where n begins with* 1.
- Is the sequence Arithmetic, Geometric, or neither?
    - *Geometric*
- Which of the two options would you say grows more quickly? Why?
    - *The penalty in Option 2 grows more quickly after a certain time because each time you are multiplying by 2 instead of just adding 5.*

Example 1 (5 minutes)

Example 1

Folklore suggests that when the creator of the game of chess showed his invention to the country's ruler, the ruler was highly impressed. He was so impressed, he told the inventor to name a prize of his choice. The inventor, being rather clever, said he would take a grain of rice on the first square of the chessboard, two grains of rice on the second square of the chessboard, four on the third square, eight on the fourth square, and so on, doubling the number of grains of rice for each successive square. The ruler was surprised, even a little offended, at such a modest price, but he ordered his treasurer to count out the rice.

a. Why is the ruler "surprised"? What makes him think the inventor requested a "modest price"?

The ruler is surprised because he hears a few grains mentioned—it seems very little, but he does not think through the effect of doubling each collection of grains; he does not know that the amount of needed rice will grow exponentially.

The treasurer took more than a week to count the rice in the ruler's store, only to notify the ruler that it would take more rice than was available in the entire kingdom. Shortly thereafter, as the story goes, the inventor became the new king.

b. Imagine the treasurer counting the needed rice for each of the 64 squares. We know that the first square is assigned a single grain of rice, and each successive square is double the number of grains of rice of the former square. The following table lists the first five assignments of grains of rice to squares on the board. How can we represent the grains of rice as exponential expressions?

Square #	Grains of Rice	Exponential Expression
1	1	2^0
2	2	2^1
3	4	2^2
4	8	2^3
5	16	2^4

c. Write the exponential expression that describes how much rice is assigned to each of the last three squares of the board.

Square #	Exponential Expression
62	2^{61}
63	2^{62}
64	2^{63}

Discussion (10 minutes): Exponential Formulas

Ask students to consider how the exponential expressions of Example 1b relate to one another.

- Why is the base of the expression 2?
  - *Since each successive square has twice the amount of rice as the former square, the factor by which the rice increases is a factor of 2.*

- What is the explicit formula for the sequence that models the number of rice grains in each square? Use n to represent the number of the square and $f(n)$ to represent the number of rice grains assigned to that square.
  - $f(n) = 2^{(n-1)}$, *where $f(n)$ represents the number of rice grains belonging to each square, and n represents the number of the square on the board.*

- Would the formula $f(n) = 2^n$ work? Why or why not?
  - *No, the formula is supposed to model the numbering scheme on the chessboard corresponding to the story.*

- What would have to change for the formula $f(n) = 2^n$ to be appropriate?
  - *If the first square started with 2 grains of rice and doubled thereafter, or if we numbered the squares as starting with square number 0 and ending on square 63, then $f(n) = 2^n$ would be appropriate.*

- Suppose instead that the first square did not begin with a single grain of rice but with 5 grains of rice, and then the number of grains was doubled with each successive square. Write the sequence of numbers representing the number of grains of rice for the first five squares.
  - $5, 10, 20, 40, 80$

- Suppose we wanted to represent these numbers using exponents? Would we still require the use of the powers of 2?
  - *Yes.* $5 = 5(2^0), 10 = 5(2^1), 20 = 5(2^2), 40 = 5(2^3), 80 = 5(2^4)$

- Generalize the pattern of these exponential expressions into an explicit formula for the sequence. How does it compare to the formula in the case where we began with a single grain of rice in the first square?
  - $f(n) = 5(2^{(n-1)})$, *the powers of 2 cause the doubling effect, and the 5 represents the initial 5 grains of rice.*

- Generalize the formula even further. Write a formula for a sequence that allows for any possible value for the number of grains of rice on the first square.
  - $f(n) = a2^{n-1}$, *where a represents the number of rice grains on the first square.*

- Generalize the formula even further. What if instead of doubling the number of grains, we wanted to triple or quadruple them?
  - $f(n) = ab^{n-1}$, *where a represents the number of rice grains on the first square and b represents the factor by which the number of rice grains is multiplied on each successive square.*

- Is the sequence for this formula Geometric, Arithmetic, or neither?
  - *Geometric*

MP.4

Example 2 (10 minutes)

Note that students may, or may not, connect the points in their graphs with a smooth line or curve as shown below. Be clear with the students that we were only asked to graph the points but that it is natural to recognize the form that the points take on by modeling them with the line or curve.

Example 2

Let us understand the difference between $f(n) = 2n$ and $f(n) = 2^n$.

a. Complete the tables below, and then graph the points $(n, f(n))$ on a coordinate plane for each of the formulas.

n	$f(n) = 2n$
-2	-4
-1	-2
0	0
1	2
2	4
3	6

n	$f(n) = 2^n$
-2	$\dfrac{1}{4}$
-1	$\dfrac{1}{2}$
0	1
1	2
2	4
3	8

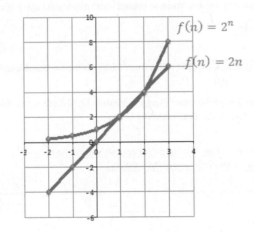

b. Describe the change in each sequence when n increases by 1 unit for each sequence.

For the sequence $f(n) = 2n$, for every increase in n by 1 unit, the $f(n)$ value increases by 2 units. For the sequence $f(n) = 2^n$, for every increase in n by 1 unit, the $f(n)$ value increases by a factor of 2.

Exercise 1 (7 minutes)

Students should attempt Exercises 1 and 2 independently and then share responses as a class.

Exercise 1

A typical thickness of toilet paper is 0.001 inches. Seems pretty thin, right? Let's see what happens when we start folding toilet paper.

a. How thick is the stack of toilet paper after 1 fold? After 2 folds? After 5 folds?

After 1 fold: $0.001(2^1) = 0.002"$

After 2 folds: $0.001(2^2) = 0.004"$

After 5 folds: $0.001(2^5) = 0.032"$

b. Write an explicit formula for the sequence that models the thickness of the folded toilet paper after n folds.

$f(n) = 0.001(2^n)$

c. After many folds will the stack of folded toilet paper pass the 1 foot mark?

After 14 folds

d. The moon is about 240,000 miles from Earth. Compare the thickness of the toilet paper folded 50 times to the distance from Earth.

Toilet paper folded 50 times is approximately 17,769,885 miles thick. That is approximately 74 times the distance between the Earth and the moon.

Watch the following video "<u>How folding paper can get you to the moon</u>"
(<u>http://www.youtube.com/watch?v=AmFMJC45f1Q</u>)

Exercise 2 (3 minutes)

Exercise 2

A rare coin appreciates at a rate of 5.2% a year. If the initial value of the coin is $500, after how many years will its value cross the $3,000 mark? Show the formula that will model the value of the coin after t years.

The value of the coin will cross the $3,000 *mark after 35 years;* $f(t) = 500(1.052)^t$.

Closing (2 minutes)

- Consider the sequences $G(n) = ab^n$, where n begins at 0 and $A(n) = a + bn$, where n begins at 0. Assume that $b > 1$.

- Which sequence will have the larger 0th term? Does it depend on what values are chosen for a and b?

  □ *Both sequences will have the same* 0th *term; the term will be* a, *regardless of what values are chosen for* a *and* b.

Exit Ticket (3 minutes)

Name _____   Date_____

Lesson 5: The Power of Exponential Growth

Exit Ticket

Chain emails are emails with a message suggesting you will have good luck if you forward the email on to others. Suppose a student started a chain email by sending the message to 3 friends and asking those friends to each send the same email to 3 more friends exactly 1 day after they received it.

a. Write an explicit formula for the sequence that models the number of people who will receive the email on the nth day. (Let the first day be the day the original email was sent.) Assume everyone who receives the email follows the directions.

b. Which day will be the first day that the number of people receiving the email exceeds 100?

Exit Ticket Sample Solutions

Chain emails are emails with a message suggesting you will have good luck if you forward the email on to others. Suppose a student started a chain email by sending the message to 3 friends and asking those friends to each send the same email to 3 more friends exactly 1 day after they received it.

a.   Write an explicit formula for the sequence that models the number of people who will receive the email on the nth day. (Let the first day be the day the original email was sent.) Assume everyone who receives the email follows the directions.

$f(n) = 3^n, \ n \geq 1$

b.   Which day will be the first day that the number of people receiving the email exceeds 100?

On the 5th day.

Problem Set Sample Solutions

1.   A bucket is put under a leaking ceiling. The amount of water in the bucket doubles every minute. After 8 minutes, the bucket is full. After how many minutes is the container half full?

7 minutes

2.   A three-bedroom house in Burbville was purchased for $190,000. If housing prices are expected to increase 1.8% annually in that town, write an explicit formula that models the price of the house in t years. Find the price of the house in 5 years.

$f(t) = 190,000(1.018)^t;$ $207,727.$

3.   A local college has increased the number of graduates by a factor of 1.045 over the previous year for every year since 1999. In 1999, 924 students graduated. What explicit formula models this situation? Approximately how many students will graduate in 2014?

$f(t) = 924(1.045)^t;$ 1,788 *graduates are expected in 2014.*

4.   The population growth rate of New York City has fluctuated tremendously in the last 200 years, the highest rate estimated at 126.8% in 1900. In 2001, the population of the city was 8,008,288, up 2.1% from 2000. If we assume that the annual population growth rate stayed at 2.1% from the year 2000 onward, in what year would we expect the population of New York City to have exceeded ten million people? Be sure to include the explicit formula you use to arrive at your answer.

$f(t) = 8,008,288(1.021)^t.$ *Based on this formula, we can expect the population of New York City to exceeded ten million people in 2012.*

5.   In 2013, a research company found that smartphone shipments (units sold) were up 32.7% worldwide from 2012, with an expectation for the trend to continue. If 959 million units were sold in 2013, how many smartphones can be expected to be sold in 2018 at the same growth rate? (Include the explicit formula for the sequence that models this growth.) Can this trend continue?

$f(t) = 959(1.327)^t;$ *Approximately 3.95 billion units are expected to be sold in 2018. No. There are a finite number of people on Earth, so this trend cannot continue.*

6. Two band mates have only 7 days to spread the word about their next performance. Jack thinks they can each pass out 100 fliers a day for 7 days and they will have done a good job in getting the news out. Meg has a different strategy. She tells 10 of her friends about the performance on the first day and asks each of her 10 friends to each tell a friend on the second day and then everyone who has heard about the concert to tell a friend on the third day and so on, for 7 days. Make an assumption that students make sure they are telling someone who has not already been told.

a. Over the first 7 days, Meg's strategy will reach fewer people than Jack's. Show that this is true.

Jack's strategy: $J(t) = 100/day \times 7\ days = 700\ people\ will\ know\ about\ the\ concert.$

Meg's strategy: $M(t) = 10(2)^{t-1}; F(7) = 640\ people\ will\ know\ about\ the\ concert.$

b. If they had been given more than 7 days, would there be a day on which Meg's strategy would begin to inform more people than Jack's strategy? If not, explain why not. If so, which day would this occur on?

On the 8th day, Meg's strategy would reach more people than Jack's: $J(t) = 800; M(8) = 1280.$

c. Knowing that she has only 7 days, how can Meg alter her strategy to reach more people than Jack does?

She can ask her ten initial friends to each tell two people each and let them tell two other people on the next day, etc.

7. On June 1, a fast-growing species of algae is accidentally introduced into a lake in a city park. It starts to grow and cover the surface of the lake in such a way that the area covered by the algae doubles every day. If it continues to grow unabated, the lake will be totally covered, and the fish in the lake will suffocate. At the rate it is growing, this will happen on June 30.

a. When will the lake be covered half way?

June 29

b. On June 26, a pedestrian who walks by the lake every day warns that the lake will be completely covered soon. Her friend just laughs. Why might her friend be skeptical of the warning?

On June 26, the lake will only be 6.25% covered. To the casual observer, it will be hard to imagine such a jump between this small percent of coverage to 100% coverage in a mere 4 more days.

c. On June 29, a clean-up crew arrives at the lake and removes almost all of the algae. When they are done, only 1% of the surface is covered with algae. How well does this solve the problem of the algae in the lake?

It only takes care of the problem for a week:

> *June 29 – 1%*
>
> *June 30 – 2%*
>
> *July 1 – 4%*
>
> *July 2 – 8%*
>
> *July 3 – 16%*
>
> *July 4 – 32%*
>
> *July 5 – 64%*

By July 6th, the lake will be completely covered with algae.

d. Write an explicit formula for the sequence that models the percentage of the surface area of the lake that is covered in algae, a, given the time in days, t, that has passed since the algae was introduced into the lake.

$$f(t) = a(2^{(t-1)})$$

Lesson 5: The Power of Exponential Growth

Date: 9/11/13

59

8. Mrs. Davis is making a poster of math formulas for her students. She takes the 8.5in × 11in paper she printed the formulas on to the photocopy machine and enlarges the image so that the length and the width are both 150% of the original. She enlarges the image a total of 3 times before she is satisfied with the size of the poster. Write an explicit formula for the sequence that models the area of the poster, A, after n enlargements. What is the area of the final image compared to the area of the original, expressed as a percent increase and rounded to the nearest percent?

The area of the original piece of paper is $93.5\ in^2$. Increasing the length and width by a factor of 1.5 increases the area by a factor of 2.25. Thus, $A(n) = 93.5(2.25)^n$. The area after 3 iterations is approximated by $93.5(11.39)$ for a result of $1065\ in^2$. The percent increase was 1139%.

Lesson 6: Exponential Growth—U.S. Population and World Population

Student Outcomes

- Students compare linear and exponential models of population growth.

Classwork

Example 1 (8 minutes)

Give students time to review the two graphs. Ask students to compare the two graphs and make conjectures about the rates of change. As the students share the conjectures with the class, respond without judgment as to accuracy, simply suggesting that we will investigate further and see which conjectures are correct.

Example 1

Callie and Joe are examining the population data in the graphs below for a history report. Their comments are as follows:

Callie: It looks like the U.S. population grew the same amount as the world population, but that can't be right, can it?

Joe: Well, I don't think they grew by the same *amount*, but they sure grew at about the same rate. Look at the slopes.

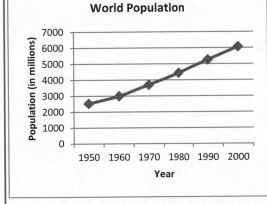

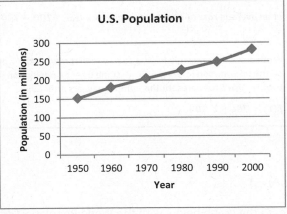

Be aware that students frequently ignore scale on graphs and may offer incorrect observations as a result. If students respond incorrectly to the prompts, direct partners or groups to discuss why the response or observation is incorrect.

a. Is Callie's observation correct? Why or why not?

No. The world population grew by a far greater amount as shown by the scale of the vertical axis.

b. Is Joe's observation correct? Why or why not?

No. Again, Joe ignored the scale, just as Callie did. The rate of change (or slope) is much greater for the world population than for the U.S. population.

c. Use the World Population graph to estimate the percent increase in world population from 1950 to 2000.

Using 2500 million for the year 1950 and 6000 million for the year 2000 gives a percent increase of 140%, obtained by computing $\dfrac{6000-2500}{2500}$.

d. Now use the U.S. Population graph to compute the percent increase in the U.S. population for the same time period.

Using 150 million for the year 1950 and 280 million for the year 2000 gives a percent increase of 87%, obtained by computing $\dfrac{280-150}{150}$.

e. How does the percent increase for the world population compare to that for the U.S. population over the same time period, 1950 to 2000?

The world population was increasing at a faster average rate than the U.S. population was.

f. Do the graphs above seem to indicate linear or exponential population growth? Explain your response.

In the time frame shown, the growth appears to be linear. The world population is increasing at an average rate of about 70 million per year. $\left(6,000-2,500=3,500;\dfrac{3,500}{50}=70\right)$ The U.S. population is increasing at an average rate of about 2.6 million per year. $\left(280-150=130;\dfrac{130}{50}=2.6\right)$

g. Write an explicit formula for the sequence that models the world population growth from 1950–2000 based on the information in the graph. Assume that the population (in millions) in 1950 was $2,500$ and in 2000 was $6,000$. Use t to represent the number of years after 1950.

$f(t) = 70t + 2,500.$

Example 2 (15 minutes)

Ask students to compare the graph below with the World Population graph Callie and Joe were using in Example 1. Again, students may respond incorrectly if they ignore scale. Requiring students to investigate and discover why their responses are incorrect will result in deeper understanding of the concept.

Joe tells Callie he has found a different world population graph that looks very different from their first one.

Example 2

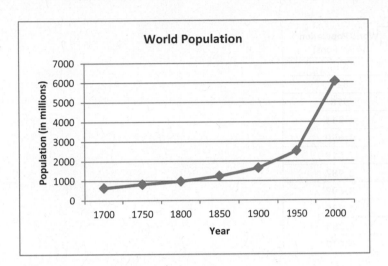

a. How is this graph similar to the World Population graph in Example 1? How is it different?

This graph uses the same vertical scale as the one for world population in Example 1. This graph is different in two ways: 1. It shows years from AD 1700 through 2000 instead of from 1950-2000, and 2. The graph itself shows that population growth took an exponential turn in approximately 1850.

b. Does the behavior of the graph from 1950–2000 match that shown on the graph in Example1?

Yes, both graphs show that 1950 world population was about 2,500 million and 2000 world population was just over 6,000 million.

c. Why is the graph from Example 1 somewhat misleading?

The graph in Example 1 makes it appear as if the world population has grown in a linear fashion when it has really grown exponentially if examined over a longer period of time.

d. An exponential formula that can be used to model the world population growth from 1950 through 2000 is as follows:

$$f(t) = 2,519(1.0177^t)$$

where 2,519 represents the world population in the year 1950, and t represents the number of years after 1950. Use this equation to calculate the world population in 1950, 1980, and 2000. How do your calculations compare with the world populations shown on the graph?

$1950 - 2,519$; $1980 - 4,264$; $2000 - 6,056$. *The amounts are similar to those shown on the graph.*

e.   Following is a table showing the world population numbers used to create the graphs above.

Year	World Population (in millions)
1700	640
1750	824
1800	978
1850	1,244
1900	1,650
1950	2,519
1960	2,982
1970	3,692
1980	4,435
1990	5,263
2000	6,070

How do the numbers in the table compare with those you calculated in part (d) above?

1950 is identical (since it was used as the base year); 1980 is reasonably close (4,264 vs. 4,435 million; about 3.9% variance); 2000 is very close (within 14 million; about 2% variance).

f.   How is the formula in part (d) above different from the formula in Example 1 part (g)? What causes the difference? Which formula more closely represents the population?

The formula in Example 1 part (g) is linear while the formula in part (d) above is exponential. The growth rate in the linear formula is a fixed 70 million increase in population each year whereas the growth rate in the exponential formula is a factor of 0.0177 or 1.77%. An exponential equation grows by a constant factor each year, while a linear equation grows by a constant difference each year. The exponential equation offers a more accurate model since the projected population numbers using this model more closely match the actual figures.

Exercises (17 minutes)

Have students work with a partner or small group to answer the exercises. Circulate to respond to group questions and to guide student responses.

Exercises

1. The table below represents the population of the U.S. (in millions) for the specified years.

Year	U.S. Population (in millions)
1800	5
1900	76
2000	282

   a. If we use the data from 1800–2000 to create an exponential equation representing the population, we generate the following formula for the sequence, where $f(t)$ represents the U.S. population and t represents the number of years after 1800.
   $$f(t) = 5(1.0204)^t$$

   Use this formula to determine the population of the U.S. in the year 2010.

   This formula yields a U.S. population of 347 million in 2010.

   b. If we use the data from 1900–2000 to create an exponential formula that models the population, we generate the following, where $f(t)$ represents the U.S. population and t represents the number of years after 1900.
   $$f(t) = 76(1.013)^t$$

   Use this formula to determine the population of the U.S. in the year 2010.

   This formula yields a U.S. population of 315 million in 2010.

   c. The actual U.S. population in the year 2010 was 309 million. Which of the above formulas better models the U.S. population for the entire span of 1800–2010? Why?

   The formula in part (b) resulted in a closer approximation of the 2010 population. Although the population of the U.S. is still increasing exponentially, the rate has slowed considerably in the last few decades. Using the population from 1800–2000 to generate the formula results in a growth factor higher than the rate of the current population growth.

   d. Complete the table below to show projected population figures for the years indicated. Use the formula from part (b) to determine the numbers.

Year	World Population (in millions)
2020	358
2050	528
2080	777

   e. Are the population figures you computed reasonable? What other factors need to be considered when projecting population?

   These numbers do not necessarily take into account changes in technology, efforts to reduce birth rates, food supply, or changes in life expectancy due to disease or scientific advances. Students may come up with a variety of responses.

2. The population of the country of Oz was $600,000$ in the year 2010. The population is expected to grow by a factor of 5% annually. The annual food supply of Oz is currently sufficient for a population of $700,000$ people and is increasing at a rate which will supply food for an additional $10,000$ people per year.

   a. Write a formula to model the population of Oz. Is your formula linear or exponential?

   $P(t) = 600,000(1.05)^t$, *with* $P(t)$ *representing population and* t *representing years after 2010. The formula is exponential.*

   b. Write a formula to model the food supply. Is the formula linear or exponential?

   $f(t) = 700,000 + 10,000t$, *with* $f(t)$ *representing the food supply in terms of number of people supplied with food and* t *representing the number of years after 2010. The equation is linear.*

   c. At what point does the population exceed the food supply? Justify your response.

   The population exceeds the food supply sometime during 2015. Students might use a table or a graph to support this response.

   d. If Oz doubled its current food supply (to 1.4 million), would shortages still take place? Explain.

   Yes; the food supply would run out during the year 2031. Again, students may justify their response using with a graph or a table.

   e. If Oz doubles both its beginning food supply and doubles the rate at which the food supply increases, would food shortages still take place? Explain.

   Yes; the food supply would run out in the year 2034. Students may justify with either a graph or a table.

Closing (2 minutes)

- Why did the equation $f(t) = 600,000(1.05)^t$ increase so much more quickly that the equation f(t) = 700,000 + 10,000t?

  □ *The first formula is exponential while the second formula is linear.*

- One use of studying population growth involves estimating food shortages. Why might we be interested in modeling population growth at a local level?

  □ *City planners may use population models to plan for road construction, school district boundaries, sewage and water facilities, and similar infrastructure issues.*

Exit Ticket (3 minutes)

Name _____   Date_____

Lesson 6: Exponential Growth—U.S. Population and World Population

Exit Ticket

Do the examples below require a linear or exponential growth model? State whether each example is linear or exponential, and write an explicit formula for the sequence that models the growth for each case. Include a description of the variables you use.

1. A savings account accumulates no interest but receives a deposit of $825 per month.

2. The value of a house increases by 1.5% per year.

3. Every year, the alligator population is $\frac{9}{7}$ of the previous year's population.

4. The temperature increases by 2° every 30 minutes from 8:00 a.m. to 3:30 p.m. each day for the month of July.

5. Every 240 minutes, $\frac{1}{3}$ of the rodent population dies.

Exit Ticket Sample Solutions

Do the examples below require a linear or exponential growth model? State linear or exponential for each, and write an explicit formula that models the growth for each case. Include a description of the variables you use.

1. A savings account, accumulating no interest with a deposit of $825 per month.

    linear; $f(t) = 825t$, where $f(t)$ represents the accumulated value in the account after t months

2. The value of a house increases by 1.5% per year.

    exponential; $f(t) = b(1.015)^t$, where b represents the beginning value of the house and $f(t)$ is the value of the house after t years.

3. Every year, the alligator population is $\frac{9}{7}$ of the previous year's population.

    exponential; $P(t) = c\left(\frac{9}{7}\right)^t$, where c represents the current population of alligators and $P(t)$ is the alligator population after t years.

4. The temperature increases by $2°$ every 30 minutes from $8{:}00$ a.m. to $3{:}30$ p.m. each day for the month of July.

    linear; $T(t) = 2t + b$; where b represents the beginning temperature and $T(t)$ is the temperature after t half-hour periods since $8{:}00\ a.m.$

5. Every 240 minutes, $\frac{1}{3}$ of the rodent population dies.

    exponential; $r(t) = p\left(\frac{2}{3}\right)^t$; where p is the current population of rodents $r(t)$ is the remaining population of rodents after t four-hour periods.

Problem Set Sample Solutions

1. Student Friendly Bank pays a simple interest rate of 2.5% per year. Neighborhood Bank pays a compound interest rate of 2.1% per year, compounded monthly.

    a. Which bank will provide the largest balance if you plan to invest $10,000$ for 10 years? For 20 years?

        Student Friendly Bank gives a larger balance at the 10-year mark. Neighborhood Bank gives a larger balance by the 20-year mark.

    b. Write an explicit formula for the sequence that models the balance of the Student Friendly Bank balance, t years after a deposit is left in the account.

        $S(t) = 10,000 + 0.025(10,000)t$

    c. Write an explicit formula for the sequence that models the balance at the Neighborhood Bank balance, m months after a deposit is left in the account.

        $$N(m) = 10,000\left(1 + \frac{0.021}{12}\right)^{12m}$$

d. Create a table of values indicating the balances in the two bank accounts from year 2 to year 20 in 2 year increments. Round each value to the nearest dollar.

Year	Student Friendly Bank (in dollars)	Neighborhood Bank (in dollars)
0	10,000	10,000
2	10,500	10,429
4	11,000	10,875
6	11,500	11,342
8	12,000	11,828
10	12,500	12,335
12	13,000	12,863
14	13,500	13,414
16	14,000	13,989
18	14,500	14,589
20	15,000	15,214

e. Which bank is a better short-term investment? Which bank is better for those leaving money in for a longer period of time? When are the investments about the same?

Student Friendly Bank; Neighborhood Bank; they are about the same by the end of year 17.

f. What type of model is Student Friendly Bank? What is the rate or ratio of change?

linear; 0.025 per year

g. What type of model is Neighborhood Bank? What is the rate or ratio of change?

exponential; $\dfrac{0.021}{12}$ per month

2. The table below represents the population of the state of New York for the years 1800–2000. Use this information to answer the questions.

Year	Population
1800	300,000
1900	7,300,000
2000	19,000,000

a. Using the year 1800 as the base year, an explicit formula for the sequence that models the population of New York is $P(t) = 300000(1.021)^t$, where t is the number of years after 1800. Using this formula, calculate the projected population of New York in 2010.

23,579,000

b. Using the year 1900 as the base year, an explicit formula for the sequence that models the population of New York is $P(t) = 7300000(1.0096)^t$, where t is the number of years after 1900. Using this equation, calculate the projected population of New York in 2010.

20,881,000

c. Using the internet (or some other source), find the population of the state of New York according to the 2010 census. Which formula yielded a more accurate prediction of the 2010 population?

The actual population of the state of New York in 2010 was 19,200,000. The formula in part (b) resulted in a more accurate prediction.

Lesson 7: Exponential Decay

Student Outcomes

- Students describe and analyze exponential decay models; they recognize that in a formula that models exponential decay, the growth factor b is less than 1; or, equivalently, when b is greater than 1, exponential formulas with negative exponents could also be used to model decay.

Classwork

Example 1 (20 minutes)

The value of a brand new car drops considerably as soon as the first purchaser completes the purchase and drives it off the lot. Generally speaking, if the buyer of a car tried to sell the car to another dealer or individual just one day after the car was bought, the buyer would not be able to sell it for what he or she paid for it. Once purchased, the car is now considered used.

Have students work Example 1 part (a) independently or in pairs.

Example 1

a.   Malik bought a new car for $15,000. As he drove it off the lot, his best friend, Will, told him that the car's value just dropped by 15% and that it would continue to depreciate 15% of its current value each year. If the car's value is now $12,750 (according to Will), what will its value be after 5 years?

Complete the table below to determine the car's value after each of the next five years.

Number of years, t, passed since driving the car off the lot	Car value after t years	15% depreciation of current car value	Car value minus the 15% depreciation
0	$12,750.00	$1,912.50	$10,837.50
1	10,837.50	1,625.63	9,211.87
2	9,211.87	1,381.78	7,830.09
3	7,830.09	1,174.51	6,655.58
4	6,655.58	998.34	5,657.24
5	5,657.24	848.59	4,808.65

Scaffold students through part (b). Allow them to try it independently and test their formulas by answering part (c). It may be helpful to allow students to work in partners or small groups. If students are not progressing, scaffold with questions like the following:

- What number could I multiply the value of the car by to get the value of the car one year later?
- What is the ratio between the value after 1 year and the start value? What is the ratio between the value after 2 years and the value after 1 year? Between year 3 and year 2? Year 4 and year 3? Year 5 and year 4?
  - *0.85*
- What does the value 0.85 have to do with a 15% decrease?
  - *It's what is left after you take off 15%. You are left with 85% of the car's value.*

MP.4

---

b. **Write an explicit formula for the sequence that models the value of Malik's car t years after driving it off the lot.**

$$v(t) = 12,750(0.85)^t$$

c. **Use the formula from part (b) to determine the value of Malik's car five years after its purchase. Round your answer to the nearest cent. Compare the value with the value in the table. Are they the same?**

$$v(t) = 12,750(0.85)^5 \approx 5,657.24 \text{ It is the same value.}$$

d. **Use the formula from part (b) to determine the value of Malik's car 7 years after its purchase. Round your answer to the nearest cent.**

$$v(t) = 12,750(0.85)^7 \approx 4,087.36$$

- Our equation looks quite similar to the formulas we used in the last two lessons for exponential growth. Is the value of the car growing though?
  - *No.*
- How can I tell just by looking at the formula that the value of the car is not growing?
  - *Because the value 0.85 shows you that the value is going to get smaller each time.*
- In this case, we call the model an **exponential decay** model. Write another example of an explicit formula that could be used in a situation of exponential decay.
- Compare your equation with a neighbor. Does your neighbor's equation accurately represent exponential decay?
- What determines whether an explicit formula is modeling exponential decay or exponential growth?
  - *The value of the growth factor, b, **determines whether an explicit formula is modeling exponential decay or exponential growth**; if $b > 1$, output will grow over time, but if $b < 1$ output will diminish over time.*

You may wish to take time now to clarify with students that the response above is only valid for exponential formulas in which the expression representing the exponent is positive for positive values of t (or whatever variable is representing time). A formula like $f(t) = 1000(2)^{-t}$, for example, would not model growth over time, but decay over time.

- What happens to the output if the growth factor of the formula is equal to 1.
  - *The output would be neither growth nor decay. The initial value would never change.*

Exercises (15 minutes)

Students work individually or with partners to complete the exercises below. Encourage students to compare answers to Exercises 2-6.

Exercises

1. Identify the initial value in each formula below, and state whether the formula models exponential growth or exponential decay. Justify your responses.

    a. $f(t) = 2 \left(\dfrac{2}{5}\right)^t$

    $a = 2.$ Decay; $b < 1$

    b. $f(t) = 2 \left(\dfrac{5}{3}\right)^t$

    $a = 2.$ *Growth; $b > 1$*

    c. $f(t) = \dfrac{2}{3}(3)^t$

    $a = \dfrac{2}{3}.$ *Growth; $b > 1$*

    d. $f(t) = \dfrac{2}{3}\left(\dfrac{1}{3}\right)^t$

    $a = \dfrac{2}{3}.$ *Decay; $b < 1$*

    e. $f(t) = \dfrac{3}{2}\left(\dfrac{2}{3}\right)^t$

    $a = \dfrac{3}{2}.$ *Decay; $b < 1$*

2. If a person takes a given dosage (d) of a particular medication, then the formula $f(t) = d\,(0.8)^t$ represents the concentration of the medication in the bloodstream t hours later. If Charlotte takes 200 mg of the medication at 6:00 a.m., how much remains in her bloodstream at 10:00 a.m.? How long does it take for the concentration to drop below 1 mg?

    81.92 mg of the medication remains in her bloodstream at 10:00 a.m.; it would take about 24 hours to drop below 1 mg.

    Note: It is expected that students will arrive at the estimate of 24 hours using a guess-and-check procedure.

3. When you breathe normally, about 12% of the air in your lungs is replaced with each breath. Write an explicit formula for the sequence that models the amount of the original air left in your lungs, given that the initial volume of air is 500 mL. Use your model to determine how much of the original 500 mL remains after 50 breaths.

    $a(n) = 500\,(1 - 0.12)^n,$ *where n is the number of breaths. After 50 breaths, only 0.83 mL of the original 500 mL remains in your lungs.*

4. Ryan bought a new computer for \$2,100. The value of the computer decreases by 50% each year. When will the value drop below \$300?

    After 3 years, the value will be \$262.50.

---

5. Kelli's mom takes a 400 mg dose of aspirin. Each hour, the amount of aspirin in a person's system decreases by about 29%. How much aspirin is left in her system after 6 hours?

   51 *mg*

6. According to the International Basketball Association (FIBA), a basketball must be inflated to a pressure such that, when it is dropped from a height of $1,800$ mm, it will rebound to a height of $1,300$ mm. Maddie decides to test the rebound-ability of her new basketball. She assumes that the ratio of each rebound height to the previous rebound height remains the same at $\frac{1,300}{1,800}$. Let $f(n)$ be the height of the basketball after n bounces. Complete the chart below to reflect the heights Maddie expects to measure.

n	$f(n)$
0	$1,800$
1	$1,300$
2	939
3	678
4	490

   a. Write the explicit formula for the sequence that models the height of Maddie's basketball after any number of bounces.

   $$f(n) = 1,800 \left(\frac{13}{18}\right)^n$$

   b. Plot the points from the table. Connect the points with a smooth curve, and then use the curve to estimate the bounce number at which the rebound height will drop below 200 mm.

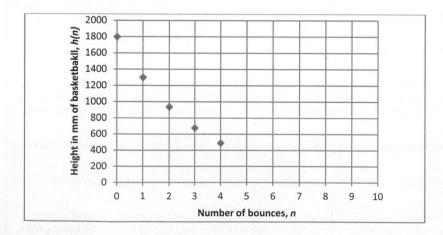

   At the 7th rebound, the rebound height falls below 200 mm.

Closing (5 minutes)

- Create a word problem that could be solved using an exponential decay model. Solve the problem yourself on a separate sheet of paper.

After students have written their word problems and solved them, check their problems before allowing the students to exchange problems for solving with another student.

Lesson Summary

The explicit formula $f(t) = ab^t$ models exponential decay, where a represents the initial value of the sequence, $b < 1$ represents the growth factor (or decay factor) per unit of time, and t represents units of time.

Exit Ticket (5 minutes)

Name _____   Date_____

Lesson 7: Exponential Decay

Exit Ticket

A huge ping-pong tournament is held in Beijing, with 65,536 participants at the start of the tournament. Each round of the tournament eliminates half the participants.

   a.   If $p(r)$ represents the number of participants remaining after r rounds of play, write a formula to model the number of participants remaining.

   b.   Use your model to determine how many participants remain after 10 rounds of play.

   c.   How many rounds of play will it take to determine the champion ping-pong player?

Exit Ticket Sample Solutions

A huge ping-pong tournament is held in Beijing, with $65,536$ participants at the start of the tournament. Each round of the tournament eliminates half the participants.

a. If $p(r)$ represents the number of participants remaining after r rounds of play, write a formula to model the number of participants remaining.

$$p(r) = 65,536 \left(\frac{1}{2}\right)^r$$

b. Use your model to determine how many participants remain after 10 rounds of play.

64 participants remain after 10 rounds.

c. How many rounds of play will it take to determine the champion ping-pong player?

It will take a total of 16 rounds to eliminate all but one player.

Problem Set Sample Solutions

1. From 2000 to 2013, the value of the U.S. dollar has been shrinking. The value can be modeled by the following formula:

$$v(t) = 1.36 \, (0.9758)^t, \text{ where } t \text{ is the number of years since } 2000.$$

a. How much was a dollar worth in the year 2005?

$\$1.20$

b. Graph the points $(t, v(t))$, for integer values of $0 \le t \le 14$.

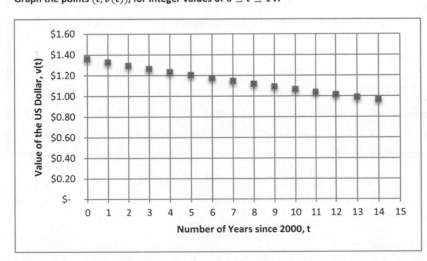

c. Estimate the year in which the value of the dollar fell below $\$1.00$.

2013

2. A construction company purchased some equipment costing $300,000$. The value of the equipment depreciates (decreases) at a rate of 14% per year.

   a. Write a formula that models the value of the equipment.

   $v(t) = 300,000 \ (0.86)^t$, *where t is the number of years after the purchase.*

   b. What is the value of the equipment after 9 years?

   $\$77,198$

   c. Graph the points $\left(t, v(t)\right)$ for integer values of $0 \leq t \leq 15$.

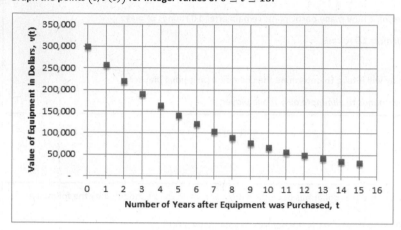

   d. Estimate when the equipment will have a value of $\$50,000$.

   After 12 *years*

3. The number of newly reported cases of HIV (in thousands) in the United States from 2000 to 2010 can be modeled by the following formula:

   $f(t) = 41(0.9842)^t$, where t is the number of years after 2000.

   a. Identify the growth factor.

   0.9842

   b. Calculate the estimated number of new HIV cases reported in 2004.

   $38,470$

c.   Graph the points $(t, f(t))$ for integer values of $0 \le t \le 10$.

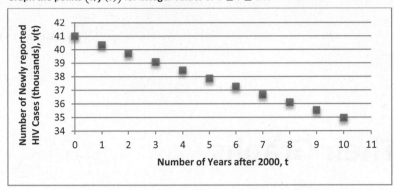

d.   During what year did the number of newly reported HIV cases drop below $36{,}000$?

2009

4.   Doug drank a soda with 130 mg of caffeine. Each hour, the caffeine in the body diminishes by about 12%.

a.   Write formula to model the amount of caffeine remaining in Doug's system.

$c(t) = 130\,(0.88)^{t}$, *where t is the number of hours after Doug drinks the beverage.*

b.   How much caffeine remains in Doug's system after 2 hours?

101 mg

c.   How long will it take for the level of caffeine in Doug's system to drop below 50 mg?

8 hours

5. 64 teams participate in a softball tournament in which half the teams are eliminated after each round of play.

a.   Write a formula to model the number of teams remaining after any given round of play.

$t(n) = 64\,(0.5)^{n}$, *where n is the number of rounds played.*

b.   How many teams remain in play after 3 rounds?

8 teams

c.   How many rounds of play will it take to determine which team wins the tournament?

6 rounds

6.   Sam bought a used car for $\$8{,}000$. He boasted that he got a great deal since the value of the car two years ago (when it was new) was $\$15{,}000$. His friend, Derek, was skeptical, stating that the value of a car typically depreciates about 25% per year, so Sam got a bad deal.

a.   Use Derek's logic to write a formula for the value of Sam's car. Use t for the total age of the car in years.

$v(t) = 15{,}000\,(0.75)^{t}$

b.   Who is right, Sam or Derek?

Sam is right. According to Derek's formula, the value of Sam's car after two years is $\$8{,}437.50$. If Sam paid only $\$8{,}000$ for the car, he did get a "great" deal.

Topic B:

Functions and Their Graphs

F-IF.A.1, F-IF.A.2, F-IF.B.4, F-IF.B.5, F-IF.C.7a

Focus Standard:	F-IF.A.1	Understand that a function from one set (called the domain) to another set (called the range) assigns to each element of the domain exactly one element of the range. If f is a function and x is an element of its domain, then $f(x)$ denotes the output of f corresponding to the input x. The graph of f is the graph of the equation $y = f(x)$.
	F-IF.A.2	Use function notation, evaluate functions for inputs in their domains, and interpret statements that use function notation in terms of a context.
	F-IF.B.4	For a function that models a relationship between two quantities, interpret key features of graphs and tables in terms of the quantities, and sketch graphs showing key features given a verbal description of the relationship. *Key features include: intercepts; intervals where the function is increasing, decreasing, positive, or negative; relative maximums and minimums; symmetries; end behavior; and periodicity.*★
	F-IF.B.5	Relate the domain of a function to its graph and, where applicable, to the quantitative relationship it describes. *For example, if the function h(n) gives the number of person-hours it takes to assemble n engines in a factory, then the positive integers would be an appropriate domain for the function.*★
	F-IF.C.7a	Graph functions expressed symbolically and show key features of the graph, by hand in simple cases and using technology for more complicated cases.★
		a. Graph linear and quadratic functions and show intercepts, maxima, and minima.

Instructional Days:	7
Lesson 8:	Why Stay with Whole Numbers?
Lesson 9-10:	Representing, Naming, and Evaluating Functions
Lesson 11:	The Graph of a Function
Lesson 12:	The Graph of the Equation $y = f(x)$
Lesson 13:	Interpreting the Graph of a Function
Lesson 14:	Linear and Exponential Models—Comparing Growth Rates

In Lesson 8, students consider that the notation they have been using to write explicit formulas for sequences can be applied to situations where the inputs are not whole numbers. In Lessons 9 and 10, they revisit the notion of function that was introduced in Grade 8. They are now prepared to use function notation as they write functions, interpret statements about functions and evaluate functions for inputs in their domains. They formalize their understanding of a function as a correspondence between two sets, X and Y, in which each element of X is matched (or assigned) to one and only one element of Y, and add the understanding that the set X is called the *domain*, and the set Y is called the *range.*

Students study the graphs of functions in Lessons 11-14 of this topic. In Lesson 11, students learn the meaning of the graph of a function, f, as the set of all points $(x, f(x))$ in the plane, such that x is in the domain of f and $f(x)$ is the value assigned to x by the correspondence of the function. Students use plain English language to write the instructions needed to plot the graph of a function. The instructions are written in a way similar to writing computer "pseudo code"—before actually writing the computer programs. In Lesson 12, students learn that the graph of $y = f(x)$ is the set of all points (x, y) in the plane that satisfy the equation $y = f(x)$ and conclude that it is the same as the graph of the function explored in Lesson 11. In Lesson 13, students use a graphic of the planned landing sequence Mars Curiosity Rover to create graphs of specific aspects of the landing sequence— altitude over time, and velocity over time—and use the graphs to examine the meaning of increasing and decreasing functions. Finally, Lesson 14 capitalizes on students' new knowledge of functions and their graphs to contrast linear and exponential functions and the growth rates which they model.

Lesson 8: Why Stay With Whole Numbers?

Student Outcomes

- Students use function notation, evaluate functions for inputs in their domains, and interpret statements that use function notation in terms of a context.

- Students create functions that represent a geometric situation and relate the domain of a function to its graph and to the relationship it describes.

Lesson Notes

This lesson builds on the work of Topic A by continuing to relate sequences to formulas or functions without explicitly defining function or function notation (however, students are using this notation and have been since Topic A). This lesson builds upon students' understanding of sequences by extending familiar sequences (the square numbers and the triangular numbers) to functions whose domain extends beyond the set of whole numbers and by asking students to continually consider what makes sense given the situation. While the word "function" appears in the student outcomes and teacher notes for this lesson, this term need not be used with students until introduced formally in Lesson 9.

Classwork

Opening (2 minutes)

Introduce the lesson. For the ancient Greeks, all of mathematics was geometry. The sequence of perfect squares earned its name because these are the numbers that come about from arranging dots (or any other simple shape or object) into squares. The figurate numbers like the square, triangular, and odd numbers are used throughout this lesson. The following resource provides some additional background information on these numbers: http://mathworld.wolfram.com/FigurateNumber.html. Before moving on, make sure students understand that the number of dots represents the perfect square number and that the 1st, 2nd, 3rd represents the term number. You can ask a few quick questions to check for understanding such as "What is the fifth perfect square?" or "Which term is the number 9 in the sequence of perfect squares?" or "Is 64 a term in this sequence? If so, which term is it? How do you know?"

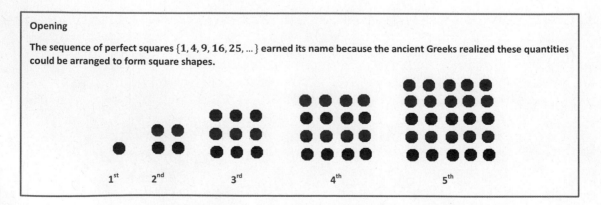

Opening

The sequence of perfect squares $\{1, 4, 9, 16, 25, \dots\}$ earned its name because the ancient Greeks realized these quantities could be arranged to form square shapes.

Opening Exercise (3 minutes)

Students should work this opening exercise with a partner. They should be familiar with the notation from previous lessons. Ask for a few students to explain how they solved this problem. Before moving on, make sure all students have the correct formula.

> **Opening Exercise**
>
> If $S(n)$ denotes the nth square number, what is a formula for $S(n)$?
>
> $S(n) = n^2$

Discussion (5 minutes)

Lead a discussion on the meaning of $S(50)$, $S(16)$, $S(0)$, $S(\pi)$, $S(2.35)$, etc. Lead the class to the result that while we can certainly compute a value for $S(\pi)$ using the formula $S(n) = n^2$, the values are only meaningful if we stretch our notion of a square number to imagine a square with a fractional side length. When we move away from non-negative integer inputs, however, the ordered set of $S(n)$ values for $n > 0$ no longer forms a sequence according to the definition of a sequence. In the next lesson, we will introduce the concept of a function and its definition. An important point is that the *input* value has meaning in a situation. Similarly, the *output* value must also be meaningful. The next exercise introduces that idea.

- In this situation, what does $S(50)$ mean? What would this number look like?
    - *The 50th square number. The value is 2500. It would be a 50 row by 50 column arrangement of dots.*
- In this situation, what does $S(0)$ mean? $S(\pi)$? $S(2.35)$?
    - *Using the formula $S(0) = 0$. In this situation, you cannot form a square with 0 dots or create a square with sides of length 0 unit. The others could be evaluated using the formula, and we would have to alter our meaning of square numbers. Instead of an arrangement of dots, we could think of a square number as the area of a square with a side measure of n units. It would be difficult to represent these numbers with arrangements of dots.*
- In this situation, what does $S(-1)$ mean?
    - *Using the formula, $S(-1) = 1$. Perhaps it would mean we constructed a square on the number line whose side was the distance between the number 0 and the number -1.*

Exercises 1–11 (15 minutes)

In this exercise, students consider different possible square numbers. They prove whether or not a given number is a term in the sequence of perfect squares.

> **Exercises**
>
> 1. Prove whether or not 169 is a perfect square.
>
>   *169 is a perfect square because it can be arranged into a 13 row by 13 column array of dots.*

2. Prove whether or not 200 is a perfect square.

If 200 was a perfect square, then there is a positive integer a such that $a^2 = 200$. But since $14^2 = 196$ and $15^2 = 225$, we have $14 < a < 15$, which means a cannot be an integer. Hence, 200 is not a perfect square because it cannot be arranged into an n row by n column array of dots.

3. If $S(n) = 225$, then what is n?

$n = 15$ because $15 \times 15 = 225$.

4. Which term is the number 400 in the sequence of perfect squares? How do you know?

Since $400 = 20 \times 20$, this number would be the $20th$ term in the sequence.

Before moving on, make sure students understand that Exercises 2–4 are basically asking the same question.

In Exercise 5, students consider a formula where the meaningful input values would be the set of positive real numbers.

Instead of arranging dots into squares, suppose we extend our thinking to consider squares of side length x cm.

5. Create formula for the area $A(x)$ cm² of a square of side length x cm. $A(x) = $ _____

$A(x) = x^2$

6. Use the formula to determine the area of squares with side lengths of 3 cm, 10.5 cm, and π cm.

$A(3) = 9; A(10.5) = 110.25; A(\pi) = \pi^2$

7. What does $A(0)$ mean?

In this situation, $A(0)$ has no physical meaning since you cannot have a square whose sides measure 0 cm.

8. What does $A(-10)$ and $A(\sqrt{2})$ mean?

In this situation, $A(-10)$ has no physical meaning since a square cannot have sides whose measure is negative. $A(\sqrt{2})$ does have meaning although it would be impossible to measure that side length physically with a ruler. The only way for the input to be negative is if we redefine what the input value represents—perhaps we just want to find the square of a number and not relate it to a geometric figure at all.

Finally, students consider the sequence of triangular numbers. Encourage students to work in small groups on this question. Circulate around the room as students are working. Keep encouraging students to consider how the sequence is growing from one term to the next or to consider the *dimensions* of the triangles as they work to uncover the formula for this sequence. When reporting out, encourage students to use the $T(n)$ notation rather than subscript notation to represent the n th term. You can also provide scaffolding for this problem by asking students to first draw and determine the 6th, 7th, and 8th triangular numbers. You can also point out that this arrangement also provides a formula for the sum of the first n counting numbers. For example, the 4th triangular number is $4 + 3 + 2 + 1 = 10$ *or* $1 + 2 + 3 + 4 = 10$.

Lesson 8: Why Stay With Whole Numbers?
Date: 9/11/13

84

You may need to give students hints. One hint is to put two *triangles* of dots together to form an n by $n + 1$ rectangle, as in the picture in the answer of Exercise 12 below. Another hint is to notice that $T(n) = 1 + 2 + 3 + \cdots + n$ can also be written as $T(n) = n + (n - 1) + (n - 2) + \cdots + 1$. Adding these together gives $2T(n) = (n + 1) + (n + 1) + (n + 1) + \cdots + (n + 1)$ or $2T(n) = n(n + 1)$. Dividing by 2 gives $T(n) = \frac{n(n+1)}{2}$. For example, $T(4) = \frac{4(5)}{2}$ because

$$
\begin{aligned}
T(4) &= 1 + 2 + 3 + 4 \\
+\ T(4) &= 4 + 3 + 2 + 1 \\
\hline
2T(4) &= 5 + 5 + 5 + 5
\end{aligned}
$$

The triangular numbers are the numbers that arise from arranging dots into triangular figures as shown:

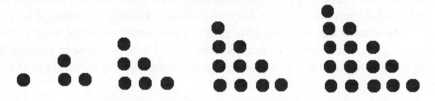

9.　What is the 100th triangular number?

　　It would be $100(101)$ divided by 2 or 5050 using the idea displayed in the picture in problem 12 below.

10.　Find a formula for $T(n)$, the n th triangular number (starting with $n = 1$).

$$T(n) = \frac{n(n + 1)}{2}$$

11.　How can you be sure your formula works?

　　By substituting a term number into the formula, you get the correct number of dots in that figure. The formula also works because each triangular number is exactly half of a rectangular arrangement of dots whose dimensions are n by $n + 1$. For example:

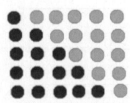

Discussion (3 minutes)

Reinforce with students that just like in the square number sequence, $T(50)$ is meaningful because it represents the 50th triangular number, but in this situation, $T(280.3)$ will only be meaningful if we consider the figures to be triangles instead of arrangements of dots. Ask students to consider a situation where $T(280.3)$ would be meaningful. Ask for a few ideas. Then pose this problem:

- Can you think of a situation where $T(280.3)$ would be meaningful?
  - *It would only be meaningful if the situation allowed for decimal inputs.*

- Sketch a right triangle whose base is 1 cm less than its height where the height cannot be a whole number. What is the area of your triangle?

  - *Student triangles should have dimensions such as* 15.7 *cm and* 14.7 *cm. The area would be* 15.7 × 14.7/2 *cm².*

Show the class that the formula for $T(x) = \frac{x(x+1)}{2}$ gives the correct area for a triangle whose base x is one less than its height.

Exercise 12 (5 minutes)

In this exercise, students compare the graphs of the formulas for the sequence of triangular numbers and the triangle area formula from the discussion. The first function should have a discrete domain. The second function should be continuous with a domain of $x > 0$. As you debrief this exercise, make sure students understand that while both graphs have points in common such as (1,1) and (2,3), the situation dictates whether or not it makes sense to connect the points on the graphs. These exercises are setting the stage for a more complete understanding of the graph of a function to be developed in Lesson 12.

12. Create a graph of the sequence of triangular numbers, $(n) = \frac{n(n+1)}{2}$, where n is a positive integer.

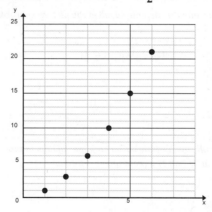

13. Create a graph of the triangle area formula $T(x) = \frac{x(x+1)}{2}$, where x is any positive real number.

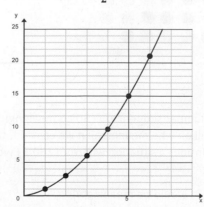

COMMON CORE™

Lesson 8:   Why Stay With Whole Numbers?
Date: 9/11/13

86

> 14. How are your two graphs alike? How are they different?
>
>   *The graph of exercise 12 is not connected because the input values must be positive integers. The graph of exercise 13 is connected because the area of a triangle can be any positive real number. Both graphs have points in common at the positive integer input values. Neither graph is a linear or an exponential function.*

Closing (2 minutes)

This lesson begins to tie several ideas together including sequences from the first part of this module, the function standards from eighth grade, and work with equations and formulas from Algebra 1 and earlier grades. Therefore, the term function has not been used explicitly in this lesson. Both of the ideas summarized here will be revisited with a more formal definition in a later lesson.

- Formulas that represent a sequence of numbers have a set of *inputs*; each input number is used to represent the term number. The outputs of the formula listed in order form the sequence.

- Formulas that represent different situations such as the area of a square of side x can have a set of *inputs* consisting of different subsets of the real number system. The set of inputs that makes sense depends on the situation, as does the set of outputs.

Exit Ticket (5 minutes)

The Exit Ticket provides a linear geometric arrangement of numbers for students to consider.

COMMON CORE   Lesson 8:   Why Stay With Whole Numbers?
Date: 9/11/13

87

Name _____ Date_____

Lesson 8: Why Stay With Whole Numbers?

Recall that an odd number is a number that is one more than or one less than twice an integer. Consider the sequence formed by the odd numbers $\{1,3,5,7, \dots\}$.

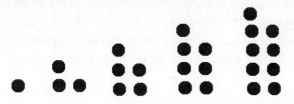

1. Find a formula for $0(n)$, the nth odd number starting with $n = 1$?

2. Write a convincing argument that 121 is an odd number.

3. What is the meaning of $0(17)$?

COMMON CORE™

Lesson 8:   Why Stay With Whole Numbers?
Date: 9/11/13

88

Exit Ticket Sample Solutions

Recall that an odd number is a number that is one more than or one less than twice an integer. Consider the sequence formed by the odd numbers $\{1, 3, 5, 7, \dots\}$.

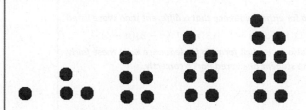

1. Find a formula for $O(n)$, the n th odd number starting with $n = 1$?

   $O(n) = 2n - 1$

2. Write a convincing argument that 121 is an odd number.

   121 is an odd number because it can be represented as $2(60) + 1$ (one more than twice an integer) or as a column of 60 dots next to a column of 61 dots. Let $n = 61$. Then $O(61) = 2(61) - 1 = 121$.

3. What is the meaning of $O(17)$?

   That represents the 17th term of the sequence. That number is $2(17) - 1$ or 33.

Problem Set Sample Solutions

1. The first four terms of two different sequences are shown below. Sequence A is given in the table and sequence B is graphed as a set of ordered pairs.

n	$A(n)$
1	15
2	31
3	47
4	63

   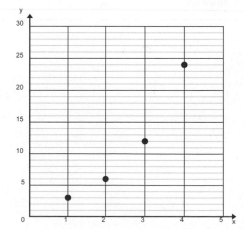

   a. Create an explicit formula for each sequence.

      $A(n) = 15 + 16(n - 1)$ *where n is an integer greater than 0.* $B(n) = 3(2^n)$ *where n is an integer greater than 0.*

COMMON CORE™

Lesson 8:   Why Stay With Whole Numbers?
Date: 9/11/13

89

b. **Which sequence will be the first to exceed 500? How do you know?**

Most likely students will create explicit formulas like the answers in Part a. In that case, sequence B will be the first to exceed 500 because it is growing by a factor of 2. Sequence A is growing by a constant difference of 16. $B = \{3, 6, 9, 18, 36, 72, 144, 288, 576\}$. $B(n)$ exceeds 500 for $n > 8$. On the other hand, $A(9) = 15 + (16)8 = 143$, which is not even close to 500.

You may find a student who develops an explicit formula for either sequence that is different than those listed in the answer to Part a. For example, $B(n) = -\frac{1}{6}(n-2)(n-3)(n-4) + 3(n-1)(n-3)(n-4) - 6(n-1)(n-2)(n-4) + 4(n-1)(n-2)(n-3)$ is also an explicit formula for sequence B. In these fairly unique cases, you may have to check by hand to see if the student answered Part b correctly.

2. **A tile pattern is shown below.**

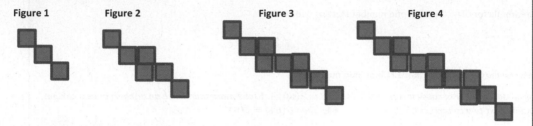

Figure 1   Figure 2   Figure 3   Figure 4

a. **How is this pattern growing?**

Each figure contains 3 more tiles than the previous figure.

b. **Create an explicit formula that could be used to determine the number of squares in the n th figure.**

$F(n) = 3n$ where n is an integer.

c. **Evaluate your formula for $n = 0$ and $n = 2.5$. Draw Figure 0 and Figure 2.5, and explain how you decided to create your drawings.**

$F(0) = 0$ and $F(2.5) = 7.5$. You could draw no squares for figure 0. You could draw 7 squares and ½ of a square for figure 2.5.

COMMON CORE

Lesson 8:   Why Stay With Whole Numbers?
Date: 9/11/13

90

3. The first four terms of a geometric sequence are graphed as a set of ordered pairs.

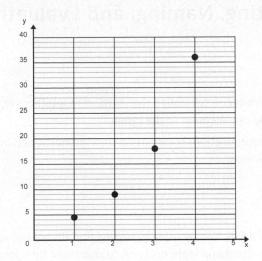

a. What is an explicit formula for this sequence?

$A(n) = 4.5(2)^{n-1}$ *for* $n > 0$.

b. Explain the meaning of the ordered pair $(3, 18)$.

It means that the 3rd term in the sequence is 18, *or* $A(3) = 18$.

c. As of July 2013, Justin Bieber had over $42,000,000$ twitter followers. Suppose the sequence represents the number of people that follow your new twitter account each week since you started tweeting. If your followers keep growing in the same manner, when will you exceed 1,000,000 followers?

This sequence will exceed $1,000,000$ *followers when* $n > 19$. *At some time in the 19th week, I would have* $1,000,000$ *followers.*

COMMON CORE

Lesson 8:   Why Stay With Whole Numbers?
Date: 9/11/13

91

Lesson 9: Representing, Naming, and Evaluating Functions

Student Outcomes

- Students understand that a function from one set (called the domain) to another set (called the range) assigns each element of the domain to exactly one element of the range.

- Students use function notation, evaluate functions for inputs in their domains, and interpret statements that use function notation in terms of a context.

Lesson Notes

This lesson begins by developing the concept of a function by using examples that do not include numbers. Students compare their work to a precise definition of function and learn notation to represent functions. Some of the notation may look different than a typical high school textbook, but it is needed for discussions of transformations (which are functions) in grades 10, 11, and 12, and it is standard notation used in college mathematics lessons. The definition of function logically builds upon the work students have done with matching and correspondence in elementary and middle grades. The definitions presented in the FAQs on functions for teachers below form the foundation of the next few lessons in this topic. Please review these carefully to help you understand the structure of the Topic B lessons.

I like the description of function that uses the word "rule." Why is this a description not a definition? While there is nothing wrong with stating a rule to define a function, such as, "Let $f(x) = x^2$ where x can be any real number," the word "rule" only describes a certain type of function. This description is good enough for introducing the idea behind functions in grade 8 (where the word rule can be used), but it is completely inadequate for helping students recognize situations when there may be a functional relationship between two sets or two types of quantities (students can overlook important functional relationships simply because the relationships do not fit into the prefabricated linear, quadratic, or exponential "rules").

The Common Core State Standards expect students to recognize when there is a functional relationship between two sets and build a function that models that relationship (cf. F-IF.3 and F-BF.1). The first step towards identifying a functional relationship is for students to recognize a correspondence. To understand the definition of correspondence, recall that the Cartesian product $X \times Y$ is the set of all ordered pairs (x, y) for which x is in the set X and y is in the set Y (for example, the Cartesian coordinate plane is the set $\mathbb{R} \times \mathbb{R}$ where $\mathbb{R}$ stands for the set of all real numbers).

> **CORRESPONDENCE BETWEEN TWO SETS**. A *correspondence between two sets X and Y* is a subset of ordered pairs (x, y) of the Cartesian product $X \times Y$; an element x in X is *matched to* (or *corresponds to*) an element y in Y if and only if the ordered pair (x, y) is an element of the subset.

The phrasing in the definition of correspondence seems too difficult for my students. Do I have to use that phrasing with my students? This phrasing is obviously *not* student-friendly; do not try to teach the phrasing above to your students. However, the *idea* behind the definition is quite intuitive and can be explained using simple pictures (see the Opening Exercise below). In fact, students have worked with correspondences and named them as correspondences many times already in the elementary curriculum, *A Story of Units*, and middle school curriculum, *A Story of Ratios*.

	Lesson 9:	Representing, Naming, and Evaluating Functions		92
	Date:	9/11/13		

- Students have been *matching* elements in two sets from kindergarten, i.e., displaying correspondences by drawing lines between two columns of related pictures/words.

- In sixth and seventh grade, students learned that a proportional relationship is a one-to-one correspondence between two types of quantities given by the formula $y = kx$.

- In seventh grade, students learned that a figure S' is a scale drawing of another figure S if there is a special type of one-to-one correspondence between the two figures.

- In eighth grade, students learned that rotations, reflections, translations, and dilations of the plane are one-to-one correspondences between points in the plane and their images under the transformation.

All of the correspondences above are examples of functions, but not all correspondences are functions in general. Functions satisfy an extra property that makes the correspondence *predictive* in the sense that once we model a real-life situation with a function, we can often use that function to make predictions about its future behavior. Thus, for students to recognize a functional relationship, they need to recognize that there is a correspondence and see that the correspondence matches each element of the first set with an element of the second set. Once they know the relationship is functional in nature, they can search for *the rule* that describes the functional relationship.

What is the difference between a generic correspondence and a function? Note that in a generic correspondence, each point of X is matched to zero, one, or many points of Y. The idea behind functions is to restrict correspondences to those that pick out only one point of Y for each point of X.

> **FUNCTION.** A *function* is a correspondence between two sets, X and Y, in which each element of X is matched[1] to one and only one element of Y. The set X is called the *domain of the function*.

(The set Y is called the *codomain of the function*, but it is not important to stress the use of this word. We will define a much more important word, *range*, below.)

The notation $f: X \to Y$ is used to name the function and describes both X and Y. If x is an element in the domain X of a function $f: X \to Y$, then x is matched to an element of Y called $f(x)$. We say $f(x)$ is the value in Y that denotes the *output* or *image* of f corresponding to the *input* x. To signify the input/output relationship of x and $f(x)$, we write

$$x \mapsto f(x),$$

for "x is matched to $f(x)$" or "x maps to $f(x)$." The $\mapsto$ arrow is meant to remind students of the segment they drew in their matching exercises since kindergarten. The arrow also signifies that x is matched to one and only one element, $f(x)$. Thus, a way to define the squaring function for real numbers, for example, would be to state, "Let $f: \mathbb{R} \to \mathbb{R}$ be the function such that $x \mapsto x^2$." This statement describes both the domain and codomain and explains how to find an output given an input.

> **RANGE OR IMAGE OF A FUNCTION.** The *range (or image)* of a function $f: X \to Y$ is the subset of Y, often denoted $f(X)$, defined by the following property: y is an element of $f(X)$ if and only if there is an x in X such that $f(x) = y$.

---

[1] "matched" can be replaced with "assigned" after students understand that each point of x is matched to exactly one point of y.

In other words, the image of a function is the set of points in Y such that each point is the image of a point in the domain. If $f: \mathbb{R} \rightarrow \mathbb{R}$ is the function such that $x \mapsto x^2$, then the range of f is the set of all nonnegative real numbers. In cases where the range is a subset of the codomain, it is customary to restrict the codomain to the range. Hence, by setting $R = \{x \in \mathbb{R} \mid x \geq 0\}$, the example above becomes, "$f: \mathbb{R} \rightarrow R$ is the function such that $x \mapsto x^2$." Because this is a common feature in high school mathematics, the notion of "codomain" is usually replaced by the word "range" instead.

Note that to define a function, it is absolutely necessary to define both the domain and the values the function can take. A function does not exist without reference to a domain and range! However, because the set (or subset) of real numbers is the *predominate* domain and range of functions considered in Algebra I, it is sometimes taken as a convention (which means it needs to be explicitly explained to students) that a function without a domain or range specified means that the unmentioned sets are the real numbers or subsets of the set of real numbers. Sometimes we use the term *real function* or *real-valued function* to describe a function whose values are real numbers—whose range is a subset of the real numbers.

Do I have to use the notation, "$f: \mathbb{R} \rightarrow R$ is the function such that $x \mapsto x^2$," or can I just say, "Let $f(x) = x^2$?" For the vast majority of purposes in Algebra I (see the FAQs in Lesson 10), we encourage the use of the phrase, "Let $f(x) = x^2$ where x can be any real number," or when the domain is obviously the real numbers, simply, "Let $f(x) = x^2$." However, the other notation is also useful when it is important to describe the domain and range explicitly (as you will see in many of the examples of Lesson 9). Since the longer notation is also used in college classrooms, you will be preparing your students for their university experience if you use it from time to time.

When are two functions equal or equivalent? Students often work with equivalent functions without realizing they are doing so. For example, every time a student writes a trigonometric identity they are invoking the idea of equivalent functions. In fact, whenever students rewrite a function in a different form (*e.g.*, from vertex form of a quadratic function to factored form) they are invoking the idea of equivalent functions.

> **EQUIVALENT FUNCTIONS.** Two functions, $f: X \rightarrow Y$ and $g: X \rightarrow Y$, are said to be *equivalent* (and written $f = g$) if they have the same domain X, take values in the same set Y, and for each x in X, $f(x) = g(x)$.

In order to check whether or not two functions f and g are equivalent, first pick an element x in their common domain X and determine whether the two elements $f(x)$ and $g(x)$ are the same value in Y, and then do the same for every other element x in X. The point is that one checks each and every value one element at a time—nothing varies.

Equivalent functions are closely tied to the idea of equivalent expressions. In fact, it is far better to use equivalent functions to state when two expressions are equivalent because equivalent functions naturally include information about domain and range. It was for this reason we limited the notion of equivalent expressions to just algebraic expressions in Module 1. Now, in Module 3, students learn about equivalent functions, and from this point on, the curriculum will use equivalent functions to describe when two expressions are equivalent.

> **IDENTITY.** An *identity* is a statement that two functions are equivalent.

This definition, for example, makes it clear that the following statement is an identity:

$$\tan x = \frac{\sin x}{\cos x} \text{ for all } x \neq \frac{\pi}{2} + \pi k, \text{ where } k \text{ is an integer.}$$

Lesson 9:   Representing, Naming, and Evaluating Functions
Date: 9/11/13

94

Classwork

Opening Exercise (3 minutes)

This exercise activates student thinking about the process of matching elements from one set (the pictures) to elements of another set (the words). This idea of correspondence is critical to understanding the concept of function and the formal definition of function to be presented in this lesson.

Opening Exercise

Match each picture to the correct word by drawing an arrow from the word to the picture.

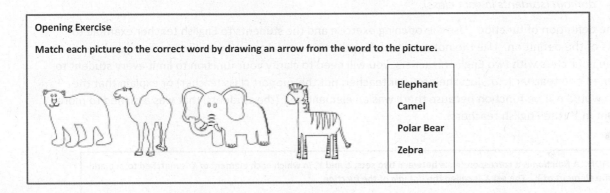

| Elephant |
| Camel |
| Polar Bear |
| Zebra |

Introduce that there is a correspondence between the pictures and the words that name them based on our joint understanding of animals. However, you might point out that while students might have naturally matched the pictures with the words there are certainly other ways to pair the pictures and words. For example, match the pictures to the words left to right and then top to bottom. According to this convention, the polar bear picture would be assigned to the word elephant. Even a simple example like this will begin to build the concept of function in students' minds that there must be a set of inputs (domain) paired with a set of outputs (range) according to some criteria. As these lessons develop, you will introduce algebraic functions, and students will learn that by substituting every value in the domain of a function into all instances of the variable in an algebraic expression and evaluating that expression, we can determine the $f(x)$ value associated with each x in the domain.

Discussion (10 minutes)

Put the names of students (or a subset of students) in your class on the board. Then put the names of the English teachers in your school on the board. Have students match each student to their assigned English teacher. Ask the class to come up with a way to organize their work. Some might suggest drawing arrows again, while others might suggest a table. Be clear that in this case we are starting with students and assigning them to an English teacher, not the other way around.

- How can you organize this information in a way that makes sense?

  □ *You can use arrows or you could pair the student and teacher names like an ordered pair of numbers. Put the student first and the teacher second in the ordered pair.*

- How does this example relate back to the opening exercise?

  □ *In this example, we matched students to teachers. In the opening exercise, we matched a picture to a word. Both of these problems involved matching one thing in the first group to one thing in the second group.*

- Did every student get assigned to an English teacher? Did any students have more than one English teacher?

  □ *Student responses will vary. Most students enrolled in Algebra One would have an English class as well. Some students may have more than one teacher if they are in a support class or are repeating a class. In this case, the correspondence would NOT be a function.*

- Are there any English teachers at this school that did not have a student from this class assigned to them?

  □ *It is okay if not every member of the codomain (the English teachers) is not assigned to a specific domain (students in your class).*

Then present the definition of function. Use the opening exercise and the students to English teacher example to explain the parts of the definition. Use the notation to define the two functions we have discussed. If you happen to have a student in your class with two English teachers, you will need to clarify your function to limit every student to only being assigned one teacher (*e.g.*, just their regular teacher, not the support class teacher) or explain that the correspondence would not be function because there was an element in X (the students) that was assigned to more than one element in Y (the English teachers).

FUNCTION. A *function* is a correspondence between two sets, X and Y, in which each element of X is matched to one and only one element of Y. The set X is called the *domain of the function*.

The notation $f: X \to Y$ is used to name the function and describes both X and Y. If x is an element in the domain X of a function $f: X \to Y$, then x is matched to an element of Y called $f(x)$. We say $f(x)$ is the value in Y that denotes the *output* or *image* of f corresponding to the *input x*.

The *range (or image)* of a function $f: X \to Y$ is the subset of Y, denoted $f(X)$, defined by the following property: y is an element of $f(X)$ if and only if there is an x in X such that $f(x) = y$.

Use the definition to name functions. Do these examples as a whole class. Be sure to emphasize that you cannot define a function without also defining its domain and range. The definition talks about the output or image of f corresponding to the input x. The range is a subset of Y composed of the output or image values of f that correspond to each x in the domain X.

Example 1 (3 minutes)

The domain of this function is the set of pictures. The range is the set of words. Each picture was assigned to exactly one word.

Example 1

Define the opening exercise using function notation. State the domain and the range.

$f: \{animals\ pictured\} \to \{words\ listed\}^2$

Assign each animal to its proper name.

Domain: the four animal pictures

Range: {elephant, giraffe, polar bear, zebra}

---

2 Remind students that "{" means "The set of," so "{animals pictured}" means, "The set of animals pictured."

Example 2 (3 minutes)

This example will be a function as long as no students in your class have two different English teachers. This example will also provide you with the opportunity to distinguish between the set Y (all the English teachers in your school) and the range (or image) of the function, which will most likely be a subset of Y (the English teachers of the students in your class). An English teacher only becomes a member of the range when they are assigned to a student.

> **Example 2**
>
> Is the assignment of students to English teachers an example of a function? If yes, define it using function notation, and state the domain and the range.
>
> $f: \{students\ in\ your\ class\} \to \{English\ teachers\ at\ your\ school\}$
>
> *Assign students in this class to the English teacher according to their class schedule.*
>
> *Domain: the students in this class*
>
> *Range: the English teachers in the school whose students are in your class*

Discussion (5 minutes)

This next portion of the lesson presents students with functions using the notation and asks them to interpret them. Introduce the father function by recording the function below on the board. This function assigns all people to their biological father. The domain is all people. The codomain is all males, and the range is the subset of the males who have fathered a child.

$f: \{people\} \to \{men\}$

Assign all people to their biological father.

Domain: all people

Range: men who are fathers

Pose the following questions:

- What is the meaning of $f(Tom) = Peter$?
  - *Tom is Peter's son.*
- What would it mean to say $f(Tom) = Tom$?
  - *Tom is his own son/father. Wait—that is impossible! What did they probably mean? Maybe: $f(Tom\ II) = Tom\ I$ (the son is named after the father). Point out: elements in a set need to have unique identifiers to avoid confusion.*
- Suppose Ana's father is George. How could we write that using function notation?
  - *$f(Ana) = George$.*
- Suppose we defined a new function that assigned fathers to their children. Would this be an example of a function?
  - *This would not be an example of a function because many men have more than one child. So each element of the domain (fathers) might be assigned to more than one output (children).*

Example 3 (5 minutes)

In the next example, students will work with sets of numbers. Notice that the ordered pairs describe the correspondence between the elements of the domain and the elements of the range. Be sure to emphasize that we could describe the correspondence in words, but using the ordered pairs is a more efficient way to associate the elements in the domain to the elements in the range. (For students to see the correspondence, you might have them create a matching picture like in the opening exercise.) One of the examples is not a function, and one is a function. This example also introduces another letter, g, to name a function.

Example 3

Let $X = \{1, 2, 3, 4\}$ and $Y = \{5, 6, 7, 8, 9\}$. f and g are defined below.

$f : X \rightarrow Y$ $g : X \rightarrow Y$

$f = \{(1, 7), (2, 5), (3, 6), (4, 7)\}$ $g = \{(1, 5), (2, 6), (1, 8), (2, 9), (3, 7)\}$

Is f a function? If yes, what is the domain and what is the range? If no, explain why f is not a function.

Yes, f is a function because each element of the domain is matched to exactly one element of the range. The domain is {1,2,3,4} and the range is {5,6,7}.

Is g a function? If yes, what is the domain and range? If no, explain why g is not a function.

No, g is not a function because an element of the domain is assigned to more than one element of the range. For example, the 1 is matched to both 5 and 8.

What is $f(2)$?

$f(2) = 5$ *since 2 is matched to 5.*

If $f(x) = 7$, then what might x be?

If $f(x) = 7$, then $x = 1$ or $x = 4$.

Use the last question to make two points: (1) A function only guarantees that there is one output for every input; it does not guarantee that there is one input for every output. (2) That guarantee is one of the reasons why functions are so useful—by knowing that a function predicts exactly one output for every input, we can use functions to create models of real–life systems and make predictions about the behavior of the system using the model.

Exercises (10 minutes)

In these exercises, students will consider examples that relate to themselves. Make adjustments as needed to adapt this problem to your school setting. Have students work in small groups and present their solutions after giving them time to work the exercises. The solutions are given assuming a high school with Grades 9-12. If your school does not assign ID numbers, you could suggest another unique identifying number like a student's telephone number (**do not** use Social Security Number, as this is federally protected information).

Lesson 9:	Representing, Naming, and Evaluating Functions
Date:	9/11/13

Exercises

1. Define f to assign each student at your school a unique ID number.

   $f:\{students\ in\ your\ school\} \rightarrow \{whole\ numbers\}$

   Assign each student a unique ID number

   a. Is this an example of a function? Use the definition to explain why or why not.

   Yes. Each student in the school is assigned a unique student ID number. Every student only gets one ID number.

   b. Suppose $f(Hilda) = 350123$. What does that mean?

   This means that Hilda's ID number is 350123.

   c. Write your name and student ID number using function notation.

   Solutions will vary but should follow the format $f(Name) = Number$.

2. Let g assign each student at your school to a grade level.

   a. Is this an example of a function? Explain your reasoning.

   Yes, this is a function because each student is assigned a single grade level. No students can be in both 9th and 10th grade.

   b. Express this relationship using function notation and state the domain and the range.

   $g:\{students\ in\ the\ school\} \rightarrow \{grade\ level\}$

   Assign each student to a grade level.

   Domain: All of the students enrolled in the school

   Range: $\{9, 10, 11, 12\}$

3. Let h be the function that assigns each student ID number to a grade level.

   $h:\{student\ ID\ number\} \rightarrow \{grade\ level\}$

   Assign each student ID number to the student's current grade level.

   a. Describe the domain and range of this function.

   Domain: the set of all numbers used as student IDs at my school

   Range: $\{9, 10, 11, 12\}$

   b. Record several ordered pairs $(x, f(x))$ that represent yourself and students in your group or class.

   Solutions will vary but should be of the form (Student ID number, grade level).

   c. Jonny says, "This is not a function because every ninth grader is assigned the same range value of 9. The range only has 4 numbers {9, 10, 11, 12}, but the domain has a number for every student in our school." Explain to Jonny why he is incorrect.

   The definition of a function says each element in the domain is assigned to one element in the range. Assigning the same range value repeatedly does not violate the definition of a function. In fact, the situation would still be a function if there was only 1 element in the range.

Closing (1 minute)

Pose the following question for closing.

- What are the essential parts of a function?
  - *There are three parts: A set of domain values, a set of range values, and a method for assigning each element of the domain to exactly one element of the range.*

Exit Ticket (5 minutes)

Students consider two situations and must recognize that the second one is not a function.

Name _____   Date_____

Lesson 9: Representing, Naming, and Evaluating Functions

Exit Ticket

1. Given f as described below.

$$f: \{whole\ numbers\} \rightarrow \{whole\ numbers\}$$
Assign each whole number to its largest place value digit.

For example, $f(4) = 4$, $f(14) = 4$, and $f(194) = 9$.

a.   What is the domain and range of f?

b.   What is $f(257)$?

c.   What is $f(0)$?

d.   What is $f(999)$?

e.   Find a value of x that makes the equation $f(x) = 7$ a true statement.

2. Is the correspondence described below a function? Explain your reasoning.

$$M: \{women\} \rightarrow \{people\}$$
Assign each woman their child.

COMMON CORE™

Lesson 9:
Date:

Representing, Naming, and Evaluating Functions
9/11/13

101

Exit Ticket Sample Solutions

1. Given *f* as described below.

   $f: \{whole\ numbers\} \rightarrow \{whole\ numbers\}$

   Assign each whole number to its largest place value digit.

   For example, $f(4) = 4$, $f(14) = 4$, and $f(194) = 9$.

   a. What is the domain and range of *f*?

   Domain: all whole numbers; Range: $\{0, 1, 2, 3, 4, 5, 6, 7, 8, 9\}$

   b. What is $f(257)$?

   7

   c. What is $f(0)$?

   0

   d. What is $f(999)$?

   9

   e. Find a value of *x* that makes the equation $f(x) = 7$ a true statement.

   Answers will vary. The largest digit in the number must be 7. The value must be a whole number that includes the digit 7. Examples: $f(457) = 7$, *but* $f(79)$ *does not equal 7.*

2. Is the correspondence described below a function? Explain your reasoning.

   $$M: \{women\} \rightarrow \{people\}$$
   Assign each woman their child.

   This is not a function because a woman who is a mother could have more than one child.

Problem Set Sample Solutions

1. Which of the following are examples of a function? Justify your answers.

   a. The assignment of the members of a football team to jersey numbers.

   Yes. Each team member gets only 1 jersey number.

   b. The assignment of U.S. citizens to Social Security Numbers.

   Yes. Each U.S. citizen who has applied for and received a social security number gets only 1 number. Note: The domain is not necessarily all U.S. citizens, but those who applied for and received a SSN.

Lesson 9: Representing, Naming, and Evaluating Functions
Date: 9/11/13

c.   The assignment of students to locker numbers.

Yes. (The answer could be no if a student claims that certain students get assigned two or more lockers such as one for books and one for PE clothes.)

d.   The assignment of the residents of a house to the street addresses.

Yes. People do not have more than one street address for the house in which they live. Even if a person has more than one house, they have only one residence.

e.   The assignment of zip codes to residences.

No. One zip code is assigned to multiple residences.

f.   The assignment of residences to zip codes.

Yes. Each residence is assigned only 1 zip code.

g.   The assignment of teachers to the students enrolled in each of their classes.

No. Each teacher is assigned multiple students in each class.

h.   The assignment of all real numbers to the next integer equal to or greater than the number.

Yes. Each real number is assigned to exactly one integer.

i.   The assignment of each rational number to the product of its numerator and denominator.

No. While the product of any two numbers is a single number, there is no single way to write a rational number: $\frac{1}{3} = \frac{2}{6} = \frac{3}{9} = \cdots$, so there is no single product. A rational number in reduced form, i.e., the GCF of the numerator and denominator is 1, could be used to define a function.

2.   Sequences are functions. The domain is the set of all term numbers (which is usually the positive integers), and the range is the set of terms of the sequence. For example, the sequence 1, 4, 9, 16, 25, 36,… of perfect squares is the function:

$$Let\ f: \{positive\ integers\} \rightarrow \{perfect\ squares\}$$
$$Assign\ each\ term\ number\ to\ the\ square\ of\ that\ number.$$

a.   What is $f(3)$? What does it mean?

$f(3) = 9$. It is the value of the 3ʳᵈ square number. 9 dots can be arranged in a 3 by 3 square array.

b.   What is the solution to the equation $f(x) = 49$? What is the meaning of this solution?

The solution is $x = 7$. It means that the 7ᵗʰ square number is 49, or the number 49 is the 7ᵗʰ term in the square number sequence.

c.   According to this definition, is -3 in the domain of f? Explain why or why not.

No. The domain is the set of positive integers, and -3 is negative number.

d.   According to this definition, is 50 in the range of f? Explain why or why not.

It is not in the range of the function f because 50 is not a perfect square.

3. Write each sequence as a function.

Student responses to the following problems can vary. A sample solution is provided.

a. {1, 3, 6, 10, 15, 21, 28}

Let $f: \{1, 2, 3, 4, 5, 6, 7\} \rightarrow \{1, 3, 6, 10, 15, 21, 28\}$

Assign each term number to the sum of the counting numbers from 1 to the term number.

b. {1, 3, 5, 7, 9,...}

Let $f: \{positive\ integers\} \rightarrow \{positive\ odd\ integers\}$

Assign each positive integer to the number 1 less than double the integer.

c. $a_{n+1} = 3a_n$, $a_1 = 1$ where n is a positive integer greater than or equal to 1.

Let $f: \{positive\ integers\} \rightarrow \{positive\ integers\}$

Assign to each positive integer the value of 3 raised to the power of that integer minus 1.

Lesson 10: Representing, Naming, and Evaluating Functions

Student Outcomes

- Students understand that a function from one set (called the domain) to another set (called the range) assigns each element of the domain to exactly one element of the range and understand that if f is a function and x is an element of its domain, then $f(x)$ denotes the output of f corresponding to the input x.
- Students use function notation, evaluate functions for inputs in their domains, and interpret statements that use function notation in terms of a context.

Lesson Notes

This lesson is a continuation of the work from Lesson 9. In this lesson, we develop the idea of using a formula to define a function (e.g., the function f, where $f(x) = x^2$) and lead students to fully understand why we can use the equal sign (=) in this way to define a function. The lesson also includes exercises that build fluency with evaluating functions, identifying the domain and the range based on the definition of an algebraic function, and interpreting functions in context. The definitions and FAQs for teachers below will be important to today's lesson. We start with a definition of polynomial function:

> POLYNOMIAL FUNCTION. Given a polynomial expression in one variable, a *polynomial function* is a function $f: \mathbb{R} \to \mathbb{R}$ such that for each real number x in the domain, $f(x)$ is the value found by substituting the number x into all instances of the variable symbol in the polynomial expression and evaluating.

It can be shown that if a function $f: \mathbb{R} \to \mathbb{R}$ is a nonzero polynomial function, then there is some non-negative integer n and collection of real numbers $a_0, a_1, a_2, \ldots, a_n$ with $a_n \neq 0$ such that the function satisfies the equation,

$$f(x) = a_n x^n + a_{n-1} x^{n-1} + \cdots + a_1 x + a_0,$$

for every real number x in the domain. The equation is sometimes called the *standard form of the polynomial function.*

Why can we use an equation to define a function? The definition of polynomial function purposefully describes, given a number in the domain, how to determine the value in the range using an expression. It *does not* say, for example (using the squaring function), that $f(x) = x^2$. Why? Because $f(x) = x^2$ is an equation, and equations are about truth values and solutions sets. The equal sign is generally reserved in mathematics for defining equations. However, *most* users of mathematics, for better or for worse, treat statements like $f(x) = x^2$ as *a formula for defining the function f.*

It turns out that using the equal sign to define a function in this way is justifiable but only if students understand that it is a special convention regarding the use of the equal sign. Here is the reasoning behind the convention (using the squaring function named by f as an example): For every number x in the domain $\mathbb{R}$ of real numbers, x is assigned the value of the expression x^2, and it is also assigned, by definition, the value $f(x)$:

$$x \mapsto x^2,$$
$$x \mapsto f(x).$$

Furthermore, since both of these statements are true for all x in the domain, the equation $f(x) = x^2$ must be true for all x. Hence, we do not lose any information by using the convention, "Let $f(x) = x^2$, where x can be any real number,"

to define the function f. We are merely stating a formula for f and specifying its domain (the formula and domain then specify the range). Of course, the statement is often abbreviated to just, "Let $f(x) = x^2$." Such an abbreviation assumes (and therefore needs to be taught to students explicitly) that the domain of the function is all real numbers and that the range is a subset of all real numbers.

Using the convention above to define and name functions, we often define a function by setting it equal to the expression, and say, for example, "Let $f(x) = 3x^2 + 5x + 8$, where x can be any real number," or say, "The function has the form $f(x) = ax^2 + bx + c$ for constants a, b, c with $a \neq 0$ and where x can be any real number." Depending on the context, one either views these statements as defining the function (or form of the function) using a formula or generating an identity statement that is true for all x in the domain.

As we alluded to above, we can use any algebraic expression to define a function. In this way, students see that the work that they did in Module 1 on algebraic expressions directly expands the universe of functions available to them in Module 3.

> **ALGEBRAIC FUNCTION.** Given an algebraic expression in one variable, an *algebraic function* is a function $f : X \to \mathbb{R}$ such that for each real number x in the domain X, $f(x)$ is the value found by substituting the number x into all instances of the variable symbol in the algebraic expression and evaluating.

For algebraic functions, it is customary (and often implicitly assumed) to let the domain X be the largest subset of the real numbers where the algebraic expression can be evaluated to get numbers. This assumption should also be made explicit to students.

Classwork

Opening Exercise (5 minutes)

This exercise activates prior knowledge about ways to represent a relationship between two sets of numbers. It is intended to set the stage for defining a function using an algebraic expression.

Opening Exercise

Study the 4 representations of a function below. How are these representations alike? How are they different?

These representations are alike because they all match the same pairs of numbers $(0, 1)$, $(1, 2)$, $(2, 4)$, $(3, 8)$, $(4, 16)$, and $(5, 32)$. They are different because they describe the domain, range, and correspondence differently. The table and the function look similar; the input and output are related to domain and range of a function. Evaluating the expression for the given x values returns the output values in the table, and the sequence also generates the output values for the first 6 terms starting at $n = 0$.

TABLE:

Input	0	1	2	3	4	5
Output	1	2	4	8	16	32

FUNCTION:

Let $f: \{0, 1, 2, 3, 4, 5\} \to \{1, 2, 4, 8, 16, 32\}$ such that $x \mapsto 2^x$.

SEQUENCE:

Let $a_{n+1} = 2a_n, a_0 = 1$ for $0 \le n \le 5$ where n is an integer.

DIAGRAM:

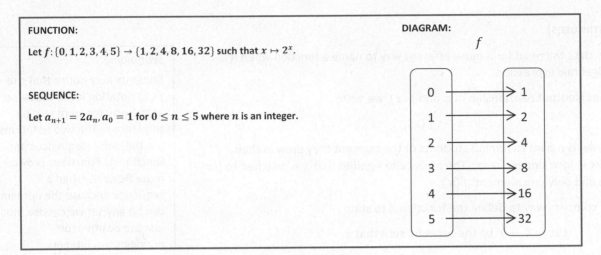

As you review student responses, lead a discussion that highlights the fact that the sequence provides a formula that we can use to quickly generate the terms of the sequence. Ask the class what the explicit formula for this sequence would be. (It would be $a_n = 2^n$ for $0 \le n \le 5$, where n is an integer.) Remind students that a formula provides an efficient way to describe a sequence of numbers. An explicit formula uses an algebraic expression whose variable is a placeholder for the term number. In a similar fashion, a function can also be defined using algebraic expressions where the variable is a placeholder for an element in the domain. Close this discussion by explaining that perhaps these representations are not so different after all and can all come together under the definition of a function.

Exercise 1 (5 minutes)

This exercise begins to transition students to the idea that we can use an algebraic expression to help us figure out how to match the elements in the domain of a function to the elements in the range.

Exercise 1

Let $X = \{0, 1, 2, 3, 4, 5\}$. Complete the following table using the definition of f.

$$f: X \to Y$$

Assign each x in X to the expression 2^x.

What are $f(0), f(1), f(2), f(3), f(4)$, and $f(5)$?

$f(0) = 1, f(1) = 2, f(2) = 4, f(3) = 8, f(4) = 16$, and $f(5) = 32$.

What is the range of f?

$\{1, 2, 4, 8, 16, 32\}$

Briefly discuss student solutions. Point out that the two questions have essentially the same answer. Some students may not have evaluated 2^x (listing $2^0, 2^1, 2^2, \dots$ instead). Point out that technically, evaluating the expression is part of finding the value in the range. One of the goals of this lesson is to define algebraic functions. We will see that evaluating the expression is part of the definition.

Discussion (7 minutes)

Discuss with the class the need for a more efficient way to name a function when it is defined by an algebraic expression.

To signify the input/output relationship of x and $f(x)$, we write

$$x \mapsto f(x),$$

where the $\mapsto$ arrow is meant to remind students of the segment they drew in their matching exercises since kindergarten. The arrow also signifies that x is matched to (or *mapped* to) one and only one element, $f(x)$.

The precise and compact way to define the function is to state

Let $f: X \to Y$ be the function such that $x \mapsto 2^x$.

Display this definition on the board, and have students record it on their student pages. Explain the use of the arrow symbol $\mapsto$ as well.

> *Scaffolding:*
> Students may notice that the $f(x)$ notation looks the same as the way we were writing sequences. The two notations are the same (sequences are functions). Functions provide more flexibility than a sequence because the domain can be any set we choose, not just the positive (or nonnegative) integers.

- Suppose we let the domain of f be the set of integers. What is the range?
  - *The range would be the powers of 2 for integer exponents, $\{\dots, \frac{1}{4}, \frac{1}{2}, 1, 2, 4, 8, 16, 32, \dots\}$.*
- Suppose we let the domain of f be the set of all real numbers. What subset of the real numbers would be the range of f?
  - *The range would be all positive real numbers.*
- There are two important parts when we define a function using an algebraic expression. The first part is substituting each element x of the domain into the expression and then *evaluating* that expression to obtain the corresponding range element $f(x)$. Typically we would say $f(3)$ is 8, not 2^3 (although both $f(3) = 8$ and $f(3) = 2^3$ are true equations). Make it clear to students that going forward we must *substitute and evaluate* to find each range element.

Exercise 2 (8 minutes)

This exercise works with the squaring function and relates student thinking back to Lesson 9. Have students work with a partner on this exercise. Debrief as a whole class, and make sure to establish the connection that a sequence can be thought of as a function whose domain is the set of or a subset of the non-negative integers. The work in the opening exercise also emphasizes this point.

Exercise 2

The squaring function is defined as follows:

Let $f: X \to Y$ be the function such that $x \mapsto x^2$, where X is the set of all real numbers.

What are $f(0), f(3), f(-2), f(\sqrt{3}), f(-2.5), f\left(\frac{2}{3}\right), f(a)$, and $f(3 + a)$?

$f(0) = 0, f(3) = 9, f(-2) = 4, f(\sqrt{3}) = 3, f(-2.5) = 6.25, f\left(\frac{2}{3}\right) = \frac{4}{9}$. To understand $f(a)$, remind students that x is a placeholder or a blank: $(\_) \mapsto (\_)^2$, so $f(a) = a^2$, and $f(3 + a) = (3 + a)^2$ or $f(3 + a) = 9 + 6a + a^2$.

> What is the range of f?
>
> *All real numbers greater than or equal to 0.*
>
> What subset of the real numbers could be used as the domain of the squaring function to create a range with the same output values as the sequence of square numbers $\{1, 4, 9, 16, 25, \dots\}$ from Lesson 9?
>
> *Let X be the set of nonzero integers. Both the set of nonzero integers and the set of positive integers can both be domains for the squaring function. Are there any others? Example: $\{1, -2, 3, -4, 5, \dots\}$. Have a discussion with your class about why they might want to restrict the domain to just the positive integers. Example: If we wish to think about it as a sequence, we might want to restrict the domain in such a way.*

Exercise 3 (8 minutes)

This exercise is designed to prepare students to understand the convention of defining a function by stating, "Let $f(x) = x^2$, where x can be any real number." The issue is that the statement $f(x) = x^2$ uses an "=" sign, so it is defining an equation—not a function—and equations are about truth values and solution sets. However, the exercise below shows that this equation is true for all values of x in the domain of f, so defining a function by setting it equal to an expression is justifiable. Set this up by directing attention to the opening exercise and asking students to decide whether or not the equation is true for each x in the domain of f. Talk through the justification for $x = 0$.

Exercise 3

Recall that an equation can either be true or false. Using the function defined by $f: \{0, 1, 2, 3, 4, 5\} \to \{1, 2, 4, 8, 16, 32\}$ such that $x \mapsto 2^x$, determine whether the equation $f(x) = 2^x$ is true or false for each x in the domain of f.

x	Is the equation $f(x) = 2^x$ true or false?	Justification
0	True	Substitute 0 into the equation. $$f(0) = 2^0$$ $$1 = 2^0$$ The 1 on the left side comes from the definition of f, and the value of 2^0 is also 1, so the equation is true.
1	True	Substitute 1 into the equation. $$f(1) = 2^1$$ $$2 = 2^1$$ The 2 on the left side comes from the definition of f, and the value of 2^1 on the right is also 2, so the equation is true.
2	True	See above with $x = 2$.
3	True	See above with $x = 3$.
4	True	See above with $x = 4$.
5	True	See above with $x = 5$.

If the domain of f were extended to all real numbers, would the equation still be true for each x in the domain of f? Explain your thinking.

Yes. Since f maps each $x \mapsto 2^x$, and we agreed to substitute and evaluate the expression to determine the range value for each x in the domain, the equation will always be true for every real number x.

By the same reasoning as in the exercise, the function

$$f:\{real\ numbers\} \to \{real\ numbers\}\ such\ that\ x \mapsto x^2$$

satisfies the equation $f(x) = x^2$ for all real numbers x. Conversely, if some function g satisfies an equation, say for example, $g(x) = 3^x$ for all real numbers x, then g must be defined by the statement

$$g:\{real\ numbers\} \to \{real\ numbers\}\ such\ that\ x \mapsto 3^x.$$

In other words, we lose absolutely nothing in defining a function by setting it equal to an expression, as in, "Let $f(x) = x^3$, where x can be any real number." Not only is this notation more convenient for defining functions with real domains and ranges,[1] the statement $f(x) = x^3$ can be thought of as a formula and can be thought of as an equation as well.

Exercise 4 (Optional if time allows)

> **Exercise 4**
>
> Write three different polynomial functions such that $f(3) = 2$.
>
> $f(x) = x^2 - 7$
>
> $f(x) = x^2 - x - 4$
>
> $f(x) = -3x + 11$

Exercise 5 (3 minutes)

Students evaluate a function and use their work to identify an appropriate domain and range. Based on their work in Grade 8 and in Module 1, students should recall that the radicand should be a non-negative real number. Have them work in pairs or groups on this exercise. Debrief as a whole class, and make sure students record the appropriate domain and range. There are many ways to represent the domain and range intervals as a subset of the real numbers. Some students may describe them in words while others may use an inequality such as $x \geq 2$ to identify the domain.

> **Exercise 5**
>
> The domain and range of this function are not specified. Evaluate the function for several values of x. What subset of the real numbers would represent the domain of this function? What subset of the real numbers would represent its range?
>
> $$Let\ f(x) = \sqrt{x - 2}$$
>
> $f(2) = 0, f(5) = \sqrt{3}, f(1) = \sqrt{-1}$. *The square root of a negative number is not a real number. Therefore, the domain of this function must be real numbers greater than or equal to 2. The range is real numbers greater than or equal to 0 since the principal square root of a number is always positive. Using set notation, the domain would be $D: x \in [2, \infty)$ and the range would be $R: f(x) \in [0, \infty)$.*

---

[1] Students will see the other notation is useful for transformations in 10th, 11th, and 12th grades.

Closing (4 minutes)

Discuss the lesson summary, and then proceed to the exit ticket to check for understanding. Make sure students understand that the domain of a function is assumed to be all real numbers unless we specify otherwise.

Lesson Summary

ALGEBRAIC FUNCTION. Given an algebraic expression in one variable, an *algebraic function* is a function $f: D \rightarrow Y$ such that for each real number x in the domain D, $f(x)$ is the value found by substituting the number x into all instances of the variable symbol in the algebraic expression and evaluating.

The following notation will be used to define functions going forward. If a domain is not specified it will be assumed to be the set of all real numbers.

For the squaring function, we say   Let $f(x) = x^2$.

For the exponential function with base 2, we say   Let $f(x) = 2^x$.

When the domain is limited by the expression or the situation to be a subset of the real numbers, it must be specified when the function is defined.

For the square root function, we say   Let $f(x) = \sqrt{x}$ for $x \geq 0$.

To define the first 5 triangular numbers, we say   Let $f(x) = \frac{x(x+1)}{2}$ for $1 \leq x \leq 5$ where x is an integer.

Depending on the context, one either views the statement "$f(x) = \sqrt{x}$" as part of defining the function f or as an equation that is true for all x in the domain of f or as a formula.

Exit Ticket (5 minutes)

Students evaluate algebraic functions, identify domain and range, and interpret the meaning of functions in context.

Name _____   Date_____

Lesson 10: Representing, Naming, and Evaluating Functions

Exit Ticket

1. Let $f(x) = 4(3)^x$. Complete the table shown below.

x	-1	0	1	2	3
$f(x)$					

2. Jenna knits scarves and then sells them on Etsy, an online marketplace. Let $C(x) = 4x + 20$ represent the cost C in dollars to produce from 0 to 6 scarves.

    a. Create a table to show the relationship between the number of scarves x and the cost C.

    b. What are the domain and range of C?

    c. What is the meaning of $C(3)$?

    d. What is the meaning of the solution to the equation $C(x) = 40$?

Exit Ticket Sample Solutions

1. Let $f(x) = 4(3)^x$. Complete the table shown below.

x	-1	0	1	2	3
$f(x)$	4/3	4	12	36	108

2. Jenna knits scarves and then sells them on Etsy, an online marketplace. Let $C(x) = 4x + 20$ represent the cost C in dollars to produce from 0 to 6 scarves.

   a. Create a table to show the relationship between the number of scarves x and the cost C.

x, Number of scarves	1	2	3	4	5	6
$C(x)$, Cost in dollars	24	28	32	36	40	44

   b. What are the domain and range of C?

   $\{1, 2, 3, 4, 5, 6\}$ *and* $\{24, 28, 32, 36, 40, 44\}$.

   c. What is the meaning of $C(3)$?

   The cost to produce 3 scarves.

   d. What is the meaning of the solution to the equation $C(x) = 40$?

   The number of scarves Jenna can knit for a cost of $40.

Problem Set Sample Solutions

These problems build fluency with identifying the range of a function given its domain and with evaluating functions for various elements in the domain. Students may express the domain and range using the notation shown below or using an alternative method such as an inequality. The following solutions indicate an understanding of the objectives of this lesson:

1. Let $f(x) = 6x - 3$, and let $g(x) = 0.5(4)^x$. Find the value of each function for the given input.

   a. $f(0)$ -3 j. $g(0)$ 0.5

   b. $f(-10)$ -63 k. $g(-1)$ $\frac{1}{8}$

   c. $f(2)$ 9 l. $g(2)$ 8

   d. $f(0.01)$ -2.94 m. $g(-3)$ $\frac{1}{128}$

   e. $f(11.25)$ 64.5 n. $g(4)$ 128

   f. $f(-\sqrt{2})$ *approx.* -11.49 o. $g(\sqrt{2})$ *approx.* 3.55

   g. $f\left(\frac{5}{3}\right)$ 7 p. $g\left(\frac{1}{2}\right)$ 1

   h. $f(1) + f(2)$ 12 q. $g(2) + g(1)$ 10

   i. $f(6) - f(2)$ 24 r. $g(6) - g(2)$ $2,040$

2. Since a variable is a placeholder, we can substitute letters that stand for numbers in for x. Let $f(x) = 6x - 3$, and let $g(x) = 0.5(4)^x$, and suppose a, b, c, and h are real numbers. Find the value of each function for the given input.

a.	$f(a)$	$6a - 3$	h.	$g(b)$	$0.5(4)^b$
b.	$f(2a)$	$12a - 3$	i.	$g(b + 3)$	$32(4)^b$
c.	$f(b + c)$	$6b + 6c - 3$	j.	$g(3b)$	$0.5(64)^b$
d.	$f(2 + h)$	$9 + 6h$	k.	$g(b - 3)$	$\frac{1}{128}(4)^b$
e.	$f(a + h)$	$6a + 6h - 3$	l.	$g(b + c)$	$0.5(4)^{b+c}$ or $0.5(4)^b(4)^c$
f.	$f(a + 1) - f(a)$	6	m.	$g(b + 1) - g(b)$	$\frac{3}{2}(4^b)$
g.	$f(a + h) - f(a)$	$6h$			

3. What is the range of each function given below?

a. Let $f(x) = 9x - 1$.

   Range: all real numbers.

b. Let $g(x) = 3^{2x}$.

   Range: all positive real numbers.

c. Let $f(x) = x^2 - 4$.

   Range: $f(x) \in [-4, \infty)$.

d. Let $h(x) = \sqrt{x} + 2$.

   Range: $h(x) \in [2, \infty)$.

e. Let $a(x) = x + 2$ such that x is a positive integer.

   Range: $a(x)$ is a positive integer greater than 2.

f. Let $g(x) = 5^x$ for $0 \le x \le 4$.

   Range: $1 \le g(x) \le 625$.

4. Provide a suitable domain and range to complete the definition of each function.

a. Let $f(x) = 2x + 3$.

   Domain: all real numbers; Range: all real numbers.

b. Let $f(x) = 2^x$.

   Domain: all real numbers; Range: all positive real numbers.

c. Let $C(x) = 9x + 130$, where $C(x)$ is the number of calories in a sandwich containing x grams of fat.

   Domain: all non-negative real numbers; Range: all real numbers greater than or equal to 130.

d. Let $B(x) = 100(2)^x$, where $B(x)$ is the number of bacteria at time x hours over the course of one day.

   Domain: $x \in [0, 24]$; Range: $B(x) = [100, 100 \cdot 2^{24}]$.

5. Let $f: X \to Y$, where X and Y are the set of all real numbers and x and h are real numbers.

   a. Find a function f such that the equation $f(x + h) = f(x) + f(h)$ is not true for all values of x and h. Justify your reasoning.

   Let $f(x) = x^2$. Then, $f(h) = h^2$ and $f(x + h) = (x + h)^2$. The equation $(x + h)^2 = x^2 + h^2$ is not true because the expression $(x + h)^2$ is equivalent to $x^2 + 2xh + h^2$.

   b. Find a function f such that equation $f(x + h) = f(x) + f(h)$ is true for all values of x and h. Justify your reasoning.

   Let $f(x) = 2x$. Then $f(x + h) = 2(x + h)$ and $f(h) = 2h$. By the distributive property, $2(x + h) = 2x + 2h$, and that is equal to $f(x) + f(h)$.

   c. Let $(x) = 2^x$. Find a value for x and a value for h that makes $f(x + h) = f(x) + f(h)$ a true number sentence.

   If $x = 1$ and $h = 1$, then the equation $f(x + h) = f(x) + f(h)$ can be transformed into $2^{1+1} = 2^1 + 2^1$, which is a true number sentence because both expressions are equal to 4.

6. Given the function f whose domain is the set of real numbers, let $f(x) = 1$ if x is a rational number, and let $f(x) = 0$ if x is an irrational number.

   a. Explain why f is a function.

   Each element of the domain (the real numbers) is assigned to one element in the range (the number 0 OR the number 1).

   b. What is the range of f?

   Range: $\{0, 1\}$.

   c. Evaluate f for each domain value shown below.

x	2/3	0	-5	$\sqrt{2}$	π
$f(x)$	1	1	1	0	0

   d. List three possible solutions to the equation $f(x) = 0$.

   Answers will vary: $\sqrt{5}, \sqrt{8}, -\sqrt{3}$.

Lesson 11: The Graph of a Function

Student Outcomes

- Students understand set builder notation for the graph of a real-valued function: $\{(x, f(x)) \mid x \in D\}$.
- Students learn techniques for graphing functions and relate the domain of a function to its graph.

Lesson Notes

The lesson continues to develop the notions of input and output from Lesson 9 and 10: if f is a function and x is an element of its domain, then $f(x)$ denotes the output of f corresponding to the input x. In particular, this lesson is designed to make sense of the definition of the *graph of f*, which is quite different than the definition of the *graph of the equation $y = f(x)$* covered in the next lesson. The ultimate goal is to show that the "graph of f" and the "graph of $y = f(x)$" both define the same set in the Cartesian plane. The argument that shows that these two sets are the same uses an idea that is very similar to the "vertical line test."

Lessons 11 and 12 also address directly two concepts that are usually "swept under the rug" in K–12 mathematics and in ignoring, can create confusion about algebra in students' minds. One is the universal quantifier "for all." What does it mean and how can students develop concept images about it? (It is one of the two major universal quantifiers in mathematics—the other is "there exists.") The other concept is the meaning of a variable symbol. Many wrong descriptions invoke the adage, "A variable is a quantity that varies." A variable is neither a quantity, nor does it vary. As we saw in Module 1, it is merely a placeholder for a number from a specified set (the domain of the variable).

In this lesson, we build concept images of *for all* and *variable* using the idea of pseudo code—code that mimics computer programs. In doing so, we see *for all* as a for-next loop and *variables* as actual placeholders that are replaced with numbers in a systematic way. See the end of this lesson for more tips on Lessons 11 and 12.

A teacher knowledgeable in computer programming could easily turn the pseudo code in these lessons into actual computer programs. (The pseudo code was designed with the capabilities of Mathematica in mind, but any programming language would do.) ***Regardless, the pseudo code presented in this lesson is purposely designed to be particularly simple and easy to explain to students***. If the pseudo code is unduly challenging for students, consider "translating" the code for each example into set-builder notation either in advance or as a class. The first example has the following features:

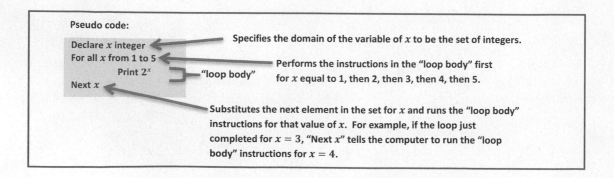

Note about the lesson pace: Every new example or exercise in this lesson usually inserts just 1 more line of pseudo code into the previous exercise or example. Use this continuity to your advantage in developing your lesson plans. For instance, you can just modify the example that is already on the board for each new example.

Classwork

Classwork

In Module 1, you graphed equations such as $y = 10 - 4x$ by plotting the points in the Cartesian plane by picking x values and then using the equation to find the y value for each x value. The number of order pairs you plotted to get the general shape of the graph depended on the type of equation (linear, quadratic, etc.). The graph of the equation was then a representation of the solution set, which could be described using set notation.

In this lesson, we extend set notation slightly to describe the graph of a function. In doing so, we explain a way to think about set notation for the graph of a function that mimics the instructions a tablet or laptop might perform to "draw" a graph on its screen.

Example 1 (5 minutes)

Example 1

Computer programs are essentially instructions to computers on what to do when the user (you!) makes a request. For example, when you type a letter on your smart phone, the smart phone follows a specified set of instructions to draw that letter on the screen and record it in memory (as part of an email, for example). One of the simplest types of instructions a computer can perform is a *for-next loop*. Below is code for a program that prints the first 5 powers of 2:

```
Declare x integer
For all x from 1 to 5
         Print 2^x
Next x
```

The output of this program code is

```
2
4
8
16
32
```

- Go through the code with your students as if you and the class were a "computer."

Here is a description of the instructions: First, x is quantified as an integer, which means the variable can only take on integer values and cannot take on values like $\frac{1}{3}$ or $\sqrt{2}$. The "For" statement begins the loop, starting with $x = 1$. The instructions between "For" and "Next" are performed for the value $x = 1$, which in this case is just to "Print 2." (Print means "print to the computer screen.") Then the computer performs the instructions again for the next x ($x = 2$), i.e., "Print 4," and so on until the computer performs the instructions for $x = 5$, i.e., "Print 32."

Have students study the pseudo code and output and then ask the following:

- What is the domain of the variable x?
  - *Integers.*
- If f is a function given by evaluating the expression 2^x for a number x, what is the domain of the function given by the program?
  - *The set $\{1, 2, 3, 4, 5\}$.*
- What is the range of f?
  - *The set $\{2, 4, 8, 16, 32\}$.*

Point out to your students the similarity between mathematics and programming. In fact, it should come as no great surprise that many of the first computers and programming languages were invented by mathematicians. If you have time, feel free to discuss Blaise Pascal's Calculator, Gottfried Leibniz's Stepped Reckoner, and the life of George Boole (using articles found on *Wikipedia*).

Exercise 1 (3 minutes)

Exercise 1

Perform the instructions in the following programming code as if *you were a computer and your paper was the computer screen*:

```
Declare x integer
For all x from 2 to 8
        Print 2x + 3
Next x
```

Answer:
7
9
11
13
15
17
19

Example 2 (4 minutes)

Example 2

We can use almost the same code to build a set: first, we start with a set with 0 elements in it (called the *empty set*) and then increase the size of the set by appending one new element to it in each for-next step:

```
Declare x integer
Initialize G as {}
For all x from 2 to 8
        Append 2x + 3 to G
        Print G
Next x
```

Go through the code step-by-step with your students as if you and the class were a computer.

> Note that G is printed to the screen after each new number is appended. Thus, the output shows how the set "builds":
>
> $\{7\}$
> $\{7, 9\}$
> $\{7, 9, 11\}$
> $\{7, 9, 11, 13\}$
> $\{7, 9, 11, 13, 15\}$
> $\{7, 9, 11, 13, 15, 17\}$
> $\{7, 9, 11, 13, 15, 17, 19\}$

Exercise 2 (4 minutes)

> **Exercise 2**
>
> We can also build a set by appending ordered pairs. Perform the instructions in the following programming code as if *you were a computer and your paper was the computer screen* (the first couple are done for you):
>
> ```
> Declare x integer
> Initialize G as {}
> For all x from 2 to 8
>         Append (x, 2x + 3) to G
> Next x
> Print G
> ```
>
> Output:
> $\{(2, 7), (3, 9),$ _____ $\}$
>
> *Answer:* $\{(2, 7), (3, 9), (4, 11), (5, 13), (6, 15), (7, 17), (8, 19)\}$.

▪ Ask students why the set G is only printed once and not multiple times like in the previous example.

  □ *Answer: Because the "Print G" command comes after the for-next loop has completed.*

Example 3 (4 minutes)

> **Example 3**
>
> Instead of "Printing" the set G to the screen, we can use another command, "Plot," to plot the points on a Cartesian plane.
>
> ```
> Declare x integer
> Initialize G as {}
> For all x from 2 to 8
>         Append (x, 2x + 3) to G
> Next x
> Plot G
> ```

Output:

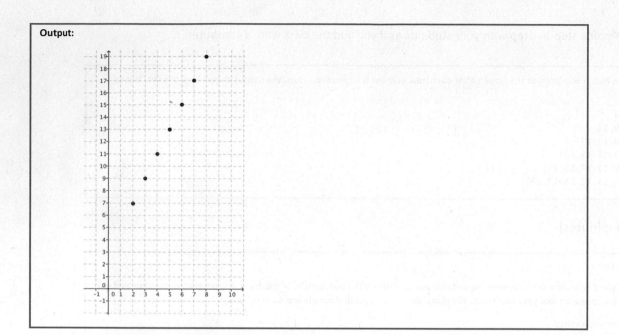

Some graphing calculators actually slow the computer down on purpose to give the human eye a sense of it plotting or drawing each point. If you have such a graphing calculator, graph an example with your students.

Make the point that, inside each for-next step, the variable has been replaced by a number at the beginning of the loop and that number does not change until all the instructions between the "For" and "Next" are completed for that step ("Next x" calls for a new number to be substituted into x).

In mathematics, the programming code above can be compactly written using set notation, as follows:

$$\{(x, 2x + 3) \mid x \text{ integer and } 2 \leq x \leq 8\}.$$

This set notation is an abbreviation for "The set of all points $(x, 2x + 3)$ such that x is an integer and $2 \leq x \leq 8$." Notice how the set of ordered pairs generated by the for-next code above,

$$\{(2, 7), (3, 9), (4, 11), (5, 13), (6, 15), (7, 17), (8, 19)\},$$

also satisfies the requirements described by $\{(x, 2x + 3) \mid x \text{ integer}, 2 \leq x \leq 8\}$. It is for this reason that the set notation of the form

$$\{\text{type of element} \mid \text{condition on each element}\}$$

is sometimes called *set-builder notation*—because it can be thought of as building the set just like the for-next code.

If time permits, have students check that the set generated by the for-next instructions is exactly the same as the set described using the set-builder notation.

Discussion (7 minutes)

Discussion

We can now upgrade our notion of a for-next loop by doing a thought experiment: Imagine a for-next loop that steps through *all* real numbers in an interval (not just the integers). No computer can actually do this—computers can only do a finite number of calculations. But our human brains are far superior to that of any computer, and we can easily imagine what that might look like. Here is some sample code:

Students have misconceptions about how a graphing calculator generates a graph on its screen. Many students actually think that the computer is running through every real number, instead of the finite set of numbers needed to pixelate just the pixels needed to display the graph on the screen.

```
Declare x real
Let f(x) = 2x + 3
Initialize G as {}
For all x such that 2 ≤ x ≤ 8
          Append (x, f(x)) to G
Next x
Plot G
```

The output of this thought code is the graph of f for all real numbers x in the interval $2 \le x \le 8$:

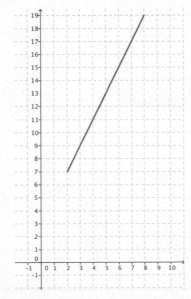

Point out to students that a couple parts of the code have changed from the previous examples: (1) The variable x is now quantified as a real number, not an integer. (2) For clarity, we named the function $f(x) = 2x + 3$, where the function f has domain $2 \le x \le 8$ and range $7 \le f(x) \le 19$. (3) The loop starts with the input value $x = 2$ and appends $(2, f(2))$ to G, and now we *imagine* that it steps one-by-one through every real number x between 2 and 8, each time appending $(x, f(x))$ to the set G. Finally, the loop finishes with appending $(8, f(8))$ to G.

The resulting set G, thought of as a geometric figure plotted in the Cartesian coordinate plane, is called the *graph of f*. In this example, the graph of f is a line segment.

Exercise 3 (10 minutes)

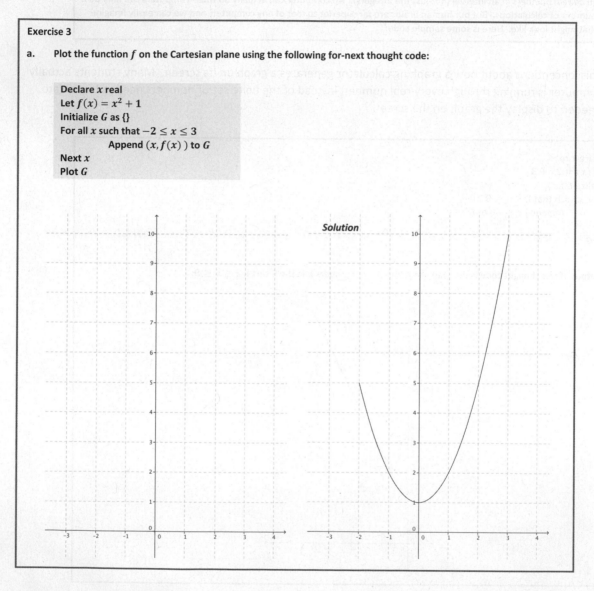

Exercise 3

a. Plot the function f on the Cartesian plane using the following for-next thought code:

```
Declare x real
Let f(x) = x² + 1
Initialize G as {}
For all x such that −2 ≤ x ≤ 3
        Append (x, f(x)) to G
Next x
Plot G
```

Walk around the class and provide help on how to plot the function $f(x) = x^2 + 1$ in the given domain. Remind students that the way we humans "draw" a graph is different than the way a computer draws a graph. We usually pick a few points (end points of the domain interval, the point (0, y-intercept), etc.), plot them first to get the general shape of the graph, and then "connect-the-dots" with an appropriate curve. Students have already done this for some time now but not in the context of $(x, f(x))$. Their biggest challenge will likely be working with function notation to get the y-coordinate for a given x-coordinate.

b. For each step of the for-next loop, what is the input value?

The number x.

c. For each step of the for-next loop, what is the output value?

f(x) or the value of x² + 1.

d. What is the domain of the function f?

The interval −2 ≤ x ≤ 3.

e. What is the range of the function f?

The interval 1 ≤ f(x) ≤ 10 for all x in the domain.

- If time allows, ask students to describe in words how the thought code works.

  □ *Answer: First, the domain of the variable x is stated as the real numbers, the formula for f is given, and the set G is initialized with nothing in it. Then the for-next loop goes through each number between −2 and 3 inclusive and appends the point (x, f(x)) to the set G. After every point is appended to G, the graph of f is plotted on the Cartesian plane.*

Closing (5 minutes)

Closing

The set G built from the for-next thought code in Exercise 4 can also be compactly written in mathematics using set notation:

$$\{(x, x^2 + 1) \mid x \text{ real}, -2 \leq x \leq 3\}.$$

When this set is thought of as plotted in the Cartesian plane, it is the same graph. When you see this set notation in your homework and/or future studies, it is helpful to imagine this set-builder notation as describing a for-next loop.

In general, if $f: D \rightarrow Y$ is a function with domain D, then its *graph* is the set of all ordered pairs,

$$\{(x, f(x)) \mid x \in D\},$$

thought of as a geometric figure in the Cartesian coordinate plane. (The symbol $\in$ simply means "in." The statement $x \in D$ is read, "x in D.")

Lesson Summary

Graph of f: Given a function f whose domain D and the range are subsets of the real numbers, the graph of f is the set of ordered pairs in the Cartesian plane given by

$$\{(x, f(x)) \mid x \in D\}.$$

Exit Ticket (3 minutes)

	Lesson 11:	The Graph of a Function
	Date:	9/11/13

123

To the teacher: Further tips about this lesson and the next. Lesson 11 and Lesson 12 use programming code to develop distinctly *mathematical concepts*. In particular:

- The lessons are designed to give a conceptual image to the meaning "for all," which is a concept that is often used but rarely (if at all) explained.

- The lessons are designed to help students develop a conceptual image of a variable as a placeholder—that students have complete control over what can be substituted into the placeholder (just as the programmer does when he/she instructs the computer to call the "next x").

- The pseudo code in Lesson 11 and the pseudo code in Lesson 12 help students to understand that the "graph of f" and the "graph of $y = f(x)$" are differently generated sets. The first set is generated with just a straight for-next loop, and the second set is generated by a nested for-next loop that tests every point in the plane to see if it is a solution to $y = f(x)$. It is study of how the two "computer programs" are different that helps students see that the way the sets are generated is different.

- The pseudo code in Lesson 12 for generating the graph of $y = f(x)$ is also another way for students to envision how the points in the graph of any equation in two variables can be generated (like $x^2 + y^2 = 100$). In particular, it explains why we set "y" equal to "$f(x)$." The notation $y = f(x)$ can appear strange to students at first: students might wonder, "In eighth grade we said that $y = x^2$ was a function. Now, in ninth grade, we say $f(x) = x^2$ is a function, so what is so special about $y = f(x)$? Doesn't that just mean $x^2 = x^2$?" The pseudo code helps students see that f is a name for a function and that $y = f(x)$ is an equation in the sense of Module 1.

- It is through the study of the two types of programs that the two differently generated graphs can be shown to be the same set; that is, the graph of f is the same set as the graph of $y = f(x)$. The critical issue that helps equate the two sets is a discussion about the definition of function and why the definition guarantees that there is only one y-value for each x-value. The pseudo code is designed to help you make this point.

- Without saying so, Lesson 11 suggests how graphs are created when students use their graphing calculators. (The "Plot" function is just another for-next loop that pixelates certain pixels on the screen to form the graph.) The lessons are designed to help demystify these "little black boxes" and to plant the seed in your students' heads that programming computers may not be as hard as they thought.

- Finally, the long division algorithm is the first nontrivial algorithm students learn. Up to this point in their education, it is also one of the only algorithms they have learned. The pseudo code in these two lessons gives students a chance to see other types of useful algorithms that are also easy to understand.

Name _____   Date_____

Lesson 11: The Graph of a Function

Exit Ticket

1. Perform the instructions for the following programming code as if *you were a computer and your paper was the computer screen*.

    ```
    Declare x integer
    Let f(x) = 2x + 1
    Initialize G as {}
    For all x from −3 to 2
            Append (x, f(x) ) to G
    Next x
    Plot G
    ```

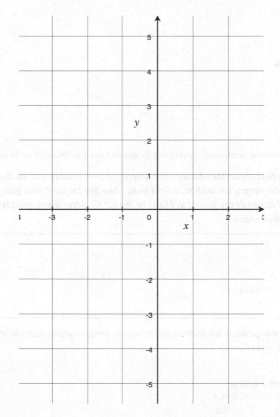

2. Write three or four sentences describing in words how the thought code works.

Exit Ticket Sample Solutions

1. Perform the instructions for the following programming code as if *you were a computer and your paper was the computer screen*.

> Declare x integer
> Let $f(x) = 2x + 1$
> Initialize G as {}
> For all x from -3 to 2
>   Append $(x, f(x))$ to G
> Next x
> Plot G

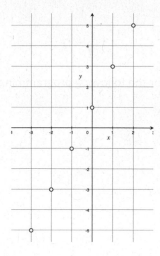

2. Write three or four sentences describing in words how the thought code works.

   Answer: The first three lines declare the domain of the variable x to be the integers, specifies the formula for f, and sets G to be the empty set with no points in it. Then the for-next loop goes through each integer between -3 and 2 inclusive and appends the point $(x, f(x))$ to the set G. After every point is appended to G, the graph of f is plotted on the Cartesian plane.

Problem Set Sample Solutions

1. Perform the instructions for each of the following programming codes as if *you were a computer and your paper was the computer screen*.

   a.
   > Declare x integer
   > For all x from 0 to 4
   >   Print $2x$
   > Next x

   Answer: $0, 2, 4, 6, 8$

   b.
   > Declare x integer
   > For all x from 0 to 10
   >   Print $2x + 1$
   > Next x

   Answer: $1, 3, 5, 7, 9, 11, 13, 15, 17, 19, 21$

c.

```
Declare x integer
For all x from 2 to 8
        Print x²
Next x
```

Answer: 4, 9, 25, 36, 49, 64

d.

```
Declare x integer
For all x from 0 to 4
        Print 10 · 3ˣ
Next x
```

Answer: 10, 30, 90, 270, 810

2. Perform the instructions for each of the following programming codes as if *you were a computer and your paper was the computer screen.*

a.

```
Declare x integer
Let f(x) = (x + 1)(x − 1) − x²
Initialize G as {}
For all x from −3 to 3
        Append (x, f(x)) to G
Next x
Plot G
```

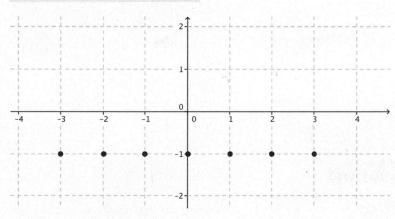

b.

```
Declare x integer
Let f(x) = 3^{-x}
Initialize G as {}
For all x from −3 to 3
        Append (x, f(x)) to G
Next x
Plot G
```

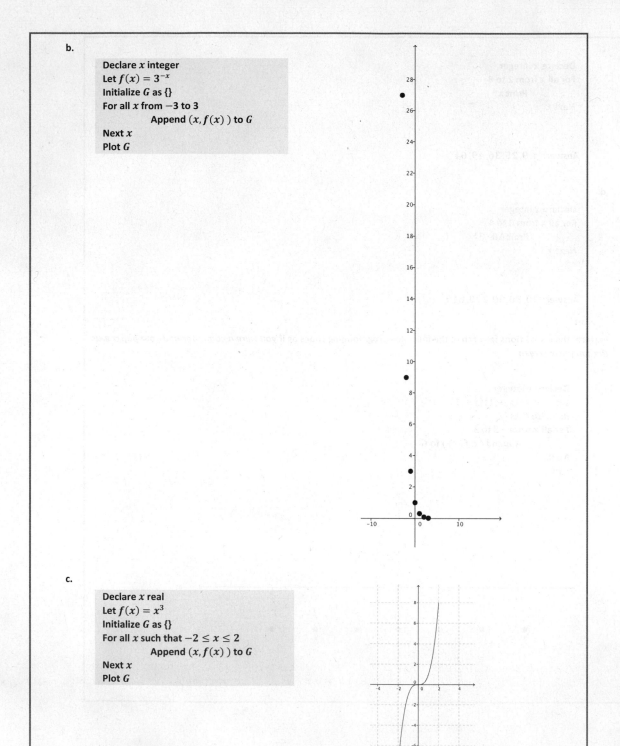

c.

```
Declare x real
Let f(x) = x^3
Initialize G as {}
For all x such that −2 ≤ x ≤ 2
        Append (x, f(x)) to G
Next x
Plot G
```

3. Answer the following questions about the "thought code:"

> Declare x real
> Let $f(x) = (x - 2)(x - 4)$
> Initialize G as $\{\}$
> For all x such that $0 \le x \le 5$
>   Append $(x, f(x))$ to G
> Next x
> Plot G

a. What is the domain of the function f?

   Answer: $0 \le x \le 5$.

b. Plot the graph of f according to the instructions in the thought code.

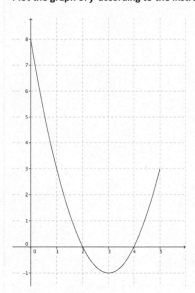

c. Look at your graph of f. What is the range of f?

   Answer: $-1 \le f(x) \le 8$ for all x in the domain.

d. Write three or four sentences describing in words how the thought code works.

   Answer: First, the domain of the variable x is stated as the real numbers, the formula for f is given, and the set G is initialized with nothing in it. Then the for-next loop goes through each number between 0 and 5 inclusive and appends the point $(x, f(x))$ to the set G. After every point is appended to G, the graph of f is plotted on the Cartesian plane.

4. Sketch the graph of the functions defined by the following formulas, and write the graph of f as a set using set-builder notation. (Hint: Assume the domain is all real numbers unless specified in the problem.)

a. $f(x) = x + 2$

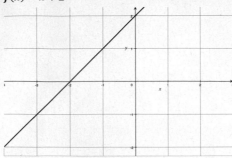

Graph of $f = \{(x, x + 2) \mid x \, real\}$

b. $f(x) = 3x + 2$

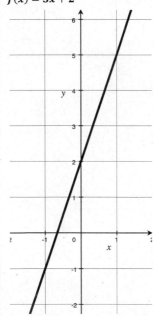

Graph of $f = \{(x, 3x + 2) \mid x \, real\}$

c. $f(x) = 3x - 2$

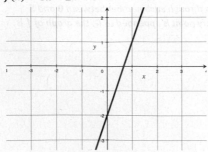

Graph of $f = \{(x, 3x - 2) \mid x \, real\}$

d. $f(x) = -3x - 2$

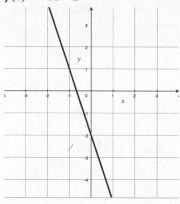

Graph of f = $\{(x, -3x - 2) \mid x\ real\}$

e. $f(x) = -3x + 2$

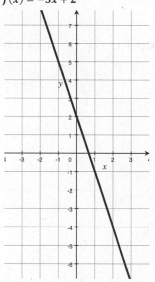

Graph of f = $\{(x, -3x + 2) \mid x\ real\}$

f. $f(x) = -\frac{1}{3}x + 2, -3 \leq x \leq 3$

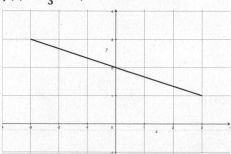

Graph of f = $\left\{\left(x, -\frac{1}{3}x + 2\right) \mid x\ real, -3 \leq x \leq 3\right\}$ *or Graph of f* = $\left\{\left(x, -\frac{1}{3}x + 2\right) \mid -3 \leq x \leq 3\right\}$

g. $f(x) = (x + 1)^2 - x^2, \quad -2 \le x \le 5$

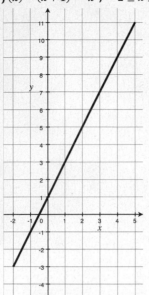

Graph of f = $\{(x, (x + 1)^2 - x^2) \mid x\,real, -2 \le x \le 5\}$ or Graph of f = $\{(x, (x + 1)^2 - x^2) \mid -2 \le x \le 5\}$

h. $f(x) = (x + 1)^2 - (x - 1)^2, \quad -2 \le x \le 4$

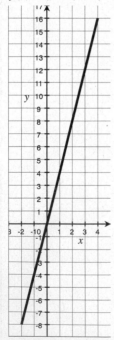

Graph of f = $\{(x, (x + 1)^2 - (x - 1)^2) \mid x\,real, -2 \le x \le 4\}$ or
Graph of f = $\{(x, (x + 1)^2 - (x - 1)^2) \mid -2 \le x \le 4\}$

5.   The figure shows the graph of $f(x) = -5x + c$.

A(0,7)

O   B

a.   Find the value of c.

Answer: $c = 7$.

b.   If the graph of f intersects the x-axis at B, find the coordinates of B.

Answer: $B\left(\frac{7}{5}, 0\right)$.

6.   The figure shows the graph of $f(x) = \frac{1}{2}x + c$.

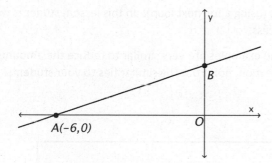

B

A(-6,0)   O

a.   Find the value of c.

Answer: $c = 3$.

b.   If the graph of f intersects the y-axis at B, find the coordinates of B.

Answer: $B(0, 3)$

c.   Find the area of triangle $\triangle AOB$.

Answer: 9 square units.

Lesson 12: The Graph of the Equation $y = f(x)$

Student Outcomes

- Students understand the meaning of the graph of $y = f(x)$, namely $\{(x, y) \mid x \in D \ and \ y = f(x)\}$.
- Students understand the definitions of when a function is increasing or decreasing.

Lesson Notes

This lesson is designed to make sense of the definition of the *graph of the equation $y = f(x)$*, which is quite different from the definition of the *graph of f* covered in the previous lesson. The ultimate goal is to show that the "graph of f" and the "graph of $y = f(x)$" both define the same set in the Cartesian plane. The argument that shows that these two sets are the same uses an idea that is very similar to the "vertical line test."

Lesson 12 also addresses directly three concepts that are usually "swept under the rug" in K–12 mathematics and in ignoring, can create confusion about algebra in students' minds. The first two concepts are described in the Lesson Notes of Lesson 11. This lesson uses pseudo code to build a concept image of a solution set that is different from the "sifting" and "gateway" concept images used in Module 1. In doing so, we once again show how number sentences play an important role in testing for solutions in the solution set to an equation—that equations are always about numbers, not about letters.

In the last lesson, the graph of f was created by a generative process (using a for-next loop). In this lesson, students will see that the graph of $y = f(x)$ is created by an "if-then" testing process.

Note about lesson pace: Just like the last lesson, use the fact that the examples are very similar to reduce the amount of "writing on the board" you will have to do. If you use computer projection, point out the similarities to your students.

Classwork

> **Classwork**
>
> In Module 1, you graphed equations such as $4x + y = 10$ by plotting the points on the Cartesian coordinate plane that corresponded to all of the ordered pairs of numbers (x, y) that were in the solution set. We called the geometric figure that resulted from plotting those points in the plane the "graph of the equation in two variables."
>
> In this lesson, we extend this notion of the graph of an equation to the graph of $y = f(x)$ for a function f. In doing so, we use computer "thought code" to describe the process of generating the ordered pairs in the graph of $y = f(x)$.

If necessary, recall for your students the steps to describe the solution set of an equation using set notation from Module 1. For example, to describe the set of solutions to the equation $w^2 = 4$, we use

$$\{w \ real \mid w^2 = 4\},$$

where "{" means "the set of" and the vertical bar "|" means "such that." Therefore, the set notation reads, "The set of all real numbers w such that $w^2 = 4$ is true." In this case, this set is $\{-2, 2\}$, which we imagined was created by stepping through all real numbers and finding solutions using the following "sifting" or "gateway" procedure: Substitute each real number in for w into the equation; if the resulting number sentence is true for that number, include the number in the solution set; otherwise discard it.

Example 1 (4 minutes)

Example 1

In the previous lesson, we studied a simple type of instruction that computers perform called a for-next loop. Another simple type of instruction is an *if-then statement*. Below is example code of a program that tests for and prints "True" when $x + 2 = 4$; otherwise it prints "False."

```
Declare x integer
For all x from 1 to 4
    If x + 2 = 4 then
        Print True
    else
        Print False
    Endif
Next x
```

The output of this program code is:

False
True
False
False

Ask your students to interpret the output: can you describe how to relate it back to the code? Then go through the code step-by-step with your students as if you and the class were a "computer."

> Notice that the if-then statement in the code above is really just testing whether each number in the loop is in the solution set!

Example 2 (4 minutes)

Before going through the code step-by-step with your students, ask your students to "translate the code into English." For example, ask what the effect the declaration of x as an integer has on the "for" statement? (It limits x to the numbers 0, 1, 2, 3, 4.) In general, is it possible that the set G could be empty after the for-next loop? (Yes.)

Example 2

Perform the instructions in the following programming code as if *you were a computer and your paper was the computer screen*:

```
Declare x integer
Initialize G as {}
For all x from 0 to 4
    If x² − 4x + 5 = 2 then
        Append x to G
    else
        Do NOT append x to G
    Endif
Next x
Print G
```

Output: $\{1, 3\}$

Go through the code step-by-step with your students as if you and the class were a "computer."

	Lesson 12:	The Graph of the Equation $y = f(x)$
	Date:	9/11/13

135

Discussion (2 minutes)

> **Discussion**
>
> Compare the for-next/if-then code above to the following set-builder notation we used to describe solution sets in Module 1:
>
> $$\{x \text{ integer} \mid 0 \le x \le 4 \text{ and } x^2 - 4x + 5 = 2\}.$$
>
> Check to see that the set-builder notation also generates the set $\{1, 3\}$. *Whenever you see set-builder notation to describe a set, a powerful way to interpret that notation is to think of the set as being generated by a "program" like the for-next/if-then code above.*

Point out all of the similarities between the set-builder notation and the pseudo code above. For example, where is the variable specified as an integer in both? During each step of the loop, x is an actual number (0, then 1, then 2, ...); hence, it is possible to determine whether the equation $x^2 - 4x + 5 = 2$ is true or false. Similarly, what does it mean for $0 \le x \le 4$ and $x^2 - 4x + 5 = 2$ to both be true? (We will replace "x integer" later in the lesson with (x, y), replace "$0 \le x \le 4$" with $x \in D$, and "$x^2 - 4x + 5 = 2$" with $y = f(x)$.)

Exercise 1 (10 minutes)

> **Exercise 1**
>
> Next we write code that generates a graph of a *two variable equation* $y = x(x - 2)(x + 2)$ for x in $\{-2, -1, 0, 1, 2\}$ and y in $\{-3, 0, 3\}$. The solution set of this equation is generated by testing each ordered pair (x, y) in the set,
>
> $$\{(-2, -3), (-2, 0), (-2, 3), (-1, -3), (-1, 0), (-1, 3), \ldots, (2, -3), (2, 0), (2, 3)\},$$
>
> to see if it is a solution to the equation $y = x(x - 2)(x + 2)$. Then the graph is just the plot of solutions in the Cartesian plane. We can instruct a computer to find these points and plot them using the following program:
>
>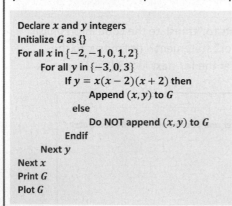
>
>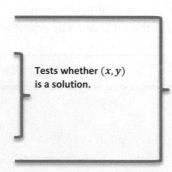
>
> Tests whether (x, y) is a solution.
>
> Loops through each y for $x = -2$, then for $x = -1$, and so on (see arrows in table below).
>
> a.   Use the table below to record the decisions a computer would make when following the program instructions above. Fill in each cell with "Yes" or "No" depending on whether the ordered pair (x, y) would be appended or not. (The step where $x = -2$ has been done for you.)
>
> | | $x = -2$ | $x = -1$ | $x = 0$ | $x = 1$ | $x = 2$ |
> |---|---|---|---|---|---|
> | $y = 3$ | No | Yes | No | No | No |
> | $y = 0$ | Yes | No | Yes | No | Yes |
> | $y = -3$ | No | No | No | Yes | No |

Help students understand the nested for-next loop: First, $x = -2$ is kept fixed while y loops through -3, 0, and 3. The "Next x" command then fixes $x = -1$ while y again steps through -3, 0, and 3. This continues until $x = 2$ and $y = 3$. Arrows are drawn on your table to indicate the order of this process.

---

b. **What would be the output to the "Print G" command? (The first ordered pair is listed for you.)**

Output:
$\{ \ (-2, 0) \ \ , \underline{\hspace{2cm}}, \underline{\hspace{2cm}}, \underline{\hspace{2cm}}, \underline{\hspace{2cm}} \}$

$\{(-2, 0), \quad (-1, 3), \quad (0, 0), \quad (1, 3), \quad (2, 0)\}$

c. **Plot the solution set G in the Cartesian plane. (The first ordered pair in G has been plotted for you.)**

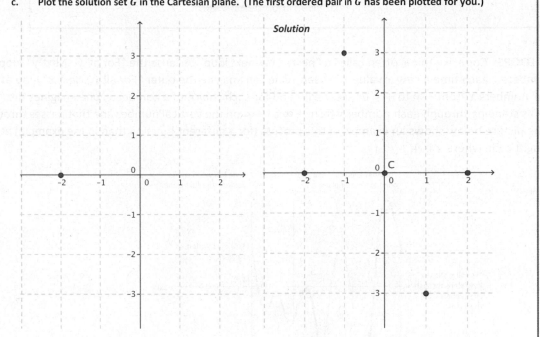

Point out that the "Yes" answers in the table show a similar pattern as the students' graphs. The point that you want to make is that this code checks *every* ordered pair in the domain and range and appends only those to the set G that solve the equation. In the next exercise, we will see that this is the same as set-builder notation.

Exercise 2 (15 minutes)

Exercise 2

The program code in Exercise 3 is a way to imagine how set-builder notation generates solution sets and figures in the plane. Given a function $f(x) = x(x - 2)(x - 3)$ with domain and range all real numbers, a slight modification of the program code above can be used to generate the graph of the equation $y = f(x)$:

$$\{(x, y) \mid x \text{ real } \text{ and } y = f(x)\}.$$

Even though the code below cannot be run on a computer, we can run the following "thought code" in our minds:

Declare x and y real
Let $f(x) = x(x-2)(x+2)$
Initialize G as {}
For all x in the real numbers
    For all y in the real numbers
        If $y = f(x)$ then
            Append (x, y) to G
        else
            Do NOT append (x, y) to G
        Endif
    Next y
Next x
Plot G

Tests whether (x, y) is a solution to $y = x(x-2)(x+2)$.

For each x value, the code loops through all y values.

NESTED FOR-NEXT LOOPS: Code like this is often called a "nested for-next loop" because the "For all y…Next y" loop runs through all numbers y each time a new x value is chosen. One can imagine the outer "For all x…Next x" loop as stepping through all numbers x from $-\infty$ to $+\infty$ on the x-axis, and for each choice of a number x, one imagines the "For all y…Next y" code as stepping through each number y from $-\infty$ to $+\infty$ on the vertical number line that passes through the point $(x, 0)$. The picture below shows an example of this process (for a different function than in the example) at the step in the thought code where x is 4:

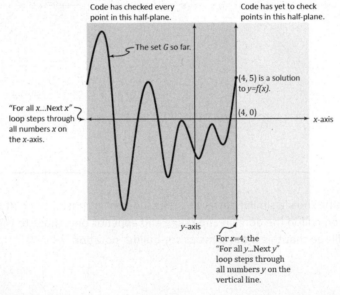

Code has checked every point in this half-plane.

Code has yet to check points in this half-plane.

The set G so far.

$(4, 5)$ is a solution to $y=f(x)$.

$(4, 0)$

x-axis

"For all x…Next x" loop steps through all numbers x on the x-axis.

y-axis

For $x=4$, the "For all y…Next y" loop steps through all numbers y on the vertical line.

In this way the "thought code" above checks every single point (x, y) in the Cartesian coordinate plane to see if it is a solution to the equation $y = f(x)$.

a.   Plot G on the Cartesian plane (the figure drawn is called the graph of $y = f(x)$).

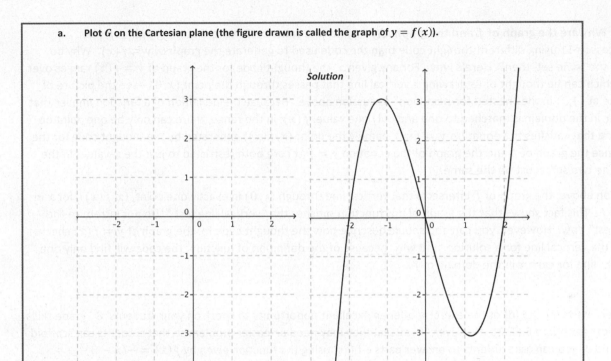

Solution

Walk around and help students construct the graph in groups of two or individually by generating a table of order pairs, plotting those points, and then "connect-the-dots" between the points with a smooth curve. Remind students that they can use their work from Exercise 1 to get started. Note: While they do not have to generate the table in the same way that the thought code builds the set G, once students have generated a table, ask them what order the thought code would have found the points in their table.

b.   Describe how the "thought code" is similar to the set-builder notation $\{(x, y) \mid x\text{ real} \text{ and } y = f(x)\}$.

Answer: *Both generate sets by checking every point (x, y) in the Cartesian plane, searching for points (x, y) for which the equation $y = x(x - 2)(x + 2)$ is true.*

■   Go over this answer with your students. Ask for:

Domain of f: all real numbers.

Range of f: all real numbers.

The thought code describes a systematic way of imagining how all of the points in the graph of $y = f(x)$ are found. However, the set $\{(x, y) \mid x\text{ real} \text{ and } y = f(x)\}$ should be thought of as the *end result* of the thought code; that is, the set contains all the points of the graph of $y = f(x)$. In this way, we can think of the set $\{(x, y) \mid x\text{ real} \text{ and } y = f(x)\}$ as the actual figure in the plane. (Students have already been introduced to this type of thinking in 8th grade using the simple example of associating a line as a geometric figure to the graph of a solution set of a linear equation. We will need this type of thinking in later grades to describe parabolas as graphs of quadratic functions, for example.)

IMPORTANT: Why are the graph of f and the graph of $y = f(x)$ the same set? Note that the graph of f was generated in Lesson 11 using different thought code than the code used to generate the graph of $y = f(x)$. Why do they generate the same set, then? Here's why: For any given x, the thought code for the graph of $y = f(x)$ ranges over all y values, which can be thought of as drawing a vertical line that passes through the point $(x, 0)$—see the picture of the vertical line at $(4, 0)$ in the "nested for-next loop" discussion above. Because the definition of a function implies that each number x in the domain is matched to one and only one value, $f(x)$, in the range, there can only be one point on that vertical line that satisfies the equation $y = f(x)$, namely the point $(x, f(x))$ generated by the thought code for the graph of f. Since the graph of f and the graph of the equation $y = f(x)$ are both restricted to just the x-values in the domain of f, the two sets must be the same.

In the discussion above, the graph of f intersects that vertical line through $(x, 0)$ in exactly one point, $(x, f(x))$, for x in the domain of f. This fact shows that the graph of any function satisfies the "vertical line test." Do not introduce the "vertical line test" now. However, you can and should describe how the thought code for the graph of $y = f(x)$ checks each point on the vertical line for a solution, and why, because of the definition of function, the code will find only one solution on that line for each x in the domain of f.

Note to teacher: Parts (c) and (d) of the exercise offer an excellent opportunity to check on your students' 8th grade skills with square roots (standard 8.EE.2). However, if you feel they may need an easier problem so that students can scaffold up to parts c and d, you can ask students to answer parts c-f first using the function given by $f(x) = -(x - 3)^2 + 4$.

---

c. A *relative maximum* for the function f occurs at the x-coordinate of $\left(-\frac{2}{3}\sqrt{3}, \frac{16}{9}\sqrt{3}\right)$. Substitute this point into the equation $y = x(x^2 - 4)$ to check that it is a solution to $y = f(x)$, and then plot the point on your graph.

Answer: Check that $\frac{16}{9}\sqrt{3} = -\frac{2}{3}\sqrt{3}\left(\left(-\frac{2}{3}\sqrt{3}\right)^2 - 4\right)$ is a true number sentence. Divide both sides by $\sqrt{3}$, multiply both sides by $\frac{9}{2}$, and evaluate the square to get $8 = -3\left(\frac{4}{3} - 4\right)$. Distributing the -3 shows that $\left(-\frac{2}{3}\sqrt{3}, \frac{16}{9}\sqrt{3}\right)$ is a solution.

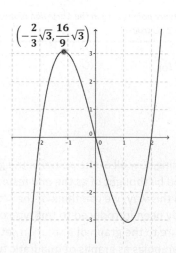

You may need to remind students that $x(x - 2)(x + 2) = x(x^2 - 4)$. If time permits, allow them to use their calculators to see that the point $\left(-\frac{2}{3}\sqrt{3}, \frac{16}{9}\sqrt{3}\right)$ really is the point they plotted on their graph.

d. A *relative minimum* for the function f occurs at the x-coordinate of $\left(\frac{2}{3}\sqrt{3}, -\frac{16}{9}\sqrt{3}\right)$. A similar calculation as you did above shows that this point is also a solution to $y = f(x)$. Plot this point on your graph.

Answer: Students should plot the point $\left(\frac{2}{3}\sqrt{3}, -\frac{16}{9}\sqrt{3}\right)$ on their graphs approximately at $(1.15, -3.08)$.

e. Look at your graph. On what interval(s) is the function f decreasing?

Answer: $-\frac{2}{3}\sqrt{3} \le x \le \frac{2}{3}\sqrt{3}$ or $\left[-\frac{2}{3}\sqrt{3}, \frac{2}{3}\sqrt{3}\right]$.

f. Look at your graph. On what interval(s) is the function f increasing?

Answer: $x \le -\frac{2}{3}\sqrt{3}$ or $\frac{2}{3}\sqrt{3} \le x$ or $\left(-\infty, -\frac{2}{3}\sqrt{3}\right]$ or $\left[\frac{2}{3}\sqrt{3}, \infty\right)$.

Closing (2 minutes)

Lesson Summary

- **Graph of $y = f(x)$.** Given a function f whose domain D and the range are subsets of the real numbers, the *graph of $y = f(x)$* is the set of ordered pairs (x, y) in the Cartesian plane given by

$$\{(x, y) \mid x \in D \text{ and } y = f(x)\}.$$

When we write $\{(x, y) \mid y = f(x)\}$ for the graph of $y = f(x)$, it is understood that the domain is the largest set of real numbers for which the function f is defined.

- The graph of f is the same as the graph of the equation $y = f(x)$.

- **Increasing/Decreasing.** Given a function f whose domain and range are subsets of the real numbers and I is an interval contained within the domain, the function is called *increasing on the interval I* if

$$f(x_1) < f(x_2) \text{ whenever } x_1 < x_2 \text{ in } I.$$

It is called *decreasing on the interval I* if

$$f(x_1) > f(x_2) \text{ whenever } x_1 < x_2 \text{ in } I.$$

Exit Ticket (8 minutes)

Name _____ Date _____

Lesson 12: The Graph of the Equation $y = f(x)$

Exit Ticket

1. Perform the instructions in the following programming code as if *you were a computer and your paper was the computer screen*:

```
Declare x integer
For all x from 2 to 7
    If x + 2 = 7 then
        Print True
    else
        Print False
    Endif
Next x
```

2. Let $f(x) = -\frac{1}{2}x + 2$ for x in the domain $0 \le x \le 2$.

    a. Write out in words the meaning of the set notation:

    $$\{(x, y) \mid 0 \le x \le 2 \text{ and } y = f(x)\}.$$

    b. Sketch the graph of $y = f(x)$.

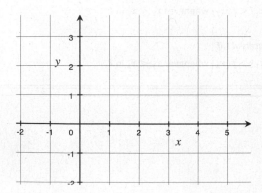

Exit Ticket Sample Solutions

1. Perform the instructions in the following programming code as if *you were a computer and your paper was the computer screen*:

```
Declare x integer
For all x from 2 to 7
        If x + 2 = 7 then
                Print True
        else
                Print False
        Endif
Next x
```

Answer: False, False, False, True, False, False.

2. Let $f(x) = -\frac{1}{2}x + 2$ for x in the domain $0 \le x \le 2$.

   a. Write out in words the meaning of the set notation:
   $$\{(x, y) \mid 0 \le x \le 2 \text{ and } y = f(x)\}.$$

   Answer: The set of all points (x, y) in the Cartesian plane such that x is between 0 and 2 inclusively and $y = -\frac{1}{2}x + 2$ is true.

   b. Sketch the graph of $y = f(x)$.

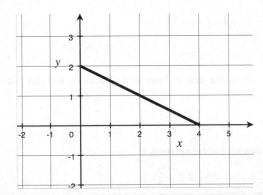

Problem Set Sample Solutions

1. Perform the instructions in the following programming code as if *you were a computer and your paper was the computer screen*:

```
Declare x integer
For all x from 1 to 6
      If x² − 2 = 7 then
            Print True
      else
            Print False
      Endif
Next x
```

Answer: False, False, True, False, False, False.

2. Answer the following questions about the computer programming code:

```
Declare x integer
Initialize G as {}
For all x from −3 to 3
      If 2ˣ + 2⁻ˣ = 17/4 then
            Append x to G
      else
            Do NOT append x to G
      Endif
Next x
Print G
```

a. Perform the instructions in the programming code as if you were a computer and your paper was the computer screen:

Answer: $\{-2, 2\}$.

b. Write a description of the set G using set-builder notation.

Answer: $\{x \ integer \mid -3 \le x \le 3 \ and \ 2^x + 2^{-x} = \frac{9}{4}\}$.

3. Answer the following questions about the computer programming code:

Declare x and y integers
Initialize G as {}
For all x in $\{0, 1, 2, 3\}$
    For all y in $\{0, 1, 2, 3\}$
        If $y = \sqrt{4 + 20x - 19x^2 + 4x^3}$ then
            Append (x, y) to G
        else
            Do NOT append (x, y) to G
        Endif
    Next y
Next x
Plot G

a. Use the table below to record the decisions a computer would make when following the program instructions above. Fill in each cell with "Yes" or "No" depending on whether the ordered pair (x, y) would be appended or not.

	$x = 0$	$x = 1$	$x = 2$	$x = 3$
$y = 3$	No	Yes	No	No
$y = 2$	Yes	No	No	No
$y = 1$	No	No	No	Yes
$y = 0$	No	No	Yes	No

b. Plot the set G in the Cartesian plane.

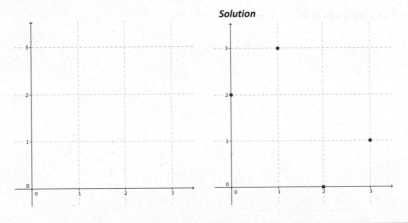

Solution

4. Answer the following questions about the "thought code":

```
Declare x and y real
Let f(x) = −2x + 8
Initialize G as {}
For all x in the real numbers
    For all y in the real numbers
        If y = f(x) then
            Append (x, y) to G
        else
            Do NOT append (x, y) to G
        Endif
    Next y
Next x
Plot G
```

a. What is the domain of the function $f(x) = -2x + 8$?

Answer: all real numbers.

b. What is the range of the function $f(x) = -2x + 8$?

Answer: all real numbers.

c. Write the set G generated by the "thought code" in set-builder notation.

Answer: $\{(x, y) \mid y = -2x + 8\}$.

d. Plot the set G to obtain the graph of the function $f(x) = -2x + 8$.

Answer:

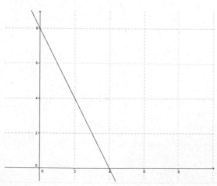

e. The function $f(x) = -2x + 8$ is clearly a decreasing function on the domain of the real numbers. Show that the function satisfies the definition of decreasing for the points 8 and 10 on the number line, i.e., show that since $8 < 10$, then $f(8) > f(10)$.

Answer: $f(8) = -8$ *and* $f(10) = -12$. *Since* $-8 > -12$, $f(8) > f(10)$.

5. Sketch the graph of the functions defined by the following formulas and write the graph of $y = f(x)$ as a set using set-builder notation. (Hint: For each function below you can assume the domain is all real numbers.)

    a. $f(x) = -\frac{1}{2}x + 6$

    b. $f(x) = x^2 + 3$

    c. $f(x) = x^2 - 5x + 6$

    d. $f(x) = x^3 - x$

    e. $f(x) = -x^2 + x - 1$

    f. $f(x) = (x - 3)^2 + 2$

    g. $f(x) = x^3 - 2x^2 + 3$

6. Answer the following questions about the set:

    $$\{(x, y) \mid 0 \le x \le 2 \text{ and } y = 9 - 4x^2\}$$

    a.   The equation can be rewritten in the form $y = f(x)$ where $f(x) = 9 - 4x^2$. What are the domain and range of the function f specified by the set?

    i.   Domain:

         Answer: $0 \le x \le 2$.

    ii. Range:

         Answer: $-7 \le y \le 9$ *or* $-7 \le f(x) \le 9$ *for x in the domain.*

    b.   Write "thought code" like in Exercise 4 that will generate and then plot the set.

         Answer:

         Declare x and y real
         Let $f(x) = 9 - 4x^2$
         Initialize G as {}
         For all x such that $0 \le x \le 2$
                 For all y such that $-5 \le y \le 9$
                         If $y = f(x)$ *then*
                                 Append (x, y) *to G*
                     else
                                 Do NOT append (x, y) *to G*
                         Endif
                 Next y
         Next x
         Plot G

7. Answer the following about the graph of a function below:

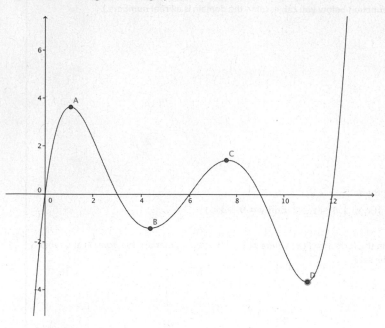

a. Which points (A, B, C, or D) are relative maximums?

    Answer: A and C.

b. Which points (A, B, C, or D) are relative minimums?

    Answer: B and D.

c. Name any interval where the function is increasing.

    Answers will vary. Example: $[5, 7]$.

d. Name any interval where the function is decreasing.

    Answers will vary. Example: $[2, 4]$.

Lesson 13: Interpreting Graphs of Functions

Student Outcomes

- Students create tables and graphs of functions and interpret key features including intercepts, increasing and decreasing intervals, and positive and negative intervals.

Lesson Notes

This lesson uses a graphic created to show the general public the landing sequence for the Mars Curiosity Rover which landed successfully on Mars in August 2012. For more information, visit http://mars.jpl.nasa.gov/msl/. For an article related to the graphic in this lesson see http://www.nasa.gov/mission_pages/msl/multimedia/gallery/pia13282.html. Here is an animation that details Curiosity's descent: http://mars.jpl.nasa.gov/msl/mission/timeline/edl/. The first three minutes of this video show a simulation of the landing sequence http://www.jpl.nasa.gov/video/index.php?id=1001. Students are presented with a problem: Does this graphic really represent the path of the Curiosity Rover as it landed on Mars? And, how can we estimate the altitude and velocity of the Curiosity Rover at any time in the landing sequence? To formulate their model, students will have to create either numeric or graphical representations of height and velocity. They will need to consider the quantities and make sense of the data shared in this graphic. During this lesson, you will be presenting them with vocabulary to help them interpret the graphs they create. To further create context for this lesson, you can share this article from *Wired* http://www.wired.com/thisdayintech/2010/11/1110mars-climate-observer-report/ with your students. It explains an earlier mishap by NASA that cost billions of dollars and two lost explorers that was due to a measurement conversion error. Scientists carefully model all aspects of space travel using mathematical functions, but if they do not attend to precision, it can lead to big mistakes.

Classwork

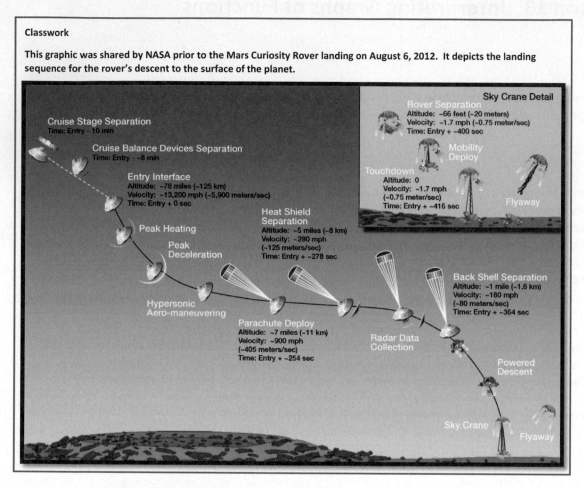

> Classwork
>
> This graphic was shared by NASA prior to the Mars Curiosity Rover landing on August 6, 2012. It depicts the landing sequence for the rover's descent to the surface of the planet.

If students are having a difficult time reading the information on this graphic, go to the website and share the link or project the image in your classroom. (There is also a printer-friendly graphic at the end of this lesson.)

Discussion (5 minutes)

PROBLEM: Read through the problem as a whole class, and have students begin to discuss how they will create a model. Suggested discussion questions to further clarify their work are listed below.

- What information is available to you in this graphic?
    - *The graphic contains the altitude and velocity at various times. Various landing stages are named. Time 0 is at the point called Entry Interface.*
- What information is in the box in the upper right corner?
    - *This box contains detailed information about the final seconds of the landing sequence.*

- Why are there negative time values? Should other quantities be measured with negative numbers?
  - *The creators of this graphic are referencing time since entry interface began. The time associated with stages before this stage would be negative. Velocities shown are all positive, but a calculation of average velocity using the altitude as the distance function shows that the velocities listed in the graphic really should be negative. Direct your students to use negative values for velocities.*
- What does this symbol ~ mean?
  - *This symbol means approximately.*
- Which units, metric or customary, will make this problem easier to understand?
  - *Depends: 13,200 mph is easier to comprehend when the Curiosity Rover is moving fast, but 0.75 meters/sec is easier to comprehend when the Curiosity Rover is just about to land. In general, it is easier to be more accurate with metric units; they also work naturally with the decimal system (since the metric system is based upon powers of 10). For reasons like these, metric units are the preferred system of measurements in science, industry, and engineering. You might suggest to your students that metric units may be easier to graph since time is measured in seconds and the velocity is measured in meters per second. If you use customary units, then miles per hour would have to be converted to feet per second or miles per second. Regardless of the choice, scaling this graph will make for interesting choices that students need to attend to.*

> Does this graphic really represent the landing path of the Curiosity Rover? Create a model that can be used to predict the altitude and velocity of the Curiosity Rover 5, 4, 3, 2, and 1 minute before landing.

Exploratory Challenge (20 mintues)

FORMULATE AND COMPUTE: During this phase of the lesson, students should work in small groups. Focus the groups on creating a tabular and graphical representation of the altitude and velocity as functions of time since entry interface began. You may have them work on large pieces of chart paper, use appropriate technology (e.g., graphing calculator or computer spreadsheet software), or use another technique of your choice to create the tables and graphs. Have each group present their findings to the rest of the class. The discussion will need to focus on the choices your students make as they construct the tables and graphs. You may want to present the option at some point to create a graph where the velocity is negative. The sample solution provided below assumes the velocity to be negative.

> **Exploratory Challenge**
>
> Create a model to help you answer the problem and estimate the altitude and velocity at various times during the landing sequence.

As groups present their work, discuss the following questions.

- How did you decide on your units? How did you decide on a scale?
  - *Answers will vary.*
- Would it make sense to connect the points on the graphs? Why?
  - *It would make sense because you could measure the velocity and altitude at any point in time during the landing sequence.*

- How would you describe the velocity graph? How would you describe the altitude graph?

  □ *The velocity graph appears below the t-axis, and it gets closer to the t-axis as time passes. The altitude gets closer to the t-axis as time passes.*

Give groups time to refine their models after seeing how other groups solved this problem. Regardless of the presentation medium, make sure students are presenting accurate graphs and tables with variables named, axes scaled, and graphs labeled and titled. Sample graphs and tables are shown below. Additional samples are provided in the Exercises section.

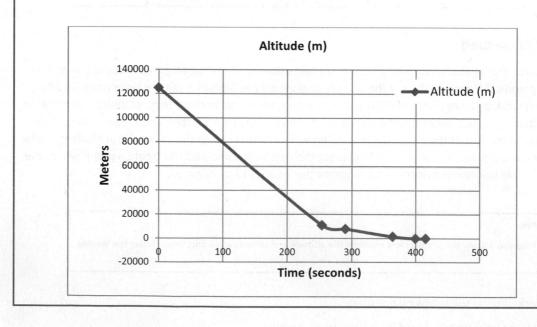

Mars Curiosity Rover Landing Sequence		
Time (s)	Altitude (m)	Velocity (m/s)
0	125000	−5900
254	11000	−405
290	8000	−125
364	1600	−80
400	20	−0.75
416	0	−0.75

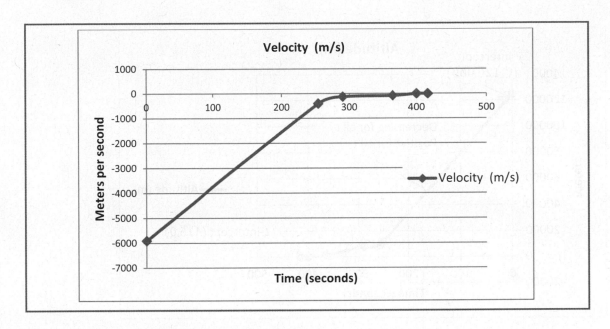

At this point we do not expect students to use the vocabulary of increasing or decreasing to describe the graphs. We will save this for the discussion.

Discussion (5 minutes)

Select one set of the student graphs. Annotate the graphs to show the intervals where the functions are increasing and decreasing, the intervals where the function's values are positive and negative, and the t- and y-intercepts. There will only be intervals where the velocity function is increasing and negative if you create a graph with negative velocity. Remind students of the definitions of increasing and decreasing functions, positive and negative shown below. A sample solution is shown after the definitions.

(Note: If you choose, you may also use this discussion to introduce interval notation. This can be done by explaining the meanings of ( ) and [ ] as exclusive and inclusive, and then asking students to sketch example intervals on a number line, such as $(3,4)$; $(-1,5]$; $[0,3]$. The intervals in this lesson may also be named by students either in words or using set-builder notation, if that is preferred.)

Let f be a function whose domain and range are the subsets of the real numbers.

- A function f is called *increasing* on an interval I if $f(x_1) < f(x_2)$ whenever $x_1 < x_2$ in I.
- A function f is called *decreasing* on an interval I if $f(x_1) > f(x_2)$ whenever $x_1 < x_2$ in I.
- A function f is called *positive* on an interval I if $f(x) > 0$ for all x in I.
- A function f is called *negative* on an interval I if $f(x) < 0$ for all x in I.

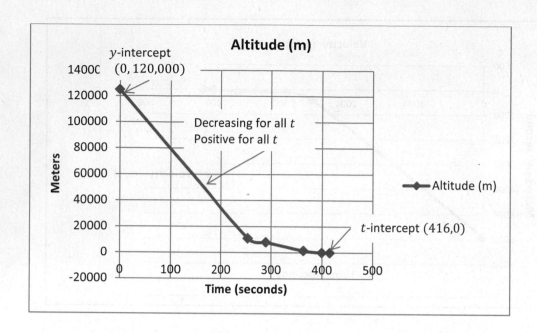

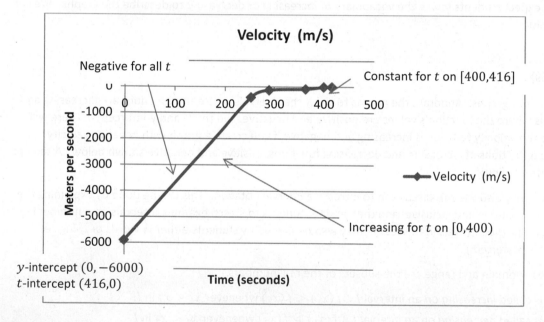

Exercises 1–6 (10 minutes)

Remind students of the original problem questions, and have them compute their results and explain how they got the answer. To generate the table in Exercise 2, students may need to produce a second graph of the last three or four data points. This is fairly easy to do if students are using technology to create their graphs. Alternatively, students could interpolate values from the tables as well. Regardless of the approach, students should be attending to precision. Work with groups to really think about and determine a good method for getting a decent estimate.

	Lesson 13:	Interpreting Graphs of Functions
	Date:	9/11/13

154

Exercises

1. Does this graphic really represent the landing path of the Curiosity Rover?

   No. The height is not scaled appropriately in this graphic. According to the video it also looks as if the Curiosity Rover rises a bit when the parachute is released and when the sky crane engages.

2. Estimate the altitude and velocity of the Curiosity Rover 5, 4, 3, 2, and 1 minute before landing. Explain how you arrived at your estimate.

   We used the graph and rounded the landing time to be at 7 minutes after entry interface. The table shows the altitude and velocity.

Time since entry interface	Altitude (miles)	Velocity (mph)
2	45	−7500
3	28	−4500
4	10	−1500
5	4	−260
6	1	−180

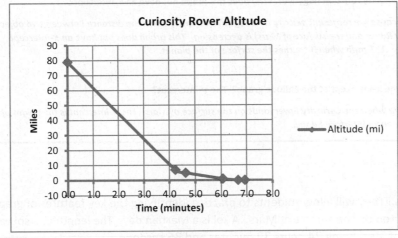

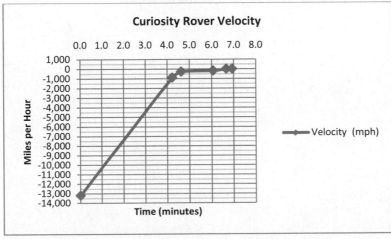

INTERPRET AND VALIDATE: To help students interpret and validate or refute their work, show one of the videos or animations listed in the lesson notes. Have them reconsider any of their solutions based on this new information, and give them time to make any revisions they deem necessary.

---

3. Based on watching the video/animation, do you think you need to revise any of your work? Explain why or why not, and then make any needed changes.

   Answers will vary. Some students might suggest that the period of rapid descent and deceleration cannot be linear. Some may suggest that their graphs take into account the period of upward motion when the parachute is released and the sky crane engages.

4. Why is the graph of the altitude function decreasing and the graph of the velocity function increasing on its domain?

   The altitude values are getting smaller as the time values are increasing. The velocity values are getting larger as the time values are increasing.

5. Why is the graph of the velocity function negative? Why does this graph not have an x-intercept?

   The graph is negative because we represent velocity as a negative quantity when the distance between two objects (in this case the Curiosity Rover and the surface of Mars) is decreasing. This graph does not have an x-intercept because it is traveling at -1.7 mph when it touches the surface of the planet.

6. What is the meaning of the x-intercept of the altitude graph? The y-intercept?

   The x-intercept is the time when the Curiosity Rover lands on the surface of Mars. The y-intercept is the height of the Curiosity Rover when entry interface begins.

Exercises 7–12

Use these exercises as time permits. They will allow students to practice identifying the key features of graphs. They involve the temperature data collected on the surface of Mars. A sol is a Martian day. The length of a sol varies as it does on Earth with the mean time of 1 sol being 24 hours 39 minutes and 35 seconds.

A Mars rover collected the following temperature data over 1.6 Martian days. A Martian day is called a sol. Use the graph to answer the following questions.

GROUND AND AIR TEMPERATURE SENSOR

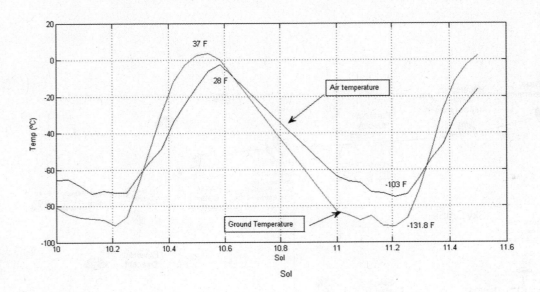

7. Approximately when does each graph change from increasing to decreasing? From decreasing to increasing?

   Increasing to decreasing: Air: approximately 10.18 and 10.59, Sol. Ground: Approximately 10.52 and 11.12 Sol.

   Decreasing to increasing: Air: approximately 10.12 Sol, 10.25 Sol, and 11.2 Sol.

8. When is the air temperature increasing?

   Air temperature is increasing on the interval [10.12, 10.18], [10.25, 10.59], and [11.2, 11.5].

9. When is the ground temperature decreasing?

   Ground temperature is decreasing on the interval [10, 10.2], [10.55, 11.1], and [11.14, 11.2].

10. What is the air temperature change on this time interval?

    The high is 28°F and the low is −103°F. That is a change of 131°F. Students might also answer in Celsius units.

11. Why do you think the ground temperature changed more than the air temperature? Is that typical on Earth?

    Student responses will vary.

12. Is there a time when the air and ground were the same temperature? Explain how you know?

    The air and ground temperature are the same at the following times: 10.3 Sol, 10.62 Sol, and 11.3 Sol.

| Lesson 13: | Interpreting Graphs of Functions | 157 |
| Date: | 9/11/13 | |

Exit Ticket (5 minutes)

Teachers: Please use this graphic if the other colored graphic does not display properly.

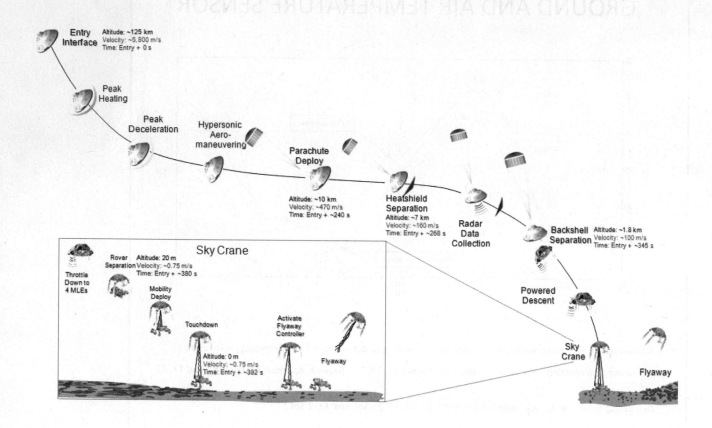

Name _____ Date_____

Lesson 13: Interpreting Graphs of Functions

Exit Ticket

1. Estimate the time intervals when mean energy use is decreasing on an average summer day. Why would power usage be decreasing during those time intervals?

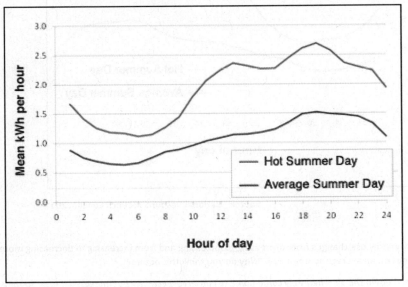

Power Usage on a Typical Summer Day in Ontario, Canada

Source: National Resource Council Canada, 2011

2. The hot summer day energy use changes from decreasing to increasing and from increasing to decreasing more frequently than it does on an average summer day. Why do you think this occurs?

Exit Ticket Sample Solutions

1. Estimate the time intervals when mean energy use is decreasing on an average summer day. Why would power usage be decreasing during those time intervals?

   Energy use is decreasing from hour 1 to hour 5 and from hour 19 to hour 24. It is nighttime when the temperatures outside are dropping.

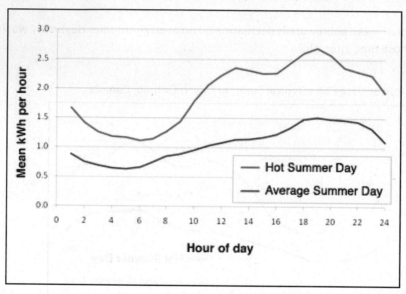

Power Usage on a Typical Summer Day in Ontario, Canada

Source: National Resource Council Canada, 2011

2. The hot summer day energy use changes from decreasing to increasing and from increasing to decreasing more frequently than it does on an average summer day. Why do you think this occurs?

   Perhaps people turned down the air when they came home to conserve electricity but increased it later so they could sleep because the temperature still had not cooled down.

Problem Set Sample Solutions

The first exercise in the problem set asks students to summarize their lesson in a written report to conclude the modeling cycle.

1. Create a short written report summarizing your work on the Mars Curiosity Rover Problem. Include your answers to the original problem questions and at least one recommendation for further research on this topic or additional questions you have about the situation.

   Student responses will vary.

2. Consider the sky crane descent portion of the landing sequence.

   a. Create a linear function to model the Curiosity Rover's altitude as a function of time. (What two points did you choose to create your function? Why?)

   For the function f, let $f(t)$ represent the altitude at time t. $f(t) = -\frac{20}{16}(t - 416)$.

   b. Compare the slope of your function to the velocity. Should they be equal? Explain why or why not.

   The slope of the linear function and velocity in the graphic are not equal. If we assume that the velocity is constant (which it is not), then they would be equal.

   c. Use your linear model to determine the altitude one minute before landing. How does it compare to your earlier estimate. Explain any differences you found.

   The model predicts 75 meters. The earlier estimate was 1 mile (1.6 km) and was close to a given data point. The model would only be a good predictor during the sky crane phase of landing.

3. The exponential function $g(t) = 125(0.99)^t$ could be used to model the altitude of the Curiosity Rover during its rapid descent. Do you think this model would be better or worse than the one your group created? Explain your reasoning.

   Answers will vary depending on the class graphs. It might be better because the Curiosity Rover did not descend at a constant rate, so a curve would make more sense than a line.

4. For each graph below, identify the increasing and decreasing intervals, the positive and negative intervals, and the intercepts.

   a. *Decreasing interval $[-5, 4.2]$, positive interval $[-5, 2)$, negative interval $(2, 4.2]$, y-intercept $(0, 3)$, x-intercept $(2, 0)$.*

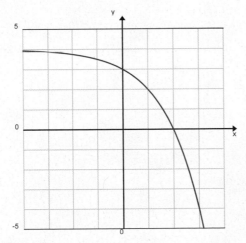

b. *Increasing intervals* $[0, 2)$, $(5, 8]$, *decreasing interval* $[2, 5]$, *positive intervals* $[0, 3.7)$, $(6, 8]$, *negative interval* $(3.7, 6)$, *y-intercept* $(0, 2)$, *x-intercept* $(3.7, 0)$ *and* $(6, 0)$.

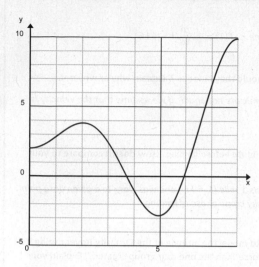

Lesson 14: Linear and Exponential Models—Comparing Growth Rates

Student Outcomes

- Students compare linear and exponential models by focusing on how the models change over intervals of equal length. Students observe from tables that a function that grows exponentially will eventually exceed a function that grows linearly.

Classwork

Example 1 (12 minutes)

Example 1

Linear Functions

a. Sketch points $P_1 = (0, 4)$ and $P_2 = (4, 12)$. Are there values of m and b such that the graph of the linear function described by $f(x) = mx + b$ contains P_1 and P_2? If so, find those values. If not, explain why they do not exist.

The graph of the linear function contains $(0, 4)$ when the y-intercept, b, is equal to 4. So all the linear functions whose graphs contain $(0, 4)$ are represented by

$$f(x) = mx + 4, \text{ where } m \text{ is a real number.}$$

For the graph of f to also contain $(4, 12)$,

$$12 = m(4) + 4$$
$$m = 2$$

The linear function whose graph passes through $(0, 4)$ and $(4, -1)$ is

$$f(x) = 2x + 4.$$

b. Sketch $P_1 = (0, 4)$ and $P_2 = (0, -2)$. Are there values of m and b so that the graph of a linear function described by $f(x) = mx + b$ contains P_1 and P_2? If so, find those values. If not, explain why they do not exist.

For a function f, for each value of x, there can only be one $f(x)$ value. Therefore, there is no linear function $f(x) = mx + b$ that contains P_1 and P_2 since each point has two different $f(x)$ values for the same x value.

<u>Exponential Functions</u>

Graphs (c) and (d) are both graphs of an exponential function of the form $g(x) = ab^x$. Rewrite the function $g(x)$ using the values of a and b required for the graph shown to be a graph of g.

c. $g(x) = 2(2)^x$

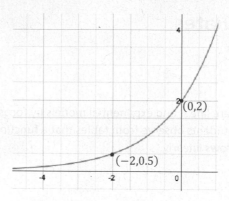

d. $g(x) = 3\left(\dfrac{3}{2}\right)^x$

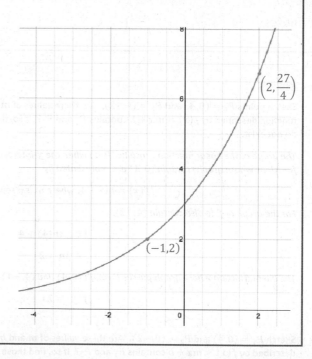

Discussion (5 minutes)

Discuss the rates of change in the Example 1.

- Consider Example 1a. Restrict the linear function $f(x) = 2x + 4$ to the positive integers, and consider the sequence $f(0), f(1), f(2),...$, i.e., the sequence $4, 6, 8, ...$ Ask students what they observe about this sequence, looking for the answer, "Each term is always the sum of the previous term and 2."

  Suggest they prove that statement by showing $f(n + 1) = f(n) + 2$: for n a positive integer, $f(n + 1) = 2(n + 1) + 4 = 2n + 2 + 4 = (2n + 4) + 2$. Since $f(n) = 2n + 4$, we see that $f(n + 1) = f(n) + 2$.

  In particular, the recursion formula $f(n + 1) = f(n) + 2$ shows that the linear function grows additively by 2 over intervals of length 1 (i.e., the length of the intervals between consecutive integers). This fact holds for any interval of length 1 (the equation $f(x + 1) = f(x) + 2$ holds for any real number x, not just integers).

  Similarly, for any linear function of the form $f(x) = mx + b$, that linear function grows additively by m over any interval of length 1. In fact, it grows additively by md over any interval of length l (if time permits, have students prove this by calculating $f(x + l) - f(x)$!).

- Now consider Example 1c. Restrict the exponential function $g(x) = 2(2^x)$ to the positive integers, and consider the sequence $g(0), g(1), g(2), g(3),...$, i.e., the sequence $2, 4, 8, 16, ...$ Ask students what they observe about this sequence, looking for the answer, "Each term is always the product of the previous term and 2."

  Suggest they prove that statement by showing $g(n + 1) = g(n) \cdot 2$: for n a positive integer, $g(n + 1) = 2(2^{n+1}) = 2(2^n 2^1) = [2(2^n)] \cdot 2$. Since $g(n) = 2(2^n)$, we see that $g(n + 1) = g(n) \cdot 2$.

  In particular, the recursion formula $g(n + 1) = g(n) \cdot 2$ shows that the exponential function grows multiplicatively by 2 over intervals of length 1 (i.e., the length of the intervals between consecutive integers). This fact holds for any interval of length 1 (the equation $g(x + 1) = g(x) \cdot 2$ holds for any real number x, not just integers).

  Similarly, for any exponential function of the form $f(x) = ab^x$, that exponential function grows multiplicatively by b over any interval of length 1.

- Moral: linear functions grow additively while exponential functions grow multiplicatively.

> *Scaffolding:*
>
> - For students performing above grade level: Ask students to make and test a conjecture about how an exponential function grows multiplicatively over any interval of length l.
>
> Answer:
> $$g(x + l) = g(x) \cdot b^l$$

Example 2 (15 minutes)

Example 2

A lab researcher records the growth of the population of a yeast colony and finds that the population doubles every hour.

a. Complete the researcher's table of data:

Hours into study	0	1	2	3	4
Yeast colony population (thousands)	5	10	20	40	80

b. What is the exponential function that models the growth of the colony's population?

$$P(t) = 5(2)^t$$

c. Several hours into the study, the researcher looks at the data and wishes there were more frequent measurements. Knowing that the colony doubles every hour, how can the researcher determine the population in half-hour increments? Explain.

Let x represent the factor by which the population grows in half an hour. Since the population grows by the same factor in the next half hour, also x, the population will grow by x^2 in 1 hour. However the colony's population doubles every hour:

$$x^2 = 2$$

$$x = \sqrt{2}$$

The researcher should multiply the population by $\sqrt{2}$ every half hour.

d. Complete the new table that includes half hour increments.

Hours into study	0	$\frac{1}{2}$	1	$\frac{3}{2}$	2	$\frac{5}{2}$	3
Yeast colony population (thousands)	5	7.071	10	14.142	20	28.284	40

e. How would the calculation for the data change for time increments of 20 minutes? Explain.

Now let x represent the factor by which the population grows in 20 minutes. Since the population grows by the same factor in the next 20 minutes and the 20 minutes after that, the population will grow by x^3 in 1 hour. Since the colony's population doubles every hour:

$$x^3 = 2$$

$$x = \sqrt[3]{2}$$

The researcher should multiply the population by $\sqrt[3]{2}$ every 20 minutes.

f. Complete the new table that includes 20 minute increments.

Hours into study	0	$\frac{1}{3}$	$\frac{2}{3}$	1	$\frac{4}{3}$	$\frac{5}{3}$	2
Yeast colony population (thousands)	5	6.3	7.937	10	12.599	15.874	20

g.   The researcher's lab assistant studies the data recorded and makes the following claim:

Since the population doubles in 1 hour, then half that growth happens in the first half hour and the second half of that growth happens in the second half hour. We should be able to find the population at $t = \frac{1}{2}$ by taking the average of the populations at $t = 0$ and $t = 1$.

Is the assistant's reasoning correct? Compare this strategy to your work in parts (c) and (e).

The assistant's reasoning is not correct. By the assistant's reasoning, the population growth at the first half hour mark would be $t\left(\frac{1}{2}\right) = 7.5$ because then the population would have grown by 2.5 thousand cells from 5 thousand cells in the first half hour and another 2.5 thousand cells to 10 thousand cells in the second half hour. This is linear growth, or the same amount of population growth n each half hour. However the percent growth by the assistant's growth is 50% from $t = 0$ to $t = 1$ and 33% from $t = 0$ to $t = 1$. For the population to double in 1 hour, there must be constant percent growth in each half hour.

To the teacher: You might have a student who says that the assistant is correct if he is using the geometric mean. Recall that the geometric mean of two numbers is the square root of their product. In this case, it is $\sqrt{5 \times 10} \approx 7.071$, which is the same value as the half hour mark in part d. Explore with your students the connection between the answer in part (c) and definition of the geometric mean. Does the geometric mean give the same value as other half hour marks in the table to part (d)?

Example 3 (8 minutes)

Example 3

A California Population Projection Engineer in 1920 was tasked with finding a model that predicts the state's population growth. He modeled the population growth as a function of time, t years since 1900. Census data shows that the population in 1900, in thousands, was $1,490$. In 1920, the population of the state of California was $3,554$ thousand. He decided to explore both a linear and an exponential model.

a.   Use the data provided to determine the equation of the linear function that models the population growth from 1900 to 1920.

$f(t) = 103.2t + 1,490$

> *Scaffolding:*
>
> Encourage students to use graphing calculators to determine the linear and exponential regression functions. The steps for finding the exponential regression are listed below.

b.   Use the data provided and your calculator to determine the equation of the exponential function that models the population growth.

$g(t) = 1,490(1.044)^t$

c.   Use the two functions to predict the population for the following years:

	Projected Population based on Linear Function, $f(t)$ (thousands)	Projected Population based on Exponential Function, $g(t)$ (thousands)	Census Population Data and Intercensal Estimates for California (thousands)
1935	5,102	6,725	6,175
1960	7,682	19,734	15,717
2010	12,842	169,919	37,253

d.   Which function is a better model for the population growth of California in 1935 and in 1960?

The exponential model.

e.   Does either model closely predict the population for 2010? What phenomenon explains the real population value?

Neither model closely predicts the population. After a population boom from 1900–1960, the population growth slows down. The following graph shows census and intercensal estimates for California's population between 1900 and 2010.

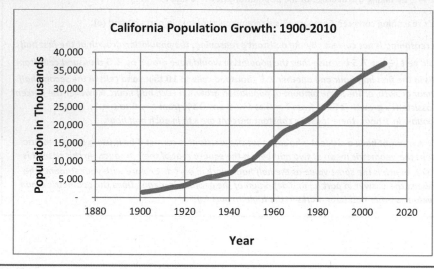

California Population Growth: 1900-2010

Closing (2 minutes)

Lesson Summary

- Given a linear function of the form $L(x) = mx + k$ and an exponential function of the form $E(x) = ab^x$ for x a real number and constants $m, k, a,$ and b, consider the sequence given by $L(n)$ and the sequence given by $E(n)$ where $n = 1, 2, 3, 4, \dots$. Both of these sequences can be written recursively:

  $$L(n + 1) = L(n) + m \text{ and } L(0) = k, \text{ and}$$
  $$E(n + 1) = E(n) \cdot b \text{ and } E(0) = a.$$

  The first sequence shows that a linear function grows additively by the same summand m over equal length intervals (i.e., the intervals between consecutive integers). The second sequence shows that an exponential function grows multiplicatively by the same factor b over equal length intervals (i.e., the intervals between consecutive integers).

- An increasing exponential function will eventually exceed any linear function. That is, if $f(x) = ab^x$ is an exponential function with $a > 1$ and $b > 0$, and $g(x) = mx + k$ is a linear function, then there is a real number M such that for all $x > M$, then $f(x) > g(x)$. Sometimes this is not apparent in a graph displayed on a graphing calculator; that is because the graphing window does not show enough of the graphs for us to see the sharp rise of the exponential function in contrast with the linear function.

Exit Ticket (3 minutes)

Lesson 14:   Linear and Exponential Models—Comparing Growth Rates
Date: 9/11/13

168

Name _____   Date_____

Lesson 14: Linear and Exponential Models—Comparing Growth Rates

Exit Ticket

A big company settles its new headquarters in a small city. The city council plans road construction based on traffic increasing at a linear rate, but based on the company's massive expansion, traffic is really increasing exponentially.

What will be the repercussions of the city council's current plans? Include what you know about linear and exponential growth in your discussion.

Exit Ticket Sample Solutions

A big company settles its new headquarters in a small city. The city council plans road construction based on traffic increasing at a linear rate, but based on the company's massive expansion, traffic is really increasing exponentially.

What will be the repercussions of the city council's current plans? Include what you know about linear and exponential growth in your discussion.

The city will not have the roads or capacity to handle the kind of traffic that will exist. Even if the linear growth of traffic initially outruns the exponential growth, eventually the exponential growth will catch up and exceed it. This means people will sit in traffic longer and the city will be generally congested for longer than if it had been planned for much heavier traffic flow.

Problem Set Sample Solutions

1. When a ball bounces up and down, the maximum height it reaches decreases with each bounce in a predictable way. Suppose for a particular type of squash ball dropped on a squash court, the maximum height, $h(x)$, after x number of bounces can be represented by $h(x) = 65\left(\frac{1}{3}\right)^x$. How many times higher is the height after the first bounce compared to the height after the third bounce?

9 times higher

Graph the points $(x, h(x))$ for x-values of $0, 1, 2, 3, 4, 5$.

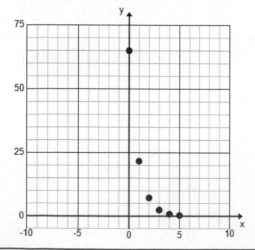

2. Australia experienced a major pest problem in the early 20th century. The pest? Rabbits. In 1859, 24 rabbits were released by Thomas Austin at Barwon Park. In 1926, there were an estimated 10 billion rabbits in Australia. Needless to say, the Australian government spent a tremendous amount of time and money to get the rabbit problem under control. (To find more on this topic, visit Australia's Department of Environment and Primary Industries website under Agriculture.)

    a. Based only on the information above, write an exponential function that would model Australia's rabbit population growth.

    $R(t) = 24(1.3448)^t.$

    b. The model you created from the data in the problem is obviously a huge simplification from the actual function of the number of rabbits in any given year from 1859 to 1926. Name at least one complicating factor (about rabbits) that might make the graph of your function look quite different than the graph of the actual function.

    Ex. A drought could have wiped out a huge percentage of rabbits in a single year, showing a dip in the graph of the actual function.

3. After graduating from college, Jane has two job offers to consider. Job A is compensated at $100,000 a year but with no hope of ever having an increase in pay. Jane knows a few of her peers are getting that kind of an offer right out of college. Job B is for a social media start-up, which guarantees a mere $10,000 a year. The founder is sure the concept of the company will be the next big thing in social networking and promises a pay increase of 25% at the beginning of each new year.

    a. Which job will have a greater annual salary at the beginning of the 5th year? By approximately how much?

    Job A, $100,000 vs. $24,400, a difference of about $75,600.

    b. Which job will have a greater annual salary at the beginning of the 10th year? By approximately how much?

    Job A, $100K vs. $74.5K, a difference of about $25.5K.

    c. Which job will have a greater annual salary at the beginning of the 20th year? By approximately how much?

    Job B, $694K vs. $100K, a difference of about $594K.

    d. If you were in Jane's shoes, which job would you take?

    Answers will vary. Encourage students to voice reasons for each position. Note: The accumulated total after n years for Job B is $B(n) = (40K)(1.25^n - 1)$, and the accumulated total for Job A is $A(n) = (100K)n$. After 16.9 years, Job B begins to have a bigger total financial payoff than Job A.

4. The population of a town in 2007 is $15,000$ people. The town has gotten its fresh water supply from a nearby lake and river system with the capacity to provide water for up to $30,000$ people. Due to its proximity to a big city and a freeway, the town's population has begun to grow more quickly than in the past. The table below shows the population counts for each year from 2007 to 2012.

    a. Write a function of x that closely matches these data points for x-values of $0, 1, 2, \ldots, 5$.

Year	Years past 2007	Population of the town
2007	0	15,000
2008	1	15,600
2009	2	16,224
2010	3	16,873
2011	4	17,548
2012	5	18,250

    The value of the ratio of population in one year to the population in the previous year appears to be the same for any two consecutive years in the table. The value of the ratio is 1.04, so a function that would model this data for x-values of $0, 1, 2, 3, 4, 5$, is $f(x) = 15,000(1.04)^x$.

    b. Assume the function is a good model for the population growth from 2012 to 2032. At what year during the time frame 2012 to 2032 will the water supply be inadequate for the population?

    If this model continues to hold true, the population will be larger than $30,000$ when x is 18, which corresponds to the year 2025.

Name _____   Date _____

1. The diagram below shows how tables and chairs are arranged in the school cafeteria. One table can seat 4 people, and tables can be pushed together. When two tables are pushed together, 6 people can sit around the table.

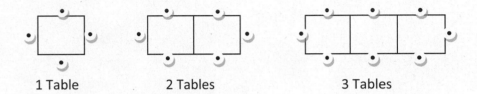

     1 Table   2 Tables   3 Tables

a. Complete this table to show the relationship between the number of tables, n, and the number of students, S, that can be seated around the table.

n (tables)						
S (students)						

b. If we made a sequence where the first term of the sequence was the number of students that can fit at 1 table, the 2nd term where the number that could fit at 2 tables, etc, would the sequence be arithmetic, geometric, or neither? Explain your reasoning.

c. Create an explicit formula for a sequence that models this situation. Use $n = 1$ as the first term, representing how many students can sit at 1 table. How do the constants in your formula relate to the situation?

d. Using this seating arrangement, how many students could fit around 15 tables pushed together in a row?

The cafeteria needs to provide seating for 189 students. They can fit up to 15 rows of tables in the cafeteria. Each row can contain at most 9 tables but could contain less than that. The tables on each row must be pushed together. Students will still be seated around the tables as described earlier.

e. If they use exactly 9 tables pushed together to make each row, how many rows will they need to seat 189 students, and how many tables will they have used to make those rows?

f. Is it possible to seat the 189 students with fewer total tables? If so, what is the fewest number of tables needed? How many tables would be used in each row? (Remember that the tables on each row must be pushed together.) Explain your thinking.

2. Sydney was studying the following functions:

$$f(x) = 2x + 4 \text{ and } g(x) = 2(2^x) + 4$$

She said that linear functions and exponential functions are basically the same. She made her statement based on plotting points at $x = 0$ and $x = 1$ and graphing the functions.

Help Sydney understand the difference between linear functions and exponential functions by comparing and constrasting f and g. Support your answer with a written explanation that includes use of the average rate of change and supporting tables and/or graphs of these functions.

3. Dots can be arranged in rectangular shapes like the one shown below.

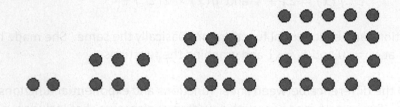

Shape 1   Shape 2   Shape 3   Shape 4 . . . . .

a. Assuming the trend continues, draw the next three shapes in this particular sequence of rectangles. How many dots are in each of the shapes you drew?

The numbers that represent the number of dots in this sequence of rectangular shapes are called rectangular numbers. For example, 2 is the first rectangular number and 6 is the 2nd rectangular number.

b. What is the 50th rectangular number? Explain how you arrived at your answer.

c. Write a recursive formula for the rectangular numbers.

d. Write an explicit formula for the rectangular numbers.

e. Could an explicit formula for the nth rectangular number be considered a function? Explain why or why not. If yes, what would be the domain and range of the function?

4. Stephen is assigning parts for the school musical.

a. Suppose there are 20 students participating, and he has 20 roles available. If each of the 20 students will be assigned to exactly one role in the play, and each role will be played by only one student, is the assignment of the roles to the students in this way certain to be an example of a function? Explain why or why not. If yes, state the domain and range of the function.

The school musical also has a pit orchestra.

b. Suppose there are 10 instrumental parts but only 7 musicians in the orchestra. The conductor assigns an instrumental part to each musician. Some musicians will have to cover two instrumental parts, but no two musicians will have the same instrumental part. If the instrumental parts are the domain and the musicians are the range, is the assignment of instrumental parts to musicians as described sure to be an example of a function? Explain why or why not. If so, what would be the meaning of $A(Piano) = Scott$?

c. Suppose there are 10 instrumental parts but 13 musicians in the orchestra. The conductor assigns an instrumental part to each musician. Some instrumental parts will have two musicians assigned so that all the musicians have instrumental parts. When two musicians are assigned to one part, they alternate who plays at each performance of the play. If the instrumental parts are the domain, and the musicians are the range, is the assignment of instrumental parts to musicians as described sure to be an example of a function? Explain why or why not. If so, what would be the meaning of $A(Piano) = Scott$?

5. The population of a remote island has been experiencing a decline since the year 1950. Scientists used census data from 1950 and 1970 to model the declining population. In 1950 the population was 2350. In 1962 the population was 1270. They chose an exponential decay model and arrived at the function: $p(x) = 2350(0.95)^x, x \geq 0$, where x is the number of years since 1950. The graph of this function is given below.

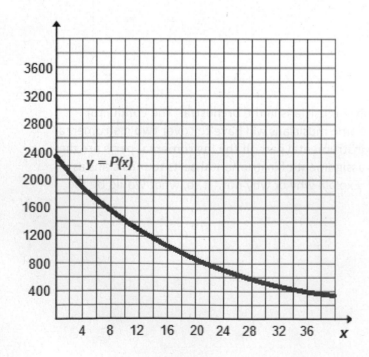

a. What is the y-intercept of the graph? Interpret its meaning in the context of the problem.

b. Over what intervals is the function increasing? What does your answer mean within the context of the problem?

c. Over what intervals is the function decreasing? What does your answer mean within the context of the problem?

Another group of scientists argues that the decline in population would be better modeled by a linear function. They use the same two data points to arrive at a linear function.

d. Write the linear function that this second group of scientists would have used.

e. What is an appropriate domain for the function? Explain your choice within the context of the problem.

f. Graph the function on the coordinate plane.

g. What is the x-intercept of the function? Interpret its meaning in the context of the problem.

A Progression Toward Mastery

Assessment Task Item		STEP 1 Missing or incorrect answer and little evidence of reasoning or application of mathematics to solve the problem	STEP 2 Missing or incorrect answer but evidence of some reasoning or application of mathematics to solve the problem	STEP 3 A correct answer with some evidence of reasoning or application of mathematics to solve the problem, or an incorrect answer with substantial evidence of solid reasoning or application of mathematics to solve the problem	STEP 4 A correct answer supported by substantial evidence of solid reasoning or application of mathematics to solve the problem
1	a – d F-BF.A.1a F-LE.A.1 F-LE.A.2 F-LE.A.3 F-IF.A.2	Student is unable to identify the sequence as arithmetic and unable to create an explicit formula for finding the number of students that can be seated at n tables.	Student is able to recognize the sequence as arithmetic, but displays a logic error in the explicit formula for the sequence. Student may also have errors in the table, the relating of constants in the formula to context, or in the computation of how many students can sit at 15 tables pushed together.	Student is able to recognize the sequence as arithmetic, and create an explicit formula for the sequence. Student has one or more errors in the table, the relating of constants in the formula to context, or in the computation of how many students can sit at 15 tables pushed together.	Student provides correct entries for the table and explains that the sequence is arithmetic because each successive term is two more than the last term. Student writes an explicit formula for the sequence using an appropriate sequence notation, such as $f(n)$ or a_n, and correctly relates the constants of their formula to the context of the problem. Student correctly determines that 32 students can sit at 15 tables pushed together in a row.
	e F-IF.A.2 MP 1 MP 4	Student is not able to demonstrate how to determine the number of students that can sit at 9 tables pushed together.	Student makes calculation errors that lead to an incorrect answer, but demonstrates some understanding of how to determine the number of students that can sit at 9 tables pushed together, and some understanding of the need to divide 189 by 20 to see that it takes more	Student articulates that 10 rows of 9 tables are needed to seat 189 students, but fails to answer the question of how many tables that would be.	Student articulates that 10 rows of 9 tables are needed to seat 189 students, and that 10 rows of 9 tables would be 90 tables.

Module 3:   Linear and Exponential Functions
Date: 9/11/13

181

			than 9 rows or 10 rows.		
	f F-IF.A.2 MP 1 MP 4	Student demonstrates very little reasoning skills in their attempted answer.	Student demonstrates some correct reasoning but is unable to arrive at one of the possible arrangements that use only 80 tables distributed across 15 rows.	Student chooses an arrangement of 80 tables distributed across 15 rows in one of any of the many possible configurations.	Student articulates that any arrangement involving 80 tables distributed among all 15 rows would use the minimum number of tables.
2	F-IF.B.5 F-IF.B.6 F-BF.A.1a F-LE.A.1 F-LE.A.2 F-LE.A.3	Student provides incorrect or insufficient tables, graphs, and written explanation.	Student provides a table and/or a graph that may have minor errors but does not provide a correct written explanation, OR student provides a limited written explanation but does not support the answer with tables or graphs.	Student demonstrates that the functions are not the same with accurate tables or graphs and provides a limited written explanation that does not thoroughly describe the differences in the rates of change of the functions, OR student has errors in his or her table or graphs but provides a thorough written explanation that references the rates of change of the functions.	Student demonstrates that the functions are not the same with accurate tables or graphs and provides a thorough written explanation that includes accurate references to the rates of change of the functions.
3	**a** F-IF.A.3 F-BF.A.1a	Student does not demonstrate any understanding of the pattern of the sequence described in the problem.	Student has a significant error or omission in the task but demonstrates some understanding of the pattern of the sequence described in the problem.	Student has a minor error or omission in the task but demonstrates clear understanding of the pattern of the sequence described in the problem.	Sequence is continued correctly three times <u>AND</u> correct number of dots is given.
	b F-IF.A.3 F-BF.A.1a	Student demonstrates no understanding of using the pattern to find the 50th term.	Student attempts to use the pattern to find the 50th term but has a flaw in this or her reasoning and therefore arrives at an incorrect answer.	Student correctly answers 2550 but does not provide an explanation based on sound reasoning, or makes a calculation error, but provides an explanation based on sound reasoning.	Student correctly answers 2550 and displays sound reasoning as they explain using the pattern of the sequence to arrive at the answer.
	c-d F-IF.A.3 F-BF.A.1a	Student work demonstrates no or very little understanding needed to write recursive or explicit formulas for this sequence.	Student is only able to provide either the recursive or the explicit formula and may have provided an explicit formula when it asked for a recursive formula or vice versa, <u>OR</u>, student demonstrates	Student provides correct formulas but uses an explicit formula where it asked for a recursive one, and a recursive one where it asked for an explicit one, <u>OR</u> the student provides the correct formulas in each	Student provides a correct recursive formula for part (c) and a correct explicit formula for part (d), each using either function notation such as f(n) or subscript notation such as an. Student also provides the necessary

Module 3: | Linear and Exponential Functions
Date: | 9/11/13

			that he or she understands the difference between a recursive formula and an explicit one by providing formulas for both, but the formulas provided are incorrect. Student may or may not have provided the necessary declaration of the initial term number in each case, and for the initial term value in the recursive case.	case, but neglects to provide the necessary declaration of the initial term number in each case, and for the initial term value in the recursive case.	declaration of the initial term number in each case, and for the initial term value in the recursive case.
	e F-IF.A.2 F-IF.A.3	Student leaves the question blank or answers that it is not a function.	Student answers that it is a function but gives insufficient reasoning. Or is unable to identify the domain and range.	Student answers that it is a function but makes minor errors or omissions in his or her reasoning, or makes errors in naming of the domain and range.	Student answers that it is a function and gives sufficient reasoning, stating the domain and the range accurately.
4	**a** F-IF.A.1 F-IF.A.2	Student indicates it is not a function and provides no reasoning or incorrect reasoning, indicating he or she does not have sufficient understanding of what is required for a relation to be a function.	Student reasoning indicates he or she understands what is required for a relation to be a function, but is not able to discern that this relation is a function, OR, student indicates it is a function but does not provide sufficient explanation and/or omits the naming of the domain and range.	Student identifies the relation as a function but provides an explanation and/or identification of the domain and range that contains minor errors or omissions.	Student identifies the relation as a function and provides a thorough explanation of how this situation meets the criteria for a function: that every input is assigned to one and only one output and student chooses either the list of students or the list of roles as the domain and the other list as the range.
	b F-IF.A.1 F-IF.A.2	Student indicates it is not a function and provides no reasoning or incorrect reasoning, indicating he or she does not have sufficient understanding of what is required for a relation to be a function.	Student reasoning indicates he or she understands what is required for a relation to be a function but is not able to discern that this relation is a function, OR, student indicates it is a function but does not provide sufficient explanation and/or omits or incorrectly interprets the meaning of $A(piano) = Scott$.	Student identifies the relation as a function but provides an explanation and/or interpretation of $A(piano) = Scott$ that contains minor errors or omissions.	Student identifies the relation as a function and provides a thorough explanation of how this situation meets the criteria for a function: that every input is assigned to one and only one output and student interprets $A(piano) = Scott$ to mean that the part of the piano is being played by Scott.

	c **F-IF.A.1** **F-IF.A.2**	Student indicates it is a function and provides no reasoning or incorrect reasoning, indicating he or she does not have sufficient understanding of what is required for a relation to be a function.	Student reasoning indicates he or she understands what is required for a relation to be a function but is not able to discern that this relation is not a function, OR, student indicates it is not a function but does not provide sufficient explanation.	Student identifies the relation is not a function but provides an explanation that contains minor errors or omissions.	Student identifies the relation is not a function and provides a thorough explanation of how this situation does not meet the criteria for a function: that every input is assigned to one and only one output.
5	**a** **F-IF.B.4**	Student is unable to correctly identify the y-intercept.	Student identifies that the y-intercept is the point (0, 2350) but fails to correctly relate the point to the context of the problem.	Student identifies that the y-intercept is the point (0, 2350) and relates 2350 to the population when $x = 0$, but fails to relate $x = 0$ to the year 1950.	Student identifies that the y-intercept is the point (0, 2350) and relates the point to the context that in 1950 the population was 2350.
	b – c **F-IF.B.4**	Student is unable to correctly identify that the function is always decreasing, never increasing.	Student identifies that there are no intervals for which the function is increasing that it is decreasing over its entire domain, but student does not correctly interpret this answer in the context of the problem.	Student identifies that there are no intervals for which the function is increasing, that it is decreasing over its entire domain, and student interprets this answer in the context of the problem, but has minor errors or omissions in the language used to answer the questions.	Student identifies that there are no intervals for which the function is increasing, that it is decreasing over its entire domain, and student interprets this answer in the context of the problem, using mathematically correct language and sound reasoning.
	d, f, g **F-BF.A.1a** **F-IF.B.4** **F-IF.C.7a**	Student does not use the two data points, and/or does not create a linear equation using the two points; therefore, the graph and/or x-intercept of parts (f) and (g) are likely incorrect.	Student attempts to use the two data points to write a linear function but makes a significant error in arriving at the equation of the line. Student graphs the equation he or she created and attempts to identify an x-intercept but may have identified the y-intercept instead.	Student uses the two data points to write the linear function correctly using either function notation or an equation in two variables but may have made a computational error in arriving at the slope (it is evident that the student understands how to compute slope). Student graphs the function created but may have extended the graph beyond the domain identified in part (e). Student identifies the x-intercept, relating it to the context of the problem.	Student uses the two data points to write the linear function correctly using either function notation or an equation in two variables. Student graphs the function correctly depicting only the domain values identified in part e, and correctly identifies the x-intercept, relating it to the context of the problem.

	e F-IF.B.5	Student does not demonstrate sound reasoning in restricting the domain given the context of the problem.	Student restricts the domain and explains the answer by either considering that we only wish to start in the year 1950, or considering that it does not make sense to continue the model when the population has fallen below zero, but does not consider both factors.	Student restricts the domain and explains the answer by considering that we only wish to start in the year 1950, or considering that it does not make sense to continue the model when the population has fallen below zero, but student makes an error in calculating the end points of the interval for the domain.	Student restricts the domain and explains the answer by considering that we only wish to start in the year 1950, or considering that it does not make sense to continue the model when the population has fallen below zero, and student and correctly calculates the end points of the interval for the domain.

1. The diagram below shows how tables and chairs are arranged in the school cafeteria. One table can seat 4 people, and tables can be pushed together. When two tables are pushed together, 6 people can sit around the table.

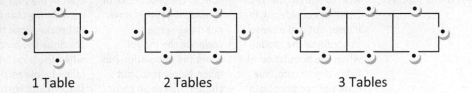

| 1 Table | 2 Tables | 3 Tables |

a. Complete this table to show the relationship between the number of tables, *n,* and the number of students, *S,* that can be seated around the table.

n (tables)	1	2	3	4	5	6
S (students)	4	6	8	10	12	14

a. If we made a sequence where the first term of the sequence was the number of students that can fit at 1 table, the 2nd term where the number that could fit at 2 tables, etc, would the sequence be arithmetic, geometric, or neither? Explain your reasoning.

It would be an arithmetic sequence because every term is 2 more than the previous term.

b. Create an explicit formula for a sequence that models this situation. How do the constants in your equation relate to the situation?

$f(n) = 4 + 2(n - 1)$

4 is the number of students that can be seated at one table by itself.

2 is the number of additional students that can be seated each time a table is added.

c. Using this seating arrangement, how many students could fit around 15 tables pushed together in a row?

$f(15) = 4 + 2(15 - 1) = 32$

The cafeteria needs to provide seating for 189 students. They can fit up to 15 rows of tables in the cafeteria. Each row can contain at most 9 tables but could contain less than that. The tables on each row must be pushed together. Students will still be seated around the tables as described earlier.

d.   If they use exactly 9 tables pushed together to make each row, how many rows will they need to seat 189 students, and how many tables will they have used to make those rows?

$$f(9) = 4 + 2(9 - 1) = 20$$

9 tables pushed together seats 20 students.

It will take 10 rows to get enough rows to seat 189 students.

10 rows of 9 tables each is 90 tables.

e.   Is it possible to seat the 189 students with fewer total tables? If so, what is the fewest number of tables needed? How many tables would be used in each row? (Remember that the tables on each row must be pushed together.) Explain your thinking.

Yes, they would use the fewest tables to seat the 189 students if they used all of the 15 rows, because with each new row, you get the added benefit of the 2 students that sit on each end of the row.

Any arrangement that uses 80 total tables spread among all 15 rows will be the best. *There will be 1 extra seat, but no extra tables.*

*One solution that evens out the rows pretty well but still uses as few tables as possible would be 5 **rows of 6 tables** and 10 **rows of 5 tables**.*

*Another example that has very uneven rows would be 8 **rows of 9 tables**, 1 **row of 2 tables**, and 6 **rows of 1 table**.*

2. Sydney was studying the following functions:

$$f(x) = 2x + 4 \text{ and } g(x) = 2(2^x) + 4$$

She said that linear functions and exponential functions are basically the same. She made her statement based on plotting points at $x = 0$ and $x = 1$ and graphing the functions.

Help Sydney understand the difference between linear functions and exponential functions by comparing and constrasting f and g. Support your answer with a written explanation that includes use of the average rate of change and supporting tables and/or graphs of these functions.

x	f(x)	Avg rate of change of f(x) from previous x-value to this one	g(x)	Avg rate of change of g(x) from previous x-value to this one
0	4		6	
1	6	2	8	2
2	8	2	12	4
3	10	2	20	8
4	12	2	36	16
5	14	2	68	32

Linear functions have a constant rate of change. f(x) increases by 2 units for every 1 unit that x increases. Exponential functions do not have a constant rate of change. The rate of change of g(x) is increasing as x increases. The average rate of change across an x interval of length 1 doubles for each successive x interval of length 1. No matter how large the rate of change is for the linear function, there is a x-value at which the rate of change for the exponential function will exceed the rate of change for the linear function.

3. Dots can be arranged in rectangular shapes like the one shown below.

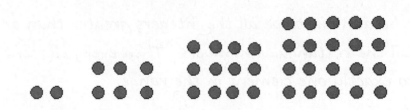

    Shape 1   Shape 2   Shape 3   Shape 4 . . . . .

    a. Assuming the trend continues, draw the next three shapes in this sequence of rectangles. How
        many dots are in each shape?

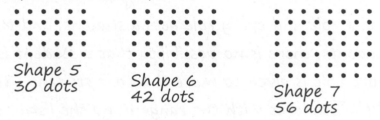

    Shape 5
    30 dots
                    Shape 6
                    42 dots
                                Shape 7
                                56 dots

    The numbers that represent the number of dots in each rectangular shape are called rectangular
    numbers. For example, 2 is the first rectangular number and 6 is the 2nd rectangular number.

    b. What is the 50th rectangular number? Explain how you arrived at your answer.

        50(51) = 2550

        The 1st figure had 1 row and 2 columns, giving 1(2) dots. The 2nd figure had 2
        rows and 3 columns, giving 2(3) dots. The pattern for the nth figure is n rows
        and n+1 columns. So, the 50th figure will have 50(51) dots.

    c. Write a recursive formula for the rectangular numbers.

        f(1) = 2 = 1•2   f(n) = f(n−1) + 2n; natural number n>1, and f(1) = 2
        f(2) = 6 = 2•3 = f(1) + 4
        f(3) = 12 = 3•4 = f(2) + 6
        f(4) = 20 = 4•5 = f(3) + 8

    d. Write an explicit formula for the rectangular numbers.

        f(n) = n(n+1); natural number n > 0.

e. Could an explicit formula for the nth rectangular number be considered a function? Explain why or why not. If yes, what would be the domain and range of the function?

> Yes, consider the domain to be all the integers greater than or equal to 1, and the range to all the rectangular numbers. Then every element in the domain corresponds to exactly one element in the range.

4. Stephen is assigning parts for the school musical.

a. Suppose there are 20 students participating, and he has 20 roles available. If each of the 20 students will be assigned to exactly one role in the play, and each role will be played by only one student, is the assignment of the roles to the students in this way certain to be an example of a function? Explain why or why not. If yes, state the domain and range of the function.

> Yes, since every student gets a role and every role gets a student, and there are exactly 20 roles and 20 students, there is no possibility that a student is given more than one role, or that a role is given to more than one student. Therefore, the domain could be the list of students with the range being the list of roles, or we could consider the domain to be the list of roles and the range to be the list of students. Either way you would have an example of a function.

The school musical also has a pit orchestra.

a. Suppose there are 10 instrumental parts but only 7 musicians in the orchestra. The conductor assigns an instrumental part to each musician. Some musicians will have to cover two instrumental parts, but no two musicians will have the same instrumental part. If the instrumental parts are the domain and the musicians are the range, is the assignment of instrumental parts to musicians as described sure to be an example of a function? Explain why or why not. If so, what would be the meaning of $A(Piano) = Scott$?

> Yes, each element of the domain (the instrumental parts) are assigned to one and only one element in the range (the musicians).
>
> A(Piano) = Scott means that the part of the piano is being played by Scott.

b. Suppose there are 10 instrumental parts but 13 musicians in the orchestra. The conductor assigns an instrumental part to each musician. Some instrumental parts will have two musicians assigned, so that all the musicians have instrumental parts. When two musicians are assigned to one part, they alternate who plays at each performance of the play. If the instrumental parts are the domain and the musicians are the range, is the assignment of instrumental parts to musicians as described sure to be an example of a function? Explain why or why not. If so, what would be the meaning of $A(Piano) = Scott$?

> *No, if the instrumental parts are the domain, then it cannot be an example of a function because there are 3 cases where one element in the domain (the instrumental parts) will be assigned to more than one element of the range (the musicians).*

5. The population of a remote island has been experiencing a decline since the year 1950. Scientists used census data from 1950 and 1970 to model the declining population. In 1950 the population was 2350. In 1962 the population was 1270. They chose an exponential decay model and arrived at the function, $p(x) = 2350(.95)^x, x \geq 0$, where x is the number of years since 1950. The graph of this function is given below.

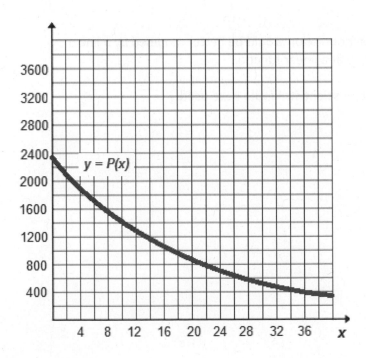

a.   What is the y-intercept of the graph? Interpret its meaning in the context of the problem.

>   The y-intercept is the point (O, 2350). When x is O, there have been O years since 1950, so in the year 1950, the population was 2350.

b.   Over what intervals is the function increasing? What does your answer mean within the context of the problem?

>   There are no intervals in the domain where it is increasing. This means that the population is always decreasing, never increasing.

c.   Over what intervals is the function decreasing? What does your answer mean within the context of the problem?

>   The function is decreasing over its entire domain: [O, ∞). This means that the population will continue to decline, except eventually when the function value is close to zero; then essentially the population will be zero from that point forward.

Another group of scientists argues that the decline in population would be better modeled by a linear function. They use the same two data points to arrive at a linear function.

d.   Write the linear function that this second group of scientists would have used.

> $L(x) = \frac{(1270-2350)}{12} x + 2350$
>
> $L(x) = -90x + 2350$

e. What is an appropriate domain for the function? Explain your choice within the context of the problem.

> D: $0 \le x \le 26\frac{1}{9}$
>
> We are only modeling the decline of the population which scientist say started in 1950, so that means x starts at 0 years past 1950. Once the population hits zero, which occurs $26\frac{1}{9}$ years past 1950, the model no longer makes sense because population cannot be a negative number.

f. Graph the function on the coordinate plane.

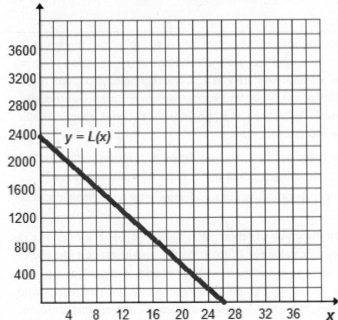

g. What is the x-intercept of the function? Interpret its meaning in the context of the problem.

> $\left(26\frac{1}{9}, 0\right)$
>
> At $26\frac{1}{9}$ years past 1950, in the year 1976, the population will be zero.

Topic C:

Transformations of Functions

A-REI.D.11, F-IF.C.7a, F-BF.B.3

Focus Standard:	A-REI.D.11	Explain why the x-coordinates of the points where the graphs of the equations $y = f(x)$ and $y = g(x)$ intersect are the solutions of the equation $f(x) = g(x)$; find the solutions approximately, e.g., using technology to graph the functions, make tables of values, or find successive approximations. Include cases where $f(x)$ and/or $g(x)$ are linear, polynomial, rational, absolute value, exponential, and logarithmic functions.★
	F-IF.C.7a	Graph functions expressed symbolically and show key features of the graph, by hand in simple cases and using technology for more complicated cases.★
		a. Graph linear and quadratic functions and show intercepts, maxima, and minima.
	F-BF.B.3	Identify the effect on the graph of replacing $f(x)$ by $f(x) + k, k\,f(x), f(kx)$, and $f(x + k)$ for specific values of k (both positive and negative); find the value of k given the graphs. Experiment with cases and illustrate an explanation of the effects on the graph using technology. *Include recognizing even and odd functions from their graphs and algebraic expressions for them.*
Instructional Days:	6	
Lesson 15:	Piecewise Functions	
Lesson 16:	Graphs Can Solve Equations Too	
Lessons 17-20:	Four Interesting Transformations of Functions	

Lesson 15 of this Topic formalizes the study of piecewise functions that began in Module 1. The study of piecewise functions in this lesson includes step functions and the absolute value function. Piecewise functions work nicely in the remaining lessons of this topic beginning with Lesson 16, where students learn that an equation $f(x) = g(x)$, such as $|x - 3| + 1 = |2x - 4|$, can be solved by finding the intersection points of the graphs of $y = f(x)$ and $y = g(x)$. Students use technology in this lesson to create the graphs and observe their intersection points. Next, in Lessons 17-20 students use piecewise functions as they explore four transformations of functions: $f(x) + k, f(x + k), kf(x)$, and $f(kx)$.

Lesson 15: Piecewise Functions

Student Outcomes

- Students examine the features of piecewise functions including the absolute value function and step functions.
- Students understand that the graph of a function f is the graph of the equation $y = f(x)$.

Lesson Notes

This lesson has two main purposes: The first is to continue the work from Lessons 11–13 regarding the interplay between graphs, equations and functions; the second is to expose students to piecewise functions in general and the absolute value and step functions, specifically. Lessons 12 and 13 established the meaning of the graph of a function and the graph of the equation $y = f(x)$. This lesson continues to clarify that these two sets are one and the same. Students consider two important functions used in later lessons and classes: the absolute value function and the greatest integer function.

Classwork

Opening (2 minutes)

Recall that the absolute value of a number is the distance from 0 of a point on the number line. Because we are measuring distance, the absolute value of a non-zero number is always positive. For example, $|-3| = 3$ because the point -3, located 3 units to the left of 0 on the real number line is 3 units away from 0. Absolute value can also be used to define the distance between any two points on the real number line. For example, $|5 - 8| = 3$ because there are 3 units between the numbers 5 and 8 on the real number line.

Opening Exercise (3 minutes) (optional)

> **Opening Exercise**
>
> For each real number a, the *absolute value of* a is the distance between 0 and a on the number line and is denoted $|a|$.
>
> 1. Solve each one variable equation.
>
>   a. $|x| = 6$ b. $|x - 5| = 4$ c. $2|x + 3| = -10$
>
> $\{-6, 6\}$ $\{9, 1\}$ **No solution.**
>
> 2. Determine at least five solutions for each two-variable equation. Make sure some of the solutions include negative values for either x or y.
>
>   a. $y = |x|$ $\{(-2, 2), (-1, 1), (0, 0), (1, 1), (2, 2)\}$
>
>   b. $y = |x - 5|$ $\{(-1, 6), (0, 5), (1, 4), (5, 0), (6, 1)\}$
>
>   c. $x = |y|$ $\{(1, 1), (1, -1), (0, 0), (2, 2), (2, -2)\}$

> **Scaffolding:**
>
> Much of this exploration relies on students accessing their knowledge from the beginning of this unit and from Module 1. Provide additional support as needed to reteach these ideas if students are struggling to work the exploration independently.

Exploratory Challenge 1 (15 minutes)

Have students work parts (a) – (d) in small groups. As you circulate, check to see that the groups are creating graphs. Remind them that the domain of the variables for these equations is all real numbers so their graphs should be continuous. Make sure groups are plotting (0,0) for parts (a) and (c) and (5,0) for part (b). After a few minutes, have different groups share their responses. Provide time for groups to revise their graphs as needed.

Part (d) offers an example of MP.6 as students must communicate their findings using precise language. A student example with particularly strong language may be highlighted for the benefit of the class.

Exploratory Challenge 1

For parts (a) – (c) create graphs of the solution set of each two-variable equation from Opening Exercise 2.

a. $y = |x|$

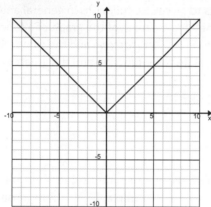

b. $y = |x - 5|$

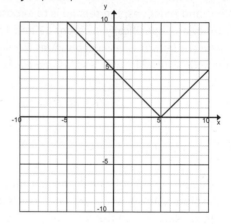

c. $x = |y|$

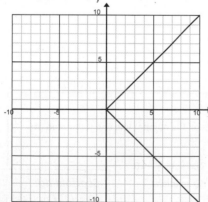

d. Write a brief summary comparing and contrasting the three solution sets and their graphs.

The graphs of parts (a) and (b) are the same except that part (b) has point of the 'vee' (the vertex of angle) at (5, 0) instead of (0, 0). The other for part (c) looks like a 90° clockwise rotation of the graph from part (a) about the point (0, 0). The points in the solution sets to parts (a) and (b) are a function but the points in the solution set for part (c) are not.

Lesson 15: Piecewise Functions
Date: 9/12/13

The next portion asks students to consider their work so far in Module 3. Part (h) makes the connection that the graph of the equation $y = |x|$ and the graph of f, where $f(x) = |x|$ are identical. Question (j) is there to help students understand that the graph of $y = f(x)$ and the graph of a two-variable equation (in x and y) are only identical if the elements of the equation's solution set define a function in x to begin with.

For parts (e) – (j) consider the function $f(x) = |x|$ where x can be any real number.

e. Explain the meaning of the function f in your own words.

This function assigns every real number to its absolute value, which is the distance the point is located from 0 on the real number line. Each number and its opposite will have the same range element. The number 0 will be assigned to 0.

f. State the domain and range of this function.

Domain: all real numbers. Range: all non-negative real numbers.

g. Create a graph of the function f. You might start by listing several ordered pairs that represent the corresponding domain and range elements.

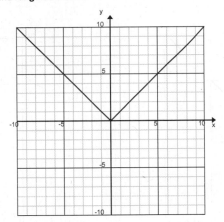

h. How does the graph of the absolute value function compare to the graph of $y = |x|$?

The two graphs are identical. They are identical because each ordered pair in the function would make the equation $y = |x|$ a true number sentence if the domain value were substituted for x and the range value was substituted for y. Therefore the graph of the function is the graph of the solution set of the equation.

i. Define a function whose graph would be identical to the graph of $y = |x - 5|$?

Let $g(x) = |x - 5|$ where x can be any real number.

j. Could you define a function whose graph would be identical to the graph of $x = |y|$? Explain your reasoning.

No. The graph of $x = |y|$ does not meet the definition of a graph of a function. If it were the graph of a function (say, the function h), it would be the set of ordered pairs $\{(x, h(x)) \mid x \in D\}$, which means there would be only one y-value for each x in the domain D. However, in the graph of $x = |y|$ there is a number x (in fact, there are infinitely many x's) associated with two different y-values: $(3, 3)$ and $(3, -3)$ are both solutions to the equation $x = |y|$.

As you debrief questions (h)–(j) as a whole group, lead a discussion that includes a summary of the following information. When we create the graph of the solution set to a two-variable equation, we use essentially the same process as when we create the graph of $y = f(x)$. We sift through all the (x, y) pairs in the Cartesian plane and plot only those pairs that make a true number sentence. The difference between the two processes is that when we graph $y = f(x)$, each x value in the domain of f will be paired with only one y value. When graphing a two-variable equation, there is no such restriction placed on the ordered pairs that return a true number sentence. The process of creating the graph of a function f yields the same results as graphing the solution set to the equation $y = f(x)$ except we run through the set of domain values, determine the corresponding range value and then plot that ordered pair. Since each x in the domain is paired with exactly one y in the range, the resulting graphs will be the same. For this reason, we often use the variable symbol y and the function name $f(x)$ interchangeably when we talk about the graph of a function or two-variable equation solved for y. The caveat is that the two-variable equation must have a solution set where each x is paired with only one y.

k. Let $f_1(x) = -x$ for $x < 0$ and let $f_2(x) = x$ for ≥ 0. Graph the functions f_1 and f_2 on the same Cartesian plane. How does the graph of these two functions compare to the graph in Exercise 7?

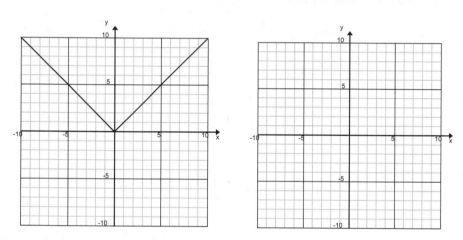

The graph of these two functions when graphed on the same Cartesian plane is identical to the graph of the absolute value function.

Close this portion of the lesson with the following definition of the absolute value function as a piecewise function.

Definition:

The *absolute value function* f is defined by setting $f(x) = |x|$ for all real numbers. Another way to write f is as a piecewise linear function:

$$f(x) = \begin{cases} -x & x < 0 \\ x & x \geq 0 \end{cases}$$

Example 1 (5 minutes)

This example shows students how to express a translation of the absolute value function as a piecewise function. Students create a graph of this function:

Example 1

Let $g(x) = |x - 5|$. **The graph of g is the same as the graph of the equation** $y = |x - 5|$ **you drew in Exercise 3. Use the redrawn graph below to re-write the function g as a piecewise function.**

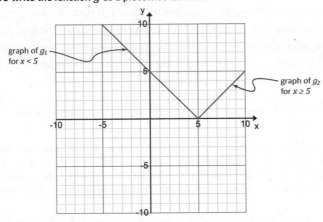

graph of g_1
for $x < 5$

graph of g_2
for $x \geq 5$

Explain that we will need to derive the equations of both lines to write g as a piecewise function.

Label the graph of the linear function with negative slope by g_1 and the graph of the linear function with positive slope by g_2 as in the picture above.

Function g_1: Slope of g_1 is –1 (why?), and the y-intercept is 5, therefore $g_1(x) = -x + 5$.

Function g_2: Slope of g_2 is 1 (why?), and the y-intercept is –5 (why?), therefore $g_2(x) = x - 5$.

Writing g as a piecewise function is just a matter of collecting all of the different "pieces" and the intervals upon which they are defined:

$$g(x) = \begin{cases} -x + 5 & x < 5 \\ x - 5 & x \geq 5 \end{cases}$$

- How does this graph compare to the graph of the translated absolute value function?
    - *The graphs are congruent, but the graph of g has been translated to the right 5 units. (Using terms like "congruent" and "translated" reinforce concepts from 8th grade and prepare students for geometry.)*
- How can you use your knowledge of the graph of $f(x) = |x|$ to quickly determine the graph of $g(x) = |x - 5|$?
    - *Watch where the vertex of the graph of f has been translated. In this case, $g(x) = |x - 5|$ has translated the vertex point from $(0,0)$ to $(5,0)$. Then, graph a line with a slope of – 1 for the piece where $x < 5$ and a line with a slope of 1 for the piece, where $x > 5$.*
- Can we interpret in words what this function does?
    - *The range values are found by finding the distance between each domain element and the number 5 on the number line.*

Exploratory Challenge 2 (8 minutes)

This exploration introduces the two types of step functions and a third function that is related to them: the floor function (also known as the greatest integer function), the ceiling function, and the sawtooth function. The notation that one often sees for the greatest integer function is $f(x) = [\![x]\!]$. Gauss first introduced the greatest integer function in the early 1800s. Later, Iverson defined the floor and ceiling functions and introduced the notation you see below in 1962. Both notations are used in mathematics. These functions are used in computer programming languages amongst other applications. Be sure to explain the notation.

Questions (b) and (c) will help students understand how the range values for each function are generated. In question (c), students will begin to understand that all real numbers in the interval have the same y-value. Clarify for students why the interval is closed at the left endpoint and open at the right endpoint. If students are struggling to create graphs, you may need to finish this exploration as a whole class. Before closing the lesson, make sure each student has a correct graph of the functions.

Exploratory Challenge 2

The *floor* of a real number x, denoted by $\lfloor x \rfloor$, is the largest integer not greater than x. The *ceiling* of a real number x, denoted by $\lceil x \rceil$, is the smallest integer not less than x. The *sawtooth* number of a positive number is the "fractional part" of the number that is to the right of its floor on the number line. In general, for a real number x, the sawtooth number of x is the value of the expression $x - \lfloor x \rfloor$. Each of these expressions can be thought of as functions with domain the set of real numbers.

a. Complete the following table to help you understand how these functions assign elements of the domain to elements of the range. The first and second rows have been done for you.

x	$floor(x) = \lfloor x \rfloor$	$ceiling(x) = \lceil x \rceil$	$sawtooth(x) = x - \lfloor x \rfloor$
4.8	4	5	0.8
-1.3	-2	-1	0.7
2.2	2	3	0.2
6	6	6	0
-3	-3	-3	0
$-\dfrac{2}{3}$	-1	0	$\dfrac{1}{3}$
π	3	4	$\pi - 3$

b. Create a graph of each function.

$floor(x) = \lfloor x \rfloor$ $ceiling(x) = \lceil x \rceil$ $sawtooth(x) = x - \lfloor x \rfloor$

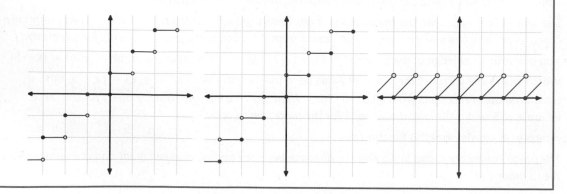

Lesson 15:   Piecewise Functions
Date: 9/12/13

c.   For the floor function, what would be the range value for all real numbers x on the interval $[0, 1)$? The interval $(1, 2]$? The interval $[-2, -1)$? The interval $[1.5, 2.5]$?

        Floor: $\{0\}$*, Ceiling:* $\{0, 1\}$*, Sawtooth:* $[0, 1)$*.*
        Floor: $\{1, 2\}$*, Ceiling:* $\{2\}$*, Sawtooth:* $[0, 1)$*.*
        Floor: $\{-2\}$*, Ceiling:* $\{-2, -1\}$*, Sawtooth:* $[0, 1)$*.*
        Floor: $\{1, 2\}$*, Ceiling:* $\{2, 3\}$*, Sawtooth:* $[0, 1)$*.*

Closing (2 minutes)

- You can use different expressions to define a function over different subsets of the domain. These are called piecewise functions. The absolute value function and step functions can be represented as piecewise functions.

- The graph of a function f and the graph of the equation $y = f(x)$ are the same.

Relevant Vocabulary

PIECEWISE-LINEAR FUNCTION. Given a number of non-overlapping intervals on the real number line, a *(real) piecewise-linear function* is a function from the union of the intervals to the set of real numbers such that the function is defined by (possibly different) linear functions on each interval.

ABSOLUTE VALUE FUNCTION. The absolute value of a number x, denoted by $|x|$, is the distance between 0 and x on the number line. The *absolute value function* is the piecewise-linear function such that for each real number x, the value of the function is $|x|$.

We often name the absolute value function by saying, "Let $f(x) = |x|$ for all real numbers x."

FLOOR FUNCTION. The *floor* of a real number x, denoted by $\lfloor x \rfloor$, is the largest integer not greater than x. The *floor function* is the piecewise-linear function such that for each real number x, the value of the function is $\lfloor x \rfloor$.

We often name the floor function by saying, "Let $f(x) = \lfloor x \rfloor$ for all real numbers x."

CEILING FUNCTION. The *ceiling* of a real number x, denoted by $\lceil x \rceil$, is the smallest integer not less than x. The *ceiling function* is the piecewise-linear function such that for each real number x, the value of the function is $\lceil x \rceil$.

We often name the ceiling function by saying, "Let $f(x) = \lceil x \rceil$ for all real numbers x."

SAWTOOTH FUNCTION. The *sawtooth function* is the piecewise-linear function such that for each real number x, the value of the function is given by the expression $x - \lfloor x \rfloor$.

The sawtooth function assigns to each positive number the part of the number (the non-integer part) that is to the right of the floor of the number on the number line. That is, if we let $f(x) = x - \lfloor x \rfloor$ for all real numbers x then $f\left(\frac{1}{3}\right) = \frac{1}{3}, f\left(1\frac{1}{3}\right) = \frac{1}{3}, f(1000.02) = 0.02, f(-0.3) = 0.7$, etc.

Exit Ticket (5 minutes)

Name _____   Date_____

Lesson 15: Piecewise Functions

Exit Ticket

Each graph shown below represents the solution set to a two-variable equation.

Graph A   Graph B   Graph C

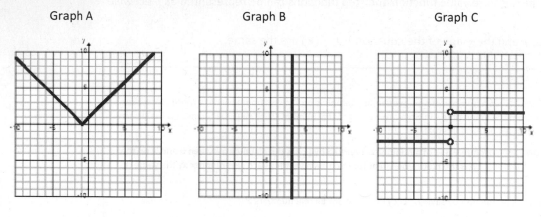

1. Which of these graphs could be represented by a function? Explain your reasoning.

2. For each one that can be represented by a function, define a piecewise function whose graph would be identical to the solution set shown.

Exit Ticket Sample Solutions

1. Which of these graphs could be represented by a function? Explain your reasoning.

    Graphs A and C could be represented by a function because each x in the domain is paired with exactly one y in the range.

2. For each one that can be represented by a function, define a piecewise function whose graph would be identical to the solution set shown.

    Graph A: $f(x) = \begin{cases} -x - 1, & x < -1 \\ x + 1, & x \geq -1 \end{cases}$

    Graph C: $f(x) = \begin{cases} -2, & x < 0 \\ 0, & x = 0 \\ 2, & x > 0 \end{cases}$

Problem Set Sample Solutions

These problems build student familiarity with piecewise functions and continue to reinforce the definition of function. The following solutions indicate an understanding of the objectives of this lesson:

1. Explain why the sawtooth function, $sawtooth(x) = x - \lfloor x \rfloor$ for all real numbers x, takes only the "fractional part" of a number when the number is positive.

    If you subtract the integer part of a number from the number, only the "fractional part" will remain.

2. Let $g(x) = \lceil x \rceil - \lfloor x \rfloor$ where x can be any real number. In otherwords, g is the difference between the ceiling and floor functions. Express g as a piecewise function.

    $$g(x) = \begin{cases} 0 & x \text{ is an integer} \\ 1 & x \text{ is not an integer} \end{cases}$$

3. The Heaviside function is defined using the formula below.

    $$H(x) = \begin{cases} -1, & x < 0 \\ 0, & x = 0 \\ 1, & x > 0 \end{cases}$$

    Graph this function and state its domain and range.

    Domain: All real numbers.

    Range: $\{-1, 0, 1\}$.

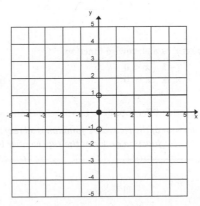

4. The following piecewise function is an example of a step function.

$$S(x) = \begin{cases} 3 & -5 \le x < -2 \\ 1 & -2 \le x < 3 \\ 2 & 3 \le x \le 5 \end{cases}$$

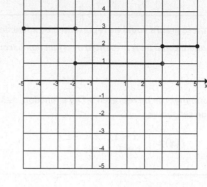

a. Graph this function and state the domain and range.

Domain: $[-5, 5]$, *Range:* $\{1, 2, 3\}$.

b. Why is this type of function is called a step function?

The horizontal line segments step up and down like steps.

5. Let $f(x) = \frac{|x|}{x}$ where x can be any real number except 0.

a. Why is the number 0 excluded from the domain of f?

If $x = 0$ then the expression would not be defined.

b. What is the range of f?

$\{-1, 1\}$.

c. Create a graph of f.

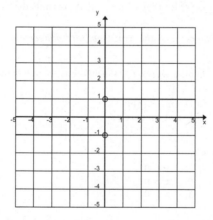

d. Express f as a piecewise function.

$$f(x) = \begin{cases} -1 & x < 0 \\ 1 & x > 0 \end{cases}$$

e. What is the difference between this function and the Heaviside function?

The domain of the Heaviside function is all real numbers. The Heaviside function has a value of 0 when $x = 0$. This function excludes the real number 0 from the domain.

6. Graph the following piecewise functions for the specified domain.

    a. $f(x) = |x + 3|$ for $-5 \leq x \leq 3$

    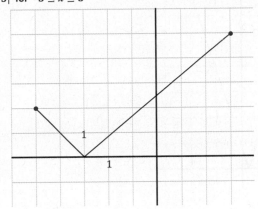

    b. $f(x) = |2x|$ for $-3 \leq x \leq 3$

    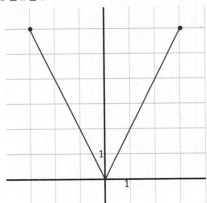

    c. $f(x) = |2x - 5|$ for $0 \leq x \leq 5$

    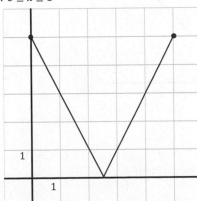

d. $f(x) = |3x + 1|$ for $-2 \leq x \leq 2$

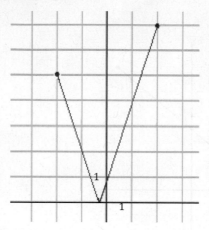

e. $f(x) = |x| + x$ for $-4 \leq x \leq 3$

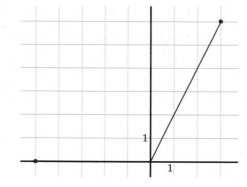

f. $f(x) = \begin{cases} x & if\ x \leq 0 \\ x + 1 & if\ x > 0 \end{cases}$

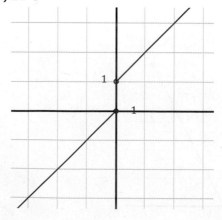

g.　$f(x) = \begin{cases} 2x + 3 & if\ x < -1 \\ 3 - x & if\ x \geq -1 \end{cases}$

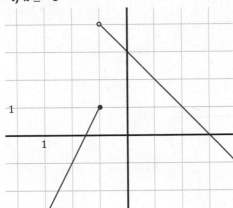

7.　Write a piecewise function for each graph below.

a.

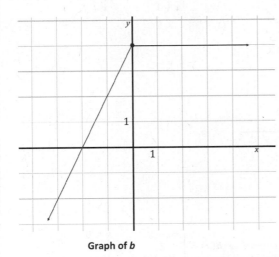

Graph of b

Answer

$b(x) = \begin{cases} 2x + 4 & x < 0 \\ 4 & x \geq 0 \end{cases}$

b.

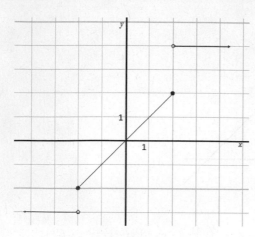

$$p(x) = \begin{cases} -3 & x \le -2 \\ 1 & -2 \le x < 2 \\ 2 & x > 2 \end{cases}$$

Graph of p

c.

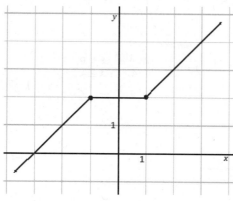

$$k(x) = \begin{cases} x + 3 & x < -1 \\ 2 & -2 \le x < 2 \\ x + 1 & x > 2 \end{cases}$$

Graph of k

d.

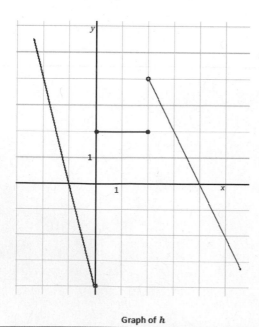

$$h(x) = \begin{cases} 4x - 3 & x < 0 \\ 2 & 0 \le x \le 2 \\ -2x + 8 & x > 2 \end{cases}$$

Graph of h

Lesson 16: Graphs Can Solve Equations Too

Student Outcomes

- Students discover that the multi-step and exact way of solving $|2x - 5| = |3x + 1|$ using algebra can sometimes be avoided by recognizing that an equation of the form $f(x) = g(x)$ can be solved visually by looking for the intersection points of the graphs of $y = f(x)$ and $y = g(x)$.

Lesson Notes

This lesson focuses on A.REI.11 which emphasizes that the x-coordinates of the intersection points of the graphs of two functions f and g are the solutions to the equation $f(x) = g(x)$. This lesson ties work from Module 1 on solving systems of two-variable equations to work with functions and leads students to the understanding of what the solution set to a one-variable equation can be.

Classwork

Opening Exercises 1–3 (5 minutes)

In the opening, instruct students to solve for x in the equation by isolating the absolute value expression and separating the solution into two cases: one for the absolute value expression that represents distance from 0 in the positive direction of the number line, and one for the distance from 0 in the negative direction. In Exercise 2, we introduce the functions f and g somewhat artificially and consider the graphs $y = f(x)$ and $y = g(x)$. Students quickly recognize that this series of artificial moves actually has a solid purpose: to solve for x visually using the graphs of functions. After the labor required in Exercise 1, students should appreciate this clever way of solving for x.

Opening Exercises 1–3

1. **Solve for x in the following equation:** $|x + 2| - 3 = 0.5x + 1$

$$|x + 2| = 0.5x + 4$$

$x + 2 = 0.5x + 4$	or	$x + 2 = -(0.5x + 4)$
$0.5x = 2$	or	$1.5x = -6$
$x = 4$	or	$x = -4$

2. Now let $f(x) = |x + 2| - 3$ and $g(x) = 0.5x + 1$. When does $f(x) = g(x)$? To answer this, first graph $y = f(x)$ and $y = g(x)$ on the same set of axes.

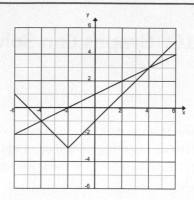

3. When does $f(x) = g(x)$? What is the visual significance of the points where $f(x) = g(x)$?

   $f(x) = g(x)$ when $x = 4$ and when $x = -4$; $(4, 3)$ and $(-4, -1)$. The points where $f(x) = g(x)$ are the intersections of the graphs of f and g.

4. Is each intersection point (x, y) an element of the graph f and an element of the graph of g? In other words, do the functions f and g really have the same value when $x = 4$? What about when $x = -4$?

   Yes. You can determine this by substituting $x = -4$ and $x = 4$ into both f and g.

   $$-1 = |-4 + 2| - 3 \qquad\qquad 3 = |4 + 2| - 3$$
   $$-1 = 2 - 3 \qquad\qquad\qquad 3 = 6 - 3$$
   $$-1 = -1 \qquad\qquad\qquad\quad 3 = 3$$

   $f(x)$ and $g(x)$ have the same value at each x.

Be sure to review the solutions to these problems with the entire class before moving on. Before sharing as whole group, give students time to compare their answers with a partner.

Discussion (8 minutes)

Lead a discussion that ties together the work in the opening exercises. The idea here is to create an equation $f(x) = g(x)$ and show that the x-coordinates of the intersection points are the solution set to this equation. This example will draw on MP.7 as students will need to look closely to determine the connection between the functions and equations involved.

First summarize what we know from the opening exercise. Ask students to discuss this with a partner and then call on a few people to share their thoughts. Make sure the following point is clear to the class:

- For functions f and g, we have found special ordered pairs that (1) are points in the intersection of the graph of f and the graph of g, that (2) are solutions to a system of equations given by the equations $y = f(x)$ and $y = g(x)$, and (3) where the x-value satisfies the equation $f(x) = g(x)$.

Write this equation on the board. Ask students to use the solutions from the opening exercise to answer the following:

- Are the x-coordinates of the intersection points solutions to this equation?

  □ *Yes, when I substituted the x-coordinates into the equation I got a true number sentence.*

| Lesson 16: | Graphs Can Solve Equations Too |
| Date: | 9/12/13 |

210

- Are the y-coordinates of the intersection points solutions to this equation?
    - *No, when I substituted the y-coordinates into the equation I got a false number sentence.*
- Do you think there are any other solutions to this equation? How could you be sure?
    - *I don't think so, because each side of the equation is one of the functions shown in the graphs. The shape of the graph makes me think that there are no other intersection points. We could algebraically solve the equation to prove that these are the only solutions.*

Give students (in groups of three or four) time to debate the next discussion question. Have different students share their thinking with the whole class.

- Is it always true that the x-coordinates of the intersection points of the graphs of two functions will be the solution set to the equation $f(x) = g(x)$?
    - *Yes. To create the graphs of f and g we cycle through some of the domain values x and plot the pairs $(x, f(x))$ and $(x, g(x))$. The points that these two functions have in common will have x-values that satisfy the equation $f(x) = g(x)$ because this equation asks us to find the domain elements x that make the range elements $f(x)$ and $g(x)$ equal.*
- What is the advantage of solving an equation graphically by finding intersection points in this manner?
    - *It can be helpful when the equations are complicated or impossible to solve algebraically. It will also be useful when estimating solutions is enough to solve a problem. The graphically estimated solutions might give insight into ways to solve the equation algebraically.*

Example 1 (8 minutes)

This example provides an opportunity to model explicitly how to use graphs of functions to solve an equation. As you work with students, guide them to label the graphs similarly to what is shown in the solutions below. This will reinforce proper vocabulary. In this guided example, students will complete the graphs of the functions and then fill in the blanks as you discuss as a whole class. This exercise should reinforce the previous discussion.

Example 1

Solve this equation by graphing two functions on the same Cartesian plane: $|0.5x| - 5 = -|x - 3| + 4$

Let $f(x) = |0.5x| - 5$ and let $g(x) = -|x - 3| + 4$ where x can be any real number.

We are looking for values of x at which the functions f and g have the same output value.

Therefore, we set $y = f(x)$ and $y = g(x)$ so we can plot the graphs on the same coordinate plane :

From the graph, we see that the two intersection points are

_____ and _____.

$(-4, -3)$ *and* $(8, -1)$

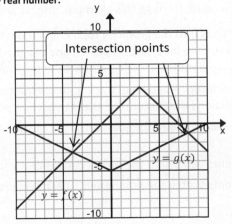

> The fact that the graphs of the functions meet at these two points means that when x is _____ both $f(x)$ and $g(x)$ are _____, or when x is _____ both $f(x)$ and $g(x)$ are _____.
>
> $-4, -3, 8, -1$
>
> Thus, the expressions $|0.5x| - 5$ and $-|x - 3| + 4$ are equal
>
> when $x =$ _____ or when $x =$ _____.
>
> $-4,\ 8$
>
> Therefore, the solution set to the original equation is _____.
>
> $\{-4, 8\}$.

After working with the class to use their knowledge from the previous lesson to create these graphs, lead a discussion that emphasizes the following:

- We are looking for values of x where the values $f(x)$ and $g(x)$ are the same. In other words, we want to identify the points $(x, f(x))$ of the graph of f and the points $(x, g(x))$ of the graph of g that are the same. This will occur where the graphs of the two functions intersect.

- We must also convince ourselves that these are the only two solutions to this equation. Pose the question: How can we be certain that these two intersection points are the only two solutions to this equation? Give students time to discuss this with a partner or in a small group. Encourage them to reason from the graphs of the functions, rather than solving the equation.

  - *For all $x < -4$ or $x > 8$, the differences in the y-values of two functions are always greater than zero. To see this, note that $f(x) - g(x) = |0.5x| - 5 - (-|x - 3| + 4) = |0.5x| + |x - 3| - 9$. The last expression is greater than zero when $|0.5x| + |x - 3| > 9$, which is certainly true for $x < -4$ or $x > 8$ (by inspection—there's no need to solve this equation due to the graph). Hence, the only solutions can occur in the interval $-4 \leq x \leq 8$, of which there are two.*

- If time permits, challenge students to experiment with sketching in the same Cartesian plane the graphs of two functions (each of which involve taking an absolute value) that intersect at 0 points, exactly 1 point, exactly two points, or an infinite number of points.

Example 2 (10 minutes)

This example requires graphing calculators or other graphing software that is capable of finding the intersection points of two graphs. As you work through this example, discuss and model how to:

- Enter functions into the graphing tool, graph them in an appropriate viewing window to see the intersection points, and use the features of the graphing technology to determine the coordinates of the intersection points.

- Show the difference between 'tracing' to the intersection point and using any built-in functions that determine the intersection point.

- Have students estimate the solutions from the graph before using the built-in features.

- Have students verify that the x-coordinates of the intersecting points are solutions to the equations.

- Have students sketch the graphs and label the coordinates of the intersection points on their handouts.

> *Scaffolding:*
>
> Refer to video lessons on the Internet for further examples and support for teaching this process using technology.

Example 2

Solve this equation graphically: $-|x - 3.5| + 4 = -0.25x - 1$

  a. Write the two functions represented by each side of the equation.

  Let $f(x) = -|x - 3.5| + 4$ and let $g(x) = -0.25x - 1$, where x can be any real number.

  b. Graph the functions in an appropriate viewing window.

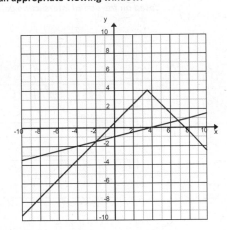

  c. Determine the intersection points of the two functions.

  $(-2, -1.5)$ and $(6.8, 0.7)$

  d. Verify that the x-coordinates of the intersection points are solutions to the equation.

  Let $x = 2$ then

  $-|-2 - 3.5| + 4 = -0.25(-2) - 1$

  $-5.5 + 4 = 0.5 - 1$

  $-0.5 = -0.5$

  Let $x = 6.75$ then

  $-|6.8 - 3.5| + 4 = -0.25(6.8) - 1$

  $-3.3 + 4 = 1.7 - 1$

  $0.7 = 0.7$

Exercises 1–5 (8 minutes)

Students practice using graphs of functions to solve equations. Students should work through these exercises in small groups and discuss their solutions as they work. Circulate among groups providing assistance as needed.

Exercises 1–5

Use graphs to find approximate values of the solution set for each equation. Use technology to support your work. Explain how each of your solutions relates to the graph. Check your solutions using the equation.

1. $3 - 2x = |x - 5|$

$x = -2$, *the intersection point is* $(-2, 7)$.

2. $2(1.5)^x = 2 + 1.5x$

First solution is $x = 0$, *from the point* $(0, 2)$;

Second solution answers will vary, x is about 2.7 *or* 2.8, *based on the actual intersection point of* $(2.776, 6.164)$

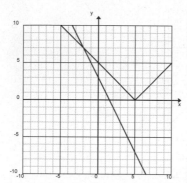

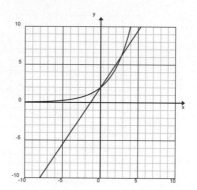

3. The graphs of the functions f and g are shown.

   a. Use the graph to *approximate* the solution(s) to the equation $f(x) = g(x)$.

   Based on the graphs, the approximate solutions are $\{-0.7, 2\}$.

   b. Let $f(x) = x^2$ and let $g(x) = 2^x$. Find *all* solutions to the equation $f(x) = g(x)$. Verify any exact solutions that you determine using the definitions of f and g. Explain how you arrived at your solutions.

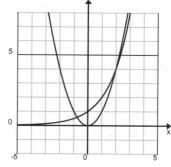

By guessing and checking, $x = 4$ *is also a solution of the equation because* $f(4) = 16$ *and* $g(4) = 16$. *Since the graph of the exponential function is increasing and increases more rapidly than the squaring function, there will only be 3 solutions to this equation. The exact solutions are* $x = 2$ *and* $x = 4$ *and an approximate solution is* $x = -0.7$.

4. The graphs of f, a function that involves taking an absolute value, and g, a linear function, are shown to the right. Both functions are defined over all real values for x. Tami concluded that the equation $f(x) = g(x)$ has no solution.

   Do you agree or disagree? Explain your reasoning.

   I disagree with Tami because we cannot see enough of this graph. The graph of the function shown to the left has a slope of 5. The graph of the function shown to the right has a slope greater than 5. Therefore, these two functions will intersect somewhere in the first quadrant. We would have to 'zoom out' to see the intersection point.

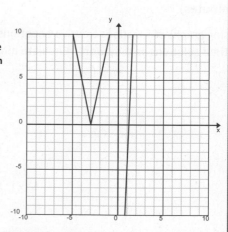

5. The graphs of f (a function that involves taking the absolute value) and g (an exponential function) are shown below. Sharon said the solution set to the equation $f(x) = g(x)$ is exactly $\{-7, 5\}$.

    Do you agree or disagree with Sharon? Explain your reasoning.

    I disagree with Sharon. We could say that the solution set is approximately $\{-7, 5\}$ but without having the actual equation or formulas for the two functions we cannot be sure the x-values of the intersection points are exactly -7 and 5.

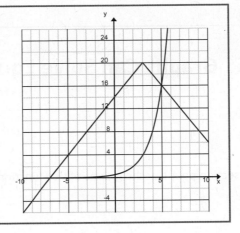

Closing (2 minutes)

In the last two exercises, students reflect on the limitations of solving an equation graphically. Debrief these exercises as a whole class and encourage different groups to present their reasoning to the entire class. Clarify any misconceptions before moving on, and give students time to revise their work. In Exercise 4, it is clear that there is an intersection point that is not visible in the viewing window provided. In Exercise 5, the intersection points would need to be estimated. If we do not have the exact algebraic solutions of the equation, then we can only estimate the solution set using graphs.

Exit Ticket (5 minutes)

Name _____   Date_____

Lesson 16: Graphs Can Solve Equations Too

Exit Ticket

1. How do intersection points of the graphs of two functions f and g relate of the solution to an equation in the form $f(x) = g(x)$?

2. What are some benefits of solving equations graphically? What are some limitations?

Exit Ticket Sample Solutions

1. How do intersection points of the graphs of two functions f and g relate to the solution to an equation in the form $f(x) = g(x)$?

   The x-coordinates of the intersection points of the graphs of two functions are the solutions of the equation.

2. What are some benefits of solving equations graphically? What are some limitations?

   Benefits: Solving equations graphically can be helpful when you don't know how to solve the equation algebraically. It can also save you some time if you have technology available. This method can only provide approximate solutions, which may be all you need. Or the approximate solutions may give you insight into how to solve the equation algebraically.

   Limitations: You cannot be sure you have found all the solutions to an equation unless you can reason about the graphs of the functions themselves and convince yourself that no other intersection points are possible. The solutions found graphically rely on eyeballing. There is no guarantee that they are exact solutions; sometimes they are, other times they are just decent approximations.

Problem Set Sample Solutions

1. Solve the following equations graphically. Verify the solution set using the original equations.

   a. $2x - 4 = \sqrt{x + 5}$

   Approximately 3.4538

   b. $|x| = x^2$

   $\{-1, 0, 1\}$

   c. $x + 2 = x^3 - 2x - 4$

   Approximately 2.3553

   d. $|3x - 4| = 5 - |x - 2|$

   $\{0.25, 2.75\}$

   e. $0.5x^3 - 4 = 3x + 1$

   Approximately 3.0467

   f. $6\left(\frac{1}{2}\right)^{5x} = 10 - 6x$

   Approximately -0.1765 and 1.6636

In each exercise, the graphs of the functions f and g are shown on the same Cartesian plane. Estimate the solution set to the equation $f(x) = g(x)$. Assume that the graphs of the two functions only intersect at the points shown on the graph.

2.

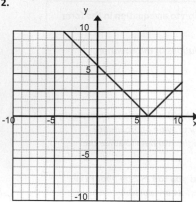

$\{3, 9\}$

3.

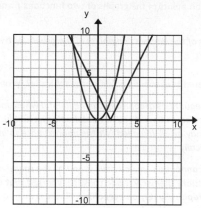

$\{-3, 1\}$

4.

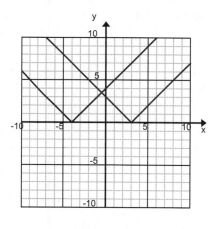

$\left\{\dfrac{1}{2}\right\}$

5.

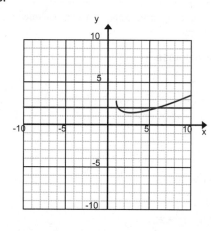

$\{1.2, 6\}$

6. The graph below shows Glenn's distance from home as he rode his bicycle to school, which is just down his street. His next-door neighbor Pablo, who lives 100 m closer to the school, leaves his house at the same time as Glenn. He walks at a constant velocity and they both arrive at school at the same time.

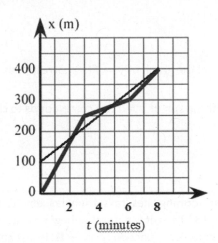

a. Graph a linear function that represents Pablo's distance from Glenn's home as a function of time.

b. Estimate when the two boys pass each other.

    They cross paths at about 2 minutes and 5 minutes. I can tell that by finding the x-coordinates of the intersection points of the graphs of the functions.

c. Write piecewise-linear functions to represent each boy's distance and use them to verify your answer to part (b).

$P(t) = 100 + 37.5t$

$$G(t) = \begin{cases} \dfrac{250}{3}t & 0 \le t \le 3 \\ 200 + \dfrac{50}{3}t & 3 < t \le 6 \\ 50t & 6 < t \le 8 \end{cases}$$

At about 2 minutes: $100 + \dfrac{75}{2}t = \dfrac{250}{3}t$ *or* $600 + 225t = 500t$ *or* $275t = 600$ *or* $t = \dfrac{24}{11}$ *min.*

At about 5 minutes: $100 + \dfrac{75}{2}t = 200 + \dfrac{50}{3}t$ *or* $225t = 600 + 100t$ *or* $125t = 600$ *or* $t = \dfrac{24}{5} = 4.8$ *min.*

Lesson 17: Four Interesting Transformations of Functions

Student Outcomes

- Students examine that a vertical translation of the graph of $y = f(x)$ corresponds to changing the equation from $y = f(x)$ to $y = f(x) + k$.
- Students examine that a vertical scaling of the graph of $y = f(x)$ corresponds to changing the equation from $y = f(x)$ to $y = kf(x)$.

Lesson Notes

Students enter Algebra 1 having experience with transforming lines, rays, triangles, etc., using translations, rotations, reflections, and dilations from Grade 8 Modules 2 and 3. Thus, it is natural to begin a discussion of transformations of functions by transforming graphs of functions—the graph of a function, $f : \mathbb{R} \to \mathbb{R}$, is just another geometric figure in the (Cartesian) plane. Students use language such as, "a translation 2 units to the left," or, "a vertical stretch by a scale factor of 3," to describe how the original graph of the function is transformed into the new graph geometrically.

As students apply their Grade 8 geometry skills to the graph of the equation $y = f(x)$, they realize that the translation of the graph to the right by 4 units is given by the graph of the equation $y = f(x - 4)$. This recognition, in turn, leads to the idea of a transformation of a function. (i.e., a new function such that the graph of it is the transformation of the original graph of $y = f(x)$.) In the example described, it is the function given by $g(x) = f(x - 4)$ for any real number x such that $x - 4$ is in the domain of f.

Since the transformation of the function is itself another function (and not a graph), we must use function language to describe the transformation. A function f cannot be translated up, down, right or left (even though its graph can). Rather, students can use function language such as: "For the same inputs, the values of the transformed function are two times as large as the values of the original function."

These lessons encourage fluidity in both the language associated with transformations of graphs, and the language associated with transformations of functions. While a formal definition for the transformation of a function is not included, teachers are encouraged use language precisely as students work to develop the notion of transformation of a function and relate it to their understanding of transformations of graphical objects.

In the exploratory challenge, you may highlight MP.3 by asking students to make a conjecture about the effect of k. This challenge also calls on students to employ MP.8, as they will generalize the effect of k through repeated graphing.

Classwork

Exploratory Challenge 1/Example 1 (12 minutes)

Let $f(x) = |x|$ for all real numbers x. Students explore the effect on the graph of $y = f(x)$ by changing the equation $y = f(x)$ to $y = f(x) + k$ for given values of k.

Exploratory Challenge 1/Example 1

Let $f(x) = |x|$, $g(x) = f(x) - 3$, $h(x) = f(x) + 2$ for any real number x.

1. Write an explicit formula for $g(x)$ in terms of $|x|$ (i.e., without using $f(x)$ notation):

$g(x) = |x| - 3$

2. Write an explicit formula for $h(x)$ in terms of $|x|$ (i.e., without using $f(x)$ notation):

$h(x) = |x| + 2$

3. Complete the table of values for these functions.

x	$f(x) = |x|$	$g(x) = f(x) - 3$	$h(x) = f(x) + 2$
-3	3	0	5
-2	2	-1	4
-1	1	-2	3
0	0	-3	2
1	1	-2	3
2	2	-1	4
3	3	0	5

4. Graph all three equations: $y = f(x)$, $y = f(x) - 3$, and $y = f(x) + 2$.

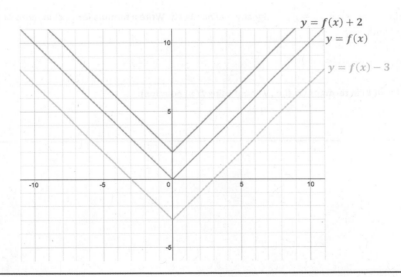

5. What is the relationship between the graph of $y = f(x)$ and the graph of $y = f(x) + k$?

For values of k, where $k > 0$, for every point $(x, f(x))$ that satisfies the equation $y = f(x)$, there is a corresponding point $(x, f(x) + k)$ on the graph, located k units above $(x, f(x))$ that satisfies the equation $y = f(x) + k$. The graph of $y = f(x) + k$ is the vertical translation of the graph of $y = f(x)$ by k units upward.

For values of k, where $k < 0$, for every point $(x, f(x))$ that satisfies the equation $y = f(x)$, there is a corresponding point $(x, f(x) + k)$ on the graph, located k units below $(x, f(x))$ that satisfies the equation $y = f(x) + k$. The graph of $y = f(x) + k$ is the vertical translation of the graph of $y = f(x)$ by k units downward.

The use of transformation language like "vertical translation" is purposeful. The Common Core State Standards require students to spend a lot of time talking about translations, rotations, reflections, and dilations in Grade 8. They will spend more time in Grade 10. Reinforcing this vocabulary will help to link these grades together.

6. How do the values of g and h relate to the values of f?

For each x in the domain of f and g, the value of $g(x)$ is 3 less than the value of $f(x)$. For each x in the domain of f and h, the value of $h(x)$ is 2 more than the value of $f(x)$.

Discussion (3 minutes)

Students should finish Example 1 with the understanding that the graph of a function g found by adding a number to another function, as in $g(x) = f(x) + k$, is the translation of the graph of the function f vertically by k units (positively or negatively depending on the sign of k).

Exploratory Challenge 2/Example 2 (12 minutes)

Let $f(x) = |x|$ for any real number x. Students explore the effect on the graph of $y = f(x)$ by changing the equation $y = f(x)$ to $y = kf(x)$ for given values of k.

Exploratory Challenge 2/Example 2

1. Let $f(x) = |x|$, $g(x) = 2f(x)$, $h(x) = \frac{1}{2}f(x)$ for any real number x. Write a formula for $g(x)$ in terms of $|x|$ (i.e., without using $f(x)$ notation):

   $g(x) = 2|x|$

2. Write a formula for $h(x)$ in terms of $|x|$ (i.e., without using $f(x)$ notation):

   $h(x) = \frac{1}{2}|x|$

3. Complete the table of values for these functions.

x	$f(x) = |x|$	$g(x) = 2f(x)$	$h(x) = \frac{1}{2}f(x)$
−3	3	6	1.5
−2	2	4	1
−1	1	2	0.5
0	0	0	0
1	1	2	0.5
2	2	4	1
3	3	6	1.5

4. Graph all three equations: $y = f(x)$, $y = 2f(x)$, and $y = \frac{1}{2}f(x)$.

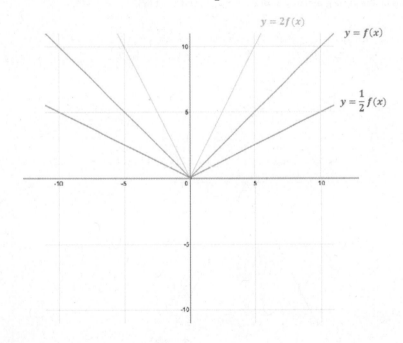

Let $p(x) = -|x|$, $q(x) = -2f(x)$, $r(x) = -\frac{1}{2}f(x)$ for any real number x.

5. Write the formula for $q(x)$ in terms of $|x|$ (i.e., without using $f(x)$ notation):

$q(x) = -2|x|$

6. Write the formula for $r(x)$ in terms of $|x|$ (i.e., without using $f(x)$ notation):

$r(x) = -\frac{1}{2}|x|$

7. Complete the table of values for the functions $p(x) = -|x|$, $q(x) = -2f(x)$, $r(x) = -\frac{1}{2}f(x)$.

x	$p(x) = -|x|$	$q = -2f(x)$	$r(x) = -\frac{1}{2}f(x)$
−3	−3	−6	−1.5
−2	−2	−4	−1
−1	−1	−2	−0.5
0	0	0	0
1	−1	−2	−0.5
2	−2	−4	−1
3	−3	−6	−1.5

8. Graph all three functions on the same graph as $y = p(x)$, $y = q(x)$, and $y = r(x)$.

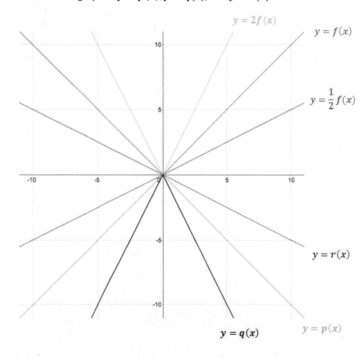

9. How is the graph of $y = f(x)$ related to the graph of $y = kf(x)$ when $k > 1$?

The graph of $y = kf(x)$ for $k > 1$ contains points (x, ky) which are related to points (x, y) in the graph of $y = f(x)$. The number ky is a multiple of y: each y-value of $y = g(x)$ is k times the y-value of $y = f(x)$. The graph of $y = kf(x)$ is a vertical scaling that appears to stretch the graph of $y = f(x)$ vertically by a factor of k.

10. How is the graph of $y = f(x)$ related to the graph of $y = kf(x)$ when $0 < k < 1$?

   The graph of $y = kf(x)$ for $0 < k < 1$ contains points (x, ky) which are related to points (x, y) in the graph of $y = f(x)$. The number ky is a fraction of y: each y-value of $y = g(x)$ is k times the y-value of $y = f(x)$. The graph of $y = kf(x)$ is a vertical scaling that appears to shrink the graph of $y = f(x)$ vertically by a factor of k.

11. How do the values of functions p, q, and r relate to the values of functions f, g, and h, respectively? What transformation of the graphs of f, g, and h represents this relationship?

   Each function is the opposite of the corresponding function. The result is that each y value of any point on the graph of $y = p(x), y = q(x)$, and $y = r(x)$ are the opposite of the y-value of the graphs of the equations $y = f(x), y = g(x)$, and $y = h(x)$. Each graph is a reflection of the corresponding graph over the x-axis.

Discussion (3 minutes)

Students should finish Example 2 with the understanding that a number, a scale factor, multiplied to a function vertically scales the original graph. For a vertical scale factor of $k > 1$, the graph is a vertical stretch of the original graph; for a vertical scale factor of k where $0 < k < 1$, the graph is a vertical shrink of the original graph. For a vertical scale factor of k where $-1 < k < 0$, the graph of the function is a reflection across the x-axis of the graph when $0 < k < 1$. Similarly, for a vertical scale factor of $k < -1$, the graph is the reflection across the x-axis of the graph when $k > 1$.

> **Scaffolding:**
>
> Gives guidance specific to this proportion of the lesson for addressing needs of diverse learners. The type of diverse learner should be specified (i.e., advanced learner, etc.)

Exercises (8 minutes)

Students complete exercises independently; then compare/discuss with partner or small group. Circulate to ensure that students grasp the effects of the given transformations.

Exercises

1. Make up your own function f by drawing the graph of it on the Cartesian plane below. Label it as the graph of the equation, $y = f(x)$. If $b(x) = f(x) - 4$ and $c(x) = \frac{1}{4} f(x)$ for every real number x, graph the equations $y = b(x)$ and $y = c(x)$ on the same Cartesian plane.

   Answers will vary. Look for and encourage students to create interesting graphs for their function f. (Functions DO NOT have to be defined by algebraic expressions— any graph that satisfies the definition of a function will do.) One such option is using $f(x) = |x|$, as shown in the example below.

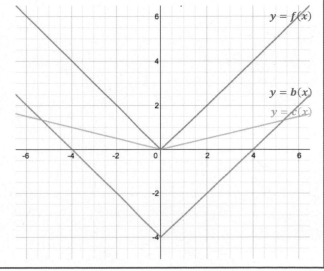

- If time permits, have students present their graphs to the class and explain how they found the graphs of $y = b(x)$ and $y = c(x)$. Pay close attention to how students explain how they found the graph of $y = c(x)$. Many might actually describe a horizontal scaling (or some other transformation that takes each point (x, y) of the graph to another point that *does not* have the same x-coordinate). Stress that multiplying the function f by k only scales the y-coordinate and leaves the x-coordinate alone.

Closing (3 minutes)

Point out that there is nothing special about using the function $f(x) = |x|$ as we did in this lesson. These transformations hold in general:

- Discuss how the graph of $y = f(x)$ can be vertically translated by positive or negative k. Draw a graph of a made up function on the board, labeled by $y = f(x)$, and show how to translate it up or down by k using the equation $y = f(x) + k$.
- Discuss how the graph of $y = f(x)$ can be vertically scaled by k for $0 < k < 1, k > 1, -1 < k < 0, k < -1$. Use the graph of $y = f(x)$ to show how to vertically scale (i.e., vertically stretch or shrink) by k units using the equation $y = kf(x)$.

Exit Ticket (5 minutes)

Name _____ Date_____

Lesson 17: Four Interesting Transformations of Functions

Exit Ticket

Let $p(x) = |x|$ for every real number x. The graph of $y = p(x)$ is shown below.

1. Let $q(x) = -\frac{1}{2}|x|$ for every real number x. Describe how to obtain the graph of $y = q(x)$ from the graph of
    $y = p(x)$. Sketch the graph of $y = q(x)$ on the same set of axes as the graph of $y = p(x)$.

2. Let $r(x) = |x| - 1$ for every real number x. Describe how to obtain the graph of $y = r(x)$ from the graph of
    $y = p(x)$. Sketch the graph of $y = r(x)$ on the same set of axes as the graphs of $y = p(x)$ and $y = q(x)$.

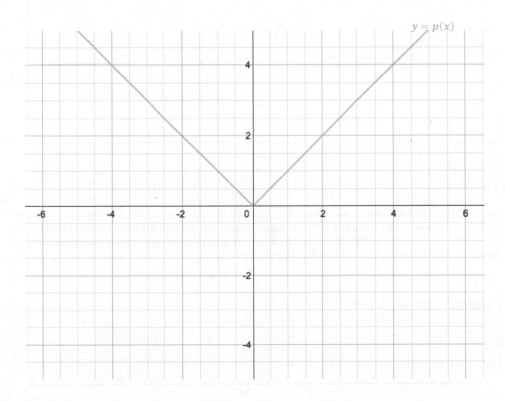

Exit Ticket Sample Solutions

Let $p(x) = |x|$ for every real number x. The graph of $y = p(x)$ is shown below.

1. Let $q(x) = -\frac{1}{2}|x|$ for every real number x. Describe how to obtain the graph of $y = q(x)$ from the graph of $y = p(x)$. Sketch the graph of $y = q(x)$ on the same set of axes as the graph of $y = p(x)$.

   Reflect and vertically scale the graph of $y = p(x)$ by plotting $\left(x, -\frac{1}{2}y\right)$ for each point (x, y) in the graph of $y = p(x)$. See the graph of $q(x)$ below.

2. Let $r(x) = |x| - 1$ for every real number x. Describe how to obtain the graph of $y = r(x)$ from the graph of $y = p(x)$. Sketch the graph of $y = r(x)$ on the same set of axes as the graphs of $y = p(x)$ and $y = q(x)$.

   Translate the graph of $y = p(x)$ vertically down 1 unit. See the graph of $y = r(x)$ below.

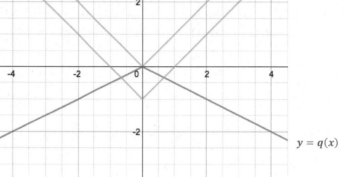

Problem Set Sample Solutions

Let $f(x) = |x|$ for every real number x. The graph of $y = f(x)$ is shown below. Describe how the graph for each function below is a transformation of the graph of $y = f(x)$. Then use this same set of axes to graph each function for problems $1 - 5$. Be sure to label each function on your graph (by $y = a(x)$, $y = b(x)$, etc.).

1. $a(x) = |x| + \frac{3}{2}$

   Translate the graph of $y = f(x)$ up 1.5 units.

2. $b(x) = -|x|$

   Reflect $y = f(x)$ across the x-axis.

3. $c(x) = 2|x|$

    Vertically scale/stretch the graph of $y = f(x)$ by doubling the output values for every input.

4. $d(x) = \frac{1}{3}|x|$

    Vertically scale/shrink the graph of $y = f(x)$ by dividing the output values by 3 for every input.

5. $e(x) = |x| - 3$

    Translate the graph of $y = f(x)$ down 3 units.

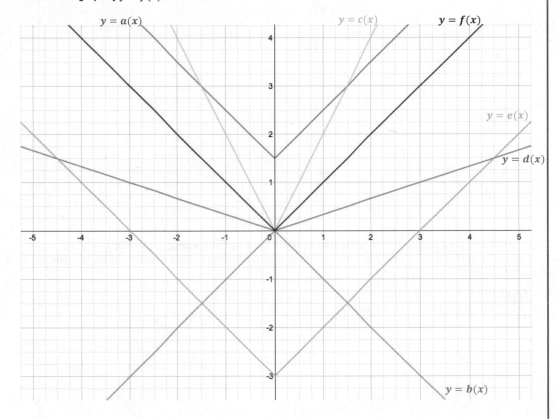

6. Let $r(x) = |x|$ and $t(x) = -2|x| + 1$ for every real number x. The graph of $y = r(x)$ is shown below. Complete the table below to generate output values for the function t; then graph the equation $y = t(x)$ on the same set of axes as the graph of $y = r(x)$.

x	$r(x) = |x|$	$t(x) = -2|x| + 1$
-2	2	-3
-1	1	-1
0	0	1
1	1	-1
2	2	-3

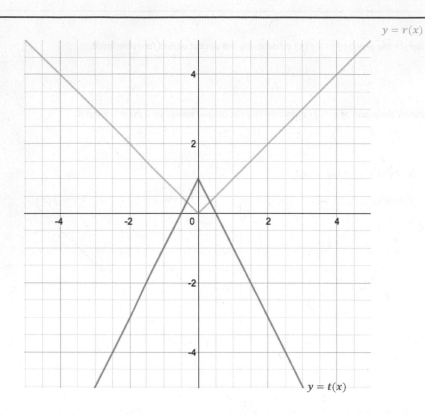

7. Let $f(x) = |x|$ for every real number x. Let m and n be functions found by transforming the graph of $y = f(x)$. Use the graphs of $y = f(x)$, $y = m(x)$ and $y = n(x)$ below to write the functions m and n in terms of the function f. (Hint: what is the k?)

$m(x) = 2f(x)$.

$n(x) = f(x) + 2$.

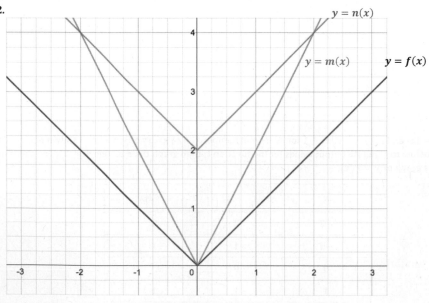

Lesson 18: Four Interesting Transformations of Functions

Student Outcomes

- Students examine that a horizontal translation of the graph of $y = f(x)$ corresponds to changing the equation from $y = f(x)$ to $y = f(x + k)$.

Lesson Notes

In Lesson 18, students examine horizontal translations (shifts) in the graph of a function and how they are represented in the equation of the function. Students will contrast the horizontal shift to the vertical shift covered in Lesson 17. They should be able to describe the transformations of the graph associated with the transformation of the function, as well as write the equation of a graph based on the translations (shifts) or vertical scalings (stretches) of another graph whose equation is known.

Classwork

Example 1 (8 minutes)

Students explore that a horizontal translation of the graph of $y = f(x)$ corresponds to changing the equation from $y = f(x)$ to $y = f(x + k)$ for given values of k. As an example of MP.3, consider asking students to make a conjecture about how they believe this placement of k will affect the graph.

Example 1

Let $f(x) = |x|$, $g(x) = f(x - 3)$, $h(x) = f(x + 2)$ where x can be any real number.

a. Write the formula for $g(x)$ in terms of $|x|$ (i.e., without using $f(x)$ notation):

$g(x) = |x - 3|$

b. Write the formula for $h(x)$ in terms of $|x|$ (i.e., without using $f(x)$ notation):

$h(x) = |x + 2|$

c. Complete the table of values for these functions.

x	$f(x) = |x|$	$g(x) = f(x - 3)$	$h(x) = f(x + 2)$
−3	3	6	1
−2	2	5	0
−1	1	4	1
0	0	3	2
1	1	2	3
2	2	1	4
3	3	3	5

---

d.   **Graph all three equations:** $y = f(x)$, $y = f(x - 3)$, **and** $y = f(x + 2)$.

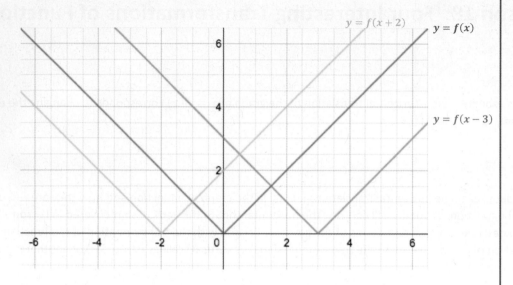

e.   **How does the graph of** $y = f(x)$ **relate to the graph of** $y = f(x - 3)$**?**

The graph of $f(x - 3)$ is the graph of $f(x)$ translated horizontally to the right 3 units.

f.   **How does the graph of** $y = f(x)$ **relate to the graph of** $y = f(x + 2)$**?**

The graph of $f(x + 2)$ is the graph of $f(x)$ translated horizontally to the left 2 units.

g.   **How does the graph of** $y = |x| - 3$ **and the graph of** $y = |x - 3|$ **relate differently to the graph of** $y = |x|$**?**

The graph of $y = |x| - 3$ translates the graph of $y = |x|$ down 3 units whereas the graph of $y = |x - 3|$ translates the graph of $y = |x|$ to the right 3 units.

h.   **How do the values of** g **and** h **relate to the values of** f**?**

The input value for g has to be 3 more than the input value for f to get the same output values. The input value for h has to be two more than the input value for f to get the same output values.

Discussion (5 minutes)

Students should finish Example 1 with the understanding that the graph of a function g found by subtracting a number k to the input of another function, as in $g(x) = f(x - k)$, is a translation of the graph of the function f horizontally by k units (positively or negatively, depending on the sign of k).

> *Scaffolding:*
>
> Gives guidance specific to this proportion of the lesson for addressing needs of diverse learners. The type of diverse learner should be specified (i.e., advanced learner, etc.)

- If we replace 3 by a number k in $g(x) = f(x - 3)$ as in Example 1 to get $g(x) = f(x - k)$, explain how to translate the graph of f to the graph of g in terms of k.

  ▫ *If $k > 0$, then the graph of f is translated to the right by $|k|$ units.*

  ▫ *If $k < 0$, then the graph of f is translated to the left by $|k|$ units.*

□   *In general, for any k, the graph of f is translated horizontally by k units (where $k > 0$ corresponds to a translation to the right and $k < 0$ corresponds to a translation to the left).*

- How does your answer for $k < 0$ make sense for $h(x) = f(x + 2)$?

    □   *We can rewrite $h(x) = f(x + 2)$ as $h(x) = f(x - (-2))$. Therefore, since $-2 < 0$, the graph of h should be the translation of the graph of f to the left by $|-2|$ units.*

- What concept from Grade 8 Geometry best describes the shifts of the graphs of the functions in Example 1?

    □   *Translation. In fact, we use the word "translate" to help you remember.*

- Students should be comfortable explaining the difference between the translations of the graphs $y = |x| + k$ and $y = |x + k|$.

- Students may confuse the direction of a horizontal translation since the equation may seem to indicate the "opposite" direction (i.e., $y = |x + 3|$ may be confused as a translation to the right because of the addition of 3 to x), especially since a vertical translation up is the transformation given by adding a positive number k to the function. Help students articulate why the horizontal translation behaves as it does.

- Consider the function $g(x) = |x - 3|$ and its graph from Example 1. There is a point $(x + 3, g(x + 3))$ on the graph of g. We have $g(x + 3) = f(x + 3 - 3) = f(x)$. Then the point $(x + 3, f(x))$ is on the graph of g. Since $(x, f(x))$ is on the graph of f and $(x + 3, f(x))$ is $(x, f(x))$ shifted 3 units to the right, we conclude that the graph of g is the graph of f translated 3 units to the right. A similar argument can be made for the graph of h.

Exercises 1–3 (15 minutes)

Have students discuss the following four exercises in pairs. Discuss the answers as a class.

Exercises 1–3

1.   Karla and Isamar are disagreeing over which way the graph of the function $g(x) = |x + 3|$ is translated relative to the graph of $f(x) = |x|$. Karla believes the graph of g is "to the right "of the graph of f, Isamar believes the graph is "to the left." Who is correct? Use the coordinates of the vertex of f and g and to support your explanation.

The graph of g is the graph of f translated to the left. The vertex of the graph of f is the point $(0, 0)$, whereas the vertex of the graph of g is the point $(-3, 0)$.

Note that in this lesson, students are working with translations of the function $f(x) = |x|$. This function was chosen because it is one of the easier functions to use in showing how translations behave—just follow what happens to the vertex. We know that $(0,0)$, or the vertex, is the point of the graph of f where the function's outputs change between decreasing and increasing. As a horizontal translation, the vertex of the graph of g will also have a y-coordinate of 0; in fact, the vertex is $(-3,0)$. Thus the graph of f is translated 3 units to the left to get the graph of g.

---

2.   Let $f(x) = |x|$ where x can be any real number. Write a formula for the function whose graph is the transformation of the graph of f given by the instructions below.

   a.   A translation right 5 units.

      $a(x) = |x - 5|$

   b.   A translation down 3 units.

      $b(x) = |x| - 3$

c.   **A vertical scaling (a vertical stretch) with scale factor of 5.**

$$c(x) = 5|x|$$

d.   **A translation left 4 units.**

$$d(x) = |x + 4|$$

e.   **A vertical scaling (a vertical shrink) with scale factor of $\frac{1}{3}$.**

$$e(x) = \frac{1}{3}|x|$$

3.   **Write the formula for the function depicted by the graph.**

a. $y = |x + 6|$

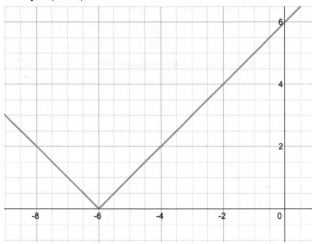

b. $y = -2|x|$

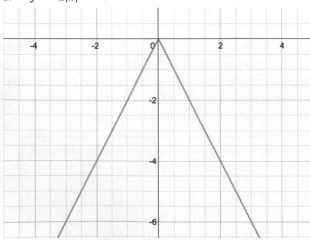

c. $y = \left| x - \dfrac{3}{2} \right|$

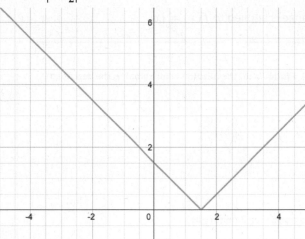

d. $y = |x| + 4$

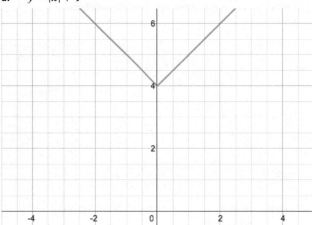

e. $y = \dfrac{1}{4}|x|$

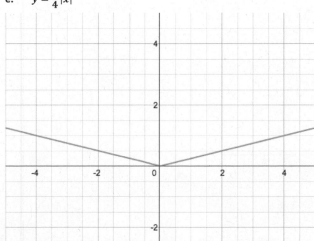

Exercises 4–5 (12 minutes)

Students now examine questions where more than one change is applied to $f(x) = |x|$.

Exercises 4–5

4. Let $f(x) = |x|$ where x can be any real number. Write a formula for the function whose graph is the described transformation of the graph of f.

    a. A translation 2 units left and 4 units down.

    $y = |x + 2| - 4$

    b. A translation 2.5 units right and 1 unit up.

    $y = |x - 2.5| + 1$

    c. A vertical scaling with scale factor $\frac{1}{2}$, and then a translation 3 units right.

    $y = \frac{1}{2}|x - 3|$

    d. A translation 5 units right and a vertical scaling by reflected across the x-axis with vertical scale factor -2.

    $y = -2|x - 5|$

5. Write the formula for the function depicted by the graph.

    a. $y = |x + 2| - 4$

    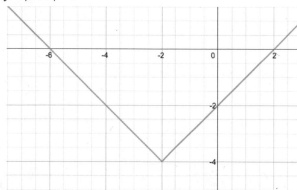

    b. $y = |x - 5| - 2$

    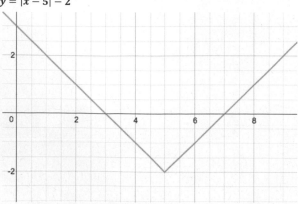

c. $y = -|x + 4|$

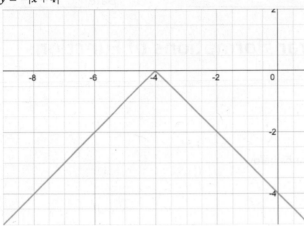

d. $y = |x - 3| + 3$

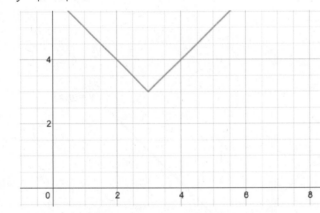

Closing (2 minutes)

- There is nothing special about using the function $f(x) = |x|$ as we did in this lesson. The effects of these transformations on the graph of a function hold true for all functions.

- How can the graph of $y = f(x)$ can be horizontally translated by positive or negative k?

- Draw a graph of a made-up function on the board, labeled by $y = f(x)$, and show how to translate it right or left by k units using the equation $y = f(x + k)$.

Exit Ticket (3 minutes)

Name _____   Date_____

Lesson 18: Four Interesting Transformations of Functions

Exit Ticket

Write the formula for the functions depicted by the graphs below:

    a. $f(x) =$ _____

    b. $g(x) =$ _____

    c. $h(x) =$ _____

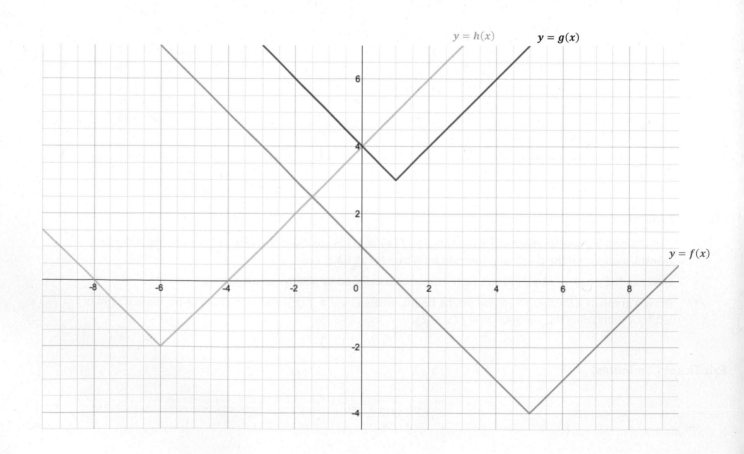

Exit Ticket Sample Solutions

Write the formula for the functions depicted by the graphs below:

a. $f(x) = |x - 5| - 4$

b. $g(x) = |x - 1| + 3$

c. $h(x) = |x + 6| - 2$

Problem Set Sample Solutions

1. Working with quadratic functions.

    a. The vertex of the quadratic function $f(x) = x^2$ is at $(0, 0)$, which is the minimum for the graph of f. Based on your work in this lessons, to where do you predict the vertex will be translated for the graphs of $g(x) = (x - 2)^2$ and $h(x) = (x + 3)^2$?

    The vertex of g will be at $(2, 0)$; The vertex of h will be at $(-3, 0)$.

    b. Complete the table of values and then graph all three functions.

x	$f(x) = x^2$	$g(x) = (x - 2)^2$	$h(x) = (x + 3)^2$
-3	3	25	0
-2	2	16	1
-1	1	9	4
0	0	4	9
1	1	1	16
2	2	0	25
3	3	1	36

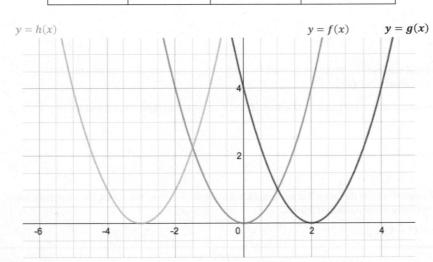

2. Let $f(x) = |x - 4|$ for every real number x. The graph of the equation $y = f(x)$ is provided on the Cartesian plane below. Transformations of the graph of $y = f(x)$ are described below. After each description, write the equation for the transformed graph. Then, sketch the graph of the equation you write for part (d).

   a. Translate the graph left 6 units and down 2 units.

   $$y = |x + 6| - 2 \ \ or \ \ y = f(x + 6) - 2$$

   b. Reflect the resulting graph from part (a) across the x-axis.

   $$y = -|x + 6| + 2 \ \ or \ \ y = -(f(x + 6) - 2)$$

   c. Scale the resulting graph from part (b) vertically by a scale factor of $\frac{1}{2}$.

   $$y = -\frac{1}{2}|x + 6| + 1 \ \ or \ \ y = -\frac{1}{2}(f(x + 6) - 2)$$

   d. Translate the resulting graph from part (c) right 3 units and up 2 units. Graph the resulting equation.

   $$y = -\frac{1}{2}|x + 3| + 3 \ \ or \ \ y = -\frac{1}{2}(f(x + 3) - 2) + 2$$

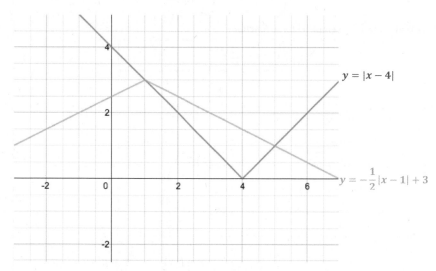

3. Let $f(x) = |x|$ for all real numbers x. Write the formula for the function represented by the described transformation of the graph of $y = f(x)$.

   a. First, a vertical stretch with scale factor $\frac{1}{3}$ is performed, then a translation right 3 units, and finally a translation down 1 unit.

   $$a(x) = \frac{1}{3}|x - 3| - 1$$

   b. First, a vertical stretch with scale factor 3 is performed, then a reflection over the x-axis, then a translation left 4 units, and finally a translation up 5 units.

   $$b(x) = -3|x + 4| + 5$$

    c. First, a reflection across the x-axis is performed, then a translation left 4 units, then a translation up 5 units, and finally a vertical stretch with scale factor 3.

$$c(x) = -3|x + 4| + 15$$

    d. Compare your answers to parts (b) and (c). Why are they different?

In part (c), the vertical stretch happens at the end, which means the graph resulting from the first three transformations is what is vertically stretched: $c(x) = 3(-|x + 4| + 5)$.

4. Write the formula for the function depicted by each graph.

    a. $a(x) = \frac{1}{2}|x - 1| - 3$

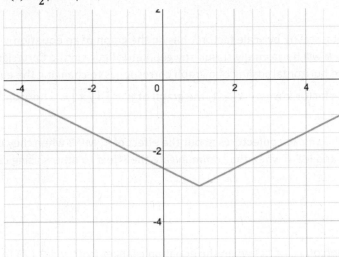

    b. $b(x) = -2|x + 3| + 4$

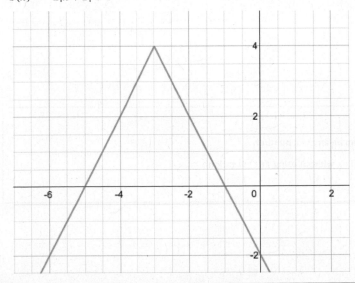

Lesson 19: Four Interesting Transformations of Functions

Student Outcomes

- Students examine that a horizontal scaling with scale factor k of the graph of $y = f(x)$ corresponds to changing the equation from $y = f(x)$ to $y = f\left(\frac{1}{k}x\right)$.

Lesson Notes

In this lesson, students study the effect a horizontal scaling by scale factor k has on the graph of an equation $y = f(x)$. For example, if $0 < k < 1$, a horizontal scaling by k will horizontally shrink any geometric figure in the Cartesian plane, including figures that are graphs of functions. The horizontal scaling of a graph corresponds to changing the equation from $y = f(x)$ to $y = f\left(\frac{1}{k}x\right)$. For values of scale factor k where $k > 1$, the graph of $y = f\left(\frac{1}{k}x\right)$ is a horizontal stretch of the graph of $y = f(x)$ by a factor of k.

In this lesson, students may employ MP.3 when they make conjectures about the effect of k, MP.8 when they use repeated reasoning to determine the effect of k, and MP.6 when the communicate the effect to others using careful language.

Classwork

Students explore the horizontal scaling of the graph of $y = f(x)$ when the equation changes from $y = f(x)$ to $y = f\left(\frac{1}{k}x\right)$ for $0 < k < 1$. In this case, students see the graph of f is a horizontal "shrink" by k. In Example 1, the scale factor for g is $k = \frac{1}{2}$, or $g(x) = f\left(\frac{1}{\frac{1}{2}}\right)x$, or $g(x) = f(2x)$.

Example 1 (8 minutes)

Example 1

Let $f(x) = x^2$ and $g(x) = f(2x)$, where x can be any real number.

a. Write the formula for g in terms of x^2 (i.e., without using $f(x)$ notation):

$$g(x) = (2x)^2$$

b.   Complete the table of values for these functions.

x	$f(x) = x^2$	$g(x) = f(2x)$
−3	9	36
−2	4	16
−1	1	4
0	0	0
1	1	4
2	4	16
3	9	36

c.   Graph both equations: $y = f(x)$ and $y = f(2x)$.

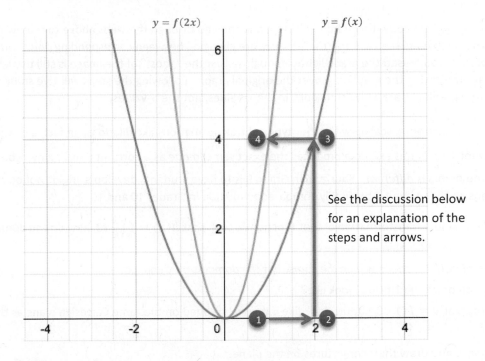

$y = f(2x)$ $y = f(x)$

See the discussion below for an explanation of the steps and arrows.

d.   How does the graph of $y = g(x)$ relate to the graph of $y = f(x)$?

The corresponding x-value of $y = g(x)$ is half of the corresponding x-value of $y = f(x)$ when $g(x) = f(x)$, the points of the graph of g are ½ the distance to the y-axis as the corresponding points of the graph of f, which makes the graph of g appear to "shrink horizontally."

e.   How are the values of f related to the values of g?

For equal outputs of f and g, the input of g only has to be half as big as the input of f.

Discussion (5 minutes)

- A horizontal scaling of a graph with scale factor $\frac{1}{2}$ will "shrink" the original graph $y = f(x)$ horizontally by $\frac{1}{2}$ and correspond to the graph of the equation $y = f\left(\frac{1}{\frac{1}{2}}x\right)$ or $y = f(2x)$, i.e., the horizontal scaling of the graph of $y = f(x)$ with scale factor $k > 0$ is the graph of the equation $y = f\left(\frac{1}{k}x\right)$.

- In Example 1, what process could be used to find the value of $g(x)$ for any given number x, using only the graph of $y = f(x)$ (not the formula for $f(x)$)?

   □ *Step 1: Find x on the x-axis.*

   □ *Step 2: Multiply x by 2 to find the number $2x$ on the x-axis.*

   □ *Step 3: Find the value of f at $2x$.*

   □ *Step 4: Move parallel to the x-axis from the point found in Step 3 until directly over/under/on x. That point is $(x, g(x))$. [These steps are numbered and illustrated in the graph above for $x = 1$.]*

Lightly erase the graph of $y = g(x)$ (already drawn from part (c)), and then go through the steps above to redraw it, picking out a few points to help students see that *only* the y-values are changing between corresponding points on the graph of f and the graph of g. If you erased the graph lightly enough so that the "ghost" of the image is still there, students will see that you are redrawing the graph of g over the original graph. Following the steps will give students a sense of how the points of the graph of f are only "shrinking" in the x-values, not the y-values.

Many students might confuse a horizontal scaling with other types of transformations like dilations. In fact, a dilation with scale factor $\frac{1}{4}$ of the graph of f in this example produces the exact same *image* as a horizontal scaling by $\frac{1}{2}$, but the correspondence between the points is *different*. Your goal in Grade 9 is to have students develop a "rigid" notion of what a vertical scaling means so that it can be profitably compared to dilation in Grades 10 and 11.

- Consider a function f, and a transformation of that function h, such that $h(x) = f\left(\frac{1}{k}x\right)$, how do the domain and range of f relate to the domain and range of h?

   □ *The range of both functions will be the same, but the domains may change.*

- What might the graph of $y = f(1,000x)$ look like?

- What might the graph of $y = f(1,000,000x)$ look like if it were graphed on the same Cartesian plane as the graphs of f and g?

Let students go up to the board and draw their conjectures on the plane.

Discussion (5 minutes)

Students explore the horizontal scaling of the graph of $y = f(x)$ when the equation changes from $y = f(x)$ to $y = f\left(\frac{1}{k}x\right)$ for $k > 1$. In this case, students see that the graph of f is horizontally "stretched" by a factor of k. In Example 2, the scale factor for g is $k = 2$, or $g(x) = f\left(\frac{1}{2}x\right)$.

Example 2 (8 minutes)

Example 2

Let $f(x) = x^2$ and $h(x) = f\left(\frac{1}{2}x\right)$, where x can be any real number.

a.   Rewrite the formula for h in terms of x^2 (i.e., without using $f(x)$ notation):

$$h(x) = \left(\frac{1}{2}x\right)^2$$

b.   Complete the table of values for these functions.

x	$f(x) = x^2$	$h(x) = f\left(\frac{1}{2}x\right)$
-3	9	2.25
-2	4	1
-1	1	0.25
0	0	0
1	1	0.25
2	4	1
3	9	2.25

c.   Graph both equations: $y = f(x)$ and $y = f\left(\frac{1}{2}x\right)$.

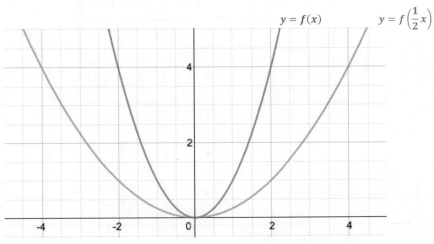

---

d. How does the graph of $y = f(x)$ relate to the graph of $y = h(x)$?

Since the corresponding x-value of $y = h(x)$ is twice the corresponding x-value of $y = f(x)$ when $g(x) = f(x)$, the points of the graph of g are 2 times the distance to the y-axis as the corresponding points of the graph of f, which makes the graph of g appear to "stretch horizontally."

e. How are the values of f related to the values of h?

To get equal outputs of each function, the input of h has to be twice the input of f.

A horizontal scale of a graph with scale factor 2 will "stretch" the original graph $y = f(x)$ horizontally by 2 and correspond to the graph of the equation $y = f\left(\frac{1}{2}x\right)$, i.e., the horizontal scale of the graph of $y = f(x)$ with scale factor $k > 0$ is once again the graph of the equation $y = f\left(\frac{1}{k}x\right)$. Follow the steps given in Discussion 1 to show students how to find the value $h(x)$ on the Cartesian plane *using only the graph of f* (not the formula for f). Emphasize that only the y-values are being scaled. When comparing $y = f(x)$ to $y = f\left(\frac{1}{k}x\right)$, the range of both functions will be the same, but the domains may change. Ask students what the graph of f might look like after a horizontal scale with scale factor $k = 10000$. Let them draw their conjecture on the graph on the board. Then ask them what the equation of the resulting graph is.

Exercise 1 (6 minutes)

Have students discuss the following exercise in pairs. Discuss the answer as a class.

Exercise 1

Complete the table of values for the given functions.

a.

x	$f(x) = 2^x$	$g(x) = 2^{(2x)}$	$h(x) = 2^{(-x)}$
-2	$\dfrac{1}{4}$	$\dfrac{1}{16}$	4
-1	$\dfrac{1}{2}$	$\dfrac{1}{4}$	2
0	1	1	1
1	2	4	$\dfrac{1}{2}$
2	4	16	$\dfrac{1}{4}$

b. Label each of the graphs with the appropriate functions from the table.

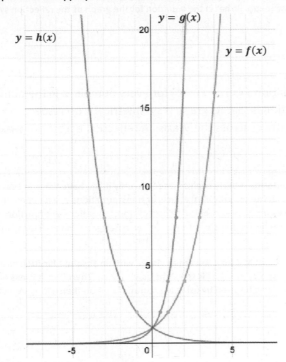

c. Describe the transformation that takes the graph of $y = f(x)$ to the graph of $y = g(x)$.

The graph of $y = g(x)$ is a horizontal scale with scale factor $\frac{1}{2}$ of the graph of $y = f(x)$.

d. Consider $y = f(x)$ and $y = h(x)$. What does negating the input do to the graph of f?

The graph of h is a reflection over the y-axis of the graph of f.

e. Write the formula of an exponential function whose graph would be a horizontal stretch relative to the graph of g.

Answers will vary. Example: $y = 2^{(0.5x)}$.

Example 3 (6 minutes)

Example 3

a. Look at the graph of $y = f(x)$ for the function $f(x) = x^2$ in Example 1 again. Would we see a difference in the graph of $y = g(x)$ if -2 was used as the scale factor instead of 2? If so, describe the difference. If not, explain why not.

There would be no difference. The function involves squaring the value within the parentheses, so the graph of $y = f(2x)$ and the graph of $y = f(-2x)$ both will be the same set as the graph of $y = g(x)$, but both correspond to different transformations: The first is a horizontal scaling with scale factor $\frac{1}{2}$, and the second is a horizontal scaling with scale factor $\frac{1}{2}$ and a reflection across the y-axis.

Lesson 19: Four Interesting Transformations of Functions
Date: 9/12/13

b.   A reflection across the y-axis takes the graph of $y = f(x)$ for the function $f(x) = x^2$ back to itself. Such a transformation is called a *reflection symmetry*. What is the equation for the graph of the reflection symmetry of the graph of $y = f(x)$?

$y = f(-x)$.

Tell students that if a function satisfies the equation $f(x) = f(-x)$ for every number x in the domain of f, it is called an *even function*. A consequence of an even function is that its graph is symmetrical with respect to the y-axis. Furthermore, the graph of $f(x) = x^2$ is symmetrical across the y-axis. A reflection across the y-axis does not change the graph.

c.   Deriving the answer to the following question is fairly sophisticated; do only if you have time: In Lessons 17 and 18, we used the function $f(x) = |x|$ to examine the graphical effects of transformations of a function. Here in Lesson 19, we use the function $f(x) = x^2$ to examine the graphical effects of transformations of a function. Based on the observations you made while graphing, why would using $f(x) = x^2$ be a better option than using the function $f(x) = |x|$?

Not all of the effects of multiplying the input of a function are as visible with an absolute function as it is with a quadratic function. For example, the graph of $y = 2|x|$ is the same as $y = |2x|$. Therefore, it is easier to see the effect of multiplying a value to the input of a function by using a quadratic function than it is by using the absolute value function.

Closing (2 minutes)

Discuss how the horizontal scaling by a scale factor of k of the graph of a function $y = f(x)$ corresponds to changing the equation of the graph from $y = f(x)$ to $y = f\left(\frac{1}{k}x\right)$. Investigate the four cases of k:

1. $k > 1$
2. $0 < k < 1$
3. $-1 < k < 0$
4. $k < -1$

Exit Ticket (5 minutes)

Name _____ Date_____

Lesson 19: Four Interesting Transformations of Functions

Exit Ticket

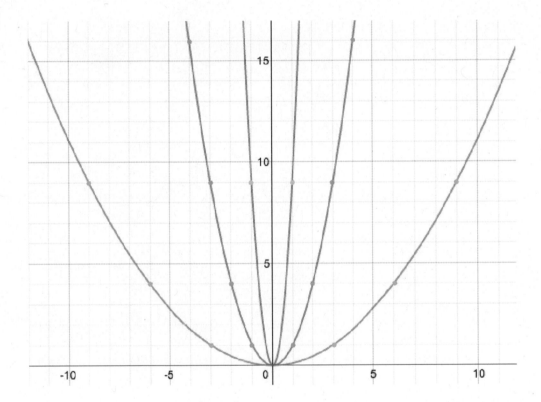

Let $f(x) = x^2$, $g(x) = (3x)^2$, and $h(x) = \left(\frac{1}{3}x\right)^2$, where x can be any real number. The graphs above are of $y = f(x)$, $y = g(x)$, and $y = h(x)$.

1. Label each graph with the appropriate equation.

2. Describe the transformation that takes the graph of $y = f(x)$ to the graph of $y = g(x)$. Use coordinates of each to illustrate an example of the correspondence.

3. Describe the transformation that takes the graph of $y = f(x)$ to the graph of $y = h(x)$. Use coordinates to illustrate an example of the correspondence.

Exit Ticket Sample Solutions

Let $f(x) = x^2$, $g(x) = (3x)^2$, and $h(x) = \left(\frac{1}{3}x\right)^2$, where x can be any real number. The graphs above are of $y = f(x)$, $y = g(x)$, and $y = h(x)$.

1. Label each graph with the appropriate equation.

   See graph.

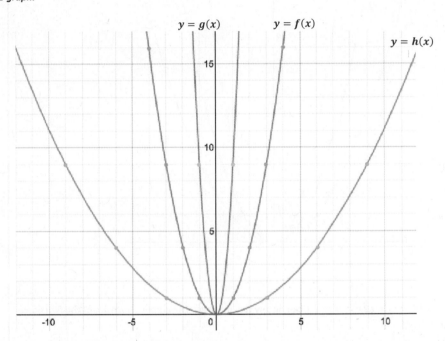

2. Describe the transformation that takes the graph of $y = f(x)$ to the graph of $y = g(x)$. Use coordinates of each to illustrate an example of the correspondence.

   The graph of $y = g(x)$ is a horizontal shrink of the graph of $y = f(x)$ with scale factor $\frac{1}{3}$. *The corresponding x-value of $y = g(x)$ is one-third of the corresponding x-value of $y = f(x)$ when $g(x) = f(x)$.* This can be illustrated with the coordinate $(1, 9)$ on $g(x)$ and the coordinate $(3, 9)$ on $f(x)$.

3. Describe the transformation that takes the graph of $y = f(x)$ to the graph of $y = h(x)$. Use coordinates to illustrate an example of the correspondence.

   The graph of $h(x)$ is a horizontal stretch of the graph of $f(x)$ with scale factor 3. *The corresponding x-value of $y = h(x)$ is three times the corresponding x-value of $y = f(x)$ when $h(x) = f(x)$.* This can be illustrated with the coordinate $(1, 1)$ on $f(x)$ and the coordinate $(3, 1)$ on $h(x)$.

Problem Set Sample Solutions

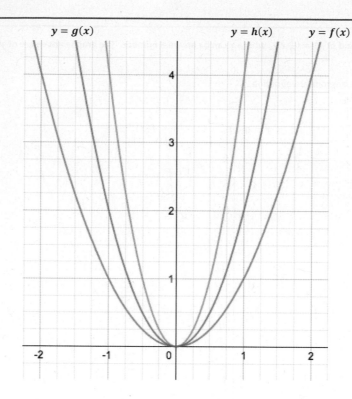

Let $f(x) = x^2$, $g(x) = 2x^2$, and $h(x) = (2x)^2$, where x can be any real number. The graphs above are of the functions $y = f(x)$, $y = g(x)$, and $y = h(x)$.

1. Label each graph with the appropriate equation.

    See graph.

2. Describe the transformation that takes the graph of $y = f(x)$ to the graph of $y = g(x)$. Use coordinates to illustrate an example of the correspondence.

    The graph of $y = g(x)$ is a vertical stretch of the graph of $y = f(x)$ by scale factor 2; for a given x-value, the value of $g(x)$ is twice as much as the value of $f(x)$.

    OR:

    The graph of $y = g(x)$ is a horizontal shrink of the graph of $y = f(x)$ by scale factor $\frac{1}{\sqrt{2}}$; it takes $\frac{1}{\sqrt{2}}$ times the input for $y = g(x)$ as compared to $y = f(x)$ to yield the same output.

3. Describe the transformation that takes the graph of $y = f(x)$ to the graph of $y = h(x)$. Use coordinates to illustrate an example of the correspondence.

    The graph of $y = h(x)$ is a horizontal shrink of the graph of $y = f(x)$ by a scale factor of ½; It takes $\frac{1}{2}$ the input for $y = h(x)$ as compared to $y = f(x)$ to yield the same output.

    OR:

    The graph of $y = h(x)$ is a vertical stretch of the graph of $y = f(x)$ by scale factor 4; for a given x-value, the value of $h(x)$ is four times as much as the value of $f(x)$.

Lesson 20: Four Interesting Transformations of Functions

Student Outcomes

- Students apply their understanding of transformations of functions and their graphs to piecewise functions.

Lesson Notes

In Lessons 17–19 students study translations and scalings of functions and their graphs. In Lesson 20, these transformations are applied in combination to piecewise functions. Students should become comfortable visualizing how the graph of a transformed piecewise function will relate to the graph of the original piecewise function.

Classwork

Opening Exercise (6 minutes)

Have students work individually or in pairs to complete the opening exercise. This exercise highlights MP.7 since it calls on students to interpret the meaning of k in the context of a graph.

Opening Exercise

Fill in the blanks of the table with the appropriate heading or descriptive information.

Graph of $y = f(x)$		Vertical			Horizontal	
Translate	$y = f(x) + k$	$k > 0$	Translate up by $|k|$ units	$y = f(x - k)$	$k > 0$	Translate right by $|k|$ units
		$k < 0$	Translate down by $|k|$ units		$k < 0$	*Translate left by $|k|$ units*
Scale by scale factor k	$y = kf(x)$	$k > 1$	*Vertical stretch by a factor of $|k|$*	$y = f\left(\frac{1}{k}x\right)$	$k > 1$	Horizontal stretch by a factor of $|k|$
		$0 < k < 1$	Vertical shrink by a factor of $|k|$		$0 < k < 1$	*Horizontal shrink by a factor of $|k|$*
		$-1 < k < 0$	Vertical shrink by a factor of $|k|$ and reflection over x-axis		$-1 < k < 0$	Horizontal shrink by a factor of $|k|$ and reflection across y-axis
		$k < -1$	*Vertical stretch by a factor of $|k|$ and reflection over x-axis*		$k < -1$	Horizontal stretch by a factor of $|k|$ and reflection over y-axis

---

In Lesson 15, we discovered how the absolute value function can be written as a piecewise function. Example 1 and the associated exercises are intended to help students reexamine how piecewise functions behave.

Example 1 (3 minutes)

Example 1

A transformation of the absolute value function, $f(x) = |x - 3|$, is rewritten here as a piecewise function. Describe in words how to graph this piecewise function.

$$f(x) = \begin{cases} -x + 3, & x < 3 \\ x - 3, & x \geq 3 \end{cases}$$

First, I would graph the line $y = -x + 3$ for x-values less than 3 and then I would graph the line $y = x - 3$ for x-values greater than or equal to 3.

Exercises 1–2 (15 minutes)

Exercises 1–2

1. Describe how to graph the following piecewise function. Then graph $y = f(x)$ below.

$$f(x) = \begin{cases} -3x - 3, & x \leq -2 \\ 0.5x + 4, & -2 < x < 2 \\ -2x + 9, & x \geq 2 \end{cases}$$

The function f can be graphed of as the line $y = -3x - 3$ for x-values less than or equal to -2, the graph of the line $y = 0.5x + 4$ for and for x-values greater than -2 and less than 2, and the graph of the line $y = -2x + 9$ for x-values greater than or equal to 2.

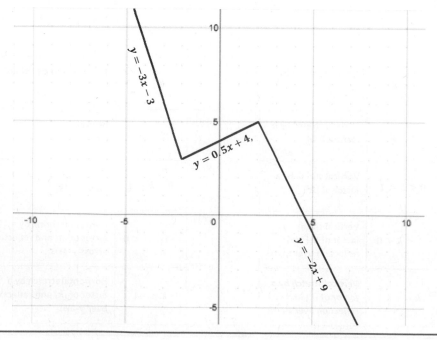

2.   Using the graph of f below, write a formula for f as a piecewise function.

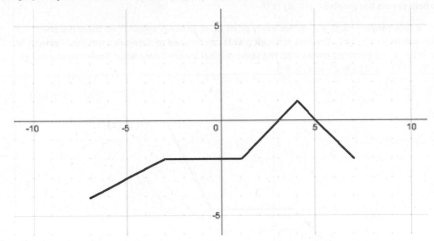

$$f(x) = \begin{cases} 0.5x - 0.5, & -7 \le x \le -3 \\ -2, & -3 < x < 1 \\ x - 3, & 1 \le x \le 4 \\ 5 - x, & 4 < x \le 7 \end{cases}$$

Or

$$f(x) = \begin{cases} 0.5x - 0.5, & -7 \le x \le -3 \\ -2, & -3 < x < 1 \\ -|x - 4| + 1, & 1 \le x \le 7 \end{cases}$$

Example 2 (10 minutes)

Students translate and scale the graph of a piecewise function.

Example 2

The graph $y = f(x)$ of a piecewise function f is shown. The domain of f is $-5 \le x \le 5$, and the range is $-1 \le y \le 3$.

a.   Mark and identify four strategic points helpful in sketching the graph of $y = f(x)$.

$(-5, -1), (-1, 1), (3, 1),$ *and* $(5, 3)$

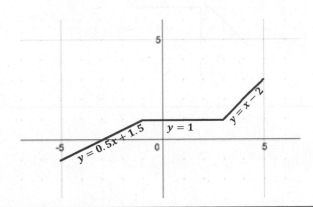

b.   Sketch the graph of $y = 2f(x)$ and state the domain and range of the transformed function. How can you use part (a) to help sketch the graph of $y = 2f(x)$?

Domain: $-5 \leq x \leq 5$, range: $-2 \leq y \leq 6$. For every point (x, y) in the graph of $f(x)$, there is a point $(x, 2y)$ on the graph of $y = 2f(x)$. The four strategic points can be used to determine the line segments in the graph of $y = 2f(x)$ by graphing points with the same original x-coordinate and 2 times the original y-coordinate $((-5, -2), (-1, 2), (3, 2),$ and $(5, 6))$.

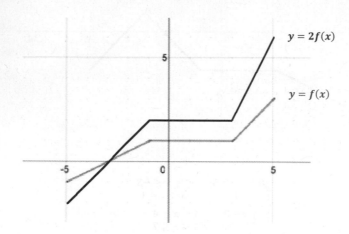

c.   A horizontal scaling with scale factor $\dfrac{1}{2}$ of the graph of $y = f(x)$ is the graph of $y = f(2x)$. Sketch the graph of $y = f(2x)$ and state the domain and range. How can you use the points identified in part (a) to help sketch $y = f(2x)$?

Domain: $-2.5 \leq x \leq 2.5$, range: $-1 \leq y \leq 3$. For every point (x, y) in the graph of $f(x)$, there is a point $(\frac{x}{2}, y)$ on the graph of $y = f(2x)$. The four strategic points can be used to determine the line segments in the graph of $y = f(2x)$ by graphing points with one-half the original x-coordinate and the original y-coordinate $((-2.5, -1), (-0.5, 1), (1.5, 1),$ and $(2.5, 3))$.

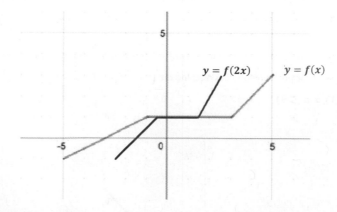

Exercises 3–4 (5 minutes)

Exercises 3–4

3. How does the range of f in Example 2 compare to the range of a transformed function g, where $g(x) = kf(x)$, when $k > 1$?

    For every point (x, y) in the graph of $y = f(x)$, there is a point (x, ky) in the graph of $y = kf(x)$, where the number ky is a multiple of each y. For values of $k > 1$, $y = kf(x)$ is a vertical scaling that appears to stretch the graph of $y = f(x)$. The original range, $-1 \le y \le 3$ for $y = f(x)$ becomes $-1k \le y \le 3k$ for the function $y = kf(x)$.

4. How does the domain of f in Example 2 compare to the domain of a transformed function g, where $g(x) = f\left(\frac{1}{k}x\right)$, when $0 < k < 1$? (Hint: How does a graph shrink when it is horizontally scaled by a factor k?)

    For every point (x, y) in the graph of $y = f(x)$, there is a point (kx, y) in the graph of $y = f\left(\frac{1}{k}x\right)$. For values of $0 < k < 1$, $y = f\left(\frac{1}{k}x\right)$ is a horizontal scaling by a factor k that appears to shrink the graph of $y = f(x)$. This means the original domain, $-5 \le x \le 5$ for $y = f(x)$ becomes $-5k \le x \le 5k$ for the function $y = f\left(\frac{1}{k}x\right)$.

Closing (2 minutes)

- The transformations that translate and scale familiar functions, like the absolute value function, also apply to piecewise functions and to any function in general.

- By focusing on strategic points in the graph of a piecewise function, we can translate and scale the entire graph of the function by manipulating the coordinates of those few points.

Exit Ticket (4 minutes)

Name _____   Date_____

Lesson 20: Four Interesting Transformations of Functions

Exit Ticket

The graph of a piecewise function f is shown below.

Let $p(x) = f(x - 2)$, $q(x) = \frac{1}{2}f(x - 2)$, and $r(x) = \frac{1}{2}f(x - 2) + 3$.

Graph $y = p(x)$, $y = q(x)$, and $y = r(x)$ on the same set of axes as the graph of $y = f(x)$.

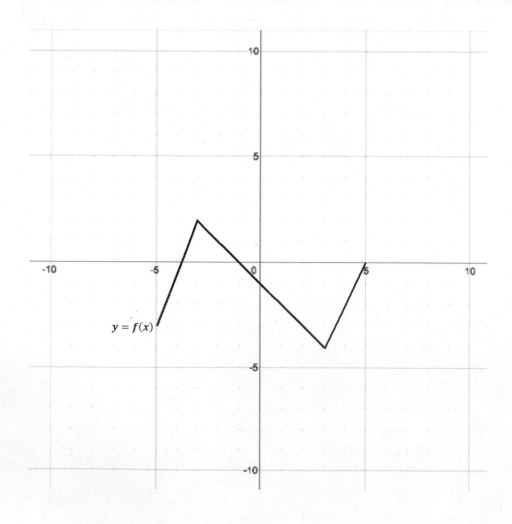

Exit Ticket Sample Solutions

The graph of a piecewise function f is shown below.

Let $p(x) = f(x-2)$, $q(x) = \frac{1}{2}f(x-2)$, and $r(x) = \frac{1}{2}f(x-2) + 3$.

Graph $y = p(x)$, $y = q(x)$, and $y = r(x)$ on the same set of axes as the graph of $y = f(x)$.

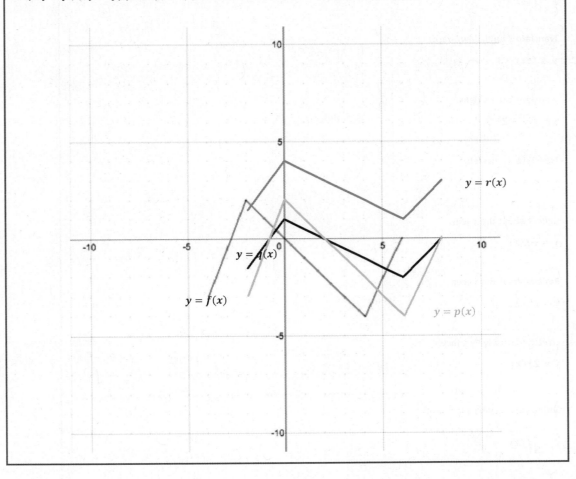

Problem Set Sample Solutions

1. Suppose the graph of f is given. Write an equation for each of the following graphs after the graph of f has been transformed as described.

   a. Translate 5 units upward.

   $$y = f(x) + 5$$

   b. Translate 3 units downward.

   $$y = f(x) - 3$$

   c. Translate 2 units right.

   $$y = f(x - 2)$$

   d. Translate 4 units left.

   $$y = f(x + 4)$$

   e. Reflect about the x-axis.

   $$y = -f(x)$$

   f. Reflect about the y-axis.

   $$y = f(-x)$$

   g. Stretch vertically by a factor of 2.

   $$y = 2f(x)$$

   h. Shrink vertically by a factor of $\frac{1}{3}$.

   $$y = \frac{1}{3}f(x)$$

   i. Shrink horizontally by a factor of $\frac{1}{3}$.

   $$y = f(3x)$$

   j. Stretch horizontally by a factor of 2.

   $$y = f\left(\frac{1}{2}x\right)$$

2. Explain how the graphs of the equations below are related to the graph of $y = f(x)$.

   a. $y = 5f(x)$

   The graph is a vertical stretch of $y = f(x)$ by a factor of 5.

b. $y = f(x - 4)$

The graph of $y = f(x)$ is translated right 4 units.

c. $y = -2f(x)$

The graph is a vertical stretch of $y = f(x)$ by a factor of 2 and reflected about the x-axis.

d. $y = f(3x)$

The graph is a horizontal shrink of $y = f(x)$ by a factor of $\frac{1}{3}$.

e. $y = 2f(x) - 5$

The graph is a vertical stretch of $y = f(x)$ by a factor of 2 and translated down 5 units.

3. The graph of the equation $y = f(x)$ is provided below. For each of the following transformations of the graph, write a formula (in terms of f) for the function that is represented by the transformation of the graph of $y = f(x)$. Then draw the transformed graph of the function on the same set of axes as the graph of $y = f(x)$.

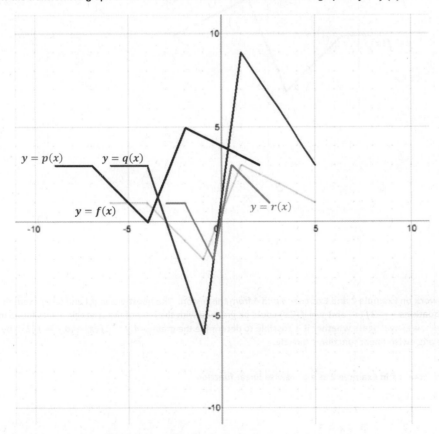

a.   A translation 3 units left and 2 units up.

$p(x) = f(x + 3) + 2$

b. A vertical stretch by a scale factor of 3.

$$q(x) = 3f(x)$$

c. A horizontal shrink by a scale factor of $\frac{1}{2}$.

$$r(x) = f(2x)$$

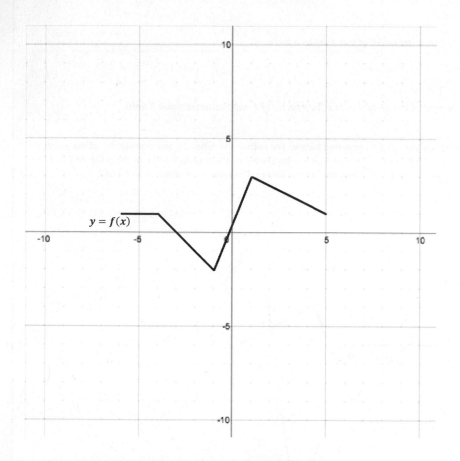

4. Reexamine your work on Example 2 and Exercises 3 and 4 from this lesson. The questions in (b) and (c) of Example 2 asked how the equations $y = 2f(x)$ and $y = f(2x)$ could be graphed with the help of the strategic points found in (a). In this problem, we investigate whether it is possible to determine the graphs of $y = 2f(x)$ and $y = f(2x)$ by working with the piecewise-linear function f directly.

a. Write the function f in Example 2 as a piecewise-linear function.

$$f(x) = \begin{cases} 0.5x + 1.5, & -5 \le x \le -1 \\ 1, & -1 < x < 3 \\ x - 2, & 3 \le x \le 5 \end{cases}$$

b.   Let $g(x) = 2f(x)$. Use the graph you sketched in Example 2(b) of $y = 2f(x)$ to write the formula for the function g as a piecewise-linear function.

$$g(x) = \begin{cases} x + 3, & -5 \leq x \leq -1 \\ 2, & -1 < x < 3 \\ 2x - 4, & 3 \leq x \leq 5 \end{cases}$$

c.   Let $h(x) = f(2x)$. Use the graph you sketched in Example 2© of $y = f(2x)$ to write the formula for the function h as a piecewise-linear function.

$$h(x) = \begin{cases} x + 1.5, & -2.5 \leq x \leq -0.5 \\ 1, & -0.5 < x < 1.5 \\ 2x - 2, & 1.5 \leq x \leq 2.5 \end{cases}$$

d.   Compare the piecewise linear functions g and h to the piecewise linear function f. Did the expressions defining each piece change? If so, how? Did the domains of each piece change? If so how?

Function g: Each piece of the formula for g is 2 times the corresponding piece of the formula for f. The domains are the same.

Function h: Each piece of the formula for h is found by substituting 2x in for x in the corresponding piece of the formula for f. The length of each interval in the domain of h is ½ the length of the corresponding interval in the domain of f.

Topic D:

Using Functions and Graphs to Solve Problems

A-CED.A.1, A-SSE.B.3c, F-IF.B.4, F-IF.B.6, F-IF.C.9, F-BF.A.1a, F-LE.A.2, F-LE.B.5

Focus Standard:	A-CED.A.1	Create equations and inequalities in one variable and use them to solve problems. *Include equations arising from linear and quadratic functions, and simple rational and exponential functions.*[★]
	A-SSE.B.3c	Choose and produce an equivalent form of an expression to reveal and explain properties of the quantity represented by the expression.[★]
		c. Use the properties of exponents to transform expressions for exponential functions. *For example the expression 1.15^2 can be rewritten as $\left(1.15^{1/12}\right)^{12t} \approx 1.012^{12t}$ to reveal the approximate equivalent monthly interest rate if the annual rate is 15%.*
	F-FI.B.4	For a function that models a relationship between two quantities, interpret key features of graphs and tables in terms of the quantities, and sketch graphs showing key features given a verbal description of the relationship. *Key features include: intercepts; intervals where the function is increasing, decreasing, positive, or negative; relative maximums and minimums; symmetries; end behavior; and periodicity.*[★]
	F-IF.B.6	Calculate and interpret the average rate of change of a function (presented symbolically or as a table) over a specified interval. Estimate the rate of change from a graph.[★]
	F-IF.C.9	Compare properties of two functions each represented in a different way (algebraically, graphically, numerically in tables, or by verbal descriptions). *For example, given a graph of one quadratic function and an algebraic expression for another, say which has the larger maximum.*
	F-BF.A.1a	Write a function that describes a relationship between two quantities.[★]
		a. Determine an explicit expression, a recursive process, or steps for calculation from a context.

	F-LE.A.2	Construct linear and exponential functions, including arithmetic and geometric sequences, given a graph, a description of a relationship, or two input-output pairs (include reading these from a table).★
	F-LE.B.5	Interpret the parameters in a linear or exponential function in terms of a context.★
Instructional Days:	4	
Lesson 21:	Comparing Linear and Exponential Models Again	
Lesson 22:	Modeling an Invasive Species Population	
Lesson 23:	Newton's Law of Cooling	
Lesson 24:	Piecewise and Step Functions in Context	

In Topic D, students explore application of functions in real world context and use exponential, linear and/or piecewise functions and their associated graphs to model the situations. The contexts include the population of an invasive species, applications of Newton's Law of Cooling, and long-term parking rates at the Albany International Airport. Students are given tabular data and/or verbal descriptions of a situation and create equations and/or scatterplots of the data. They use continuous curves fit to population data to estimate average rate of change and make predictions about future population sizes. They write functions to model temperature over time, graph the functions they have written, and use the graphs to answer questions within the context of the problem. They recognize when one function is a transformation of another within a context involving cooling substances.

Lesson 21: Comparing Linear and Exponential Functions Again

Student Outcomes

- Students create models and understand the differences between linear and exponential models that are represented in different ways.

Lesson Notes

Students have spent several lessons in this module studying linear and exponential functions. This lesson has students compare and contrast the two functions to solidify their understanding of each. Students then learn how to differentiate between the two functions by recognizing a constant rate of change or a common quotient in data tables, or by recognizing the features in their graphs or formulas.

Classwork

Opening Exercise (10 minutes)

This table format will allow students to compare linear and exponential models in several ways. This exercise reminds students what linear and exponential models are and allows them to easily see the difference between them. You can either give students the example or have them write their own for each model. Once students have finished, have them discuss their work in pairs or in groups. Tie this together with a class discussion, paying particular attention to the different wording students use and the real-world examples that they give. In a way similar to the prior lesson, students will use MP.7 to identify the meaning of structural components of each function type.

Opening Exercise		
	Linear Model	**Exponential Model**
General Form	$f(x) = ax + b$	$f(x) = a(b^x)$
Meaning of parameters a and b	a is the slope of the line, or the constant rate of change, b is the y-intercept, or the $f(x)$ value at $x = 0$.	a is the y-intercept, or the $f(x)$ value when $x = 0$, b is the base, or the constant quotient of change.
Example	$f(x) = 2x + 3$	$f(x) = 3(2^x)$
Rule for finding $f(x + 1)$ from $f(x)$	Starting at $(0, 3)$, to find $f(x + 1)$, add 2 to $f(x)$.	Starting at $(0, 3)$, to find $f(x + 1)$, multiply $f(x)$ by 2.

	Table					

Linear table:

x	$f(x)$
0	3
1	5
2	7
3	9

Exponential table:

x	$f(x)$
0	3
1	6
2	12
3	24

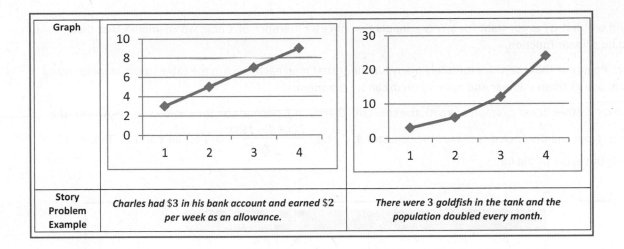

Graph		
Story Problem Example	*Charles had $3 in his bank account and earned $2 per week as an allowance.*	*There were 3 goldfish in the tank and the population doubled every month.*

Exercises 1–2 (12 minutes)

In this exercise, students complete the table for the function f and find a progression of differences of two outputs of f for two inputs that have a difference of 1 unit (i.e., they find the change in f, $\Delta f = f(x + 1) - f(x)$, where the difference between $x + 1$ and x is 1.) If $\Delta f = f(x + 1) - f(x)$ is constant for all input values x and $x + 1$ in the table, students identify the function given by the table as *potentially* linear. Similarly, when the quotient, $f(x + 1)/f(x)$, is a constant for all input values x and $x + 1$, they identify the function as *potentially* exponential. This activity can be done individually or in groups. Upon completion, a class discussion should take place.

> *Scaffolding:*
>
> If students are struggling with the type of function, have them plot the points.

Be sure that students understand the following telltale signs for recognizing linear and exponential functions from a table of input-output pairs: for each $d > 0$, consider all inputs that have a difference of d units,

- if the **difference** between their corresponding outputs is always the same constant, then the input-output pairs in the table can be modeled by a **linear** function;

- if the **quotient** between their corresponding outputs is always the same constant, then the input-output pairs in the table can be modeled by an **exponential** function.

In the exercise below, we use $d = 1$, but you can point out to students that these statements also make sense for $d = 2$, $d = 3$, etc.

Exercises 1–2

1. For each table below, assume the function f is defined for all real numbers. Calculate $\Delta f = f(x + 1) - f(x)$ in the last column in the tables below and show your work (the symbol Δ in this context means "change in"). What do you notice about Δf? Could the function be linear or exponential? Write a linear or exponential function formula that generates the same input-output pairs as given in the table.

x	$f(x)$	$\Delta f = f(x + 1) - f(x)$
1	-3	$1 - (-3) = 4$
2	1	$5 - 1 = 4$
3	5	$9 - 5 = 4$
4	9	$13 - 9 = 4$
5	13	

$f(x) = 4x - 7.$

Students should see that Δf is constant for any two inputs that have a difference of 1 unit, which implies that the function could be a linear function.

To the teacher: Point out that there are infinitely many functions that map each input in the table to the corresponding output, but only one of them is linear and none of them can be exponential.

In this example (and other linear examples like it), the constant change in f depends on the choice of d. However, the rate of change in f per the distance d is always the constant 4, that is: $\frac{f(x+d)-f(x)}{d} = 4$ for all x and d. This constant rate of change is the slope of the line.

x	$f(x)$	$\Delta f = f(x+1) - f(x)$
0	2	$6 - 2 = 4$
1	6	$18 - 6 = 12$
2	18	$54 - 18 = 36$
3	54	$162 - 54 = 108$
4	162	

If the entries in the table were considered as a geometric sequence, then the common quotient would be $r = 3$. Since $f(0) = 2$, $a = 2$. Since $f(1) = 6$, we must have $6 = 2 \cdot b$ or $b = 3$. Hence, $f(x) = 2(3^x)$.

In this table, students should see that Δf is not constant for any two inputs that have a difference of 1 unit, which implies that the function cannot be a linear function. However, there is a common quotient between inputs that have a difference of 1 unit: $\frac{6}{2} = \frac{18}{6} = \frac{54}{18} = \frac{162}{54}$. Hence the function f could be exponential.

To the teacher: Again, point out that there are infinitely many functions that map each input in the table to the corresponding output, but none of them can be linear and only one of them can be of the form $f(x) = ab^x$ (exponential).

2. Terence looked down the second column of the table below and noticed that $\frac{3}{1} = \frac{9}{3} = \frac{27}{9} = \frac{81}{27}$. Because of his observation, he claimed that the input-output pairs in this table could be modeled with an exponential function. Explain why Terence is correct or incorrect. If he is correct, write a formula for the exponential function that generates the input-output pairs given in the table. If he is incorrect, determine and write a formula for a function that generates the input-output pairs given in the table.

x	$T(x)$
0	1
1	3
4	9
13	27
40	81

Terence is incorrect. This is because the distance between consecutive x-values is not 1 (not constant).

As you walk around the classroom, some of your students may claim he is correct and use the first two input-output pairs to get the formula $T(x) = 3^{x-1}$. Ask them to see if it satisfies the remaining input-output pairs. You can guide (hint) to your students what function models this table by asking them to compute the average rate of change (you may need to recall this term for them) between input-output pairs. If they do, they will quickly see that the average rate of change is always 2. They should then be able to quickly derive the linear function $T(x) = 2x + 1$ using the first two input-out pairs. Encourage them to check their answers.

In groups, have students look at the Exercises 3 and 4. After groups have had time to discuss their solutions, have them discuss their results as a class. The purpose of these exercises is to help students understand when a situation models exponential or linear growth or decay. Exercise 4 re-emphasizes that the value of an exponential function with a base greater than 1 will always exceed any linear function for large enough positive input numbers. Exercise 4 highlights MP.3 as it calls on students to evaluate a hypothetical claim.

Exercise 3 (14 minutes)

Exercise 3

3. A river has an initial minnow population of $40,000$ that is growing at 5% per year. Due to environmental conditions, the amount of algae that minnows use for food is decreasing, supporting 1000 fewer minnows each year. Currently, there is enough algae to support $50,000$ minnows. Is the minnow population increasing linearly or exponentially? Is the amount of algae decreasing at a linear or exponential rate? In what year will the minnow population exceed the amount of algae available?

    The minnow population is increasing exponentially. The amount of algae is decreasing the food supply that can be used to support minnows linearly. Solution methods to finding when the minnow population will exceed the amount of algae may vary. Here's one solution: We need to find the number of years n such that $40(1.05)^n > 50 - n$ (why?). For $n = 3$, we get $46.3 > 47$ is false, but for $n = 4$, we get that $48.6 > 46$ is true. Hence, some time after the third year the minnow population will exceed the amount of algae available.

4. Using a calculator, Joanna made the following table and then made the following conjecture: $3x$ is always greater than $(1.02)^x$. Is Joanna correct? Explain.

x	$(1.02)^x$	$3x$
1	1.02	3
2	1.0404	6
3	1.0612	9
4	1.0824	12
5	1.1041	15

    The first function is exponential and the second is linear, so the exponential will eventually exceed the linear. (Alternatively, students could extend the table to larger values of x to show that the exponential function will eventually exceed the linear function.) $(1.02)^{500} \approx 19,957$, but $3(500) = 1,500$.

Closing (4 minutes)

▪ How can you tell whether input-output pairs in a table are describing a linear relationship or an exponential relationship?

Lesson Summary

▪ Suppose that the input-output pairs of a bivariate dataset have the following the property: for every two inputs that are a given difference apart, the difference in their corresponding outputs is constant. Then an appropriate model for that dataset could be a linear function.

▪ Suppose that the input-output pairs of a bivariate dataset have the following the property: for every two inputs that are a given difference apart, the quotient of their corresponding outputs is constant. Then an appropriate model for that dataset could be an exponential function.

▪ An increasing exponential function will eventually exceed any linear function. That is, if $f(x) = ab^x$ is an exponential function with $a > 0$ and $b > 1$, and $g(x) = mx + k$ is any linear function, then there is a real number M such that for all $x > M$, then $f(x) > g(x)$. Sometimes this is not apparent in a graph displayed on a graphing calculator; that is because the graphing window does not show enough of the graph to show the sharp rise of the exponential function in contrast with the linear function.

Exit Ticket (5 minutes)

Name _____   Date_____

Lesson 21: Comparing Linear and Exponential Functions Again

Exit Ticket

Here is a classic riddle: Mr. Smith has an apple orchard. He hires his daughter, Lucy, to pick apples and offers her two payment options.

> Option A: $1.50 per bushel of apples picked.
>
> Option B: 1 *cent* for picking one bushel, 3 *cents* for picking two bushels, 9 *cents* for picking three bushels, and so on, with the amount of money tripling for each additional bushel picked.

a.   Write a function to model each option.

b.   If Lucy picks *six* bushels of apples, which option should she choose?

c.   If Lucy picks 12 bushels of apples, which option should she choose?

d.   How many bushels of apples does Lucy need to pick to make option B better for her than option A?

Exit Ticket Sample Solutions

Here is a classic riddle: Mr. Smith has an apple orchard. He hires his daughter, Lucy, to pick apples and offers her two payment options.

Option A: $1.50 per bushel of apples picked.

Option B: 1 *cent* for picking one bushel, 3 *cents* for picking two bushels, 9*cents* for picking three bushels, and so on, with the amount of money tripling for each additional bushel picked.

a.   Write a function to model each option.

Option A: $f(x) = 1.50x$ *where x is the number of bushels of apples picked.*

Option B: $g(x) = 0.01(3^{x-1})$ *where x is the number of bushels of apples picked.*

b.   If Lucy picks *six* bushels of apples, which option should she choose?

Option A: $9   *Option B:* $2.43   *Option A is better.*

c.   If Lucy picks 12 bushels of apples, which option should she choose?

Option A: $18   *Option B:* $1,771.47   *Option B is much better.*

d.   How many bushels of apples does Lucy pick to make option B better for her than option A?

The eighth bushel picked is when the exponential function exceeds the linear function.

Problem Set Sample Solutions

For each table in Problems 1–6, classify the data as describing a linear relationship, an exponential growth relationship, an exponential decay relationship, or neither. If the relationship is linear, calculate the constant rate of change (slope), and write a formula for the linear function that models the data. If the function is exponential, calculate the common quotient for input values that are distance 1 apart, and write the formula for the exponential function that models the data. For each linear or exponential function found, graph the equation $y = f(x)$.

1.

x	$f(x)$
1	$\frac{1}{2}$
2	$\frac{1}{4}$
3	$\frac{1}{8}$
4	$\frac{1}{16}$
5	$\frac{1}{32}$

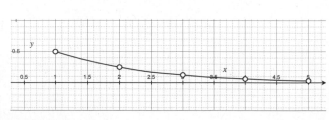

Common quotient: $\frac{1}{2}$, exponential decay, $f(x) = \left(\frac{1}{2}\right)^x$.

2.

x	$f(x)$
1	1.4
2	2.5
3	3.6
4	4.7
5	5.8

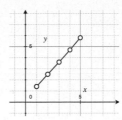

Constant rate of change: 1.1, *linear,* $f(x) = 0.3 + 1.1x$.

3.

x	$f(x)$
1	−1
2	0
3	2
4	5
5	9

Neither.

4.

x	$f(x)$
1	20
2	40
3	80
4	160
5	320

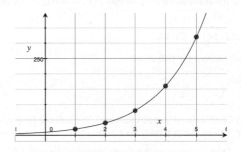

Ratio of change: 2, *exponential growth,* $f(x) = 10(2^x)$.

5.

x	$f(x)$
1	−5
2	−12
3	−19
4	−26
5	−33

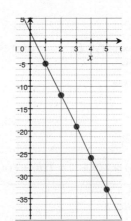

Rate of change: −7, *linear,* $f(x) = 2 − 7x$.

6.

x	$f(x)$
1	$\dfrac{1}{2}$
2	$\dfrac{1}{3}$
3	$\dfrac{1}{4}$
4	$\dfrac{1}{5}$
5	$\dfrac{1}{6}$

Neither.

7. Here is a variation on a classic riddle: Jayden has a dog-walking business. He has two plans. Plan 1 includes walking a dog once a day for a rate of $5/day. Plan 2 also includes one walk a day, but charges 1 cent for 1 day, 2 cents for 2 days, 4 cents for 3 days, 8 cents for 4 days, and continues to double for each additional day. Mrs. Maroney needs Jayden to walk her dog every day for two weeks. Which plan should she choose? Show the work to justify your answer.

Plan #1: $5 \times 14 = 70$. *She will pay* $70 *for all two weeks under Plan 1.*

Plan #2: The price can be modeled using the function $f(x) = 0.01(2^{x-1})$, *which describes the amount she pays for* x *days. Then,*

$$f(14) = 0.01(2^{14-1}) \text{ or } f(14) = 81.92.$$

She will pay $81.92 *under Plan 2 for two weeks.*

Plan 1 is the better choice.

8. Tim deposits money in a Certificate of Deposit account. The balance (in dollars) in his account t years after making the deposit is given by $T(t) = 1,000(1.06)^t$ for $t \geq 0$.

   a. Explain, in terms of the structure of the expression used to define $T(t)$, why Tim's balance can never be $999.

   $(1.06)^0 = 1$ *and positive powers of* 1.06 *are larger than 1, thus the minimum value* $T(t)$ *attains, if* $t \geq 0$, *is* $1,000$. *In the context given, a CD account grows in value over time so with a deposit of* $1,000 *the value will never drop to* $999.

   b. By what percent does the value of $T(t)$ grow each year? Explain by writing a recursive formula for the sequence $T(1), T(2), T(3)$, etc.

   Writing out the sequence, we see:

   Year 1: $1,000(1.06)^1$
   Year 2: $1,000(1.06)^2$
   Year 3: $1,000(1.06)^3$
   ...

   Thus, $T(n+1) = T(n)(1.06)$ *or* $T(n+1) = T(n) + T(n)(0.06)$, *showing that* $T(n)$ *grows by 6% a year.*

c. By what percentages does the value of $T(t)$ grow every two years? (Hint: Use your recursive formula to write $T(n + 2)$ in terms of $T(n)$.)

Since, $T(n + 1) = T(n)(1.06)$, we can write,

$$T(n + 2) = T(n + 1)(1.06)$$

$$= T(n)(1.06)(1.06),$$

or $T(n + 2) = T(n)(1.1236)$.

Hence, the amount in his account grows by 12.36% every two years.

9. Your mathematics teacher asks you to sketch a graph of the exponential function $f(x) = \left(\frac{3}{2}\right)^x$ for x, a number between 0 and 40 inclusively, using a scale of 10 units to one inch for both the x- and y-axes.

a. What are the dimensions in feet of the roll of paper you will need to sketch this graph?

The roll would need to be a bit wider than 4 in. ($\frac{1}{3}$ ft.) and, after rounding up, about $1,105,734$ in. (or $92,145$ ft.) long.

b. How many more feet of paper would you need to add to the roll in order to graph the function on the interval $0 \le x \le 41$?

It would require approximately $46,072$ more feet of paper. Teachers: look for the easy solution: $f(41) = f(40) \times 1.5 = f(40) + f(40) \times \frac{1}{2}$.

c. Find an m so that the linear function $g(x) = mx + 2$ is greater than $f(x)$ for all x such that $0 \le x \le 40$, but $f(41) > g(41)$.

There are many possible answers: any number between (roughly) $276,433.275$ and $404,536$ will do. Note that $f(40) \approx 11,057,332.32$ and $f(41) \approx 16,585,998.48$, so any slope such that $11,057,333 \le g(40)$ and $g(41) \le 16,585,998$ will do. Since $g(40) = 40m + 2$, solving $11,057,333 = 40m + 2$, or $m - 276,433.275$ might produced such a linear function. We need to check only that the function $g(x) = 276,433.275x + 2$ satisfies $f(41) > g(41)$, which it does: $g(41) = 11,333,766.275$.

Lesson 22: Modeling an Invasive Species Population

Student Outcomes

- Students apply knowledge of exponential functions and transformations of functions to a contextual situation.

Lesson Notes

The lionfish is an invasive species that began appearing in the western Atlantic Ocean in 1985 and now have large populations throughout the Caribbean as well as along eastern coastline of the United States. They have recently been spotted as far north as New York and Rhode Island. More information can be found at the site http://nas.er.usgs.gov/queries/FactSheet.aspx?speciesID=963.

To maximize class time, create groups ahead of time and place students in groups as they come in the classroom.

The focus of this lesson is on MP.4, modeling with mathematics. Additionally, students will need to employ MP.2 as they move back and forth between a real world context and an algebraic model.

> **Scaffolding:**
>
> When grouping students, consider their reading skill. Create groups ahead of time with varying ability levels so that they can assist students who may struggle with the reading comprehension aspect of this exercise.

Classwork

Opening (4 minutes)

Ask students to read through the introductory paragraph independently, or read it aloud as they read silently. After students have had a chance to read through the introductory paragraph, show them a picture of a lionfish and the interactive map at the site http://nas.er.usgs.gov/queries/SpeciesAnimatedMap.aspx?speciesID=963.

Discussion (3 minutes)

Motivate the lesson by asking students to discuss the problems inherent with introducing a non-native invasive species to a region. Why should we care about these problems?

- The lionfish has no natural predator in this region to help control its population.
- Lionfish reproduce quickly and eat large amounts of the fish around the reef or area they inhabit.

Mathematical Modeling Exercise (25 minutes)

Have students work in groups. Circulate throughout the room asking students about the problem. Make sure students are providing thorough written explanations when called for. To engage students with MP.1, set an expectation and encourage students to persist in struggling with the problem for some time without teacher assistance. If you feel students are equipped for further challenge, consider simply presenting the data and asking them to develop a model, without the scaffolding questions provided. If graphing calculators or spreadsheet software are not available, have students use points from their graph to write the equation.

- Why did you decide the data was linear/exponential?
- After seeing the scatterplot, did you change your mind?
- What do you think the graph will look like in the future? Will it keep going up? Level off? Why?

Mathematical Modeling Exercise

The lionfish is a fish that is native to the western Pacific Ocean. The lionfish began appearing in the western Atlantic Ocean in 1985. This is probably because people bought them as pets and then dumped them in waterways leading to the ocean. Because it has no natural predators in this area, the number of lionfish grew very quickly and now has large populations throughout the Caribbean as well as along the eastern coastline of the United States and the Gulf of Mexico. They have recently been spotted as far north as New York and Rhode Island.

The table below shows the number of new sightings by year reported to NAS (Nonindigenous Aquatic Species), which is a branch of the U.S. Geological Survey Department.

Year	Number of New Sightings	Total Number of Sightings
1985	1	1
1992	1	2
1995	3	5
1996	1	6
2000	6	12
2001	25	37
2002	50	87
2003	45	132
2004	57	189
2005	43	232
2006	51	283
2007	186	469
2008	173	642
2009	667	1,309
2010	1,342	2,651

1. Complete the table by recording the total number of sightings for each year.

2. Examine the total number of sightings data. Which model appears to be a better fit for the data, linear or exponential? Explain your reasoning.

    Exponential. For example, for the last three years the total number of sightings appears to have doubled each year.

3. Make a scatterplot of the year versus the total number of sightings.

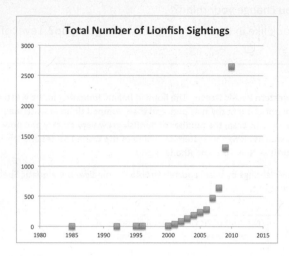

4. Based on the scatterplot, either revise your answer from Exercise 2 or explain how the scatterplot supports your answer from Exercise 2.

Answers will vary.

5. On the scatterplot, draw a smooth curve that best fits the data.

The smooth curve should look similar to the above scatterplot.

6. From your table, calculate the average rate of change in total number of sightings for each of the following time intervals.

   a. 1995–2000

   1.4

   b. 2000–2005

   44

   c. 2005–2010

   484

7. How do the average rates of change help to support your argument of whether a linear or exponential model is better suited for the data?

   If the model total number of sightings was growing linearly, then the average rate of change would be constant. Instead, it appears to be growing multiplicatively, indicating an exponential model.

> **Scaffolding:**
> This lesson could be extended to a student project. Early finishers could work on researching other non-native invasive species found in the U.S.

8. Use the regression feature of a graphing calculator to find an equation that models the number of lionfish sightings each year.

Answers will vary depending on the technology used. If the selected technology is not sensitive enough to display the equation for the exponential model, provide students with the equation below.

Exponential Model: $y = (4.602 \times 10^{-292})(1.401)^x$
Linear Model: $y = 61.15x - 122{,}000$

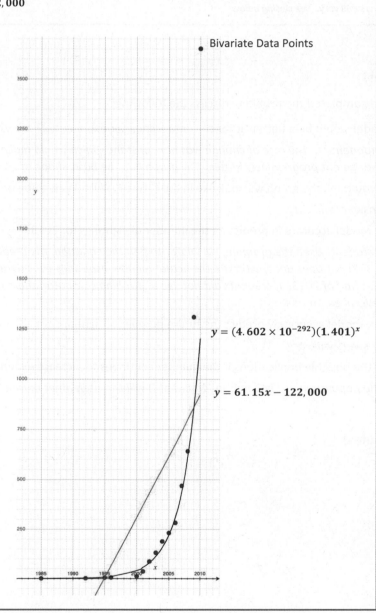

Bivariate Data Points

$$y = (4.602 \times 10^{-292})(1.401)^x$$

$$y = 61.15x - 122{,}000$$

9. Use your model to predict the total number of lionfish sightings by the end of 2013.

   Exponential: 2,273 total sightings.
   Linear: 1,095 total sightings.

10. The actual number of sightings as of July 2013 was 3,776. Does it seem that your model produced an accurate prediction? Explain.

    Answers will vary. See closing below.

Closing (8 minutes)

After students have completed the problem, discuss the following:

- Which model would be a better fit for the data – linear or exponential? Why?

  □ *Exponential. The rate of change was not constant, which would make it linear. The average rates of change got progressively larger. The graph had the basic shape of an exponential growth curve.*

- What do you think the graph will look like in the future? Will it keep going up? Level off? Why?

  □ *Answers will vary.*

- Was your model accurate in predicting the number of sightings for 2013?

  □ *If students used the graphing calculator to find the equation, the prediction is pretty close (3,147–3,307) but does underestimate the actual number especially considering that the number is only for the first half of 2013. If students did not use a graphing calculator, their answers will vary. Compare several equations.*

- Could your model accurately predict the future number of sightings?

  □ *Answers will vary.*

- What are the possible implications if the number continues to increase exponentially?

  □ *The population will become so large that it will threaten other marine life especially around coral reefs.*

Exit Ticket (5 minutes)

Name _____   Date_____

Lesson 22: Modeling an Invasive Species Population

Exit Ticket

1. For the equation found in Exercise 8, explain the parameters of the equation within the context of the problem.

2. Given each of the following, describe what features in the data or graph make it apparent that an exponential model would be more suitable than a linear model?

   a.   The table of data.

   b.   The scatterplot.

   c.   The average rates of change found in question 6.

3. Use your equation from Exercise 8 to predict the number of lionfish sightings by year 2020. Is this prediction accurate? Explain.

COMMON CORE™

Lesson 22:
Date:

Modeling an Invasive Species Population
9/12/13

281

Exit Ticket Sample Solutions

1. For the equation found in Exercise 8, explain the parameters of the equation within the context of the problem.

   $a = 4.602 \times 10^{-292}$, at $x = 0$, there were virtually no lionfish in the Atlantic Ocean.

   $b = 1.401$, the population of lionfish grew by this constant quotient of change every year.

2. Given each of the following, describe what features in the data or graph make it apparent that an exponential model would be more suitable than a linear model?

   a. The table of data.

   The values of the lionfish sightings grow by a quotient of change rather than a constant rate of change.

   b. The scatterplot.

   The shape of the scatterplot looks more like an exponential curve than a line.

   c. The average rates of change found in question 6.

   The three sets of average rates of change would have been the same, or close to the same, had the situation been more suited to a linear model.

3. Use your equation from question 8 to predict the number of lionfish sightings by year 2020. Is this prediction accurate? Explain.

   $35,060$; this answer assumes that the conditions that allowed for a constant quotient of change remain the same until 2020. This is probably not a realistic scenario, change in ocean temperature, food availability and other needs for continued exponential growth would have remain the same to yield this projected population.

Problem Set Sample Solutions

Another invasive species problem: kudzu

Kudzu, a perennial vine native to Southeast Asia, now covers a large area of the southern United States. Kudzu was promoted as a forage crop and an ornamental plant when it was introduced to the U.S. at the Philadelphia Centennial Exposition in 1876. Many southern farmers were encouraged to plant kudzu for erosion control from the mid 1930's to the mid 1950's. In 1953, kudzu was removed from the U.S. Department of Agriculture's list of permissible cover plants due to its recognition as an invasive species.

1. Look up information about kudzu in the United States on Wikipedia and write a short (1–2 pg.) report on the growth of kudzu since its introduction. In your report, choose a function (linear or exponential) to model and graph the growth of kudzu (in hectares) in the U.S. per year over the past half-century or so. Remember to cite your sources!

   To the teacher: Point out that the report is not about getting a correct answer, but how they explain and manipulate the data that they find. Hence, it is important for them to cite their sources. (Note: a rough estimate of how kudzu spreads, 50,000 hectares/year, is on the Wiki page—challenge them to find out more than that.)

Lesson 23: Newton's Law of Cooling

Student Outcomes

- Students apply knowledge of exponential functions and transformations of functions to a contextual situation.

Lesson Notes

Newton's Law of Cooling is a complex topic that appears in Physics and Calculus. Here it is simplified to focus on the idea of applying the transformations learned in Lessons 17–20 to a contextual situation. The mathematical practice in focus for this lesson is again MP.4, modeling with mathematics.

Classwork

Opening Exercise (7 minutes)

The opening exercise introduces students to the formula used in the lesson. Allow students a few minutes to read through the scenario and examine the given formula. Before they begin working, discuss each parameter of the formula as a class.

- What does T_a represent? T_0? k? $T(t)$?

Give students time to complete the problem and then discuss results.

- Why would it be important to be able to find the precise time of death?

  □ *To establish suspects, verify alibis, determine cause of death, etc.*

Opening Exercise

A detective is called to the scene of a crime where a dead body has just been found. He arrives at the scene and measures the temperature of the dead body at 9:30 p.m. After investigating the scene, he declares that the person died 10 hours prior at approximately 11:30 a.m. A crime scene investigator arrives a little later and declares that the detective is wrong. She says that the person died at approximately 6:00 a.m., 15.5 hours prior to the measurement of the body temperature. She claims she can prove it by using Newton's Law of Cooling:

$$T(t) = T_a + (T_0 - T_a) \cdot 2.718^{-kt},$$

where:

$T(t)$ is the temperature of the object after a time of t hours has elapsed,

T_a is the ambient temperature (the temperature of the surroundings), assumed to be constant, not impacted by the cooling process,

T_0 is the initial temperature of the object, and

k is the decay constant.

Scaffolding:

If students have difficulty inputting the formula in their calculators, encourage them to input the expression in separate steps, following the order of operations.

> Using the data collected at the scene, decide who is correct: the detective or the crime scene investigator.
>
> $T_a = 68°F$ (the temperature of the room)
>
> $T_0 = 98.6°F$ (the initial temperature of the body)
>
> $k = 0.1335$ (13.35 % per hour - calculated by the investigator from the data collected)
>
> Temperature of the body at 9:30 p.m. is 72°F.
>
> *If the person had died 10 hours prior to 9:30 p.m., his body temperature would be approximately 76°F. When you fill in 15.5 hours for t, the temperature is 71.865°F. This is much closer to the measured temperature of 72°F.*

Discussion (3 minutes)

Display the demonstration on Newton's Law of Cooling found at Wolfram Alpha:
http://demonstrations.wolfram.com/NewtonsLawOfCooling/

- First, at what type of graph are we looking?
  - *Exponential decay curve that has been vertically translated by an initial value.*
- Why is it still an exponential decay function when the base is greater than 1?
  - *Because the base is being raised to a negative power (graph is reflected around the y-axis).*

Allow students to drag the sliders and observe the effect of each on the graph. Keep this discussion fairly general. Students will explore this more in the modeling exercise in Module 5.

Mathematical Modeling Exercise (25 minutes)

Allow students to work through the exercise in groups. Encourage students to use the language from previous lessons on transformations such as translate, stretch, and shrink. If students ask how k is determined, explain that finding k requires algebra that they will learn Algebra II (logarithms). So, for this exercise, k is given.

> **Mathematical Modeling Exercise**
>
> Two cups of coffee are poured from the same pot. The initial temperature of the coffee is 180°F and k is 0.2337 (for time in minutes).
>
> 1. Suppose both cups are poured at the same time. Cup 1 is left sitting in the room that is 75°F, and cup 2 is taken outside where it is 42°F.
>
>   a. Use Newton's Law of Cooling to write equations for the temperature of each cup of coffee after t minutes has elapsed.
>
>   *Cup 1:* $T_1(t) = 75 + (180 - 75) \cdot 2.718^{-0.2337t}$
>
>   *Cup 2:* $T_2(t) = 42 + (180 - 42) \cdot 2.718^{-0.2337t}$

b. Graph both on the same coordinate plane and compare and contrast the two graphs.

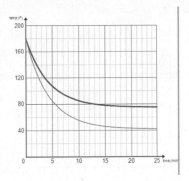

Both are decreasing exponentially and have the same y-intercept because they have the same initial temperature. The graph for cup 2 has a larger vertical stretch than cup 1, but cup 1 has a larger vertical translation, which is why they both can have the same initial temperature. The y-values of cup 2 level out lower than the corresponding y-values of cup 1 because of the lower ambient temperature.

The temperature difference (between the cup and the surroundings) drives the cooling. Larger temperature differences lead to faster cooling. This is why the outdoor cup cools much faster.

Ask students:

- Do these functions, graphs, and temperature values make sense? For example, if it is 42°F outside, can a cup of coffee ever cool to below 42°F?

  □ *No. The temperature of the cup will decrease until it is roughly the same temperature as its ambient surroundings, which the graph shows.*

c. Coffee is safe to drink when its temperature is below 140°F. Estimate how much time elapses before each cup is safe to drink.

Cup 1: Approximately 2 min.   *Cup 2: Approximately 1.5 min.*

When discussing the results, ask students how they found the answer to part (c). Some may have used the graph; some may have plugged time (in number of minutes) into the formula using trial and error. Allow students to demonstrate both methods.

2. Suppose both cups are poured at the same time, and both are left sitting in the room that is 75°F. But this time milk is immediately poured into cup 2 cooling it to an initial temperature of 162°F.

a. Use Newton's Law of Cooling to write equations for the temperature of each cup of coffee after t minutes has elapsed.

Cup 1: $T_1(t) = 75 + (180 - 75) \cdot 2.718^{-0.2337t}$

Cup 2: $T_2(t) = 75 + (162 - 75) \cdot 2.718^{-0.2337t}$

b.   Graph both on the same coordinate plane and compare and contrast the two graphs.

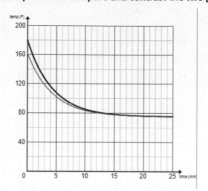

Both are decreasing exponentially and both appear to level out to approximately the same temperature (the room temperature). The graph for cup 2 has a smaller vertical stretch than cup 1 and a smaller y-intercept because of its lower starting temperature.

c.   Coffee is safe to drink when its temperature is below $140°F$. How much time elapses before each cup is safe to drink?

Cup 1: Approximately 2 min.   *Cup 2: Approximately 1 min.*

- Which should you do to drink the coffee sooner: walk outside in the 42°F temperature? Or poor milk into your coffee? Which scenario would have a greater impact on the temperature of the coffee over the long run?

  □   *At first, decreasing the initial temperature with milk has the greater impact because the coffee cools enough to drink more quickly. But, as time elapses, decreasing the ambient temperature has the greater impact because the coffee continues to cool and levels out at a lower temperature.*

3.   Suppose cup 2 is poured 5 minutes after cup 1 (the pot of coffee is maintained at $180°F$ over the 5 minutes). Both are left sitting in the room that is $75°F$.

a.   Use the equation for cup 1 found in Exercise 1 (a) to write an equation for cup 2.

   Cup 2: $T(t) = 75 + (180 - 75) \cdot 2.718^{-0.2337(t-5)}$

b.   Graph both on the same coordinate plane and describe how to obtain the graph of cup 2 from the graph of cup 1.

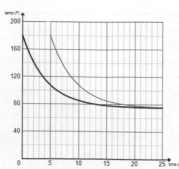

The graph of cup 2 is the graph of cup 1 shifted right 5 units.

Closing (5 minutes)

- How does changing the initial coffee temperature affect the graph?

    □ *The graph had a lower "starting point" (y-intercept). The cold milk cools the coffee quickly at first, but, compared to the hotter cup, takes longer to cool to the same temperature. This is because the cooler cup has a smaller temperature difference with the ambiance, which leads to the slower cooling rate.*

- How does changing the ambient temperature of the coffee affect the graph?

    □ *At a lower ambient temperature, the coffee cools more quickly and levels off to a lower temperature because of the cooler surrounding temperature.*

Exit Ticket (5 minutes)

Name _____   Date_____

Lesson 23: Newton's Law of Cooling

Exit Ticket

Shown below is the graph of cup 1 from the exercise completed in class. For each scenario, sketch a graph of cup 2 on the same coordinate plane.

1. Cup 2 is poured 10 minutes after cup 1 (the pot of coffee is maintained at 180°F over the 10 minutes).

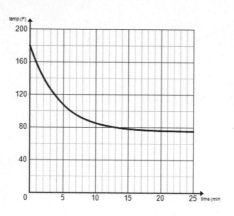

2. Cup 2 is immediately taken outside where the temperature is 90°F.

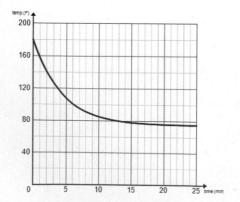

Exit Ticket Sample Solutions

Shown below is the graph of cup 1 from the exercise completed in class. For each scenario, sketch a graph of cup 2 on the same coordinate plane.

1. Cup 2 is poured 10 minutes after cup 1 (the pot of coffee is maintained at 180°F over the 10 minutes).

    Answer:

    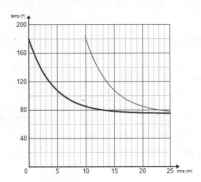

2. Cup 2 is immediately taken outside where the temperature is 90°F.

    Answer:

    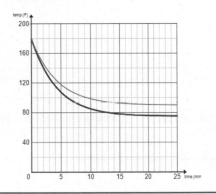

Problem Set Sample Solutions

Use the Coffee Cooling demonstration on Wolfram Alpha to write a short report on the questions that follow.
http://demonstrations.wolfram.com/TheCoffeeCoolingProblem/

1. If you want your coffee to become drinkable as quickly as possible, should you add cream immediately after pouring or wait?
2. If you want your coffee to stay warm longer, should you add cream immediately after pouring or wait?

Use results from the demonstration to support your claim.

Answers will vary, but the results may surprise students. It turns out that if you want the coffee to stay hot as long as possible then you should add the cream immediately. If you want the coffee to cool more quickly, you should wait as long as possible before adding the cream.

Lesson 24: Piecewise and Step Functions in Context

Student Outcomes

- Students create piecewise and step functions that relate to real-life situations and use those functions to solve problems.
- Students interpret graphs of piecewise and step functions in a real-life situation.

Lesson Notes

Students study airport parking rates and consider making a change to them to raise revenue for the airport. They model the parking rates with piecewise and step functions and apply transformations and function evaluation skills to solve problems about this real-life situation. The current problem is based on the rates at the Albany International Airport (http://www.albanyairport.com/parking_rates.php).

Do not assume that just because this lesson is about piecewise linear functions that it will be easy for your students. Please read through and do all the calculations carefully before teaching this lesson. By doing the calculations you will get a sense of how much time this lesson will take. To finish this modeling lesson in one day you will need to break the class into four large groups (which may be split into smaller groups that work on the same task if you wish). Depending on your student population, you may wish to break this lesson into two days.

Classwork

Opening Exercise (2 minutes)

Introduce the lesson by presenting the following two scenarios. Model how to compute the parking costs for a 2.75-hour stay.

Opening Exercise

Here are two different parking options in the city.

1-2-3 Parking	Blue Line Parking
\$6 for the 1st hr (or part of an hr) \$5 for the 2nd hr (or part of an hr) \$4 for the each hr (or part of an hr) starting with the 3rd hr	\$5 per hour up to 5 hr \$4 per hr after that

The cost of a 2.75-hr stay at 1-2-3 Parking would be \$6 + \$5 + \$4 = \$15. The cost of a 2.75-hr stay at Blue Line Parking would be \$5(2.75) = \$13.75.

Students then use the rates at each parking garage to determine which one would cost less money if they planned to stay for exactly 5.25 hours in the opening exercise.

Opening Exercise (3 minutes)

> **Opening Exercise**
>
> Which garage costs less for a 5.25-hour stay? Show your work to support your answer.
>
> *1-2-3 Parking:* $27. *Blue Line Parking:* $26.

Discussion (5 minutes)

Lead a discussion about the type of function that could be used to model the relationship between the length of the stay and the parking rates at each garage.

- What is this problem about?

    - *It is about comparing parking rates at two different lots.*

- What are the quantities in this situation?

    - *Time and money are two quantities in this situation.*

- What types of functions would model each parking plan?

    - *1-2-3 Parking would be modeled by a step function and Blue Line Parking by a piecewise function. For 1-2-3 Parking, the charge for a fraction of an hour is the same as the hourly rate so a step function would be a better model.*

- What would be the domain and what would be the range in each situation?

    - *A reasonable domain could be 0– 24 hours. The range would be the cost based on the domain. For 1-2-3, the range would be $\{6, 11, 15, 19, 23, 27 \dots\}$ and for Blue Line, the range would be $(0, 121]$.*

> **Scaffolding:**
>
> - Allow students to use technology throughout this lesson.
> - Pay careful attention to assigning proper intervals for each piece. You may need to model this more closely for your classes.

Students will revisit this opening exercise in the problem set exercises. Optionally, you may consider doing problem 1 (b) from the problem set for this lesson here.

Additional Lesson Notes

Transition to the exploratory challenge by announcing that students will spend the rest of this session working on a modeling problem. You can review the modeling cycle with your class if you wish to alert them to the distinct phases in the modeling cycle. You can activate thinking by using questions similar to the ones above to engage students in the airport parking problem.

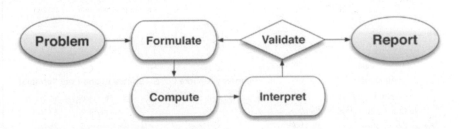

Exploratory Challenge (30 minutes)

In this portion of the lesson, students access parking rates at the Albany International Airport. They create algebraic models for the various parking structures and then analyze how much money is made on a typical day. Finally, they recommend how to adjust the rates to increase revenues by 10%. These parking rates are based upon rates that went into effect in 2008. Updated rates can be accessed by visiting the Albany International Airport website. The parking ticket data has been created for the purposes of this problem and is not based on information provided by the airport (although the data is based upon the average daily revenue generated using the figure below for total revenue in a year).

Assign each group one parking rate to model. These will all be step functions. Students will work in groups to create a function to model their assigned parking rate. Make sure each rate is assigned to at least one group. You may also encourage students to generate tables and graphs for each parking rate, both as a scaffold to help define the function algebraically and to create a richer model. Offering a variety of tools, such as graph paper, calculators, and graphing software will highlight MP.5.

If a group finishes questions 2–3 of this challenge early, it can repeat the questions for a different rate of its choice. If time permits, you could have groups graph their functions in the Cartesian plane. After all groups have completed their assigned rates, share results as a whole class. Give groups time enough to record the other models and their results for the revenue generated. Groups must then decide how to alter the price structure to get a 10% increase in average daily revenue based on the data available. Explain to groups that in a real situation, the finance department would have access to revenue data for a longer period of time and would be better able to forecast and make recommendations regarding increases in revenue. In 2008, the Albany International Airport generated over $11,000,000 in parking revenues.

Exploratory Challenge

Helena works as a summer intern at the Albany International Airport. She is studying the parking rates and various parking options. Her department needs to raise parking revenues by 10% to help address increased operating costs. The parking rates as of 2008 are displayed below. Your class will write piecewise linear functions to model each type of rate and then use those functions to develop a plan to increase parking revenues.

Parking Rates (Effective October 28, 2008)

Short Term Rates
Located on first floor of parking garage and front of the terminal

First Half Hour:	FREE
Second Half Hour:	$2.00
Each Additional Half Hour:	$1.00
Maximum Daily Rate:	$24.00

Garage Parking Rates
Located on floors two, three, four and five of the parking garage

First Hour:	$2.00
Each Additional Hour:	$2.00
Maximum Daily Rate:	$12.00
Five Consecutive Days:	$50.00
Seven Consecutive Days:	$64.00

Long Term Parking Rates
Located behind the parking garage

First Hour:	$2.00
Each Additional Hour:	$1.00
Maximum Daily Rate:	$9.00
Five Days:	$36.00
Seven Days:	$45.00

Economy Remote Lot E - Shuttle to and from Terminal

First Hour:	$1.00
Hourly Rate:	$1.00
Maximum Daily Rate:	$5.00

1. Write a piecewise linear function using step functions that models your group's assigned parking rate. Note: Like in the opening exercise, assume that if the car is there for any part of the next time period, then that period is counted in full (i.e., 3.75 hours is counted as 4 hours, 3.5 days is counted as 4 days, etc.).

SHORT-TERM

$$S(x) = \begin{cases} 0 & 0 \le x \le 0.5 \\ \lceil 2x \rceil & 0.5 < x \le 12 \\ 24 & 12 < x \le 24 \end{cases}$$

GARAGE

$$G(x) = \begin{cases} 2\lceil x \rceil & 0 < x \le 6 \\ 12\left\lceil \dfrac{x}{24} \right\rceil & 6 < x < 120 \\ 50 & 120 \le x < 168 \\ 64 & 128 \le x < 192 \end{cases}$$

LONG-TERM

$$L(x) = \begin{cases} 2 & 0 < x \le 1 \\ \lceil x \rceil + 1 & 1 < x \le 8 \\ 9\left\lceil \dfrac{x}{24} \right\rceil & 8 < x < 120 \\ 36 & 120 \le x < 168 \\ 45 & 168 \le x \le 192 \end{cases}$$

ECONOMY

$$E(x) = \begin{cases} \lceil x \rceil & 0 < x \le 5 \\ 5\left\lceil \dfrac{x}{24} \right\rceil & 5 < x \end{cases}$$

Students will definitely have questions about how to interpret the different rates. Stress the second sentence of the problem statement. Let students discuss in their groups how to interpret the rates (it is part of the formulation of the problem in the modeling cycle), but gently guide them to adopting the following guidelines after that discussion:

Short-Term Rates: Since it is free for the first $\frac{1}{2}$ hour but \$2 for the second $\frac{1}{2}$ hour, students can use just one step function to model the first 12 hours, after which the parking fee is \$12 for the day. Suggest to students that it is not necessary to go past 24 hours—that is a rare occurrence and is usually dealt with on an ad hoc basis.

Garage Rates/Long-Term Rates: For this lesson, we will assume that the charge is \$50 for Garage and \$36 for Long-Term for either 5 or 6 days (do not prorate the time). Students may write a piecewise linear function for each day up to 7 days. This is acceptable, but challenge students to use a step function instead.

Helena collected all the parking tickets from one day during the summer to help her analyze ways to increase parking revenues, and used that data to create the table shown below. The table displays the number of tickets turned in for each time and cost category at the four different parking lots.

Parking Tickets Collected on a Summer Day at the Albany International Airport

Short Term			Long Term			Parking Garage			Economy Remote		
Time on Ticket (hours)	Parking Cost ($)	Number of Tickets	Time on Ticket (hours)	Parking Cost ($)	Number of Tickets	Time on Ticket (hours)	Parking Cost ($)	Number of Tickets	Time on Ticket (hours)	Parking Cost ($)	Number of Tickets
0.5	0	400	1	2	8	1	2	8	1	1	-
1	2	600	2	3	20	2	4	12	2	2	
1.5	3	80	3	4	24	3	6	8	3	3	
2	4	64	4	5		4	8	4	4	4	
2.5	5	8	5	6		5	10	0	5	5	
3	6	24	6	7		6	12	16	5 to 24 hrs	5	84
3.5	7	4	7	8	60	6 to 24	12	156	2 days	10	112
4	8		8	9	92	2 days	24	96	3 days	15	64
4.5	9		8 to 24	9	260	3 days	36	40	4 days	20	60
5	10		2 days	18	164	4 days	48	12	5 days	25	72
5.5	11		3 days	27	12	5-6 days	50	8	6 days	30	24
6	12		4 days	36	8	7 days	64	4	7 days	35	76
6.5	13		5 days	36	20				8 days	40	28
7	14		6 days	36	36				9 days	45	8
7.5	15		7 days	45	32				10 days	50	4
8	16	4							14 days	70	8
8.5	17								18 days	90	4
9	18	8							21 days	105	4
9.5	19										
10	20										
10.5	21										
11	22										
11.5	23										
12 to 24	24	8									

For example, there were 600 short term 1-hr tickets charged $2 each. Total revenue for that type of ticket would be $1200.

Before moving groups on to tackle Exercises 3–4, lead a quick discussion around the data in the table. Ask the following questions. All of the answers to the discussion questions below are sample responses. Encourage a wide variety of reasonable responses from your students as long as they are realistic.

- What do the values in the number of tickets columns represent?
  - *The number of tickets turned in as cars left the parking area for various hours in the lots.*

- What does is the last row of the economy lot table mean?
  - *It means that 4 people left the parking lot after parking their cars there for 21 days and each paid $105.*

- How much do you think this data varies from day to day, month to month, etc.?
  - *It might vary day to day—for example, more people checking out on a Friday or fewer people traveling on the weekends. It might also vary season to season. Maybe people use the parking garage more in the winter months to avoid having their cars be covered with snow.*

- What if Helena collected this data on July 4? How would that information influence your thinking about whether or not this is a typical day's collection of parking fees.
  - *This would probably not be a typical day. Fewer people travel on holidays, so parking revenues might be less than usual.*

- What assumptions would you need to make to use this data to make a recommendation about raising yearly parking revenues by 10%?

  □ *You would need to assume that on average, approximately $8700 is collected each day and the distribution of tickets on any given day is similar to this one.*

---

2. Compute the total revenue generated by your assigned rate using the following parking ticket data.

   Total revenue for Short Term: $2,308

   Total revenue for Long Term: $10,840

   Total revenue for Parking Garage: $7,184

   Total revenue for Economy: $11,900

   Total revenue from all lots: $32,232

3. The Albany International Airport wants to increase average daily parking revenue by 10%. Make a recommendation to management of one or more parking rates to change to increase daily parking revenue by 10%. Then use the data Helena collected to show that revenue would increase by 10% if they implement the recommended change.

   A 10% increase would be a total of $35,455.20. Student solutions will vary but should be supported with a calculation showing that their changes will result in a 10% increase in parking revenue. The simplest solution would be to raise each rate by 10% across the board. However, consumers may not like the strange-looking parking rates. Another proposal would be to raise short-term rates by $0.50/half-hour and raise economy rates to $6 per day instead of $5.

Exit Ticket (5 minutes)

Students interpret a step function that represents postage costs. They create a piecewise linear function to model the data.

Name _____   Date _____

Lesson 24: Piecewise and Step Functions in Context

Exit Ticket

1. Use the graph to complete the table.

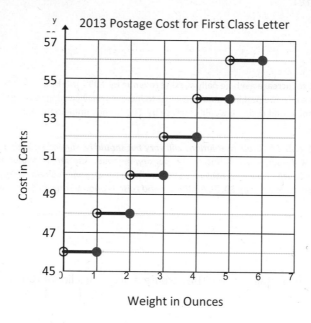

Weight in ounces, x	2	2.2	3	3.5	4
Cost of postage, $C(x)$					

2. Write a formula involving step functions that represents the cost of postage based on the graph shown above.

3. It cost Trina $0.54 to mail her letter, how many ounces did it weigh?

Exit Ticket Sample Solutions

1. Use the graph to complete the table.

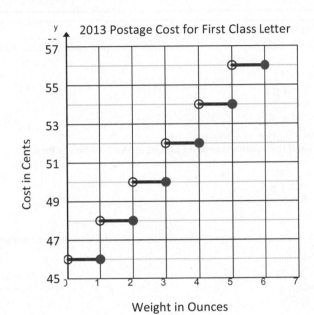

2013 Postage Cost for First Class Letter

Weight in ounces, x	2	2.2	3	3.5	4
Cost of postage, $C(x)$	48	50	50	52	52

2. Write a formula involving step functions that represents the cost of postage based on the graph shown above.

   $f(x) = 2\lceil x \rceil + 44, 0 < x \le 6$

3. It cost Trina $0.54 to mail her letter, how many ounces did it weigh?

   It weighed more than 4 oz. but less than or equal to 5 oz.

Problem Set Sample Solutions

These problems provide a variety of contexts for using piecewise and step functions to model situations. The following solutions indicate an understanding of the objectives of this lesson:

1. Recall the parking problem from the opening exercise.

   a. Write a piecewise linear function P using step functions that models the cost of parking at 1-2-3 Parking for x hrs.

   $$P(x) = \begin{cases} 6\lceil x \rceil & 0 \le x \le 1 \\ 5\lceil x - 1 \rceil + 6 & 1 < x \le 2 \\ 4\lceil x - 2 \rceil + 11 & 2 < x \end{cases}$$

   b. Write a piecewise linear function B that models the cost of parking at Blue Line parking for x hrs.

   $$B(x) = \begin{cases} 5x & 0 \le x \le 5 \\ 4(x - 5) + 25 & 5 < x \end{cases}$$

   c. Evaluate each function at 2.75 and 5.25 hrs. Do your answers agree with the work in the opening? If not, refine your model.

   $P(2.75) = 15$ *and* $B(2.75) = 13.75$,
   $P(5.25) = 27$ *and* $B(5.25) = 26$.

   d. Is there a time where both models have the same parking cost? Support your reasoning with graphs and/or equations.

   When $x = 5.5, 6.5, 7.5, \dots$

   e. Apply your knowledge of transformations to write a new function that would represent the result of a \$2 across the board increase in hourly rates at 1-2-3 Parking. (Hint: Draw its graph first and then use the graph to help you determine the step functions and domains.)

   $$P_{new}(x) = \begin{cases} (2 + 6)\lceil x \rceil & 0 \le x \le 1 \\ (2 + 5)\lceil x - 1 \rceil + 8 & 1 < x \le 2 \\ (2 + 4)\lceil x - 2 \rceil + 15) & 2 < x \end{cases}$$

2. There was no snow on the ground when it started falling at midnight at a constant rate of 1.5 inches per hour. At 4:00 a.m., it starting falling at a constant rate of 3 in. per hr. and then from 7:00 a.m. to 9:00 a.m., snow was falling at a constant rate of 2 in. per hr. It stopped snowing at 9:00 a.m. (Note—this problem models snow falling by a constant rate during each time period. In reality, the snowfall rate might be very close to constant but is unlikely to be perfectly uniform throughout any given time period.)

   a. Write a piecewise linear function that models the depth of snow as a function of time since midnight.

   Let S be a function that gives the depth of snow $S(x)$ on the ground x hours after midnight.

   $$S(x) = \begin{cases} 1.5x & 0 \le x < 4 \\ 3(x - 4) + 6 & 4 \le x < 7 \\ 2(x - 7) + 15 & 7 \le x \le 9 \end{cases}$$

b. Create a graph of the function.

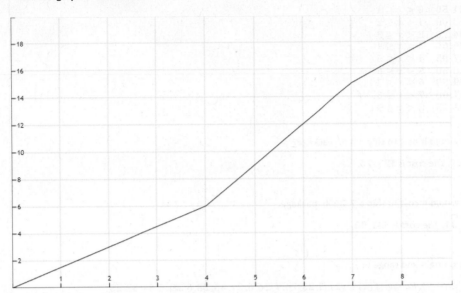

c. When was depth of the snow on the ground 8 inches deep?

$S(x) = 8$ when $3(x - 4) + 6 = 8$. *The solution of this equation is* $x = \frac{14}{3}$ *hours after midnight or at 4:40 a.m.*

d. How deep was the snow at $9:00$ a.m.?

$S(9) = 19$.

3. If you earned up to $\$113,700$ in 2013 from an employer, you Social Security tax rate was 6.2% of your income. If you earned over $\$113,700$, you pay a fixed amount of $\$7,049.40$.

a. Write a piecewise linear function to represent the 2013 Social Security taxes for incomes between $\$0$ and $\$500,000$.

Let $f(x) = \begin{cases} 0.062x, & 0 < x \le 113,700 \\ 7,049.40, & 113,700 < x \le 500,000 \end{cases}$

where x is income in dollars and $f(x)$ is the 2013 social security tax.

b. How much Social Security tax would someone who made $\$50,000$ owe?

$f(50,000) = 3,100$. *They would owe* $\$3,100$.

c. How much money would you have made if you paid $\$4000$ in social security tax in 2013.

$f(x) = 4000$ *when* $x = 64,516.129$. *You would have made* $\$64,516.13$.

d. What is the meaning of $f(150,000)$? What is the value of $f(150,000)$?

The amount of Social Security tax you would owe if you earned $\$150,000$. $f(150,000) = \$7,049.40$.

4. The function f gives the cost to ship x lbs. via Fed Ex Standard Overnight Rates to Zone 2 in 2013.

$$f(x) = \begin{cases} 21.50 & 0 < x \leq 1 \\ 23.00 & 1 < x \leq 2 \\ 24.70 & 2 < x \leq 3 \\ 26.60 & 3 < x \leq 4 \\ 27.05 & 4 < x \leq 5 \\ 28.60 & 5 < x \leq 6 \\ 29.50 & 6 < x \leq 7 \\ 31.00 & 7 < x \leq 8 \\ 32.25 & 8 < x \leq 9 \end{cases}$$

a. How much would it cost to ship a 3 lb. package?

$f(3) = 24.7$, The cost is $\$24.70$.

b. How much would it cost to ship a 7.25 lb. package.

$f(7.25) = 31$, The cost is $\$31.00$.

c. What is the domain and range of f?

Domain: $x \in (0, 9]$, Range: $f(x) \in \{21.5, 23, 24.7, 26.6, 27.05, 28.6, 29.5, 31, 32.25\}$

d. Could you use the ceiling function to write this function more concisely? Explain your reasoning.

No. The range values on the ceiling function differ by a constant amount. The rates in function f do not increase at a constant rate.

5. Use the floor or ceiling function and your knowledge of transformations to write a piecewise linear function f whose graph is shown below.

$f(x) = -\lceil x \rceil + 3$ *or* $f(x) = \lfloor -x \rfloor + 4$

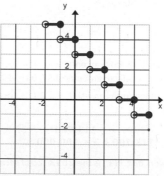

Name _____   Date _____

1. Given $h(x) = |x + 2| - 3$ and $g(x) = -|x| + 4$.

   a. Describe how to obtain the graph of g from the graph of $a(x) = |x|$ using transformations.

   b. Describe how to obtain the graph of h from the graph of $a(x) = |x|$ using transformations.

   c. Sketch the graphs of $h(x)$ and $g(x)$ on the same coordinate plane.

   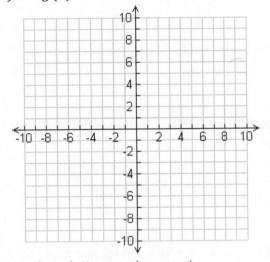

   d. Use your graphs to estimate the solutions to the equation:
   $$|x + 2| - 3 = -|x| + 4$$

   Explain how you got your answer.

   e. Were your estimations you made in part (d) correct? If yes, explain how you know. If not explain why not.

2. Let f and g be the functions given by $f(x) = x^2$ and $g(x) = x|x|$.

   a. Find $f\left(\frac{1}{3}\right)$, $g(4)$, and $g(-\sqrt{3})$.

   b. What is the domain of f?

   c. What is the range of g?

   d. Evaluate $f(-67) + g(-67)$.

   e. Compare and contrast f and g. How are they alike? How are they different?

   f. Is there a value of x, such that $f(x) + g(x) = -100$? If so, find x. If not, explain why no such value exists.

   g. Is there a value of x such that $(x) + g(x) = 50$? If so, find x. If not, explain why no such value exists.

3. A boy bought 6 guppies at the beginning of the month. One month later the number of guppies in his tank had doubled. His guppy population continued to grow in this same manner. His sister bought some tetras at the same time. The table below shows the number of tetras, t, after n months have passed since they bought the fish.

n, months	0	1	2	3
t, tetras	8	16	24	32

a. Create a function g to model the growth of the boy's guppy population, where $g(n)$ is the number of guppies at the beginning of each month, and n is the number of months that have passed since he bought the 6 guppies. What is a reasonable domain for g in this situation?

b. How many guppies will there be one year after he bought the 6 guppies?

c. Create an equation that could be solved to determine how many months after he bought the guppies there will be 100 guppies.

d. Use graphs or tables to approximate a solution to the equation from part (c). Explain how you arrived at your estimate.

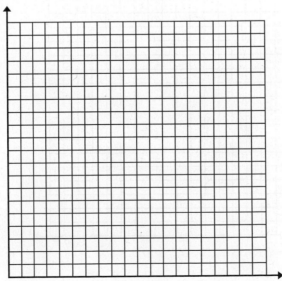

e. Create a function, t, to model the growth of the sister's tetra population, where $t(n)$ is the number of tetras after n months have passed since she bought the tetras.

f. Compare the growth of the sister's tetra population to the growth of the guppy population. Include a comparison of the average rate of change for the functions that model each population's growth over time.

g. Use graphs to estimate the number of months that will have passed when the population of guppies and tetras will be the same.

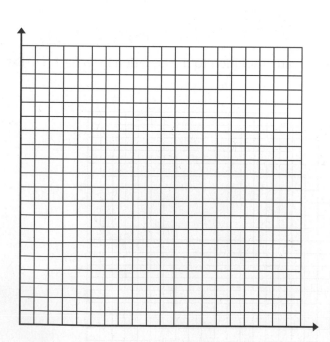

h. Use graphs or tables to explain why the guppy population will eventually exceed the tetra population even though there were more tetras to start with.

i. Write the function $g(n)$ in such a way that the percent increase in the number of fish per month can be identified. Circle or underline the expression representing percent increase in number of fish per month.

4. Regard the solid dark equilateral triangle as figure 0. Then, the first figure in this sequence is the one composed of three dark triangles, the second figure is the one composed of nine dark triangles, and so on.

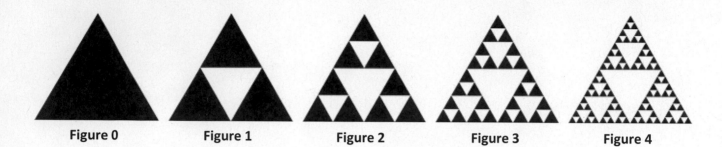

Figure 0   Figure 1   Figure 2   Figure 3   Figure 4

a. How many dark triangles are in each figure? Make a table to show this data.

n (Figure Number)					
T (# of dark triangles)					

b. Describe in words how, given the number of dark triangles in a figure, to determine the number of dark triangles in the next figure.

c. Create a function that models this sequence. What is the domain of this function?

d. Suppose the area of the solid dark triangle in Figure 0 is 1 square meter. The areas of one dark triangle in each figure form a sequence. Create an explicit formula that gives the area of just one of the dark triangles in the nth figure in the sequence?

e. The sum of the areas of all the dark triangles in Figure 0 is 1 m^2; there is only one triangle in this case. The sum of the areas of <u>all</u> the dark triangles in Figure 1 is $\frac{3}{4}$ m^2. What is the sum of the areas of <u>all</u> the dark triangles in the nth figure in the sequence? Is this total area increasing or decreasing as n increases?

f. Let $P(n)$ be the sum of the perimeters of the <u>all</u> dark triangles in the nth figure in the sequence of figures. There is a real number k so that:

$$P(n + 1) = kP(n)$$

is true for each positive whole number n. What is the value of k?

5.   The graph of a piecewise function f is shown to the right. The domain of f is $-3 \le x \le 3$.

    a.   Create an algebraic representation for f. Assume that the graph of f is composed of straight line segments.

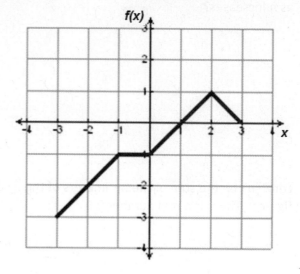

    b.   Sketch the graph of $y = 2f(x)$ and state the domain and range.

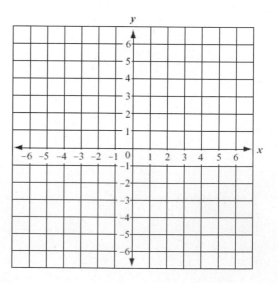

c.   Sketch the graph of $y = f(2x)$ and state the domain and range.

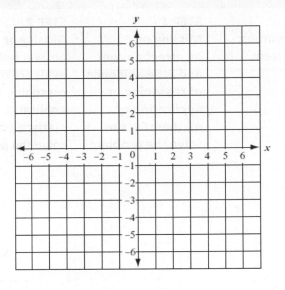

d.   How does the range of $y = f(x)$ compare to the range of $y = kf(x)$, where $k > 1$?

e.   How does the domain of $y = f(x)$ compare to the domain of $y = f(kx)$, where $k > 1$?

A Progression Toward Mastery

Assessment Task Item		STEP 1 Missing or incorrect answer and little evidence of reasoning or application of mathematics to solve the problem	STEP 2 Missing or incorrect answer but evidence of some reasoning or application of mathematics to solve the problem	STEP 3 A correct answer with some evidence of reasoning or application of mathematics to solve the problem, or an incorrect answer with substantial evidence of solid reasoning or application of mathematics to solve the problem	STEP 4 A correct answer supported by substantial evidence of solid reasoning or application of mathematics to solve the problem
1	a F-BF.B.3	Student answer is missing or entirely incorrect.	Student's descriptions of transformations are partially correct.	Student's descriptions of the transformations are correct, but there may be some minor misuse or omission of appropriate vocabulary.	Student's descriptions of the transformations are clear and correct and use appropriate vocabulary.
	b F-BF.B.3	Student answer is missing or entirely incorrect.	Student's descriptions of transformations are partially correct.	Student's descriptions of the transformations are correct, but there may be some minor misuse or omission of appropriate vocabulary.	Student's descriptions of the transformations are clear and correct and use appropriate vocabulary.
	c-e A-REI.D.11 F-BF.B.3	Student's sketches do not resemble absolute value functions, and/or student is unable to use the graphs to estimate the solutions to the equation. Student may or may not have arrived at correct solutions of the equation via another method such as trial and error.	Student's sketches resemble the graph of an absolute value function, but are inaccurate. Student shows evidence of using the intersection point of the graphs to find the solution but is unable to confirm his or her solution points; therefore, the conclusion in (e) is inconsistent with the intersection points.	Student sketches are accurate with no more than one minor error; the student shows evidence of using the intersection points to find the solutions to the equation. The conclusion in (e) is consistent with their estimated solutions but may have one error. Student's communication is clear but could include more appropriate use of vocabulary or more detail.	Student sketches are accurate and solutions in part (d) match the x-coordinates of the intersection points. The student's explanation for part (d) reflects an understanding that the process is analogous to solving the system $y = h(x)$ and $y = g(x)$. The work shown in part (e) supports his or her conclusion that estimates were or were not solutions and includes supporting explanation using appropriate vocabulary.

Module 3:   Linear and Exponential Functions
Date: 9/12/13

310

2	a F-IF.A.2	Student provides no correct answers.	Student provides only one correct answer.	Student provides two correct answers.	Student provides correct answers for all three items.
	b – c F-IF.A.1	Neither domain nor range is correct.	One of the two is identified correctly, or the student has reversed the ideas, giving the range of f when asked for domain of f, and the domain of g when asked for the range of g.	Both domain and range are correct but notation may contain minor errors.	Both domain and range are correct and use appropriate notation.
	d F-IF.A.2	Student makes a major error or omission in evaluating the expression (e.g., doesn't substitute -67 into f or g)	Student makes one or more errors in evaluating the expression.	Student evaluates the expression correctly, but work to support the answer is limited, or there is one minor error present.	Student evaluates the expression correctly and shows the work to support their answer.
	e F-IF.A.1 F-IF.A.2 F-IF.C.7a	Student makes little or no attempt to compare the two functions.	Student's comparison does not note the similarity of the two functions yielding identical outputs for positive inputs and opposite outputs for negative inputs; it may be limited to superficial features, such as one involves squaring and the other contains an absolute value.	Student recognizes that they are equal for $x = 0$ and positive x-values but may not clearly articulate that the two functions are opposites when x is negative.	Student clearly describes when that the two functions yielding identical outputs for positive inputs, and for an input of $x = 0$, and opposite outputs for negative inputs.
	f F-IF.A.1 F-IF.A.2	Student provides an incorrect conclusion, <u>OR</u> makes little or no attempt to answer.	Student identifies that there is no solution but provides little or no supporting work or explanation.	Student identifies that there is no solution and provides an explanation, but the explanation is limited or contains minor inconsistencies or errors.	Student identifies that there is no solution and provides an explanation and/or work that clearly supports valid reasoning.
	g F-IF.A.1 F-IF.A.2	Student provides an incorrect conclusion, <u>OR</u> makes little or no attempt to answer.	Student identifies that $x = 5$ is a solution but provides little or no supporting work or explanation.	Student identifies that $x = 5$ is a solution and provides an explanation, but the explanation is limited or contains minor inconsistencies/ errors.	Student identifies that $x = 5$ is a solution and provides an explanation and/or work that clearly supports valid reasoning.
3	a A-CED.A.1 F-BF.A.1a F-IF.B.5	Student does not provide an exponential function, OR student provides an exponential function that does not model the data the	Student provides a correct exponential function, but the domain is incorrect or omitted, OR student provides an exponential function	Student has made only minor errors in providing an exponential function that models the data and a domain that fits the situation.	Student provides a correct exponential function and identifies the domain to fit the situation.

Module 3:   Linear and Exponential Functions
Date: 9/12/13

		domain is incorrect or omitted.	that does not model the data but correctly identifies the domain in this situation.		
b F-IF.A.2	Student gives an incorrect answer with no supporting calculations.	Student gives an incorrect answer, but the answer is supported with the student's function from part (a).	Student has a minor calculation error in arriving at the answer. Student provides supporting work.	Student provides a correct answer with proper supporting work.
c F-BF.A.1a	Student provides no equation or gives an equation that does not demonstrate understanding of what is required to solve the problem described.	Student sets up an incorrect equation that demonstrates limited understanding of what is required to solve the problem described.	Student provides a correct answer but then simplifies it into an incorrect equation, OR student has a minor error in the equation given but demonstrates substantial understanding of what is required to solve the problem.	Student provides a correct equation that demonstrates understanding of what is required to solve the problem.
d F-IF.A.2	Student provides an equation or graph that does not reflect the correct data, OR student fails to provide an equation or graph.	Student provides a correct graph or table, but the answer to the question is either not given or incorrect.	Student provides a correct table or graph, but the answer is 4 months with an explanation that the 100 mark occurs during the 4th month.	Student provides a correct table or graph, AND the answer is correct (5 months) with a valid explanation.
e F-BF.A.1a	Student does not provide a linear function.	Student provides a function is linear but does not reflect data.	Student provides a correct linear function, but the function was either simplified incorrectly or does not use the notation, $t(n)$.	Student provides a correct linear function using the notation, $t(n)$.
f A-CED.A.2 F-IF.B.6 F-LE.A.3	Student does not demonstrate an ability to recognize and distinguish between linear and exponential growth or to compare growth rates or average rate of change of functions.	Student makes a partially correct but incomplete comparison of growth rates that does not include or incorrectly applies the concept of average rate of change.	Student makes a correct comparison of growth rates that includes an analysis of the rate of change of each function. However, student's communication contains minor errors or misuse of mathematical terms.	Student identifies that the Guppies' population will increase at a faster rate and provides a valid explanation that includes an analysis of the rate of change of each function.
g A-REI.D.11 F-IF.A.2 F-IF.C.9	Student does not provide correct graphs of the functions and is unable to provide an answer that is based on reasoning.	Student provides correct graphs but is unable to arrive at a correct answer from the graphs, OR student's graphs are incomplete or incorrect, but the student arrives	Student provides graphs that contain minor imprecisions and therefore arrives at an answer that is supportable by the graphs but incorrect.	Student provides correct graphs and arrives at an answer that is supportable by the graphs and correct.

Module 3:	Linear and Exponential Functions
Date:	9/12/13

312

			at an answer based on sound reasoning.		
	h F-IF.B.6 F-LE.A.1 F-LE.A.3	Student does not provide tables or graphs that are accurate enough to support an answer, and shows little reasoning in an explanation.	Student provides tables or graphs that are correct but provides limited or incorrect explanation of results.	Student provides tables or graphs that are correct and gives an explanation that is predominantly correct but contains minor errors or omissions in the explanation.	Student provides tables or graphs that are correct and gives a complete explanation that uses mathematical vocabulary correctly.
	i A-SSE.B.3c	Student does not provide an exponential function that shows percent increase.	Student writes an exponential function that uses an incorrect version of the growth factor, such as 0.02, 2%, 20%, or 0.20.	Student creates a correct version of the function using a growth factor expressed as 200% or expressed as 2 with a note that 2 is equivalent to 200%. Student has a minor error in notation, or in the domain, or does not specify the domain.	Student creates a correct version of the function using a growth factor expressed as 200% or expressed as 2 with a note that 2 is equivalent to 200%. Student specifies the domain correctly.
4	**a – c** F-BF.A.1a F-IF.A.3 F-LE.A.1 F-LE.A.2	Student does not fill in the table correctly and does not describe the relationship correctly. Student does not provide an exponential function.	Student completes the table correctly and describes the sequence correctly but gives an incorrect function. Student may or may not have given a correct domain.	Student completes the table correctly, and describes the sequence correctly, but has a minor error in either his or her function or domain. The function provided is exponential with a growth factor of 3. Description or notation may contain minor errors.	Student completes the table correctly, describes the sequence correctly, and provides a correct exponential function including the declaration of the domain. Student uses precise language and proper notation (either function or subscript notation) for the function.
	d F-BF.A.1a F-LE.A.1 F-LE.A.2	Student fails to provide an explicit exponential formula.	Student provides an explicit formula that is exponential but incorrect; supporting work is missing or reflects limited reasoning about the problem.	Student provides a correct explicit exponential formula. Notation or supporting work may contain minor errors.	Student provides a correct explicit exponential formula using function or subscript notation; formula and supporting work are free of errors.
	e F-BF.A.1a F-LE.A.1 F-LE.A.2	Student fails to provide an explicit exponential formula.	Student provides an explicit formula that is exponential but incorrect; supporting work is missing or reflects limited reasoning about the problem.	Student provides a correct explicit exponential formula. Notation or supporting work may contain minor errors.	Student provides a correct explicit exponential formula using function or subscript notation; formula and supporting work are free of errors.

	f F-BF.A.1a F-LE.A.1	Student provides little or no evidence of understanding how to determine the perimeter of the dark triangles nor how to recognize the common factor between two successive figures' perimeter.	Student's value of k is incorrect or not provided, but solution shows some understanding of how to determine the perimeter of the dark triangles.	Student's solution shows significant progress towards identifying that k is 3/2 but contains minor errors or is not complete. <u>OR</u> student computes an incorrect k value due to a minor error but otherwise demonstrates a way to determine k either by recognizing that the given equation is a recursive form of a geometric sequence or by approaching the problem algebraically.	Student identifies the correct value of k with enough supporting evidence of student thinking (correct table, graph, marking on diagram, or calculations) that shows how her or she arrived at the solution.
5	a F-BF.A.1a	Student does not provide a piecewise definition of the function and/or more than two expressions in the answer are incorrect.	Student provides a piecewise function in which at least one of the expressions is correct, the solution may contain errors with the intervals or notation.	Student provides a piecewise function with correct expressions, but the answer may contain minor errors with the intervals or use of function notation. OR one expression is incorrect, but intervals and use of function notation is correct.	Student provides a correctly defined piecewise function with correct intervals.
	b – c F-BF.B.3 F-IF.A.1	Student's graphs contain major errors; domain and range are missing or are inconsistent with the graphs.	Student's graph for (b) would be correct for (c) and vice versa, OR student answers either (b) or (c) correctly. Minor errors may exist in the domain and range.	Student's graphs contain one minor error. The domain and range are consistent with the graphs.	Student provides correct graphs for both (b) and (c) and provides a domain and range for each that are consistent with student graphs.
	d – e F-BF.B.3 F-IF.A.1	Both explanations and solutions are incorrect or have major conceptual errors (e.g., confusing domain and range).	Student answers contain more than one minor error, OR student answers only one of (d) and (e) correctly.	Student answer only explains how the domain/range changes; it may contain one minor error.	Student answer not only explains how the domain/range changes, but also explains how knowing $k > 1$ aids in finding the new domain/range.

Name _____   Date _____

1. Given $h(x) = |x + 2| - 3$ and $g(x) = -|x| + 4$.

   a. Describe how to obtain the graph of g from the graph of $a(x) = |x|$ using transformations.

   *To obtain the graph of **g**, reflect the graph of **a** about the x-axis and translate this graph up 4 units.*

   b. Describe how to obtain the graph of h from the graph of $a(x) = |x|$ using transformations.

   *To obtain the graph of **h**, translate the graph of **a** 2 units to the left and 3 units down.*

   c. Sketch the graphs of $h(x)$ and $g(x)$ on the same coordinate plane.

   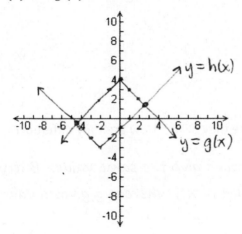

   d. Use your graphs to estimate the solutions to the equation:
   $$|x + 2| - 3 = -|x| + 4$$

   Explain how you got your answer.

   Solution: x ≈ 2.5 or x ≈ -4.5

   *The solutions are the x-coordinates of the intersection points of the graphs of **g** and **h**.*

   e. Were your estimations you made in part (d) correct? If yes, how do you know? If not explain why not.

Let x = 2.5	*Let x = -4.5*
Is $\|2.5 + 2\| - 3 = -\|2.5\| + 4$ true?	*Is $\|-4.5 + 2\| - 3 = -\|4.5\| + 4$ true?*
Yes, 4.5 − 3 = −2.5 + 4 is true.	*Yes, 2.5 − 3 = −4.5 + 4 is true.*

   Yes, the estimates are correct. They each make the equation true.

2. Let f and g be the functions given by $f(x) = x^2$ and $g(x) = x|x|$.

     a.   Find $f\left(\frac{1}{3}\right)$, $g(4)$, and $g(-\sqrt{3})$.

         f(1/3) = 1/9,   *g(4) = 16,*   *g(−√3) = −3*

     b.   What is the domain of f?

         D: all real numbers.

     c.   What is the range of g?

         R: all real numbers.

     d.   Evaluate $f(-67) + g(-67)$.

         (−67)² + −67|−67| = 0.

     e.   Compare and contrast f and g. How are they alike? How are they different?

         When x is positive, both functions give the same value. But when x is negative, f gives the always positive value of x², whereas g gives a value that is the opposite of what f gives.

     f.   Is there a value of x, such that $f(x) + g(x) = -100$? If so, find x. If not, explain why no such value exists.

         No, f and g are either both zero, giving a sum of zero, both positive, giving a positive sum, or the opposite of each other, giving a sum of zero. So, there is no way to get a negative sum.

     g.   Is there a value of x such that $(x) + g(x) = 50$? If so, find x. If not, explain why no such value exists.

         Yes, if x = 5, f(x) = g(x) = 25, thus f(x) + g(x) = 50.

3. A boy bought 6 guppies at the beginning of the month. One month later the number of guppies in his tank had doubled. His guppy population continued to grow in this same manner. His sister bought some tetras at the same time. The table below shows the number of tetras, t, after n months have passed since they bought the fish.

n, months	0	1	2	3
t, tetras	8	16	24	32

a. Create a function g to model the growth of the boy's guppy population, where g(n) is the number of guppies at the beginning of each month and n is the number of months that have passed since he bought the 6 guppies. What is a reasonable domain for g in this situation?

$g(n) = 6 \cdot 2^n$ Domain: n is a whole number.

b. How many guppies will there be one year after he bought the 6 guppies?

$g(12) = 6 \cdot 2^{12} = 24{,}576$ guppies

c. Create an equation that could be solved to determine how many months after he bought the guppies there will be 100 guppies.

$100 = 6 \cdot 2^n$

d. Use graphs or tables to approximate a solution to the equation from part c. Explain how you arrived at your estimate.

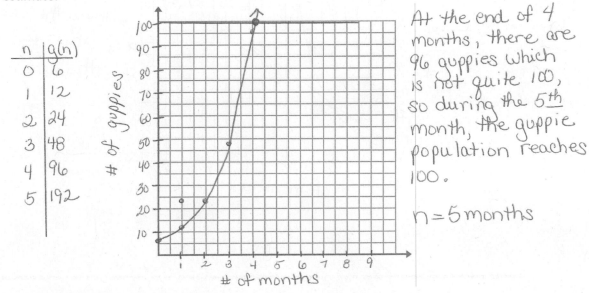

n	g(n)
0	6
1	12
2	24
3	48
4	96
5	192

At the end of 4 months, there are 96 guppies which is not quite 100, so during the 5th month, the guppie population reaches 100.

n = 5 months

e. Create a function, t, to model the growth of the sister's tetra population, where $t(n)$ is the number of tetras after n months have passed since she bought the tetras.

> $t(n) = 8(n+1)$, n is a whole number.
>
> Or, $t(n) = 8n + 8$, n is a whole number.

f. Compare the growth of the sister's tetra population to the growth of the guppy population. Include a comparison of the average rate of change for the functions that model each population's growth over time.

> The guppies' population is increasing faster than the tetras' population. Each month, the number of guppies doubles, while the number of tetra's increases by 8. The rate of change for the tetras is constant, but the rate of change for the guppies is always increasing.

g. Use graphs to estimate the number of months that will have passed when the population of guppies and tetras will be the same.

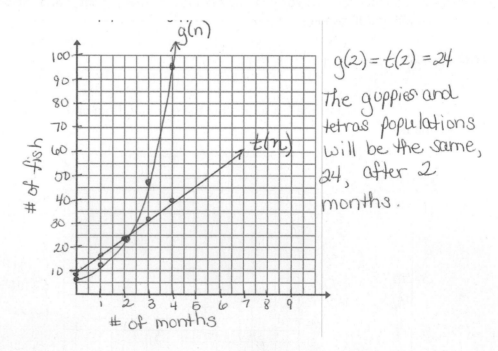

> $g(2) = t(2) = 24$
>
> The guppies and tetras populations will be the same, 24, after 2 months.

h. Use graphs or tables to explain why the guppy population will eventually exceed the tetra population even though there were more tetras to start with.

The guppy population's growth is exponential, and the tetra populations' growth is linear. The graph in part (g) shows how the population of the guppies eventually overtakes the population of the tetras. The table below shows that by the end of the 3rd month, there are more guppies than tetras.

n	0	1	2	3	4	5	
$g(n)$	6	12	24	48	96	192	*The average rate of change is doubling.*
$t(n)$	8	16	24	32	40	48	*The rate of change is constant.*

i. Write the function $g(n)$ in such a way that the percent increase in the number of fish per month can be identified. Circle or underline the expression representing percent increase in number of fish per month.

$g(n) = 6(\underline{200\%})^n$

4. Regard the solid dark equilateral triangle as figure 0. Then, the first figure in this sequence is the one composed of three dark triangles, the second figure is the one composed of nine dark triangles, and so on.

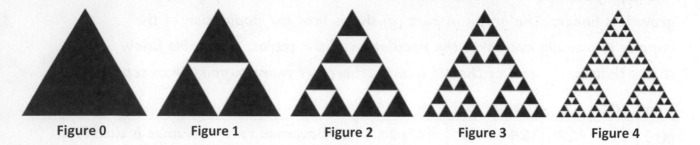

Figure 0   Figure 1   Figure 2   Figure 3   Figure 4

a. How many dark triangles are in each figure? Make a table to show this data.

n (Figure Number)	0	1	2	3	4
T (# of dark triangles)	1	3	9	27	81

b. Describe in words how, given the number of dark triangles in a figure, to determine the number of dark triangles in the next figure.

   The number of triangles in a figure is 3 times the number of triangles in the previous figure.

c. Create a function that models this sequence. What is the domain of this function?

   $T(n) = 3^n$, D: n is a whole number.

d. Suppose the area of the solid dark triangle in Figure 0 is 1 square meter. The areas of one dark triangle in each figure form a sequence. Create an explicit formula that gives the area of just one of the dark triangles in the nth figure in the sequence?

Figure, n	Area of one dark triangle, A(n)
0	1
1	1/4
2	1/16
3	1/64

$A(n) = \left(\frac{1}{4}\right)^n$

e. The sum of the areas of all the dark triangles in Figure 0 is 1 m²; there is only one triangle in this case. The sum of the areas of <u>all</u> the dark triangles in Figure 1 is ¾ m². What is the sum of the areas of <u>all</u> the dark triangles in the nth figure in the sequence? Is this total area increasing or decreasing as *n* increases?

Figure	Area in m²
0	1
1	3/4
2	9/16
3	27/64

$$T(n) = \left(\frac{3}{4}\right)^n$$

The total area is decreasing as n increases.

f. Let $P(n)$ be the sum of the perimeters of the <u>all</u> dark triangles in the nth figure in the sequence of figures. There is a real number k so that:

$$P(n + 1) = kP(n)$$

is true for each positive whole number n. What is the value of k?

Let x represent the number of meters long of one side of the triangle in Figure 0.

Figure	P(n)
0	$3x$
1	$3x + \dfrac{3}{2}x = \dfrac{9}{2}x$
2	$\dfrac{9}{2}x + \dfrac{9}{4}x = \dfrac{27}{4}x$

P is a geometric sequence and k is the ratio between any term and the previous term, so k = P(n+1)/P(n).

So, for example, for n = 0, $k = \dfrac{P(1)}{P(0)} = \dfrac{\frac{9}{2}x}{3x} = \dfrac{3}{2}$

For n = 1, $k = \dfrac{P(2)}{P(1)} = \dfrac{\frac{27}{4}x}{\frac{9}{2}x} = \dfrac{3}{2}$

K = 3/2

5. The graph of a piecewise –defined function f is shown to the right. The domain of f is $-3 \le x \le 3$.

    a. Create an algebraic representation for f. Assume that the graph of f is composed of straight line segments.

    $$f(x) = \begin{cases} x, & -3 \le x < -1 \\ -1, & -1 \le x < 0 \\ x-1, & 0 \le x < 2 \\ -x+3, & 2 \le x \le 3 \end{cases}$$

    or $f(x) = \begin{cases} x, & -3 \le x < -1 \\ -1, & -1 \le x < 0 \\ -|x-2|+1, & 0 \le x \le 3 \end{cases}$

    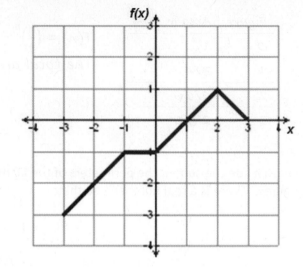

    b. Sketch the graph of $y = 2f(x)$ and state the domain and range.

    Domain: $-3 \le x \le 3$

    Range: $-6 \le y \le 2$

    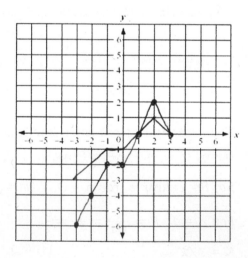

c.   Sketch the graph of $y = f(2x)$ and state the domain and range.

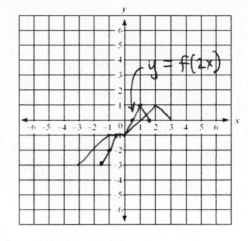

Domain: $-1.5 \leq x \leq 1.5$

Range: $-3 \leq y \leq 1$

d.   How does the range of $y = f(x)$ compare to the range of $y = kf(x)$, where $k > 1$?

Every value in the range of y = f(x) would be multiplied by k. Since k>1 we can represent this by multiplying the compound inequality that gives the range of y = f(x) by *k*, giving –3k ≤ y ≤ k.

e.   How does the domain of $y = f(x)$ compare to the domain of $y = f(kx)$, where $k > 1$?

Every value in the domain of y = f(x) would be divided by k. Since k>1 we can represent this by multiplying the compound inequality that gives the domain of y = f(x) by 1/k, giving –3/k ≤ x ≤ 3/k.

Student Materials

Lesson 1: Integer Sequences—Should You Believe in Patterns?

Classwork

Opening Exercise

Mrs. Rosenblatt gave her students what she thought was a very simple task:

What is the next number in the sequence 2, 4, 6, 8, …?

Cody: I am thinking of a "plus 2 pattern," so it continues 10, 12, 14, 16, ….

Ali: I am thinking a repeating pattern, so it continues 2, 4, 6, 8, 2, 4, 6, 8, ….

Suri: I am thinking of the units digits in the multiples of two, so it continues 2, 4, 6, 8, 0, 2, 4, 6, 8, ….

1. Are each of these valid responses?

2. What is the hundredth number in the sequence in Cody's scenario? Ali's? Suri's?

3. What is an expression in terms of n for the nth number in the sequence in Cody's scenario?

Example 1

Jerry has thought of a pattern that shows powers of two. Here are the first 6 numbers of Jerry's sequence:

$$1, 2, 4, 8, 16, 32, …$$

Write an expression for the nth number of Jerry's sequence.

Example 2

Consider the sequence that follows a "plus 3" pattern: $4, 7, 10, 13, 16, \dots$.

a. Write a formula for the sequence using both the a_n notation and the $f(n)$ notation.

b. Does the formula $f(n) = 3(n - 1) + 4$ generate the same sequence? Why might some people prefer this formula?

c. Graph the terms of the sequence as ordered pairs $(n, f(n))$ on the coordinate plane. What do you notice about the graph?

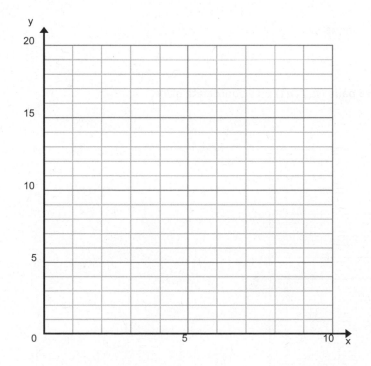

COMMON CORE™

Lesson 1:
Date:

Integer Sequences—Should You Believe in Patterns?
9/11/13

S.2

Exercises

1. Refer back to the sequence from the opening exercise. When Dr. T was asked for the next number in the sequence $2, 4, 6, 8, \ldots$, he said 17. 17?

   Yes, using the formula, $f(n) = \frac{7}{24}(n-1)^4 - \frac{7}{4}(n-1)^3 + \frac{77}{24}(n-1)^2 + \frac{1}{4}(n-1) + 2$.

   a. Does his formula actually produce the numbers 2, 4, 6, and 8?

   b. What is the 100th term in the Dr. T's sequence?

2. Consider a sequence that follows a "minus 5" pattern: $30, 25, 20, 15, \ldots$.

   a. Write a formula for the nth term of the sequence. Be sure to specify what value of n your formula starts with.

   b. Using the formula, find the 20th term of the sequence.

   c. Graph the terms of the sequence as ordered pairs $(n, f(n))$ on a coordinate plane.

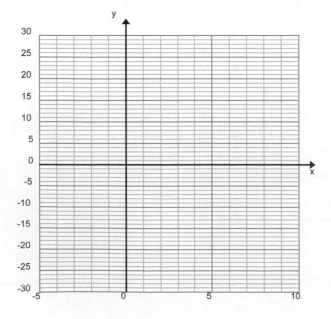

COMMON CORE™

Lesson 1:   Integer Sequences—Should You Believe in Patterns?
Date: 9/11/13

S.3

© 2013 Common Core, Inc. All rights reserved. **commoncore.org**

3. Consider a sequence that follows a "times 5" pattern: $1, 5, 25, 125, \ldots$.

    a. Write a formula for the nth term of the sequence. Be sure to specify what value of n your formula starts with.

    b. Using the formula, find the 10th term of the sequence.

    c. Graph the terms of the sequence as ordered pairs $(n, f(n))$ on a coordinate plane.

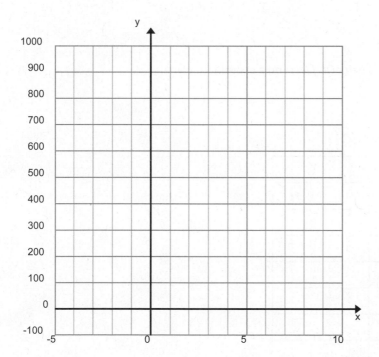

4. Consider the sequence formed by the square numbers:

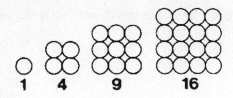

    a. Write a formula for the nth term of the sequence. Be sure to specify what value of n your formula starts with.

    b. Using the formula, find the 50th term of the sequence.

    c. Graph the terms of the sequence as ordered pairs $(n, f(n))$ on a coordinate plane.

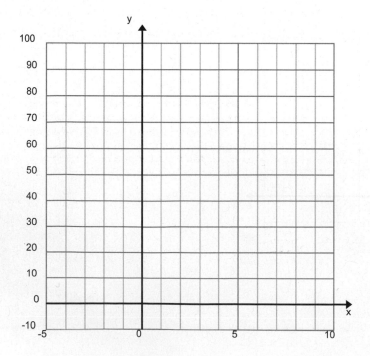

COMMON CORE™

Lesson 1:   Integer Sequences—Should You Believe in Patterns?
Date: 9/11/13

S.5

© 2013 Common Core, Inc. All rights reserved. commoncore.org

5. A standard letter-sized piece of paper has a length and width of 8.5 inches by 11 inches.

    a. Find the area of one piece of paper.

    b. If the paper were folded completely in half, what would be the area of the resulting rectangle?

    c. Write a formula for a sequence to determine the area of the paper after n folds.

    d. What would the area be after 7 folds?

Lesson Summary

A sequence can be thought of as an ordered list of elements. To define the pattern of the sequence, an explicit formula is often given, and unless specified otherwise, the first term is found by substituting 1 into the formula.

Problem Set

1. Consider a sequence generated by the formula $f(n) = 6n - 4$ starting with $n = 1$. Generate the terms $f(1), f(2), f(3), f(4)$, and $f(5)$.

2. Consider a sequence given by the formula $f(n) = \dfrac{1}{3^{n-1}}$ starting with $n = 1$. Generate the first 5 terms of the sequence.

3. Consider a sequence given by the formula $f(n) = (-1)^n \times 3$ starting with $n = 1$. Generate the first 5 terms of the sequence.

4. Here is the classic puzzle that shows that patterns need not hold true. What are the numbers counting?

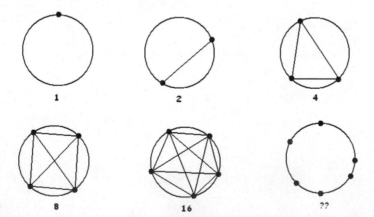

    a. Based on the sequence of numbers, predict the next number.
    b. Write a formula based on the perceived pattern.
    c. Find the next number in the sequence by actually counting.
    d. Based on your answer from c, is your model from b effective for this puzzle?

COMMON CORE™

Lesson 1:
Date:

Integer Sequences—Should You Believe in Patterns?
9/11/13

S.7

© 2013 Common Core, Inc. All rights reserved. **commoncore.org**

In problems 5-8, for each of the following sequences:

    a.   Write a formula for the nth term of the sequence. Be sure to specify what value of n your formula starts with.

    b.   Using the formula, find the 15th term of the sequence.

    c.   Graph the terms of the sequence as ordered pairs $(n, f(n))$ on a coordinate plane.

5.   The sequence follows a "plus 2" pattern: $3, 5, 7, 9, \dots$

6.   The sequence follows a "times 4" pattern: $1, 4, 16, 64, \dots$

7.   The sequence follows a "times -1" pattern: $6, -6, 6, -6, \dots$

8.   The sequence follows a "minus 3" pattern: $12, 9, 6, 3, \dots$

Lesson 2: Recursive Formulas for Sequences

Classwork

Example 1

Consider the sequence 5, 8, 11, 14, 17, ...

    a.   If you believed in patterns, what might you say is the next number in the sequence?

    b.   Write a formula for Akelia's sequence.

    c.   Explain how each part of the formula relates to the sequence.

    d.   Explain Johnny's formula.

Exercises 1–2

1.   Akelia, in a playful mood, asked Johnny: What would happen if we change the "+" sign in your formula to a "−" sign? To a "×" sign? To a "÷" sign?

    a.   What sequence does $A(n + 1) = A(n) - 3$ for $n \geq 1$ and $A(1) = 5$ generate?

    b.   What sequence does $A(n + 1) = A(n) \cdot 3$ for $n \geq 1$ and $A(1) = 5$ generate?

    c.   What sequence does $A(n + 1) = A(n) \div 3$ for $n \geq 1$ and $A(1) = 5$ generate?

2. Ben made up a recursive formula and used it to generate a sequence. He used $B(n)$ to stand for the nth term of his recursive sequence.

   a. What does $B(3)$ mean?

   b. What does $B(m)$ mean?

   c. If $B(n + 1) = 33$ and $B(n) = 28$, write a possible recursive formula involving $B(n + 1)$ and $B(n)$ that would generate 28 and 33 in the sequence.

   d. What does $2B(7) + 6$ mean?

   e. What does $B(n) + B(m)$ mean?

   f. Would it necessarily be the same as $B(n + m)$?

   g. What does $B(17) - B(16)$ mean?

Example 2

Consider a sequence given by the formula $a_n = a_{n-1} - 5$ where $a_1 = 12$ and $n \geq 1$.

    a.   List the first five terms of the sequence.

    b.   Write an explicit formula.

    c.   Find a_6 and a_{100} of the sequence.

Exercises 3–6

3.   One of the most famous sequences is the Fibonacci sequence:

    $1, 1, 2, 3, 5, 8, 13, 21, 34, \ldots$

        $f(n + 1) = f(n) + f(n - 1)$, where $f(1) = 1, f(2) = 1$, and $n \geq 2$.

    How is each term of the sequence generated?

4.   For each sequence below, an explicit formula is given. Write the first 5 terms of each sequence. Then, write a recursive formula for the sequence.

    a. $a_n = 2n + 10$ for $n \geq 1$

    b. $a_n = \left(\frac{1}{2}\right)^{n-1}$ for $n \geq 1$

5. For each sequence, write *either* an explicit or recursive formula.

   a. $1, -1, 1, -1, 1, -1, \ldots$

   b. $\dfrac{1}{2}, \dfrac{2}{3}, \dfrac{3}{4}, \dfrac{4}{5}, \ldots$

6. Lou opens a bank account. The deal he makes with his mother is that if he doubles the amount that was in the account at the beginning of each month by the end of the month, she will add an additional $5 to the account at the end of the month.

   a. Let $A(n)$ represent the amount in the account at the beginning of the nth month. Assume that he does, in fact, double the amount every month. Write a recursive formula for the amount of money in his account at the beginning of the nth month.

   b. What is the least amount he could start with in order to have $300 by the beginning of the 3rd month?

> **Lesson Summary**
>
> RECURSIVE SEQUENCE (description). An example of a *recursive sequence* is a sequence that (1) is defined by specifying the values of one or more initial terms and (2) has the property that the remaining terms satisfy a recursive formula that describes the value of a term based upon an expression in numbers, previous terms, or the index of the term.
>
> An explicit formula specifies the nth term of a sequence as an expression in n.
>
> A recursive formula specifies the nth term of a sequence as an expression in the previous term (or previous couple of terms).

Problem Set

For problems 1-4, list the first five terms of each sequence.

1. $a_{n+1} = a_n + 6$, where $a_1 = 11$ for $n \geq 1$

2. $a_n = a_{n-1} \div 2$, where $a_1 = 50$ for $n \geq 2$

3. $f(n + 1) = -2f(n) + 8$ and $f(1) = 1$ for $n \geq 1$

4. $f(n) = f(n - 1) + n$ and $f(1) = 4$ for $n \geq 2$

For problems 5-10, write a recursive formula for each sequence given or described below.

5. It follows a "plus one" pattern: $8, 9, 10, 11, 12, \ldots$.

6. It follows a "times 10" pattern: $4, 40, 400, 4000, \ldots$.

7. It has an explicit formula of $f(n) = -3n + 2$ for $n \geq 1$.

8. It has an explicit formula of $f(n) = -1(12)^{n-1}$ for $n \geq 1$.

9. Doug accepts a job where his starting salary will be $30,000 per year, and each year he will receive a raise of $3,000.

10. A bacteria culture has an initial population of 10 bacteria, and each hour the population triples in size.

Lesson 3: Arithmetic and Geometric Sequences

Classwork

Exercise 2

Think of a real–world example of an arithmetic/geometric sequence? Describe it and write its formula.

Exercise 3

If we fold a rectangular piece of paper in half multiple times and count the number of rectangles created, what type of sequence are we creating? Can you write the formula?

Lesson Summary

Two types of sequences were studied:

ARITHMETIC SEQUENCE (description). A sequence is called *arithmetic* if there is a real number d such that each term in the sequence is the sum of the previous term and d.

GEOMETRIC SEQUENCE (description). A sequence is called *geometric* if there is a real number r such that each term in the sequence is a product of the previous term and r.

Problem Set

For problems 1–4, list the first five terms of each sequence, and identify them as arithmetic or geometric.

1. $A(n + 1) = A(n) + 4$ for $n \geq 1$ and $A(1) = -2$

2. $A(n + 1) = \frac{1}{4} \cdot A(n)$ for $n \geq 1$ and $A(1) = 8$

3. $A(n + 1) = A(n) - 19$ for $n \geq 1$ and $A(1) = -6$

4. $A(n + 1) = \frac{2}{3} A(n)$ for $n \geq 1$ and $A(1) = 6$

For problems 5–8, identify the sequence as arithmetic or geometric, and write a recursive formula for the sequence. Be sure to identify your starting value.

5. $14, \ 21, \ 28, \ 35, \ldots$

6. $4, \ 40, \ 400, \ 4000, \ldots$

7. $49, \ 7, \ \frac{1}{7}, \frac{1}{49}, \ldots$

8. $-101, \ -91, \ -81, \ -71, \ldots$

9. The local football team won the championship several years ago, and since then, ticket prices have been increasing $20 per year. The year they won the championship, tickets were $50. Write a recursive formula for a sequence that will model ticket prices. Is the sequence arithmetic or geometric?

10. A radioactive substance decreases in the amount of grams by one third each year. If the starting amount of the substance in a rock is 1,452 g, write a recursive formula for a sequence that models the amount of the substance left after the end of each year. Is the sequence arithmetic or geometric?

---

11. Find an explicit form $f(n)$ for each of the following arithmetic sequences (assume a is some real number and x is some real number):

    a. $-34, -22, -10, 2, \ldots$

    b. $\dfrac{1}{5}, \dfrac{1}{10}, 0, -\dfrac{1}{10}, \ldots$

    c. $x + 4, x + 8, x + 12, x + 16, \ldots$

    d. $a, 2a + 1, 3a + 2, 4a + 3, \ldots$

12. Consider the arithmetic sequence $13, 24, 35, \ldots$.

    a.   Find an explicit form for the sequence in terms of n.

    b.   Find the 40th term.

    c.   If the nth term is 299, find the value of n.

13. If $-2, a, b, c, 14$ forms an arithmetic sequence, find the values of $a, b,$ and c.

14. $3 + x, 9 + 3x, 13 + 4x, \ldots$ is an arithmetic sequence for some real number x.

    a.   Find the value of x.

    b.   Find the 10th term of the sequence.

15. Find an explicit form $f(n)$ of the arithmetic sequence where the 2nd term is 25 and the sum of the 3rd term and 4th term is 86.

16. (Challenge) In the right triangle figure below the lengths of the sides a cm, b cm, c cm of the right triangle form a finite arithmetic sequence. If the perimeter of the triangle is 18 cm, find the values of $a, b,$ and c.

17. Find the common ratio and an explicit form in each of the following geometric sequences:

    a. $4, 12, 36, 108, \ldots$

    b. $162, 108, 72, 48, \ldots$

    c. $\dfrac{4}{3}, \dfrac{2}{3}, \dfrac{1}{3}, \dfrac{1}{6}, \ldots$

    d. $xz, x^2z^3, x^3z^5, x^4z^7, \ldots$

18. The first term in a geometric sequence is 54, and the 5th term is $\dfrac{2}{3}$. Find an explicit form for the geometric sequence.

19. If $2, a, b, -54$ forms a geometric sequence, find the values of a and b.

20. Find the explicit form $f(n)$ of a geometric sequence if $f(3) - f(1) = 48$ and $\dfrac{f(3)}{f(1)} = 9$.

Lesson 4: Why do Banks Pay YOU to Provide Their Services?

Classwork

Example 1

Kyra has been babysitting since 6th grade. She has saved $1000 and wants to open an account at the bank so that she will earn interest on her savings. Simple Bank pays simple interest at a rate of 10%. How much money will Kyra have after 1 year? After 2 years, if she does not add money to her account? After 5 years?

Raoul needs $200 to start a snow cone stand for this hot summer. He borrows the money from a bank that charges 4% simple interest a year.

   a. How much will he owe if he waits 1 year to pay back the loan? If he waits two years? 3 years? 4 years? 5 years?

   b. Write a formula for the amount he will owe after t years.

Example 2

Jack has $500 to invest. The bank offers an interest rate of 6% compounded annually. How much money will Jack have after 1 year? 2 years? 5 years? 10 years?

Example 3

If you have $200 to invest for 10 years, would you rather invest your money in a bank that pays 7% simple interest or 5% interest compounded annually? Is there anything you could change in the problem that would make you change your answer?

COMMON CORE

Lesson 4
Date:

Why do Banks Pay YOU to Provide Their Services?
9/11/13

S.19

Lesson Summary

Simple Interest – Interest is calculated once per year on the original amount borrowed or invested. The interest does not become part of the amount borrowed or owed (the principal).

Compound Interest – Interest is calculated once per period on the current amount borrowed or invested. Each period, the interest becomes a part of the principal.

Problem Set

1. $250 is invested at a bank that pays 7% simple interest. Calculate the amount of money in the account after 1 year; 3 years; 7 years; 20 years.

2. $325 is borrowed from a bank that charges 4% interest compounded annually. How much is owed after 1 year; 3 years; 7 years; 20 years?

3. Joseph has $10,000 to invest. He can go to Yankee Bank that pays 5% simple interest or Met Bank that pays 4% interest compounded annually. After how many years will Met Bank be the better choice?

Lesson 5: The Power of Exponential Growth

Classwork

Opening Exercise

Two equipment rental companies have different penalty policies for returning a piece of equipment late:

Company 1: On day 1, the penalty is $5. On day 2, the penalty is $10. On day 3, the penalty is $15. On day 4, the penalty is $20 and so on, increasing by $5 each day the equipment is late.

Company 2: On day 1, the penalty is $0.01. On day 2, the penalty is $0.02. On day 3, the penalty is $0.04. On day 4, the penalty is $0.08 and so on, doubling in amount each additional day late.

Jim rented a digger from Company 2 because he thought it had the better late return policy. The job he was doing with the digger took longer than he expected, but it did not concern him because the late penalty seemed so reasonable. When he returned the digger 15 days late, he was shocked by the penalty fee. What did he pay, and what would he have paid if he had used Company 1 instead?

Company 1		Company 2	
Day	Penalty	Day	Penalty
1		1	
2		2	
3		3	
4		4	
5		5	
6		6	
7		7	
8		8	
9		9	
10		10	
11		11	
12		12	
13		13	
14		14	
15		15	

1. Which company has a greater 15 day late charge?

2. Describe how the amount of the late charge changes from any given day to the next successive day in both companies 1 and 2.

3. How much would the late charge have been after 20 days under Company 2?

Example 1

Folklore suggests that when the creator of the game of chess showed his invention to the country's ruler, the ruler was highly impressed. He was so impressed, he told the inventor to name a prize of his choice. The inventor, being rather clever, said he would take a grain of rice on the first square of the chessboard, two grains of rice on the second square of the chessboard, four on the third square, eight on the fourth square, and so on, doubling the number of grains of rice for each successive square. The ruler was surprised, even a little offended, at such a modest price, but he ordered his treasurer to count out the rice.

   a.   Why is the ruler "surprised"? What makes him think the inventor requested a "modest price"?

The treasurer took more than a week to count the rice in the ruler's store, only to notify the ruler that it would take more rice than was available in the entire kingdom. Shortly thereafter, as the story goes, the inventor became the new king.

b. Imagine the treasurer counting the needed rice for each of the 64 squares. We know that the first square is assigned a single grain of rice, and each successive square is double the number of grains of rice of the former square. The following table lists the first five assignments of grains of rice to squares on the board. How can we represent the grains of rice as exponential expressions?

Square #	Grains of Rice	Exponential Expression
1	1	
2	2	
3	4	
4	8	
5	16	

c. Write the exponential expression that describes how much rice is assigned to each of the last three squares of the board.

Square #	Exponential Expression
62	
63	
64	

Example 2

Let us understand the difference between $f(n) = 2n$ and $f(n) = 2^n$.

a. Complete the tables below, and then graph the points $(n, f(n))$ on a coordinate plane for each of the formulas.

n	$f(n) = 2n$
-2	
-1	
0	
1	
2	
3	

n	$f(n) = 2^n$
-2	
-1	
0	
1	
2	
3	

b. Describe the change in each sequence when n increases by 1 unit for each sequence.

Exercise 1

A typical thickness of toilet paper is 0.001 inches. Seems pretty thin, right? Let's see what happens when we start folding toilet paper.

    a.   How thick is the stack of toilet paper after 1 fold? After 2 folds? After 5 folds?

    b.   Write an explicit formula for the sequence that models the thickness of the folded toilet paper after n folds.

    c.   After many folds will the stack of folded toilet paper pass the 1 foot mark?

    d.   The moon is about 240,000 miles from Earth. Compare the thickness of the toilet paper folded 50 times to the distance from Earth.

Watch the following video "How folding paper can get you to the moon"
(http://www.youtube.com/watch?v=AmFMJC45f1Q)

Exercise 2

A rare coin appreciates at a rate of 5.2% a year. If the initial value of the coin is $500, after how many years will its value cross the $3,000 mark? Show the formula that will model the value of the coin after t years.

Problem Set

1. A bucket is put under a leaking ceiling. The amount of water in the bucket doubles every minute. After 8 minutes, the bucket is full. After how many minutes is the container half full?

2. A three-bedroom house in Burbville was purchased for $190,000. If housing prices are expected to increase 1.8% annually in that town, write an explicit formula that models the price of the house in t years. Find the price of the house in 5 years.

3. A local college has increased the number of graduates by a factor of 1.045 over the previous year for every year since 1999. In 1999, 924 students graduated. What explicit formula models this situation? Approximately how many students will graduate in 2014?

4. The population growth rate of New York City has fluctuated tremendously in the last 200 years, the highest rate estimated at 126.8% in 1900. In 2001, the population of the city was 8,008,288, up 2.1% from 2000. If we assume that the annual population growth rate stayed at 2.1% from the year 2000 onward, in what year would we expect the population of New York City to have exceeded ten million people? Be sure to include the explicit formula you use to arrive at your answer.

5. In 2013, a research company found that smartphone shipments (units sold) were up 32.7% worldwide from 2012, with an expectation for the trend to continue. If 959 million units were sold in 2013, how many smartphones can be expected to be sold in 2018 at the same growth rate? (Include the explicit formula for the sequence that models this growth.) Can this trend continue?

6. Two band mates have only 7 days to spread the word about their next performance. Jack thinks they can each pass out 100 fliers a day for 7 days and they will have done a good job in getting the news out. Meg has a different strategy. She tells 10 of her friends about the performance on the first day and asks each of her 10 friends to each tell a friend on the second day and then everyone who has heard about the concert to tell a friend on the third day and so on, for 7 days. Make an assumption that students make sure they are telling someone who has not already been told.

   a. Over the first 7 days, Meg's strategy will reach fewer people than Jack's. Show that this is true.

   b. If they had been given more than 7 days, would there be a day on which Meg's strategy would begin to inform more people than Jack's strategy? If not, explain why not. If so, which day would this occur on?

   c. Knowing that she has only 7 days, how can Meg alter her strategy to reach more people than Jack does?

7. On June 1, a fast-growing species of algae is accidentally introduced into a lake in a city park. It starts to grow and cover the surface of the lake in such a way that the area covered by the algae doubles every day. If it continues to grow unabated, the lake will be totally covered, and the fish in the lake will suffocate. At the rate it is growing, this will happen on June 30.

    a. When will the lake be covered half way?

    b. On June 26, a pedestrian who walks by the lake every day warns that the lake will be completely covered soon. Her friend just laughs. Why might her friend be skeptical of the warning?

    c. On June 29, a clean-up crew arrives at the lake and removes almost all of the algae. When they are done, only 1% of the surface is covered with algae. How well does this solve the problem of the algae in the lake?

    d. Write an explicit formula for the sequence that models the percentage of the surface area of the lake that is covered in algae, a, given the time in days, t, that has passed since the algae was introduced into the lake.

8. Mrs. Davis is making a poster of math formulas for her students. She takes the 8.5in x 11in paper she printed the formulas on to the photocopy machine and enlarges the image so that the length and the width are both 150% of the original. She enlarges the image a total of 3 times before she is satisfied with the size of the poster. Write an explicit formula for the sequence that models the area of the poster, A, after n enlargements. What is the area of the final image compared to the area of the original, expressed as a percent increase and rounded to the nearest percent?

Lesson 6: Exponential Growth—U.S. Population and World Population

Classwork

Example 1

Callie and Joe are examining the population data in the graphs below for a history report. Their comments are as follows:

Callie: It looks like the U.S. population grew the same amount as the world population, but that can't be right, can it?

Joe: Well, I don't think they grew by the same *amount*, but they sure grew at about the same rate. Look at the slopes.

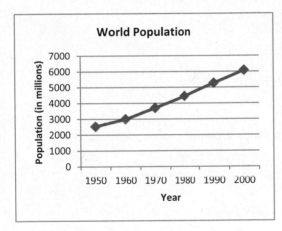

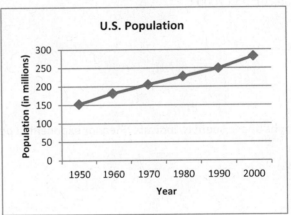

a. Is Callie's observation correct? Why or why not?

b. Is Joe's observation correct? Why or why not?

c.   Use the World Population graph to estimate the percent increase in world population from 1950 to 2000.

d.   Now use the U.S. Population graph to compute the percent increase in the U.S. population for the same time period.

e.   How does the percent increase for the world population compare to that for the U.S. population over the same time period, 1950 to 2000?

f.   Do the graphs above seem to indicate linear or exponential population growth? Explain your response.

g.   Write an explicit formula for the sequence that models the world population growth from 1950–2000 based on the information in the graph. Assume that the population (in millions) in 1950 was 2,500 and in 2000 was 6,000. Use t to represent the number of years after 1950.

Lesson 6:	Exponential Growth—U.S. Population and World Population
Date:	9/11/13

S.29

Example 2

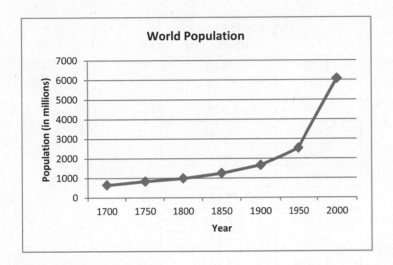

a. How is this graph similar to the World Population graph in Example 1? How is it different?

b. Does the behavior of the graph from 1950–2000 match that shown on the graph in Example 1?

c. Why is the graph from Example 1 somewhat misleading?

d. An exponential formula that can be used to model the world population growth from 1950 through 2000 is as follows:

$$f(t) = 2{,}519(1.0177^t)$$

where 2,519 represents the world population in the year 1950, and t represents the number of years after 1950. Use this equation to calculate the world population in 1950, 1980, and 2000. How do your calculations compare with the world populations shown on the graph?

e.   Following is a table showing the world population numbers used to create the graphs above.

Year	World Population (in millions)
1700	640
1750	824
1800	978
1850	1,244
1900	1,650
1950	2,519
1960	2,982
1970	3,692
1980	4,435
1990	5,263
2000	6,070

How do the numbers in the table compare with those you calculated in part (d) above?

f.   How is the formula in part (d) above different from the formula in Example 1 part (g)? What causes the difference? Which formula more closely represents the population?

Exercises

1. The table below represents the population of the U.S. (in millions) for the specified years.

Year	U.S. Population (in millions)
1800	5
1900	76
2000	282

a. If we use the data from 1800–2000 to create an exponential equation representing the population, we generate the following formula for the sequence, where $f(t)$ represents the U.S. population and t represents the number of years after 1800.

$$f(t) = 5(1.0204)^t$$

Use this formula to determine the population of the U.S. in the year 2010.

b. If we use the data from 1900–2000 to create an exponential formula that models the population, we generate the following, where $f(t)$ represents the U.S. population and t represents the number of years after 1900.

$$f(t) = 76(1.013)^t$$

Use this formula to determine the population of the U.S. in the year 2010.

c. The actual U.S. population in the year 2010 was 309 million. Which of the above formulas better models the U.S. population for the entire span of 1800–2010? Why?

d. Complete the table below to show projected population figures for the years indicated. Use the formula from part (b) to determine the numbers.

Year	World Population (in millions)
2020	
2050	
2080	

e. Are the population figures you computed reasonable? What other factors need to be considered when projecting population?

2. The population of the country of Oz was 600,000 in the year 2010. The population is expected to grow by a factor of 5% annually. The annual food supply of Oz is currently sufficient for a population of 700,000 people and is increasing at a rate which will supply food for an additional 10,000 people per year.

a. Write a formula to model the population of Oz. Is your formula linear or exponential?

b. Write a formula to model the food supply. Is the formula linear or exponential?

c. At what point does the population exceed the food supply? Justify your response.

d. If Oz doubled its current food supply (to 1.4 million), would shortages still take place? Explain.

e. If Oz doubles both its beginning food supply and doubles the rate at which the food supply increases, would food shortages still take place? Explain.

Problem Set

1. Student Friendly Bank pays a simple interest rate of 2.5% per year. Neighborhood Bank pays a compound interest rate of 2.1% per year, compounded monthly.

   a. Which bank will provide the largest balance if you plan to invest $10,000 for 10 years? For 20 years?

   b. Write an explicit formula for the sequence that models the balance of the Student Friendly Bank balance, t years after a deposit is left in the account.

   c. Write an explicit formula for the sequence that models the balance at the Neighborhood Bank balance, m months after a deposit is left in the account.

   d. Create a table of values indicating the balances in the two bank accounts from year 2 to year 20 in 2 year increments. Round each value to the nearest dollar.

Year	Student Friendly Bank (in dollars)	Neighborhood Bank (in dollars)
0		
2		
4		
6		
8		
10		
12		
14		
16		
18		
20		

   e. Which bank is a better short-term investment? Which bank is better for those leaving money in for a longer period of time? When are the investments about the same?

   f. What type of model is Student Friendly Bank? What is the rate or ratio of change?

   g. What type of model is Neighborhood Bank? What is the rate or ratio of change?

2. The table below represents the population of the state of New York for the years 1800–2000. Use this information to answer the questions.

Year	Population
1800	300,000
1900	7,300,000
2000	19,000,000

a. Using the year 1800 as the base year, an explicit formula for the sequence that models the population of New York is $P(t) = 300000(1.021)^t$, where t is the number of years after 1800.
    Using this formula, calculate the projected population of New York in 2010.

b. Using the year 1900 as the base year, an explicit formula for the sequence that models the population of New York is $P(t) = 7300000(1.0096)^t$, where t is the number of years after 1900.
    Using this equation, calculate the projected population of New York in 2010.

c. Using the internet (or some other source), find the population of the state of New York according to the 2010 census. Which formula yielded a more accurate prediction of the 2010 population?

Lesson 7: Exponential Decay

Classwork

Example 1

a. Malik bought a new car for $15,000. As he drove it off the lot, his best friend, Will, told him that the car's value just dropped by 15% and that it would continue to depreciate 15% of its current value each year. If the car's value is now $12,750 (according to Will), what will its value be after 5 years?

Complete the table below to determine the car's value after each of the next five years.

Number of years, t, passed since driving the car off the lot	Car value after t years	15% depreciation of current car value	Car value minus the 15% depreciation
0	$12,750.00	$1,912.50	$10,837.50
1	10,837.50		
2			
3			
4			
5			

b. Write an explicit formula for the sequence that models the value of Malik's car t years after driving it off the lot.

c. Use the formula from part (b) to determine the value of Malik's car five years after its purchase. Round your answer to the nearest cent. Compare the value with the value in the table. Are they the same?

d. Use the formula from part (b) to determine the value of Malik's car 7 years after its purchase. Round your answer to the nearest cent.

Exercises

1. Identify the initial value in each formula below, and state whether the formula models exponential growth or exponential decay. Justify your responses.

   a. $f(t) = 2 \left(\frac{2}{5}\right)^t$

   b. $f(t) = 2 \left(\frac{5}{3}\right)^t$

   c. $f(t) = \frac{2}{3}(3)^t$

   d. $f(t) = \frac{2}{3}\left(\frac{1}{3}\right)^t$

   e. $f(t) = \frac{3}{2}\left(\frac{2}{3}\right)^t$

2. If a person takes a given dosage (d) of a particular medication, then the formula $f(t) = d\,(0.8)^t$ represents the concentration of the medication in the bloodstream t hours later. If Charlotte takes 200 mg of the medication at $6\!:\!00$ a.m., how much remains in her bloodstream at $10\!:\!00$ a.m.? How long does it take for the concentration to drop below 1 mg?

3. When you breathe normally, about 12% of the air in your lungs is replaced with each breath. Write an explicit formula for the sequence that models the amount of the original air left in your lungs, given that the initial volume of air is 500 mL. Use your model to determine how much of the original 500 mL remains after 50 breaths.

4. Ryan bought a new computer for $2,100. The value of the computer decreases by 50% each year. When will the value drop below $300?

5. Kelli's mom takes a 400 mg dose of aspirin. Each hour, the amount of aspirin in a person's system decreases by about 29%. How much aspirin is left in her system after 6 hours?

6. According to the International Basketball Association (FIBA), a basketball must be inflated to a pressure such that, when it is dropped from a height of 1,800 mm, it will rebound to a height of 1,300 mm. Maddie decides to test the rebound-ability of her new basketball. She assumes that the ratio of each rebound height to the previous rebound height remains the same at $\dfrac{1{,}300}{1{,}800}$. Let $f(n)$ be the height of the basketball after n bounces. Complete the chart below to reflect the heights Maddie expects to measure.

n	$f(n)$
0	1,800
1	
2	
3	
4	

a. Write the explicit formula for the sequence that models the height of Maddie's basketball after any number of bounces.

b. Plot the points from the table. Connect the points with a smooth curve, and then use the curve to estimate the bounce number at which the rebound height will drop below 200 mm.

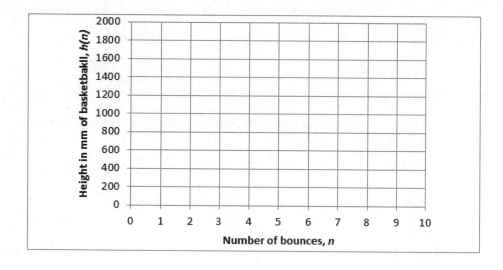

Lesson Summary

The explicit formula $f(t) = ab^t$ models exponential decay, where a represents the initial value of the sequence, $b < 1$ represents the growth factor (or decay factor) per unit of time, and t represents units of time.

Problem Set

1. From 2000 to 2013, the value of the U.S. dollar has been shrinking. The value can be modeled by the following formula:

   $v(t) = 1.36 \, (0.9758)^t$, where t is the number of years since 2000.

   a. How much was a dollar worth in the year 2005?

   b. Graph the points $(t, v(t))$, for integer values of $0 \le t \le 14$.

   c. Estimate the year in which the value of the dollar fell below $1.00.

2. A construction company purchased some equipment costing $300,000. The value of the equipment depreciates (decreases) at a rate of 14% per year.

   a. Write a formula that models the value of the equipment.

   b. What is the value of the equipment after 9 years?

   c. Graph the points $(t, v(t))$ for integer values of $0 \le t \le 15$.

   d. Estimate when the equipment will have a value of $50,000.

3. The number of newly reported cases of HIV (in thousands) in the United States from 2000 to 2010 can be modeled by the following formula:

   $f(t) = 41(0.9842)^t$, where t is the number of years after 2000.

   a. Identify the growth factor.

   b. Calculate the estimated number of new HIV cases reported in 2004.

   c. Graph the points $(t, f(t))$ for integer values of $0 \le t \le 10$.

   d. During what year did the number of newly reported HIV cases drop below 36,000?

4. Doug drank a soda with 130 mg of caffeine. Each hour, the caffeine in the body diminishes by about 12%.

   a. Write formula to model the amount of caffeine remaining in Doug's system.

   b. How much caffeine remains in Doug's system after 2 hours?

   c. How long will it take for the level of caffeine in Doug's system to drop below 50 mg?

Lesson 7:	Exponential Decay
Date:	9/11/13

S.40

5. 64 teams participate in a softball tournament in which half the teams are eliminated after each round of play.

   a. Write a formula to model the number of teams remaining after any given round of play.

   b. How many teams remain in play after 3 rounds?

   c. How many rounds of play will it take to determine which team wins the tournament?

6. Sam bought a used car for $8,000. He boasted that he got a great deal since the value of the car two years ago (when it was new) was $15,000. His friend, Derek, was skeptical, stating that the value of a car typically depreciates about 25% per year, so Sam got a bad deal.

   a. Use Derek's logic to write a formula for the value of Sam's car. Use t for the total age of the car in years.

   b. Who is right, Sam or Derek?

Lesson 8: Why Stay With Whole Numbers?

Classwork

Opening Exercise

The sequence of perfect squares $\{1,4,9,16,25, \dots\}$ earned its name because the ancient Greeks realized these quantities could be arranged to form square shapes.

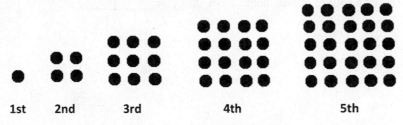

| 1st | 2nd | 3rd | 4th | 5th |

If $S(n)$ denotes the nth square number, what is a formula for $S(n)$?

Exercises

1. Prove whether or not 169 is a perfect square.

2. Prove whether or not 200 is a perfect square.

3. If $S(n) = 225$, then what is n?

4. Which term is the number 400 in the sequence of perfect squares? How do you know?

Instead of arranging dots into squares, suppose we extend our thinking to consider squares of side length x cm.

5. Create formula for the area $A(x)$ cm^2 of a square of side length x cm. $A(x) =$ _____

6. Use the formula to determine the area of squares with side lengths of 3 cm, 10.5 cm, and π cm.

7. What does $A(0)$ mean?

8. What does $A(-10)$ and $A(\sqrt{2})$ mean?

COMMON CORE™

Lesson 8:   Why Stay With Whole Numbers?
Date: 9/11/13

S.43

The triangular numbers are the numbers that arise from arranging dots into triangular figures as shown:

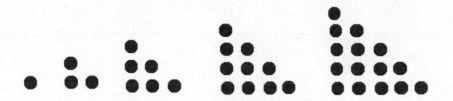

9. What is the 100th triangular number?

10. Find a formula for $T(n)$, the nth triangular number (starting with $n = 1$).

11. How can you be sure your formula works?

12. Create a graph of the sequence of triangular numbers, $T(n) = \dfrac{n(n+1)}{2}$, where n is a positive integer.

COMMON CORE™

Lesson 8:   Why Stay With Whole Numbers?
Date: 9/11/13

S.44

13. Create a graph of the triangle area formula $T(x) = \dfrac{x(x+1)}{2}$, where x is any positive real number.

14. How are your two graphs alike? How are they different?

COMMON CORE™

Lesson 8:   Why Stay With Whole Numbers?
Date: 9/11/13

S.45

Problem Set

1. The first four terms of two different sequences are shown below. Sequence A is given in the table and sequence B is graphed as a set of ordered pairs.

n	$A(n)$
1	15
2	31
3	47
4	63

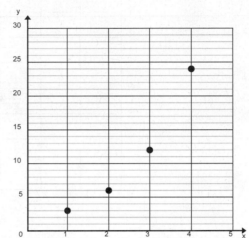

a. Create an explicit formula for each sequence.

b. Which sequence will be the first to exceed 500? How do you know?

2. A tile pattern is shown below.

Figure 1   **Figure 2**   **Figure 3**   **Figure 4**

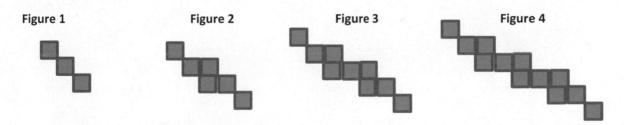

a. How is this pattern growing?

b. Create an explicit formula that could be used to determine the number of squares in the n th figure.

c. Evaluate your formula for $n = 0$ and $n = 2.5$. Draw Figure 0 and Figure 2.5, and explain how you decided to create your drawings.

3. The first four terms of a geometric sequence are graphed as a set of ordered pairs.

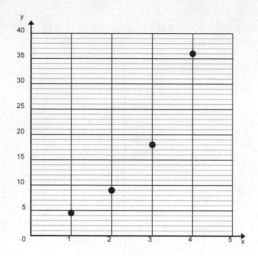

a. What is an explicit formula for this sequence?

b. Explain the meaning of the ordered pair $(3, 18)$.

c. As of July 2013, Justin Bieber had over 42,000,000 twitter followers. Suppose the sequence represents the number of people that follow your new twitter account each week since you started tweeting. If your followers keep growing in the same manner, when will you exceed 1,000,000 followers?

COMMON CORE™

Lesson 8: Why Stay With Whole Numbers?
Date: 9/11/13

S.47

Lesson 9: Representing, Naming, and Evaluating Functions

Classwork

Opening Exercise

Match each picture to the correct word by drawing an arrow from the word to the picture.

Elephant

Camel

Polar Bear

Zebra

FUNCTION. A *function* is a correspondence between two sets, X and Y, in which each element of X is matched to one and only one element of Y. The set X is called the *domain of the function*.

The notation $f: X \rightarrow Y$ is used to name the function and describes both X and Y. If x is an element in the domain X of a function $f: X \rightarrow Y$, then x is matched to an element of Y called $f(x)$. We say $f(x)$ is the value in Y that denotes the *output* or *image* of f corresponding to the *input* x.

The *range (or image)* of a function $f: X \rightarrow Y$ is the subset of Y, denoted $f(X)$, defined by the following property: y is an element of $f(X)$ if and only if there is an x in X such that $f(x) = y$.

Example 1

Define the opening exercise using function notation. State the domain and the range.

Example 2

Is the assignment of students to English teachers an example of a function? If yes, define it using function notation, and state the domain and the range.

Example 3

Let $X = \{1, 2, 3, 4\}$ and $Y = \{5, 6, 7, 8, 9\}$. f and g are defined below.

$f: X \to Y$ $g: X \to Y$

$f = \{(1,7), (2,5), (3,6), (4,7)\}$ $g = \{(1,5), (2,6), (1,8), (2,9), (3,7)\}$

Is f a function? If yes, what is the domain and what is the range? If no, explain why f is not a function.

Is g a function? If yes, what is the domain and range? If no, explain why g is not a function.

What is $f(2)$?

If $f(x) = 7$, then what might x be?

Exercises

1. Define f to assign each student at your school a unique ID number.

$$f: \{students\ in\ your\ school\} \rightarrow \{whole\ numbers\}$$

Assign each student a unique ID number

   a. Is this an example of a function? Use the definition to explain why or why not.

   b. Suppose $f(Hilda) = 350123$. What does that mean?

   c. Write your name and student ID number using function notation.

2. Let g assign each student at your school to a grade level.

   a. Is this an example of a function? Explain your reasoning.

   b. Express this relationship using function notation and state the domain and the range.

$$g: \{students\ in\ the\ school\} \rightarrow \{grade\ level\}$$

Assign each student to a grade level.

3. Let h be the function that assigns each student ID number to a grade level.

    $$h: \{student\ ID\ number\} \rightarrow \{grade\ level\}$$

    Assign each student ID number to the student's current grade level.

    a. Describe the domain and range of this function.

    b. Record several ordered pairs $(x, f(x))$ that represent yourself and students in your group or class.

    c. Jonny says, "This is not a function because every ninth grader is assigned the same range value of 9. The range only has 4 numbers {9, 10, 11, 12}, but the domain has a number for every student in our school." Explain to Jonny why he is incorrect.

Problem Set

1. Which of the following are examples of a function? Justify your answers.

    a.   The assignment of the members of a football team to jersey numbers.

    b.   The assignment of U.S. citizens to Social Security Numbers.

    c.   The assignment of students to locker numbers.

    d.   The assignment of the residents of a house to the street addresses.

    e.   The assignment of zip codes to residences.

    f.   The assignment of residences to zip codes.

    g.   The assignment of teachers to the students enrolled in each of their classes.

    h.   The assignment of all real numbers to the next integer equal to or greater than the number.

    i.   The assignment of each rational number to the product of its numerator and denominator.

2. Sequences are functions. The domain is the set of all term numbers (which is usually the positive integers), and the range is the set of terms of the sequence. For example, the sequence 1, 4, 9, 16, 25, 36,… of perfect squares is the function:

$$Let\ f: \{positive\ integers\} \rightarrow \{perfect\ squares\}$$

$$Assign\ each\ term\ number\ to\ the\ square\ of\ that\ number.$$

    a.   What is $f(3)$? What does it mean?

    b.   What is the solution to the equation $f(x) = 49$? What is the meaning of this solution?

    c.   According to this definition, is -3 in the domain of f? Explain why or why not.

    d.   According to this definition, is 50 in the range of f? Explain why or why not.

3. Write each sequence as a function.

    a.   {1, 3, 6, 10, 15, 21, 28}

    b.   {1, 3, 5, 7, 9,…}

    c. $a_{n+1} = 3a_n$, $a_1 = 1$ where n is a positive integer greater than or equal to 1.

Lesson 10: Representing, Naming, and Evaluation Functions

Classwork

Opening Exercise

Study the 4 representations of a function below. How are these representations alike? How are they different?

TABLE:

Input	0	1	2	3	4	5
Output	1	2	4	8	16	32

FUNCTION:

Let $f: \{0,1,2,3,4,5\} \rightarrow \{1,2,4,8,16,32\}$ such that $x \mapsto 2^x$.

SEQUENCE:

Let $a_{n+1} = 2a_n, a_0 = 1$ for $0 \le n \le 5$ where n is an integer.

DIAGRAM:

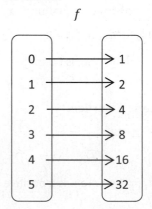

Lesson 10:	Representing, Naming, and Evaluating Functions
Date:	9/11/13

S.53

Exercise 1

Let $X = \{0,1,2,3,4,5\}$. Complete the following table using the definition of f.

$$f: X \to Y$$

Assign each x in X to the expression 2^x.

What are $f(0), f(1), f(2), f(3), f(4)$, and $f(5)$?

What is the range of f?

Exercise 2

The squaring function is defined as follows:

Let $f: X \to Y$ be the function such that $x \mapsto x^2$, where X is the set of all real numbers.

What are $f(0), f(3), f(-2), f(\sqrt{3}), f(-2.5), f\left(\frac{2}{3}\right), f(a)$, and $f(3 + a)$?

What is the range of f?

What subset of the real numbers could be used as the domain of the squaring function to create a range with the same output values as the sequence of square numbers $\{1, 4, 9, 16, 25, \ldots\}$ from Lesson 9?

Exercise 3

Recall that an equation can either be true or false. Using the function defined by $f: \{0, 1, 2, 3, 4, 5\} \rightarrow \{1, 2, 4, 8, 16, 32\}$ such that $x \mapsto 2^x$, determine whether the equation $f(x) = 2^x$ is true or false for each x in the domain of f.

x	Is the equation $f(x) = 2^x$ true or false?	Justification
0	True	Substitute 0 into the equation. $f(0) = 2^0$ $1 = 2^0$ The 1 on the left side comes from the definition of f, and the value of 2^0 is also 1, so the equation is true.
1		
2		
3		
4		
5		

If the domain of f were extended to all real numbers, would the equation still be true for each x in the domain of f? Explain your thinking.

Exercise 4

Write three different polynomial functions such that $f(3) = 2$.

Exercise 5

The domain and range of this function are not specified. Evaluate the function for several values of x. What subset of the real numbers would represent the domain of this function? What subset of the real numbers would represent its range?

$$\text{Let } f(x) = \sqrt{x - 2}$$

Lesson Summary

ALGEBRAIC FUNCTION. Given an algebraic expression in one variable, an *algebraic function* is a function $f: D \to Y$ such that for each real number x in the domain D, $f(x)$ is the value found by substituting the number x into all instances of the variable symbol in the algebraic expression and evaluating.

The following notation will be used to define functions going forward. If a domain is not specified it will be assumed to be the set of all real numbers.

For the squaring function, we say   Let $f(x) = x^2$.

For the exponential function with base 2, we say   Let $f(x) = 2^x$.

When the domain is limited by the expression or the situation to be a subset of the real numbers, it must be specified when the function is defined.

For the square root function, we say   Let $f(x) = \sqrt{x}$ for $x \geq 0$.

To define the first 5 triangular numbers, we say   Let $f(x) = \frac{x(x+1)}{2}$ for $1 \leq x \leq 5$ where x is an integer.

Depending on the context, one either views the statement "$f(x) = \sqrt{x}$" as part of defining the function f or as an equation that is true for all x in the domain of f or as a formula.

Problem Set

1. Let $f(x) = 6x - 3$, and let $g(x) = 0.5(4)^x$. Find the value of each function for the given input.

    a. $f(0)$ j. $g(0)$

    b. $f(-10)$ k. $g(-1)$

    c. $f(2)$ l. $g(2)$

    d. $f(0.01)$ m. $g(-3)$

    e. $f(11.25)$ n. $g(4)$

    f. $f(-\sqrt{2})$ o. $g(\sqrt{2})$

    g. $f\left(\frac{5}{3}\right)$ p. $g\left(\frac{1}{2}\right)$

    h. $f(1) + f(2)$ q. $g(2) + g(1)$

    i. $f(6) - f(2)$ r. $g(6) - g(2)$

2. Since a variable is a placeholder, we can substitute letters that stand for numbers in for x. Let $f(x) = 6x - 3$, and let $g(x) = 0.5(4)^x$, and suppose a, b, c, and h are real numbers. Find the value of each function for the given input.

   a. $f(a)$

   b. $f(2a)$

   c. $f(b + c)$

   d. $f(2 + h)$

   e. $f(a + h)$

   f. $f(a + 1) - f(a)$

   g. $f(a + h) - f(a)$

   h. $g(b)$

   i. $g(b + 3)$

   j. $g(3b)$

   k. $g(b - 3)$

   l. $g(b + c)$

   m. $g(b + 1) - g(b)$

3. What is the range of each function given below?

   a.   Let $f(x) = 9x - 1$.

   b.   Let $g(x) = 3^{2x}$.

   c.   Let $f(x) = x^2 - 4$.

   d.   Let $h(x) = \sqrt{x} + 2$.

   e.   Let $a(x) = x + 2$ such that x is a positive integer.

   f.   Let $g(x) = 5^x$ for $0 \le x \le 4$.

4. Provide a suitable domain and range to complete the definition of each function.

   a.   Let $f(x) = 2x + 3$.

   b.   Let $f(x) = 2^x$.

   c.   Let $C(x) = 9x + 130$, where $C(x)$ is the number of calories in a sandwich containing x grams of fat.

   d.   Let $B(x) = 100(2)^x$, where $B(x)$ is the number of bacteria at time x hours over the course of one day.

5. Let $f : X \to Y$, where X and Y are the set of all real numbers and x and h are real numbers.

   a.   Find a function f such that the equation $f(x + h) = f(x) + f(h)$ is not true for all values of x and h. Justify your reasoning.

   b.   Find a function f such that equation $f(x + h) = f(x) + f(h)$ is true for all values of x and h. Justify your reasoning.

   c.   Let $(x) = 2^x$. Find a value for x and a value for h that makes $f(x + h) = f(x) + f(h)$ a true number sentence.

---

6. Given the function f whose domain is the set of real numbers, let $f(x) = 1$ if x is a rational number, and let $f(x) = 0$ if x is an irrational number.

    a. Explain why f is a function.

    b. What is the range of f?

    c. Evaluate f for each domain value shown below.

x	2/3	0	−5	$\sqrt{2}$	π
$f(x)$					

    d. List three possible solutions to the equation $f(x) = 0$.

Lesson 11: The Graph of a Function

Classwork

Opening Exercise

In Module 1, you graphed equations such as $y = 10 - 4x$ by plotting the points in the Cartesian plane by picking x values and then using the equation to find the y value for each x value. The number of order pairs you plotted to get the general shape of the graph depended on the type of equation (linear, quadratic, etc.). The graph of the equation was then a representation of the solution set, which could be described using set notation.

In this lesson, we extend set notation slightly to describe the graph of a function. In doing so, we explain a way to think about set notation for the graph of a function that mimics the instructions a tablet or laptop might perform to "draw" a graph on its screen.

Example 1

Computer programs are essentially instructions to computers on what to do when the user (you!) makes a request. For example, when you type a letter on your smart phone, the smart phone follows a specified set of instructions to draw that letter on the screen and record it in memory (as part of an email, for example). One of the simplest types of instructions a computer can perform is a *for-next loop*. Below is code for a program that prints the first 5 powers of 2:

```
Declare x integer
For all x from 1 to 5
        Print 2^x
Next x
```

The output of this program code is

2
4
8
16
32

Here is a description of the instructions: First, x is quantified as an integer, which means the variable can only take on integer values and cannot take on values like $\frac{1}{3}$ or $\sqrt{2}$. The "For" statement begins the loop, starting with $x = 1$. The instructions between "For" and "Next" are performed for the value $x = 1$, which in this case is just to "Print 2." (Print means "print to the computer screen.") Then the computer performs the instructions again for the next x ($x = 2$), i.e., "Print 4," and so on until the computer performs the instructions for $x = 5$, i.e., "Print 32."

Exercise 1

Perform the instructions in the following programming code as if *you were a computer and your paper was the computer screen*:

```
Declare x integer
For all x from 2 to 8
        Print 2x + 3
Next x
```

Example 2

We can use almost the same code to build a set: first, we start with a set with 0 elements in it (called the *empty set*) and then increase the size of the set by appending one new element to it in each for-next step:

```
Declare x integer
Initialize G as {}
For all x from 2 to 8
        Append 2x + 3 to G
        Print G
Next x
```

Note that G is printed to the screen after each new number is appended. Thus, the output shows how the set "builds":

$\{7\}$
$\{7, 9\}$
$\{7, 9, 11\}$
$\{7, 9, 11, 13\}$
$\{7, 9, 11, 13, 15\}$
$\{7, 9, 11, 13, 15, 17\}$
$\{7, 9, 11, 13, 15, 17, 19\}$

Exercise 2

We can also build a set by appending ordered pairs. Perform the instructions in the following programming code as if *you were a computer and your paper was the computer screen* (the first couple are done for you):

> **Declare** x **integer**
> **Initialize** G **as {}**
> **For all** x **from 2 to 8**
>   **Append** $(x, 2x + 3)$ **to** G
> **Next** x
> **Print** G

Output:
{(2,7), (3,9), _____

Example 3

Instead of "Printing" the set G to the screen, we can use another command, "Plot," to plot the points on a Cartesian plane.

> **Declare** x **integer**
> **Initialize** G **as {}**
> **For all** x **from 2 to 8**
>   **Append** $(x, 2x + 3)$ **to** G
> **Next** x
> **Plot** G

Output:

In mathematics, the programming code above can be compactly written using set notation, as follows:

$$\{(x, 2x + 3) \mid x \text{ integer and } 2 \leq x \leq 8\}.$$

This set notation is an abbreviation for "The set of all points $(x, 2x + 3)$ such that x is an integer and $2 \leq x \leq 8$." Notice how the set of ordered pairs generated by the for-next code above,

$$\{(2,7), (3,9), (4,11), (5,13), (6,15), (7,17), (8,19)\},$$

also satisfies the requirements described by $\{(x, 2x + 3) \mid x \text{ integer}, 2 \leq x \leq 8\}$. It is for this reason that the set notation of the form

{type of element | condition on each element}

is sometimes called *set-builder notation*—because it can be thought of as building the set just like the for-next code.

Discussion

We can now upgrade our notion of a for-next loop by doing a thought experiment: Imagine a for-next loop that steps through *all* real numbers in an interval (not just the integers). No computer can actually do this—computers can only do a finite number of calculations. But our human brains are far superior to that of any computer, and we can easily imagine what that might look like. Here is some sample code:

```
Declare x real
Let f(x) = 2x + 3
Initialize G as {}
For all x such that 2 ≤ x ≤ 8
        Append (x, f(x)) to G
Next x
Plot G
```

The output of this thought code is the graph of f for all real numbers x in the interval $2 \leq x \leq 8$:

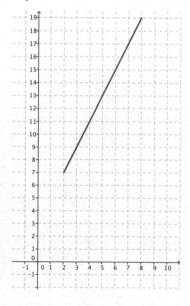

Exercise 3

1. Plot the function f on the Cartesian plane using the following for-next thought code:

> **Declare** x **real**
> **Let** $f(x) = x^2 + 1$
> **Initialize** G **as {}**
> **For all** x **such that** $-2 \leq x \leq 3$
> 　　　**Append** $(x, f(x))$ **to** G
> **Next** x
> **Plot** G

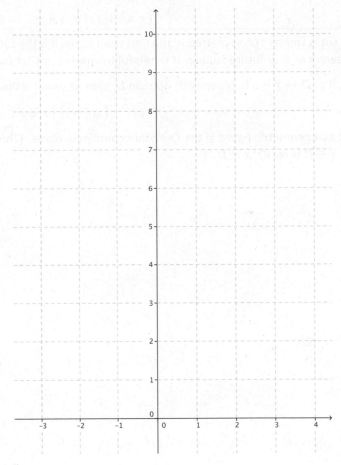

a. For each step of the for-next loop, what is the input value?

b. For each step of the for-next loop, what is the output value?

c. What is the domain of the function f?

d. What is the range of the function f?

Closing

The set G built from the for-next thought code in Exercise 4 can also be compactly written in mathematics using set notation:

$$\{(x, x^2 + 1) \mid x \text{ real}, -2 \leq x \leq 3\}.$$

When this set is thought of as plotted in the Cartesian plane, it is the same graph. When you see this set notation in your homework and/or future studies, it is helpful to imagine this set-builder notation as describing a for-next loop.

In general, if $f: D \to Y$ is a function with domain D, then its *graph* is the set of all ordered pairs,

$$\{(x, f(x)) \mid x \in D\},$$

thought of as a geometric figure in the Cartesian coordinate plane. (The symbol $\in$ simply means "in." The statement $x \in D$ is read, "x in D.")

Lesson Summary

Graph of f: Given a function f whose domain D and the range are subsets of the real numbers, the graph of f is the set of ordered pairs in the Cartesian plane given by

$$\{(x, f(x)) \mid x \in D\}.$$

Problem Set

1. Perform the instructions for each of the following programming codes as if *you were a computer and your paper was the computer screen.*

   a.
   ```
   Declare x integer
   For all x from 0 to 4
           Print 2x
   Next x
   ```

   b.
   ```
   Declare x integer
   For all x from 0 to 10
           Print 2x + 1
   Next x
   ```

   c.
   ```
   Declare x integer
   For all x from 2 to 8
           Print x²
   Next x
   ```

   d.
   ```
   Declare x integer
   For all x from 0 to 4
           Print 10 · 3ˣ
   Next x
   ```

2. Perform the instructions for each of the following programming codes as if *you were a computer and your paper was the computer screen*.

a.

> Declare x integer
> Let $f(x) = (x + 1)(x - 1) - x^2$
> Initialize G as {}
> For all x from -3 to 3
>   Append $(x, f(x))$ to G
> Next x
> Plot G

b.

> Declare x integer
> Let $f(x) = 3^{-x}$
> Initialize G as {}
> For all x from -3 to 3
>   Append $(x, f(x))$ to G
> Next x
> Plot G

c.

> Declare x real
> Let $f(x) = x^3$
> Initialize G as {}
> For all x such that $-2 \leq x \leq 2$
>   Append $(x, f(x))$ to G
> Next x
> Plot G

3. Answer the following questions about the "thought code:"

> **Declare** x **real**
> **Let** $f(x) = (x - 2)(x - 4)$
> **Initialize** G **as** {}
> **For all** x **such that** $0 \le x \le 5$
>   **Append** $(x, f(x)\,)$ **to** G
> **Next** x
> **Plot** G

a. What is the domain of the function f?

b. Plot the graph of f according to the instructions in the thought code.

c. Look at your graph of f. What is the range of f?

d. Write three or four sentences describing in words how the thought code works.

4. Sketch the graph of the functions defined by the following formulas, and write the graph of f as a set using set-builder notation. (Hint: Assume the domain is all real numbers unless specified in the problem.)

a. $f(x) = x + 2$

b. $f(x) = 3x + 2$

c. $f(x) = 3x - 2$

d. $f(x) = -3x - 2$

e. $f(x) = -3x + 2$

f. $f(x) = -\frac{1}{3}x + 2, -3 \le x \le 3$

g. $f(x) = (x + 1)^2 - x^2, \ -2 \le x \le 5$

h. $f(x) = (x + 1)^2 - (x - 1)^2, \ -2 \le x \le 4$

5. The figure shows the graph of $f(x) = -5x + c$.

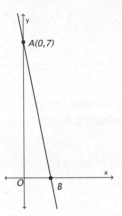

a. Find the value of c.

b. If the graph of f intersects the x-axis at B, find the coordinates of B.

6. The figure shows the graph of $f(x) = \frac{1}{2}x + c$.

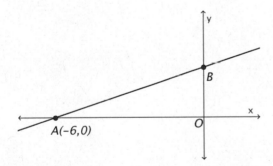

a. Find the value of c.

b. If the graph of f intersects the y-axis at B, find the coordinates of B.

c. Find the area of triangle $\triangle AOB$.

Lesson 12: The Graph of the Equation $y = f(x)$

Classwork

In Module 1, you graphed equations such as $4x + y = 10$ by plotting the points on the Cartesian coordinate plane that corresponded to all of the ordered pairs of numbers (x, y) that were in the solution set. We called the geometric figure that resulted from plotting those points in the plane the "graph of the equation in two variables."

In this lesson, we extend this notion of the graph of an equation to the graph of $y = f(x)$ for a function f. In doing so, we use computer "thought code" to describe the process of generating the ordered pairs in the graph of $y = f(x)$.

Example 1

In the previous lesson, we studied a simple type of instruction that computers perform called a for-next loop. Another simple type of instruction is an *if-then statement*. Below is example code of a program that tests for and prints "True" when $x + 2 = 4$; otherwise it prints "False."

```
Declare x integer
For all x from 1 to 4
    If x + 2 = 4 then
        Print True
    else
        Print False
    Endif
Next x
```

The output of this program code is:

False
True
False
False

Notice that the if-then statement in the code above is really just testing whether each number in the loop is in the solution set!

Example 2

Perform the instructions in the following programming code as if *you were a computer and your paper was the computer screen*:

```
Declare x integer
Initialize G as {}
For all x from 0 to 4
        If x² − 4x + 5 = 2 then
                Append x to G
        else
                Do NOT append x to G
        Endif
Next x
Print G
```

Output:

{1, 3}

Discussion

Compare the for-next/if-then code above to the following set-builder notation we used to describe solution sets in Module 1:

$$\{x \text{ integer } \mid \ 0 \leq x \leq 4 \text{ and } x^2 - 4x + 5 = 2\}.$$

Check to see that the set-builder notation also generates the set {1, 3}. *Whenever you see set-builder notation to describe a set, a powerful way to interpret that notation is to think of the set as being generated by a "program" like the for-next/if-then code above.*

Exercise 1

Next we write code that generates a graph of a *two variable equation* $y = x(x - 2)(x + 2)$ for x in $\{-2, -1, 0, 1, 2\}$ and y in $\{-3, 0, 3\}$. The solution set of this equation is generated by testing each ordered pair (x, y) in the set,

$$\{(-2, -3), (-2, 0), (-2, 3), (-1, -3), (-1, 0), (-1, 3), \ldots, (2, -3), (2, 0), (2, 3)\},$$

to see if it is a solution to the equation $y = x(x - 2)(x + 2)$. Then the graph is just the plot of solutions in the Cartesian plane. We can instruct a computer to find these points and plot them using the following program:

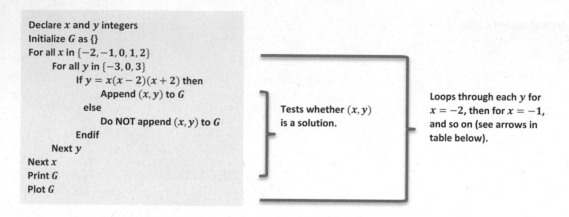

Declare x and y integers
Initialize G as {}
For all x in $\{-2, -1, 0, 1, 2\}$
    For all y in $\{-3, 0, 3\}$
        If $y = x(x - 2)(x + 2)$ then
            Append (x, y) to G
        else
            Do NOT append (x, y) to G
        Endif
    Next y
Next x
Print G
Plot G

Tests whether (x, y) is a solution.

Loops through each y for $x = -2$, then for $x = -1$, and so on (see arrows in table below).

a.   Use the table below to record the decisions a computer would make when following the program instructions above. Fill in each cell with "Yes" or "No" depending on whether the ordered pair (x, y) would be appended or not. (The step where $x = -2$ has been done for you.)

	$x = -2$	$x = -1$	$x = 0$	$x = 1$	$x = 2$
$y = 3$	No				
$y = 0$	Yes				
$y = -3$	No				

b.   What would be the output to the "Print G" command? (The first ordered pair is listed for you.)

Output:
{ $(-2, 0)$, _____, _____, _____, _____ }

c.   Plot the solution set G in the Cartesian plane. (The first ordered pair in G has been plotted for you.)

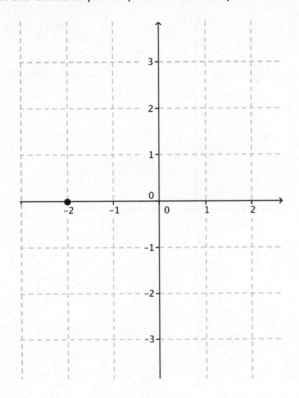

Exercise 2

The program code in Exercise 3 is a way to imagine how set-builder notation generates solution sets and figures in the plane. Given a function $f(x) = x(x - 2)(x - 3)$ with domain and range all real numbers, a slight modification of the program code above can be used to generate the graph of the equation $y = f(x)$:

$$\{(x, y) \mid x \text{ real} \text{ and } y = f(x)\}.$$

Even though the code below cannot be run on a computer, we can run the following "thought code" in our minds:

```
Declare x and y real
Let f(x) = x(x − 2)(x + 2)
Initialize G as {}
For all x in the real numbers
        For all y in the real numbers
                If y = f(x) then
                        Append (x, y) to G
                else
                        Do NOT append (x, y) to G
                Endif
        Next y
Next x
Plot G
```

Tests whether (x, y) is a solution to $y = x(x - 2)(x + 2)$.

For each x value, the code loops through all y values.

a. Plot G on the Cartesian plane (the figure drawn is called the graph of $y = f(x)$).

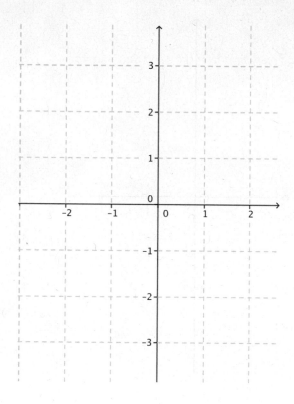

b. Describe how the "thought code" is similar to the set-builder notation $\{(x, y) \mid x \text{ real and } y = f(x)\}$.

c. A *relative maximum* for the function f occurs at the x-coordinate of $\left(-\frac{2}{3}\sqrt{3}, \frac{16}{9}\sqrt{3}\right)$. Substitute this point into the equation $y = x(x^2 - 4)$ to check that it is a solution to $y = f(x)$, and then plot the point on your graph.

d. A *relative minimum* for the function f occurs at the x-coordinate of $\left(\frac{2}{3}\sqrt{3}, -\frac{16}{9}\sqrt{3}\right)$. A similar calculation as you did above shows that this point is also a solution to $y = f(x)$. Plot this point on your graph.

e. Look at your graph. On what interval(s) is the function f decreasing?

f. Look at your graph. On what interval(s) is the function f increasing?

Lesson Summary

- Graph of $y = f(x)$. Given a function f whose domain D and the range are subsets of the real numbers, the graph of $y = f(x)$ is the set of ordered pairs (x, y) in the Cartesian plane given by

$$\{(x, y) \mid x \in D \text{ and } y = f(x)\}.$$

When we write $\{(x, y) \mid y = f(x)\}$ for the graph of $y = f(x)$, it is understood that the domain is the largest set of real numbers for which the function f is defined.

- The graph of f is the same as the graph of the equation $y = f(x)$.

- Increasing/Decreasing. Given a function f whose domain and range are subsets of the real numbers and I is an interval contained within the domain, the function is called *increasing on the interval I* if

$$f(x_1) < f(x_2) \text{ whenever } x_1 < x_2 \text{ in } I.$$

It is called decreasing on the interval I if

$$f(x_1) > f(x_2) \text{ whenever } x_1 < x_2 \text{ in } I.$$

Problem Set

1. Perform the instructions in the following programming code as if *you were a computer and your paper was the computer screen*:

```
Declare x integer
For all x from 1 to 6
     If x² − 2 = 7 then
          Print True
     else
          Print False
     Endif
Next x
```

2. Answer the following questions about the computer programming code:

```
Declare x integer
Initialize G as {}
For all x from −3 to 3
     If 2ˣ + 2⁻ˣ = 17/4 then
          Append x to G
     else
          Do NOT append x to G
     Endif
Next x
Print G
```

a. Perform the instructions in the programming code as if you were a computer and your paper was the computer screen:

b. Write a description of the set G using set-builder notation.

3. Answer the following questions about the computer programming code:

```
Declare x and y integers
Initialize G as {}
For all x in {0, 1, 2, 3}
        For all y in {0, 1, 2, 3}
                If y = √(4 + 20x − 19x² + 4x³) then
                        Append (x, y) to G
                else
                        Do NOT append (x, y) to G
                Endif
        Next y
Next x
Plot G
```

a. Use the table below to record the decisions a computer would make when following the program instructions above. Fill in each cell with "Yes" or "No" depending on whether the ordered pair (x, y) would be appended or not.

	$x = 0$	$x = 1$	$x = 2$	$x = 3$
$y = 3$				
$y = 2$				
$y = 1$				
$y = 0$				

b. Plot the set G in the Cartesian plane.

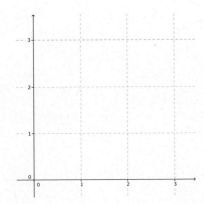

4. Answer the following questions about the "thought code":

    ```
    Declare x and y real
    Let f(x) = −2x + 8
    Initialize G as {}
    For all x in the real numbers
            For all y in the real numbers
                If y = f(x) then
                        Append (x, y) to G
                    else
                        Do NOT append (x, y) to G
                Endif
            Next y
        Next x
        Plot G
    ```

    a. What is the domain of the function $f(x) = -2x + 8$?

    b. What is the range of the function $f(x) = -2x + 8$?

    c. Write the set G generated by the "thought code" in set-builder notation.

    d. Plot the set G to obtain the graph of the function $f(x) = -2x + 8$.

    e. The function $f(x) = -2x + 8$ is clearly a decreasing function on the domain of the real numbers. Show that the function satisfies the definition of decreasing for the points 8 and 10 on the number line, i.e., show that since $8 < 10$, then $f(8) > f(10)$.

5. Sketch the graph of the functions defined by the following formulas and write the graph of $y = f(x)$ as a set using set-builder notation. (Hint: For each function below you can assume the domain is all real numbers.)

    a. $f(x) = -\frac{1}{2}x + 6$

    b. $f(x) = x^2 + 3$

    c. $f(x) = x^2 - 5x + 6$

    d. $f(x) = x^3 - x$

    e. $f(x) = -x^2 + x - 1$

    f. $f(x) = (x - 3)^2 + 2$

    g. $f(x) = x^3 - 2x^2 + 3$

6. Answer the following questions about the set:

$$\{(x, y) \mid 0 \leq x \leq 2 \text{ and } y = 9 - 4x^2\}$$

a. The equation can be rewritten in the form $y = f(x)$ where $f(x) = 9 - 4x^2$. What are the domain and range of the function f specified by the set?

   i.   Domain:

   ii. Range:

b. Write "thought code" like in Exercise 4 that will generate and then plot the set.

7. Answer the following about the graph of a function below:

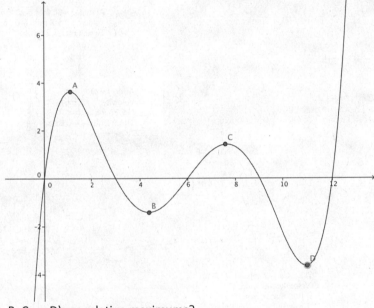

a. Which points (A, B, C, or D) are relative maximums?

b. Which points (A, B, C, or D) are relative minimums?

c. Name any interval where the function is increasing.

d. Name any interval where the function is decreasing.

Lesson 13: Interpreting Graphs of Functions

Classwork

Mathematical Modeling Exercise

This graphic was shared by NASA prior to the Mars Curiosity Rover landing on August 6, 2012. It depicts the landing sequence for the rover's descent to the surface of the planet.

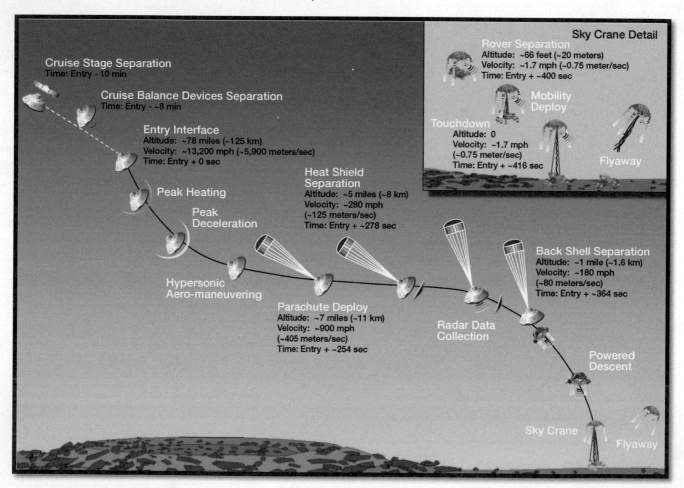

Does this graphic really represent the landing path of the Curiosity Rover? Create a model that can be used to predict the altitude and velocity of the Curiosity Rover 5, 4, 3, 2, and 1 minute before landing.

Exploratory Challenge

Create a model to help you answer the problem and estimate the altitude and velocity at various times during the landing sequence.

Exercises 1–6

1. Does this graphic really represent the landing path of the Curiosity Rover?

2. Estimate the altitude and velocity of the Curiosity Rover 5, 4, 3, 2, and 1 minute before landing. Explain how you arrived at your estimate.

3. Based on watching the video/animation, do you think you need to revise any of your work? Explain why or why not, and then make any needed changes.

4. Why is the graph of the altitude function decreasing and the graph of the velocity function increasing on its domain?

5. Why is the graph of the velocity function negative? Why does this graph not have an x-intercept?

6. What is the meaning of the x-intercept of the altitude graph? The y-intercept?

Exercises 7–12

A Mars rover collected the following temperature data over 1.6 Martian days. A Martian day is called a sol. Use the graph to answer the following questions.

GROUND AND AIR TEMPERATURE SENSOR

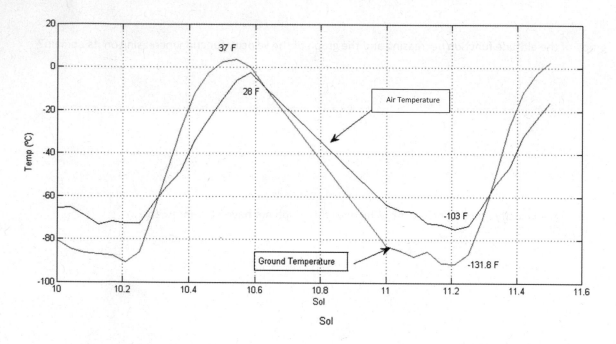

7. Approximately when does each graph change from increasing to decreasing? From decreasing to increasing?

8. When is the air temperature increasing?

9. When is the ground temperature decreasing?

10. What is the air temperature change on this time interval?

11. Why do you think the ground temperature changed more than the air temperature? Is that typical on Earth?

12. Is there a time when the air and ground were the same temperature? Explain how you know?

Problem Set

1. Create a short written report summarizing your work on the Mars Curiosity Rover Problem. Include your answers to the original problem questions and at least one recommendation for further research on this topic or additional questions you have about the situation.

2. Consider the sky crane descent portion of the landing sequence.

   a. Create a linear function to model the Curiosity Rover's altitude as a function of time. (What two points did you choose to create your function? Why?)

   b. Compare the slope of your function to the velocity. Should they be equal? Explain why or why not.

   c. Use your linear model to determine the altitude one minute before landing. How does it compare to your earlier estimate. Explain any differences you found.

3. The exponential function $g(t) = 125(0.99)^t$ could be used to model the altitude of the Curiosity Rover during its rapid descent. Do you think this model would be better or worse than the one your group created? Explain your reasoning.

4. For each graph below, identify the increasing and decreasing intervals, the positive and negative intervals, and the intercepts.

   a.

   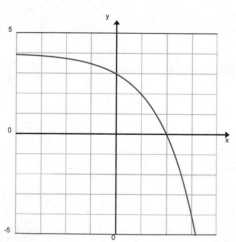

   b.

   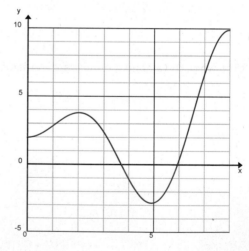

Lesson 14: Linear and Exponential Models—Comparing Growth Rates

Classwork

Example 1

<u>Linear Functions</u>

a. Sketch points $P_1 = (0,4)$ and $P_2 = (4,12)$. Are there values of m and b such that the graph of the linear function described by $f(x) = mx + b$ contains P_1 and P_2? If so, find those values. If not, explain why they do not exist.

b. Sketch $P_1 = (0,4)$ and $P_2 = (0,-2)$. Are there values of m and b so that the graph of a linear function described by $f(x) = mx + b$ contains P_1 and P_2? If so, find those values. If not, explain why they do not exist.

Exponential Functions

Graphs (c) and (d) are both graphs of an exponential function of the form $g(x) = ab^x$. Rewrite the function $g(x)$ using the values of a and b required for the graph shown to be a graph of g.

c. $g(x) =$

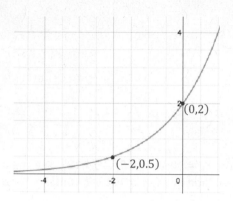

d. $g(x) =$

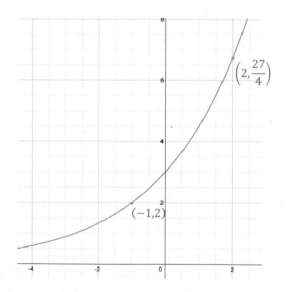

Example 2

A lab researcher records the growth of the population of a yeast colony and finds that the population doubles every hour.

a.   Complete the researcher's table of data:

Hours into study	0	1	2	3	4
Yeast colony population (thousands)	5				

b. What is the exponential function that models the growth of the colony's population?

c. Several hours into the study, the researcher looks at the data and wishes there were more frequent measurements. Knowing that the colony doubles every hour, how can the researcher determine the population in half-hour increments? Explain.

d. Complete the new table that includes half hour increments.

Hours into study	0	$\frac{1}{2}$	1	$\frac{3}{2}$	2	$\frac{5}{2}$	3
Yeast colony population (thousands)	5						

e. How would the calculation for the data change for time increments of 20 minutes? Explain.

f. Complete the new table that includes 20 minute increments.

Hours into study	0	$\frac{1}{3}$	$\frac{2}{3}$	1	$\frac{4}{3}$	$\frac{5}{3}$	2
Yeast colony population (thousands)	5						

g. The researcher's lab assistant studies the data recorded and makes the following claim:

Since the population doubles in 1 hour, then half that growth happens in the first half hour and the second half of that growth happens in the second half hour. We should be able to find the population at $t = \frac{1}{2}$ by taking the average of the populations at $t = 0$ and $t = 1$.

Is the assistant's reasoning correct? Compare this strategy to your work in parts (c) and (e).

Example 3

A California Population Projection Engineer in 1920 was tasked with finding a model that predicts the state's population growth. He modeled the population growth as a function of time, t years since 1900. Census data shows that the population in 1900, in thousands, was 1,490. In 1920, the population of the state of California was 3,554 thousand. He decided to explore both a linear and an exponential model.

a. Use the data provided to determine the equation of the linear function that models the population growth from 1900 to 1920.

b. Use the data provided and your calculator to determine the equation of the exponential function that models the population growth.

c. Use the two functions to predict the population for the following years:

	Projected Population based on Linear Function, $f(t)$ (thousands)	Projected Population based on Exponential Function, $g(t)$ (thousands)	Census Population Data and Intercensal Estimates for California (thousands)
1935			
1960			
2010			

d. Which function is a better model for the population growth of California in 1935 and in 1960?

e. Does either model closely predict the population for 2010? What phenomenon explains the real population value?

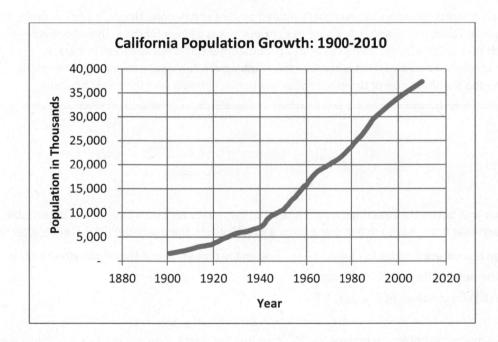

California Population Growth: 1900-2010

Lesson Summary

- Given a linear function of the form $L(x) = mx + k$ and an exponential function of the form $E(x) = ab^x$ for x a real number and constants $m, k, a,$ and b, consider the sequence given by $L(n)$ and the sequence given by $E(n)$ where $n = 1, 2, 3, 4, \ldots$. Both of these sequences can be written recursively:

$$L(n + 1) = L(n) + m \text{ and } L(0) = k, \text{ and}$$
$$E(n + 1) = E(n) \cdot b \text{ and } E(0) = a.$$

- The first sequence shows that a linear function grows additively by the same summand m over equal length intervals (i.e., the intervals between consecutive integers). The second sequence shows that an exponential function grows multiplicatively by the same factor b over equal length intervals (i.e., the intervals between consecutive integers).

- An increasing exponential function will eventually exceed any linear function. That is, if $f(x) = ab^x$ is an exponential function with $a > 1$ and $b > 0$, and $g(x) = mx + k$ is a linear function, then there is a real number M such that for all $x > M$, then $f(x) > g(x)$. Sometimes this is not apparent in a graph displayed on a graphing calculator; that is because the graphing window does not show enough of the graphs for us to see the sharp rise of the exponential function in contrast with the linear function.

Problem Set

1. When a ball bounces up and down, the maximum height it reaches decreases with each bounce in a predictable way. Suppose for a particular type of squash ball dropped on a squash court, the maximum height, $h(x)$, after x number of bounces can be represented by $h(x) = 65\left(\frac{1}{3}\right)^x$. How many times higher is the height after the first bounce compared to the height after the third bounce?

   Graph the points $(x, h(x))$ for x-values of $0, 1, 2, 3, 4, 5$.

2. Australia experienced a major pest problem in the early 20th century. The pest? Rabbits. In 1859, 24 rabbits were released by Thomas Austin at Barwon Park. In 1926, there were an estimated 10 billion rabbits in Australia. Needless to say, the Australian government spent a tremendous amount of time and money to get the rabbit problem under control. (To find more on this topic, visit Australia's Department of Environment and Primary Industries website under Agriculture.)

   a. Based only on the information above, write an exponential function that would model Australia's rabbit population growth.

   b. The model you created from the data in the problem is obviously a huge simplification from the actual function of the number of rabbits in any given year from 1859 to 1926. Name at least one complicating factor (about rabbits) that might make the graph of your function look quite different than the graph of the actual function.

3. After graduating from college, Jane has two job offers to consider. Job A is compensated at $100,000 a year but with no hope of ever having an increase in pay. Jane knows a few of her peers are getting that kind of an offer right out of college. Job B is for a social media start-up, which guarantees a mere $10,000 a year. The founder is sure the concept of the company will be the next big thing in social networking and promises a pay increase of 25% at the beginning of each new year.

   a. Which job will have a greater annual salary at the beginning of the 5th year? By approximately how much?

   b. Which job will have a greater annual salary at the beginning of the 10th year? By approximately how much?

   c. Which job will have a greater annual salary at the beginning of the 20th year? By approximately how much?

   d. If you were in Jane's shoes, which job would you take?

4. The population of a town in 2007 is 15,000 people. The town has gotten its fresh water supply from a nearby lake and river system with the capacity to provide water for up to 30,000 people. Due to its proximity to a big city and a freeway, the town's population has begun to grow more quickly than in the past. The table below shows the population counts for each year from 2007 to 2012.

   a. Write a function of x that closely matches these data points for x-values of $0, 1, 2, ..., 5$.

Year	Years past 2007	Population of the town
2007	0	15,000
2008	1	15,600
2009	2	16,224
2010	3	16,873
2011	4	17,548
2012	5	18,250

   b. Assume the function is a good model for the population growth from 2012 to 2032. At what year during the time frame 2012 to 2032 will the water supply be inadequate for the population?

Lesson 15: Piecewise Functions

Classwork

Opening Exercise

For each real number a, the *absolute value of a* is the distance between 0 and a on the number line and is denoted $|a|$.

1. Solve each one variable equation.

   a. $|x| = 6$

   b. $|x - 5| = 4$

   c. $2|x + 3| = -10$

2. Determine at least five solutions for each two-variable equation. Make sure some of the solutions include negative values for either x or y.

   a. $y = |x|$

   b. $y = |x - 5|$

   c. $x = |y|$

Exploratory Challenge 1

For parts (a) – (c) create graphs of the solution set of each two-variable equation from Opening Exercise 2.

a.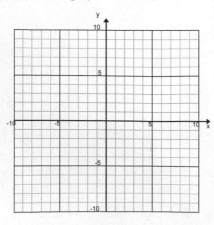

b.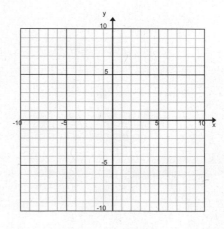

c.

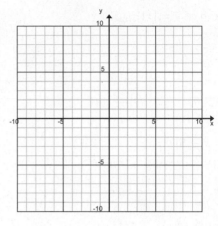

d. Write a brief summary comparing and contrasting the three solution sets and their graphs.

For parts (e) – (j) consider the function $f(x) = |x|$ where x can be any real number.

e. Explain the meaning of the function f in your own words.

f. State the domain and range of this function.

g. Create a graph of the function f. You might start by listing several ordered pairs that represent the corresponding domain and range elements.

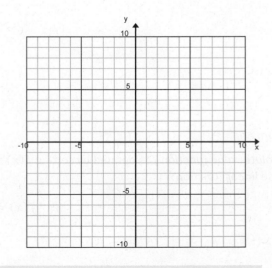

h. How does the graph of the absolute value function compare to the graph of $y = |x|$?

i. Define a function whose graph would be identical to the graph of $y = |x - 5|$?

j. Could you define a function whose graph would be identical to the graph of $x = |y|$? Explain your reasoning.

k. Let $f_1(x) = -x$ for $x < 0$ and let $f_2(x) = x$ for ≥ 0 . Graph the functions f_1 and f_2 on the same Cartesian plane. How does the graph of these two functions compare to the graph in Exercise 7?

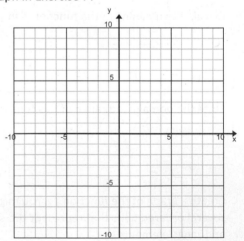

Definition:

The *absolute value function* f is defined by setting $f(x) = |x|$ for all real numbers. Another way to write f is as a piecewise linear function:

$$f(x) = \begin{cases} -x & x < 0 \\ x & x \geq 0 \end{cases}$$

Example 1

Let $g(x) = |x - 5|$. The graph of g is the same as the graph of the equation $y = |x - 5|$ you drew in Exercise 3. Use the redrawn graph below to re-write the function g as a piecewise function.

Label the graph of the linear function with negative slope by g_1 and the graph of the linear function with positive slope by g_2 as in the picture above.

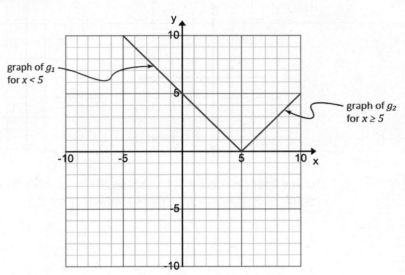

Function g_1: Slope of g_1 is -1 (why?), and the y-intercept is 5, therefore $g_1(x) = -x + 5$.

Function g_2: Slope of g_2 is 1 (why?), and the y-intercept is -5 (why?), therefore $g_2(x) = x - 5$.

Writing g as a piecewise function is just a matter of collecting all of the different "pieces" and the intervals upon which they are defined:

$$g(x) = \begin{cases} -x + 5 & x < 5 \\ x - 5 & x \geq 5 \end{cases}$$

Exploratory Challenge 2

The *floor* of a real number x, denoted by $\lfloor x \rfloor$, is the largest integer not greater than x. The *ceiling* of a real number x, denoted by $\lceil x \rceil$, is the smallest integer not less than x. The *sawtooth* number of a positive number is the "fractional part" of the number that is to the right of its floor on the number line. In general, for a real number x, the sawtooth number of x is the value of the expression $x - \lfloor x \rfloor$. Each of these expressions can be thought of as functions with domain the set of real numbers.

a. Complete the following table to help you understand how these functions assign elements of the domain to elements of the range. The first and second rows have been done for you.

x	$floor(x) = \lfloor x \rfloor$	$ceiling(x) = \lceil x \rceil$	$sawtooth(x) = x - \lfloor x \rfloor$
4.8			
-1.3			
2.2			
6			
-3			
$-\dfrac{2}{3}$			
π			

b.   Create a graph of each function.

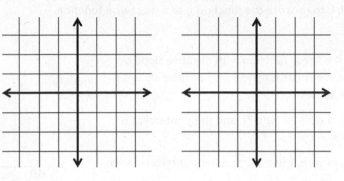

$$floor(x) = \lfloor x \rfloor \qquad ceiling(x) = \lceil x \rceil \qquad sawtooth(x) = x - \lfloor x \rfloor$$

c.   For the floor function, what would be the range value for all real numbers x on the interval $[0,1)$? The interval $(1,2]$? The interval $[-2,-1)$? The interval $[1.5,2.5]$?

Relevant Vocabulary

PIECEWISE-LINEAR FUNCTION. Given a number of non-overlapping intervals on the real number line, a *(real) piecewise-linear function* is a function from the union of the intervals to the set of real numbers such that the function is defined by (possibly different) linear functions on each interval.

ABSOLUTE VALUE FUNCTION. The absolute value of a number x, denoted by $|x|$, is the distance between 0 and x on the number line. The *absolute value function* is the piecewise-linear function such that for each real number x, the value of the function is $|x|$.

We often name the absolute value function by saying, "Let $f(x) = |x|$ for all real numbers x."

FLOOR FUNCTION. The *floor* of a real number x, denoted by $\lfloor x \rfloor$, is the largest integer not greater than x. The *floor function* is the piecewise-linear function such that for each real number x, the value of the function is $\lfloor x \rfloor$.

We often name the floor function by saying, "Let $f(x) = \lfloor x \rfloor$ for all real numbers x."

CEILING FUNCTION. The *ceiling* of a real number x, denoted by $\lceil x \rceil$, is the smallest integer not less than x. The *ceiling function* is the piecewise-linear function such that for each real number x, the value of the function is $\lceil x \rceil$.

We often name the ceiling function by saying, "Let $f(x) = \lceil x \rceil$ for all real numbers x."

SAWTOOTH FUNCTION. The *sawtooth function* is the piecewise-linear function such that for each real number x, the value of the function is given by the expression $x - \lfloor x \rfloor$.

The sawtooth function assigns to each positive number the part of the number (the non-integer part) that is to the right of the floor of the number on the number line. That is, if we let $f(x) = x - \lfloor x \rfloor$ for all real numbers x then

$$f\left(\tfrac{1}{3}\right) = \tfrac{1}{3}, f\left(1\tfrac{1}{3}\right) = \tfrac{1}{3}, f(1000.02) = 0.02, f(-0.3) = 0.7, \text{etc.}$$

Problem Set

1. Explain why the sawtooth function, $sawtooth(x) = x - \lfloor x \rfloor$ for all real numbers x, takes only the "fractional part" of a number when the number is positive.

2. Let $g(x) = \lceil x \rceil - \lfloor x \rfloor$ where x can be any real number. In otherwords, g is the difference between the ceiling and floor functions. Express g as a piecewise function.

3. The Heaviside function is defined using the formula below.
$$H(x) = \begin{cases} -1, & x < 0 \\ 0, & x = 0 \\ 1, & x > 0 \end{cases}$$
   Graph this function and state its domain and range.

4. The following piecewise function is an example of a step function.
$$S(x) = \begin{cases} 3 & -5 \leq x < -2 \\ 1 & -2 \leq x < 3 \\ 2 & 3 \leq x \leq 5 \end{cases}$$

   a. Graph this function and state the domain and range.

   b. Why is this type of function is called a step function?

5. Let $f(x) = \dfrac{|x|}{x}$ where x can be any real number except 0.

   a. Why is the number 0 excluded from the domain of f?

   b. What is the range of f?

   c. Create a graph of f.

   d. Express f as a piecewise function.

   e. What is the difference between this function and the Heaviside function?

6. Graph the following piecewise functions for the specified domain.

   a. $f(x) = |x + 3|$ for $-5 \leq x \leq 3$

   b. $f(x) = |2x|$ for $-3 \leq x \leq 3$

   c. $f(x) = |2x - 5|$ for $0 \leq x \leq 5$

   d. $f(x) = |3x + 1|$ for $-2 \leq x \leq 2$

   e. $f(x) = |x| + x$ for $-4 \leq x \leq 3$

   f. $f(x) = \begin{cases} x & if\ x \leq 0 \\ x + 1 & if\ x > 0 \end{cases}$

   g. $f(x) = \begin{cases} 2x + 3 & if\ x < -1 \\ 3 - x & if\ x \geq -1 \end{cases}$

7. Write a piecewise function for each graph below.

a.

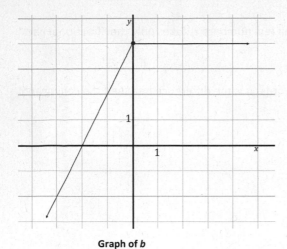

Graph of *b*

b.

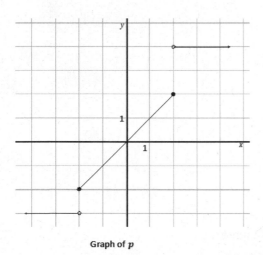

Graph of *p*

c.

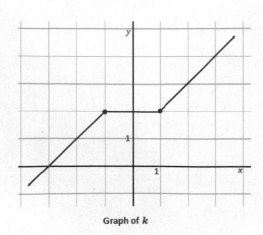

Graph of *k*

d.

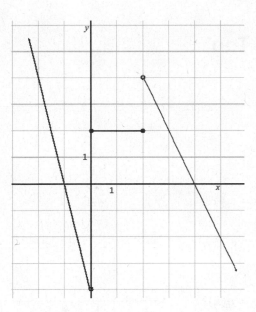

Graph of *h*

Lesson 16: Graphs Can Solve Equations Too

Classwork

Opening Exercise

1. Solve for x in the following equation: $|x + 2| - 3 = 0.5x + 1$

2. Now let $f(x) = |x + 2| - 3$ and $g(x) = 0.5x + 1$. When does $f(x) = g(x)$?
    To answer this, first graph $y = f(x)$ and $y = g(x)$ on the same set of axes.

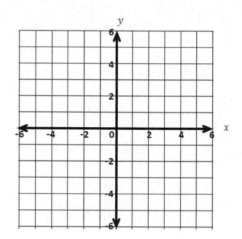

3. When does $f(x) = g(x)$? What is the visual significance of the points where
    $f(x) = g(x)$?

4. Is each intersection point (x, y) an element of the graph f and an element of the graph of g? In other words, do
    the functions f and g really have the same value when $x = 4$? What about when $x = -4$?

Example 1

Solve this equation by graphing two functions on the same Cartesian plane: $|0.5x| - 5 = -|x - 3| + 4$

Let $f(x) = |0.5x| - 5$ and let $g(x) = -|x - 3| + 4$ where x can be any real number.

We are looking for values of x at which the functions f and g have the same output value.

Therefore, we set $y = f(x)$ and $y = g(x)$ so we can plot the graphs on the same coordinate plane:

From the graph, we see that the two intersection points are

_____ and _____.

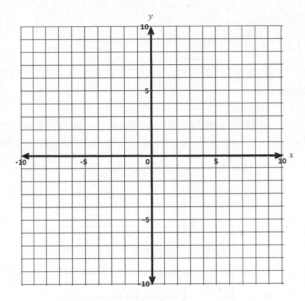

The fact that the graphs of the functions meet at these two points means that when x is _____ both $f(x)$ and $g(x)$

are _____, or when x is _____ both $f(x)$ and $g(x)$ are _____.

Thus, the expressions $|0.5x| - 5$ and $-|x - 3| + 4$ are equal when $x =$ _____ or when $x =$ _____.

Therefore, the solution set to the original equation is _____.

Example 2

Solve this equation graphically: $-|x - 3.5| + 4 = -0.25x - 1$

    a.   Write the two functions represented by each side of the equation.

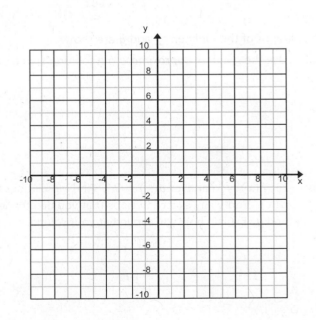

    b.   Graph the functions in an appropriate viewing window.

    c.   Determine the intersection points of the two functions.

d.   Verify that the x-coordinates of the intersection points are solutions to the equation.

Exercises 1-5

Use graphs to find approximate values of the solution set for each equation. Use technology to support your work. Explain how each of your solutions relates to the graph. Check your solutions using the equation.

1. $3 - 2x = |x - 5|$

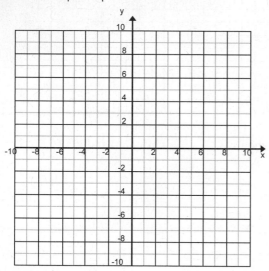

2. $2(1.5)^x = 2 + 1.5x$

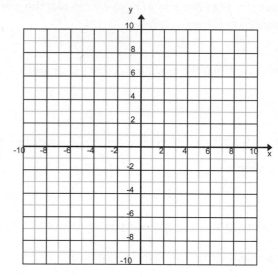

3.   The graphs of the functions f and g are shown.

a.   Use the graph to *approximate* the solution(s) to the equation $f(x) = g(x)$.

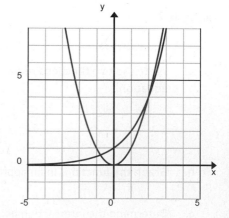

b.   Let $f(x) = x^2$ and let $g(x) = 2^x$. Find *all* solutions to the equation $f(x) = g(x)$. Verify any exact solutions that you determine using the definitions of f and g. Explain how you arrived at your solutions.

4. The graphs of f, a function that involves taking an absolute value, and g, a linear function, are shown to the right. Both functions are defined over all real values for x. Tami concluded that the equation $f(x) = g(x)$ has no solution.

   Do you agree or disagree? Explain your reasoning.

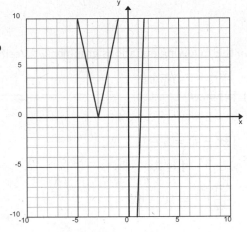

5. The graphs of f (a function that involves taking the absolute value) and g (an exponential function) are shown below. Sharon said the solution set to the equation $f(x) = g(x)$ is exactly $\{-7, 5\}$.

   Do you agree or disagree with Sharon? Explain your reasoning.

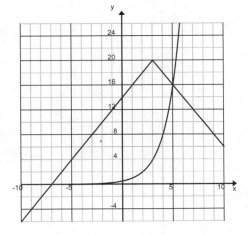

Problem Set

1. Solve the following equations graphically. Verify the solution set using the original equations.

   a. $2x - 4 = \sqrt{x + 5}$

   b. $|x| = x^2$

   c. $x + 2 = x^3 - 2x - 4$

   d. $|3x - 4| = 5 - |x - 2|$

   e. $0.5x^3 - 4 = 3x + 1$

   f. $6\left(\frac{1}{2}\right)^{5x} = 10 - 6x$

In each exercise, the graphs of the functions f and g are shown on the same Cartesian plane. Estimate the solution set to the equation $f(x) = g(x)$. Assume that the graphs of the two functions only intersect at the points shown on the graph.

2.

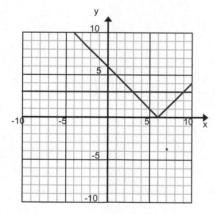

3.

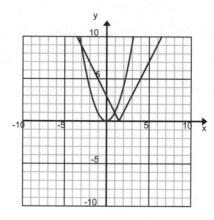

4.

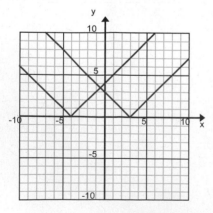

5.

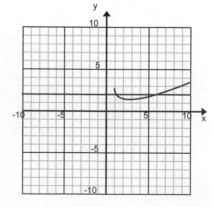

6. The graph below shows Glenn's distance from home as he rode his bicycle to school, which is just down his street. His next-door neighbor Pablo, who lives 100 m closer to the school, leaves his house at the same time as Glenn. He walks at a constant velocity and they both arrive at school at the same time.

    a. Graph a linear function that represents Pablo's distance from Glenn's home as a function of time.

    b. Estimate when the two boys pass each other.

    c. Write piecewise-linear functions to represent each boy's distance and use them to verify your answer to part (b).

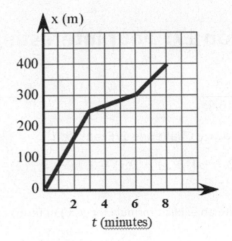

Lesson 17: Four Interesting Transformations of Functions

Classwork

Exploratory Challenge 1/Example 1

Let $f(x) = |x|$, $g(x) = f(x) - 3$, $h(x) = f(x) + 2$ for any real number x.

1. Write an explicit formula for $g(x)$ in terms of $|x|$ (i.e., without using $f(x)$ notation):

2. Write an explicit formula for $h(x)$ in terms of $|x|$ (i.e., without using $f(x)$ notation):

3. Complete the table of values for these functions.

x	$f(x) = |x|$	$g(x) = f(x) - 3$	$h(x) = f(x) + 2$
-3			
-2			
-1			
0			
1			
2			
3			

4. Graph all three equations: $y = f(x)$, $y = f(x) - 3$, and $y = f(x) + 2$.

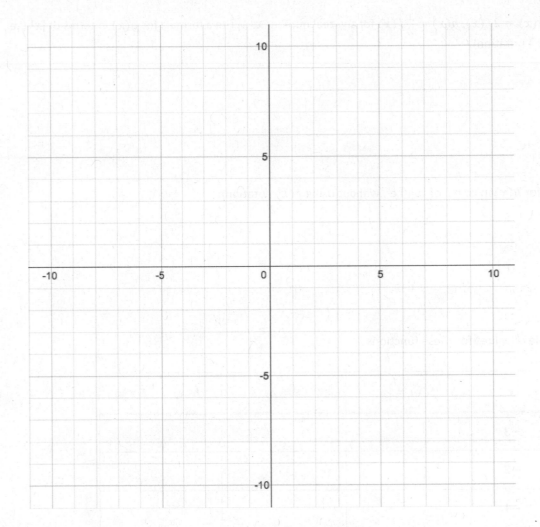

5. What is the relationship between the graph of $y = f(x)$ and the graph of $y = f(x) + k$?

6. How do the values of g and h relate to the values of f?

Exploratory Challenge 2/Example 2

1. Let $f(x) = |x|$, $g(x) = 2f(x)$, $h(x) = \frac{1}{2}f(x)$ for any real number x. Write a formula for $g(x)$ in terms of $|x|$ (i.e., without using $f(x)$ notation):

2. Write a formula for $h(x)$ in terms of $|x|$ (i.e., without using $f(x)$ notation):

3. Complete the table of values for these functions.

x	$f(x) = |x|$	$g(x) = 2f(x)$	$h(x) = \frac{1}{2}f(x)$
-3			
-2			
-1			
0			
1			
2			
3			

4. Graph all three equations: $y = f(x)$, $y = 2f(x)$, and $y = \frac{1}{2}f(x)$.

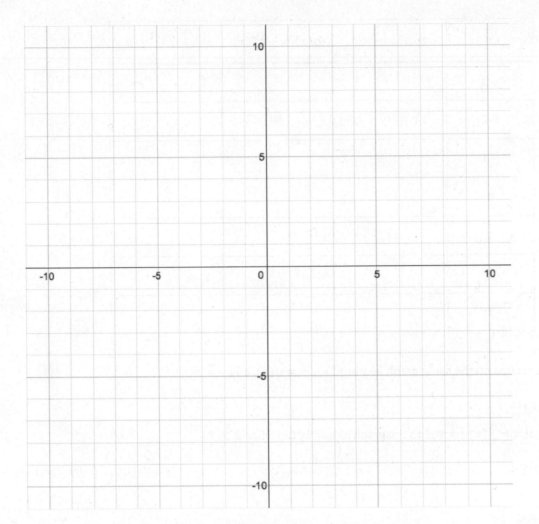

Let $p(x) = -|x|$, $q(x) = -2f(x)$, $r(x) = -\frac{1}{2}f(x)$ for any real number x.

5. Write the formula for $q(x)$ in terms of $|x|$ (i.e., without using $f(x)$ notation):

6. Write the formula for $r(x)$ in terms of $|x|$ (i.e., without using $f(x)$ notation):

7. Complete the table of values for the functions $p(x) = -|x|$, $q(x) = -2f(x)$, $r(x) = -\frac{1}{2}f(x)$.

x	$p(x) = -|x|$	$q(x) = -2f(x)$	$r(x) = -\frac{1}{2}f(x)$
-3			
-2			
-1			
0			
1			
2			
3			

8. Graph all three functions on the same graph as $y = p(x)$, $y = q(x)$, and $y = r(x)$.

9. How is the graph of $y = f(x)$ related to the graph of $y = kf(x)$ when $k > 1$?

10. How is the graph of $y = f(x)$ related to the graph of $y = kf(x)$ when $0 < k < 1$?

11. How do the values of functions p, q, and r relate to the values of functions f, g, and h, respectively? What transformation of the graphs of f, g, and h represents this relationship?

Exercises

1. Make up your own function f by drawing the graph of it on the Cartesian plane below. Label it as the graph of the equation, $y = f(x)$. If $b(x) = f(x) - 4$ and $c(x) = \frac{1}{4}f(x)$ for every real number x, graph the equations $y = b(x)$ and $y = c(x)$ on the same Cartesian plane.

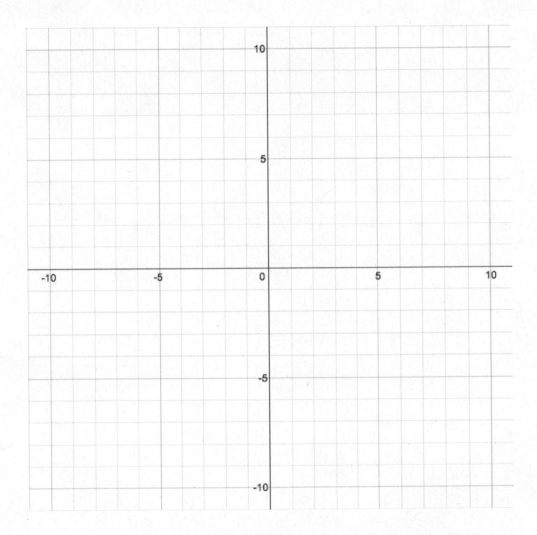

Problem Set

Let $f(x) = |x|$ for every real number x. The graph of $y = f(x)$ is shown below. Describe how the graph for each function below is a transformation of the graph of $y = f(x)$. Then use this same set of axes to graph each function for problems 1–5. Be sure to label each function on your graph (by $y = a(x)$, $y = b(x)$, etc.).

1. $a(x) = |x| + \dfrac{3}{2}$

2. $b(x) = -|x|$

3. $c(x) = 2|x|$

4. $d(x) = \dfrac{1}{3}|x|$

5. $e(x) = |x| - 3$

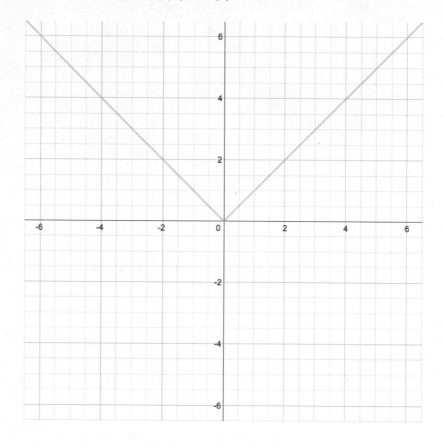

6. Let $r(x) = |x|$ and $t(x) = -2|x| + 1$ for every real number x. The graph of $y = r(x)$ is shown below. Complete the table below to generate output values for the function t; then graph the equation $y = t(x)$ on the same set of axes as the graph of $y = r(x)$.

x	$r(x) = |x|$	$t(x) = -2|x| + 1$
-2		
-1		
0		
1		
2		

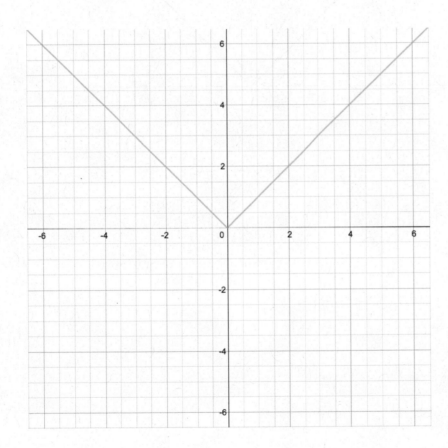

7. Let $f(x) = |x|$ for every real number x. Let m and n be functions found by transforming the graph of $y = f(x)$. Use the graphs of $y = f(x)$, $y = m(x)$ and $y = n(x)$ below to write the functions m and n in terms of the function f. (Hint: What is the k?)

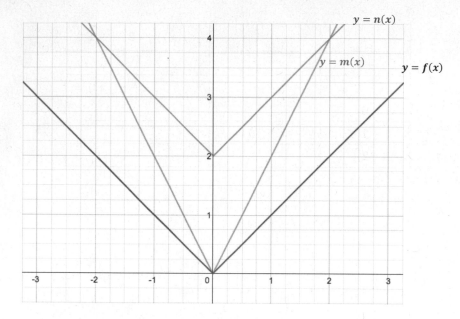

Lesson 18: Four Interesting Transformations of Functions

Classwork

Example 1

Let $f(x) = |x|$, $g(x) = f(x - 3)$, $h(x) = f(x + 2)$ where x can be any real number.

a.   Write the formula for $g(x)$ in terms of $|x|$ (i.e., without using $f(x)$ notation):

b.   Write the formula for $h(x)$ in terms of $|x|$ (i.e., without using $f(x)$ notation):

c.   Complete the table of values for these functions.

x	$f(x) = |x|$	$g(x) =$	$h(x) =$
-3			
-2			
-1			
0			
1			
2			
3			

d.   Graph all three equations: $y = f(x)$, $y = f(x - 3)$, and $y = f(x + 2)$.

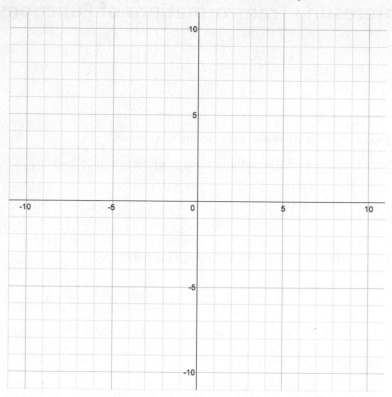

e.   How does the graph of $y = f(x)$ relate to the graph of $y = f(x - 3)$?

f.   How does the graph of $y = f(x)$ relate to the graph of $y = f(x + 2)$?

g.   How does the graph of $y = |x| - 3$ and the graph of $y = |x - 3|$ relate differently to the graph of $y = |x|$?

h.   How do the values of g and h relate to the values of f?

Exercises

1.   Karla and Isamar are disagreeing over which way the graph of the function $g(x) = |x + 3|$ is translated relative to the graph of $f(x) = |x|$. Karla believes the graph of g is "to the right "of the graph of f, Isamar believes the graph is "to the left." Who is correct? Use the coordinates of the vertex of f and g and to support your explanation.

2.   Let $f(x) = |x|$ where x can be any real number. Write a formula for the function whose graph is the transformation of the graph of f given by the instructions below.

   a.   A translation right 5 units.

   b.   A translation down 3 units.

   c.   A vertical scaling (a vertical stretch) with scale factor of 5.

   d.   A translation left 4 units.

   e.   A vertical scaling (a vertical shrink) with scale factor of $\frac{1}{3}$.

3. Write the formula for the function depicted by the graph.

a. $y =$

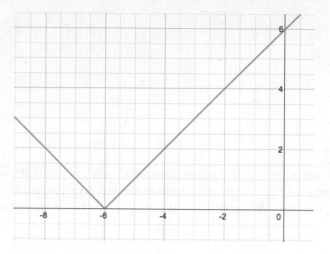

b. $y =$

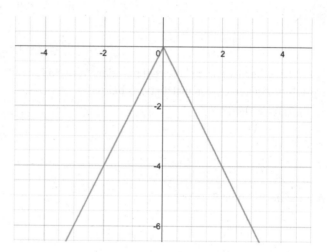

c. $y =$

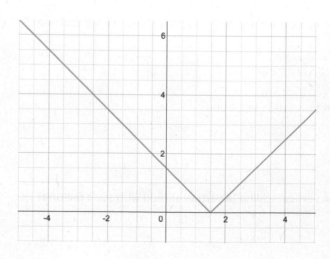

d. $y =$

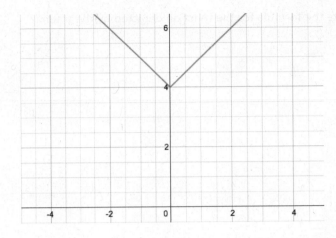

e. $y =$

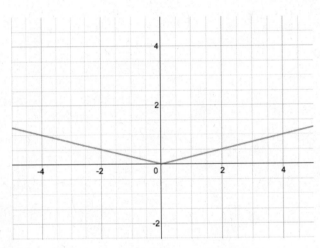

4.   Let $f(x) = |x|$ where x can be any real number. Write a formula for the function whose graph is the described transformation of the graph of f.

   a.   A translation 2 units left and 4 units down.

   b.   A translation 2.5 units right and 1 unit up.

   c.   A vertical scaling with scale factor $\frac{1}{2}$, and then a translation 3 units right.

   d.   A translation 5 units right and a vertical scaling by reflected across the x-axis with vertical scale factor -2.

5. Write the formula for the function depicted by the graph.

    a. $y =$

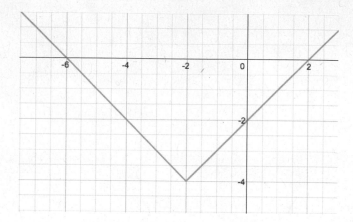

    b. $y =$

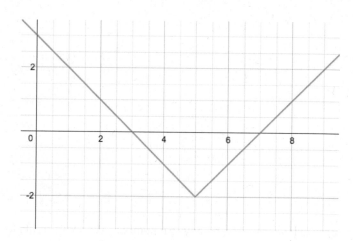

    c. $y =$

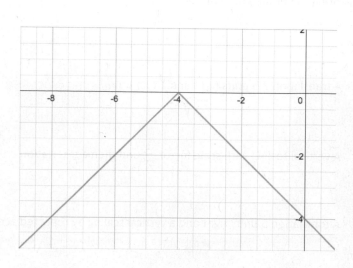

d. $y =$

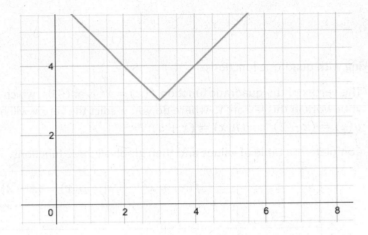

Problem Set

1. Working with quadratic functions.

    a. The vertex of the quadratic function $f(x) = x^2$ is at $(0,0)$, which is the minimum for the graph of f. Based on your work in this lesson, to where do you predict the vertex will be translated for the graphs of $g(x) = (x - 2)^2$ and $h(x) = (x + 3)^2$?

    b. Complete the table of values and then graph all three functions.

x	$f(x) = x^2$	$g(x) = (x - 2)^2$	$h(x) = (x + 3)^2$
-3			
-2			
-1			
0			
1			
2			
3			

2. Let $f(x) = |x - 4|$ for every real number x. The graph of the equation $y = f(x)$ is provided on the Cartesian plane below. Transformations of the graph of $y = f(x)$ are described below. After each description, write the equation for the transformed graph. Then, sketch the graph of the equation you write for part (d).

    a. Translate the graph left 6 units and down 2 units.

    b. Reflect the resulting graph from part (a) across the x-axis.

    c. Scale the resulting graph from part (b) vertically by a scale factor of $\frac{1}{2}$.

    d. Translate the resulting graph from part (c) right 3 units and up 2 units. Graph the resulting equation.

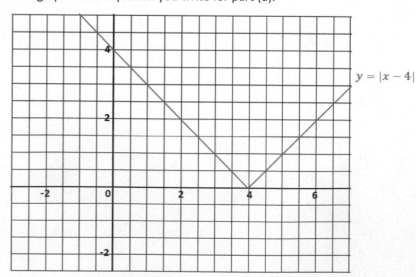

$y = |x - 4|$

3. Let $f(x) = |x|$ for all real numbers x. Write the formula for the function represented by the described transformation of the graph of $y = f(x)$.

    a. First, a vertical stretch with scale factor $\frac{1}{3}$ is performed, then a translation right 3 units, and finally a translation down 1 unit.

    b. First, a vertical stretch with scale factor 3 is performed, then a reflection over the x-axis, then a translation left 4 units, and finally a translation up 5 units.

    c. First, a reflection across the x-axis is performed, then a translation left 4 units, then a translation up 5 units, and finally a vertical stretch with scale factor 3.

    d. Compare your answers to parts (b) and (c). Why are they different?

4. Write the formula for the function depicted by each graph.

    a. $a(x) =$

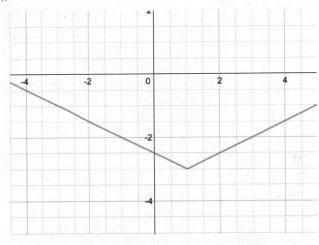

    b. $b(x) =$

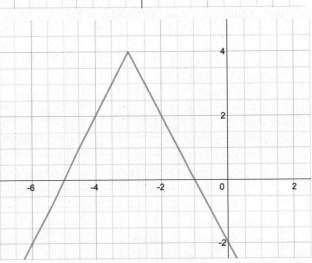

Lesson 19: Four Interesting Transformations of Functions

Classwork

Example 1

Let $f(x) = x^2$ and $g(x) = f(2x)$, where x can be any real number.

   a. Write the formula for g in terms of x^2 (i.e., without using $f(x)$ notation):

   b. Complete the table of values for these functions.

x	$f(x) = x^2$	$g(x) = f(2x)$
−3		
−2		
−1		
0		
1		
2		
3		

   c. Graph both equations: $y = f(x)$ and $y = f(2x)$.

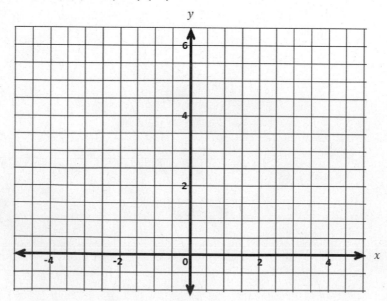

d. How does the graph of $y = g(x)$ relate to the graph of $y = f(x)$?

e. How are the values of f related to the values of g?

Example 2

Let $f(x) = x^2$ and $h(x) = f\left(\frac{1}{2}x\right)$, where x can be any real number.

a. Rewrite the formula for h in terms of x^2 (i.e., without using $f(x)$ notation):

b. Complete the table of values for these functions.

x	$f(x) = x^2$	$h(x) = f\left(\frac{1}{2}x\right)$
-3		
-2		
-1		
0		
1		
2		
3		

c.   Graph both equations: $y = f(x)$ and $y = f\left(\frac{1}{2}x\right)$.

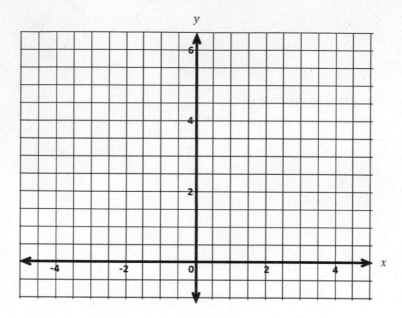

d.   How does the graph of $y = f(x)$ relate to the graph of $y = h(x)$?

e.   How are the values of f related to the values of h?

Exercise 1

Complete the table of values for the given functions.

a.

x	$f(x) = 2^x$	$g(x) = 2^{(2x)}$	$h(x) = 2^{(-x)}$
-2			
-1			
0			
1			
2			

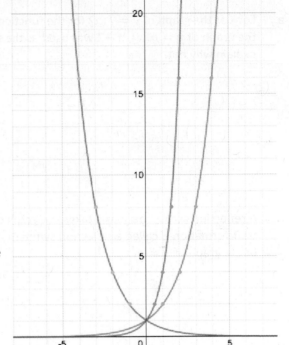

b. Label each of the graphs with the appropriate functions from the table.

c. Describe the transformation that takes the graph of $y = f(x)$ to the graph of $y = g(x)$.

d. Consider $y = f(x)$ and $y = h(x)$. What does negating the input do to the graph of f?

e. Write the formula of an exponential function whose graph would be a horizontal stretch relative to the graph of g.

Example 3

a. Look at the graph of $y = f(x)$ for the function $f(x) = x^2$ in Example 1 again. Would we see a difference in the graph of $y = g(x)$ if -2 was used as the scale factor instead of 2? If so, describe the difference. If not, explain why not.

b. A reflection across the y-axis takes the graph of $y = f(x)$ for the function $f(x) = x^2$ back to itself. Such a transformation is called a reflection symmetry. What is the equation for the graph of the reflection symmetry of the graph of $y = f(x)$?

c. Deriving the answer to the following question is fairly sophisticated; do only if you have time: In Lessons 17 and 18, we used the function $f(x) = |x|$ to examine the graphical effects of transformations of a function. Here in Lesson 19, we use the function $f(x) = x^2$ to examine the graphical effects of transformations of a function. Based on the observations you made while graphing, why would using $f(x) = x^2$ be a better option than using the function $f(x) = |x|$?

Problem Set

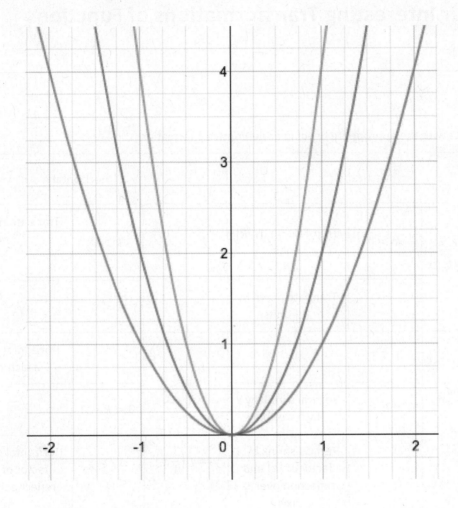

Let $f(x) = x^2$, $g(x) = 2x^2$, and $h(x) = (2x)^2$, where x can be any real number. The graphs above are of the functions $y = f(x)$, $y = g(x)$, and $y = h(x)$.

   a.   Label each graph with the appropriate equation.

   b.   Describe the transformation that takes the graph of $y = f(x)$ to the graph of $y = g(x)$. Use coordinates to illustrate an example of the correspondence.

   c.   Describe the transformation that takes the graph of $y = f(x)$ to the graph of $y = h(x)$. Use coordinates to illustrate an example of the correspondence.

Lesson 20: Four Interesting Transformations of Functions

Opening Exercise

Fill in the blanks of the table with the appropriate heading or descriptive information.

Graph of $y = f(x)$		Vertical			Horizontal	
Translate	$y = f(x) + k$	$k > 0$	Translate up by $|k|$ units		$k > 0$	Translate right by $|k|$ units
			Translate down by $|k|$ units		$k < 0$	
Scale by scale factor k		$k > 1$		$y = f\left(\frac{1}{k}x\right)$		Horizontal stretch by a factor of $|k|$
		$0 < k < 1$	Vertical shrink by a factor of $|k|$		$0 < k < 1$	
			Vertical shrink by a factor of $|k|$ and reflection over x-axis		$-1 < k < 0$	Horizontal shrink by a factor of $|k|$ and reflection across y-axis
		$k < -1$			$k < -1$	Horizontal stretch by a factor of $|k|$ and reflection over y-axis

Example 1

A transformation of the absolute value function, $f(x) = |x - 3|$, is rewritten here as a piecewise function. Describe in words how to graph this piecewise function.

$$f(x) = \begin{cases} -x + 3, & x < 3 \\ x - 3, & x \geq 3 \end{cases}$$

Exercises 1–2

1. Describe how to graph the following piecewise function. Then graph $y = f(x)$ below.

$$f(x) = \begin{cases} -3x - 3, & x \leq -2 \\ 0.5x + 4, & -2 < x < 2 \\ -2x + 9, & x \geq 2 \end{cases}$$

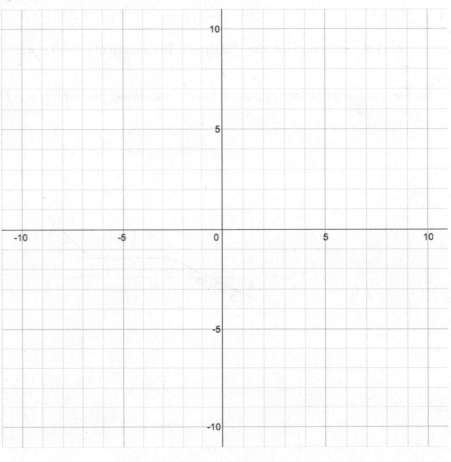

2. Using the graph of f below, write a formula for f as a piecewise function.

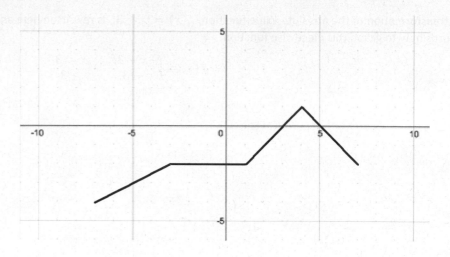

Example 2

The graph $y = f(x)$ of a piecewise function f is shown. The domain of f is $-5 \leq x \leq 5$, and the range is $-1 \leq y \leq 3$.

a. Mark and identify four strategic points helpful in sketching the graph of $y = f(x)$.

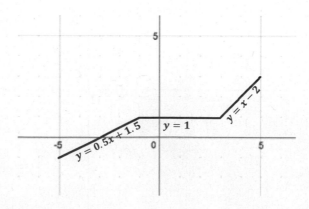

b. Sketch the graph of $y = 2f(x)$ and state the domain and range of the transformed function. How can you use part (a) to help sketch the graph of $y = 2f(x)$?

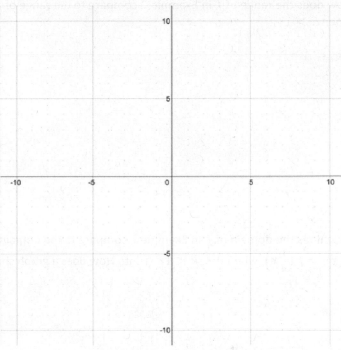

c. A horizontal scaling with scale factor $\frac{1}{2}$ of the graph of $y = f(x)$ is the graph of $y = f(2x)$. Sketch the graph of $y = f(2x)$ and state the domain and range. How can you use the points identified in part (a) to help sketch $y = f(2x)$?

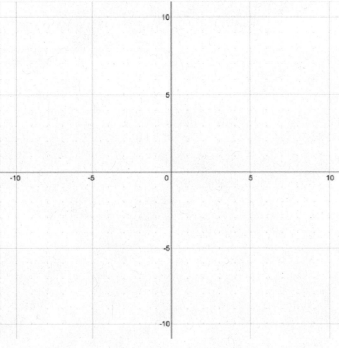

Exercises 3–4

3. How does the range of f in Example 2 compare to the range of a transformed function g, where $g(x) = kf(x)$, when $k > 1$?

4. How does the domain of f in Example 2 compare to the domain of a transformed function g, where $g(x) = f\left(\frac{1}{k}x\right)$, when $0 < k < 1$? (Hint: How does a graph shrink when it is horizontally scaled by a factor k?)

Problem Set

1. Suppose the graph of f is given. Write an equation for each of the following graphs after the graph of f has been transformed as described.

   a. Translate 5 units upward.

   b. Translate 3 units downward.

   c. Translate 2 units right.

   d. Translate 4 units left.

   e. Reflect about the x-axis.

   f. Reflect about the y-axis.

   g. Stretch vertically by a factor of 2.

   h. Shrink vertically by a factor of $\frac{1}{3}$.

   i. Shrink horizontally by a factor of $\frac{1}{3}$.

   j. Stretch horizontally by a factor of 2.

2. Explain how the graphs of the equations below are related to the graph of $y = f(x)$.

   a. $y = 5f(x)$

   b. $y = f(x - 4)$

   c. $y = -2f(x)$

   d. $y = f(3x)$

   e. $y = 2f(x) - 5$

3. The graph of the equation $y = f(x)$ is provided below. For each of the following transformations of the graph, write a formula (in terms of f) for the function that is represented by the transformation of the graph of $y = f(x)$. Then draw the transformed graph of the function on the same set of axes as the graph of $y = f(x)$.

   a. A translation 3 units left and 2 units up.

   b. A vertical stretch by a scale factor of 3.

   c. A horizontal shrink by a scale factor of $\frac{1}{2}$.

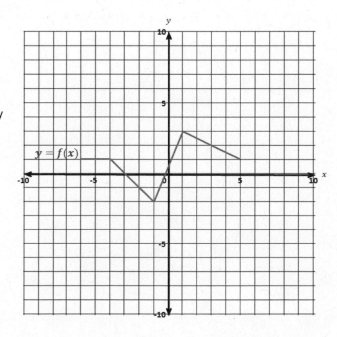

$y = f(x)$

4. Reexamine your work on Example 2 and Exercises 3 and 4 from this lesson. The questions in (b) and (c) of Example 2 asked how the equations $y = 2f(x)$ and $y = f(2x)$ could be graphed with the help of the strategic points found in (a). In this problem, we investigate whether it is possible to determine the graphs of $y = 2f(x)$ and $y = f(2x)$ by working with the piecewise-linear function f directly.

a. Write the function f in Example 2 as a piecewise-linear function.

b. Let $g(x) = 2f(x)$. Use the graph you sketched in Example 2b of $y = 2f(x)$ to write the formula for the function g as a piecewise-linear function.

c. Let $h(x) = f(2x)$. Use the graph you sketched in Example 2c of $y = f(2x)$ to write the formula for the function h as a piecewise-linear function.

d. Compare the piecewise linear functions g and h to the piecewise linear function f. Did the expressions defining each piece change? If so, how? Did the domains of each piece change? If so how?

Lesson 21: Comparing Linear and Exponential Functions Again

Classwork

Opening Exercise

	Linear Model	Exponential Model
General Form		
Meaning of parameters a and b		
Example		
Rule for finding $f(x + 1)$ from $f(x)$		
Table	<table><tr><td></td><td></td></tr><tr><td></td><td></td></tr><tr><td></td><td></td></tr><tr><td></td><td></td></tr></table>	<table><tr><td></td><td></td></tr><tr><td></td><td></td></tr><tr><td></td><td></td></tr><tr><td></td><td></td></tr></table>
Graph		
Story Problem Example		

Exercises

1. For each table below, assume the function f is defined for all real numbers. Calculate $\Delta f = f(x + 1) - f(x)$ in the last column in the tables below and show your work (the symbol Δ in this context means "change in"). What do you notice about Δf? Could the function be linear or exponential? Write a linear or exponential function formula that generates the same input-output pairs as given in the table.

x	$f(x)$	$\Delta f = f(x + 1) - f(x)$
1	−3	
2	1	
3	5	
4	9	
5	13	

x	$f(x)$	$\Delta f = f(x + 1) - f(x)$
0	2	
1	6	
2	18	
3	54	
4	162	

2. Terence looked down the second column of the table and noticed that $\dfrac{3}{1} = \dfrac{9}{3} = \dfrac{27}{3} = \dfrac{81}{27}$. Because of his observation, he claimed that the input-output pairs in this table could be modeled with an exponential function. Explain why Terence is correct or incorrect. If he is correct, write a formula for the exponential function that generates the input-output pairs given in the table. If he is incorrect, determine and write a formula for a function that generates the input-output pairs given in the table.

x	$T(x)$
0	1
1	3
4	9
13	27
40	81

3. A river has an initial minnow population of 40,000 that is growing at 5% per year. Due to environmental conditions, the amount of algae that minnows use for food is decreasing, supporting 1000 fewer minnows each year. Currently, there is enough algae to support 50,000 minnows. Is the minnow population increasing linearly or exponentially? Is the amount of algae decreasing at a linear or exponential rate? In what year will the minnow population exceed the amount of algae available?

4. Using a calculator, Joanna made the following table and then made the following conjecture: $3x$ is always greater than $(1.02)^x$. Is Joanna correct? Explain.

x	$(1.02)^x$	$3x$
1	1.02	3
2	1.0404	6
3	1.0612	9
4	1.0824	12
5	1.1041	15

Lesson Summary

- Suppose that the input-output pairs of a bivariate dataset have the following the property: for every two inputs that are a given difference apart, the difference in their corresponding outputs is constant. Then an appropriate model for that dataset could be a linear function.

- Suppose that the input-output pairs of a bivariate dataset have the following the property: for every two inputs that are a given difference apart, the quotient of their corresponding outputs is constant. Then an appropriate model for that dataset could be an exponential function.

- An increasing exponential function will eventually exceed any linear function. That is, if $f(x) = ab^x$ is an exponential function with $a > 0$ and $b > 1$, and $g(x) = mx + k$ is any linear function, then there is a real number M such that for all $x > M$, then $f(x) > g(x)$. Sometimes this is not apparent in a graph displayed on a graphing calculator; that is because the graphing window does not show enough of the graph to show the sharp rise of the exponential function in contrast with the linear function.

Problem Set

For each table in problems 1–6, classify the data as describing a linear relationship, an exponential growth relationship, an exponential decay relationship, or neither. If the relationship is linear, calculate the constant rate of change (slope), and write a formula for the linear function that models the data. If the function is exponential, calculate the common quotient for input values that are distance 1 apart, and write the formula for the exponential function that models the data. For each linear or exponential function found, graph the equation $y = f(x)$.

1.

x	$f(x)$
1	$\dfrac{1}{2}$
2	$\dfrac{1}{4}$
3	$\dfrac{1}{8}$
4	$\dfrac{1}{16}$
5	$\dfrac{1}{32}$

2.

x	$f(x)$
1	1.4
2	2.5
3	3.6
4	4.7
5	5.8

3.

x	$f(x)$
1	-1
2	0
3	2
4	5
5	9

4.

x	$f(x)$
1	20
2	40
3	80
4	160
5	320

5.

x	$f(x)$
1	-5
2	-12
3	-19
4	-26
5	-33

6.

x	$f(x)$
1	$\frac{1}{2}$
2	$\frac{1}{3}$
3	$\frac{1}{4}$
4	$\frac{1}{5}$
5	$\frac{1}{6}$

7. Here is a variation on a classic riddle: Jayden has a dog-walking business. He has two plans. Plan 1 includes walking a dog once a day for a rate of $5/day. Plan 2 also includes one walk a day, but charges 1 cent for 1 day, 2 cents for 2 days, 4 cents for 3 days, 8 cents for 4 days, and continues to double for each additional day. Mrs. Maroney needs Jayden to walk her dog every day for two weeks. Which plan should she choose? Show the work to justify your answer.

8. Tim deposits money in a Certificate of Deposit account. The balance (in dollars) in his account t years after making the deposit is given by $T(t) = 1,000(1.06)^t$ for $t \geq 0$.

   a. Explain, in terms of the structure of the expression used to define $T(t)$, why Tim's balance can never be $999.

   b. By what percent does the value of $T(t)$ grow each year? Explain by writing a recursive formula for the sequence $T(1), T(2), T(3)$, etc.

   c. By what percentages does the value of T(t) grow every two years? (Hint: Use your recursive formula to write $T(n + 2)$ in terms of $T(n)$.)

9. Your mathematics teacher asks you to sketch a graph of the exponential function $f(x) = \left(\frac{3}{2}\right)^x$ for x, a number between 0 and 40 inclusively, using a scale of 10 units to one inch for both the x- and y-axes.

   a. What are the dimensions in feet of the roll of paper you will need to sketch this graph?

   b. How many more feet of paper would you need to add to the roll in order to graph the function on the interval $0 \leq x \leq 41$?

   c. Find an m so that the linear function $g(x) = mx + 2$ is greater than $f(x)$ for all x such that $0 \leq x \leq 40$, but $f(41) > g(41)$.

Lesson 22: Modeling an Invasive Species Population

Classwork

Mathematical Modeling Exercise

The lionfish is a fish that is native to the western Pacific Ocean. The lionfish began appearing in the western Atlantic Ocean in 1985. This is probably because people bought them as pets and then dumped them in waterways leading to the ocean. Because it has no natural predators in this area, the number of lionfish grew very quickly and now has large populations throughout the Caribbean as well as along the eastern coastline of the United States and the Gulf of Mexico. They have recently been spotted as far north as New York and Rhode Island.

The table below shows the number of new sightings by year reported to NAS (Nonindigenous Aquatic Species), which is a branch of the U.S. Geological Survey Department.

Year	Number of New Sightings	Total Number of Sightings
1985	1	
1992	1	
1995	3	
1996	1	
2000	6	
2001	25	
2002	50	
2003	45	
2004	57	
2005	43	
2006	51	
2007	186	
2008	173	
2009	667	
2010	1,342	

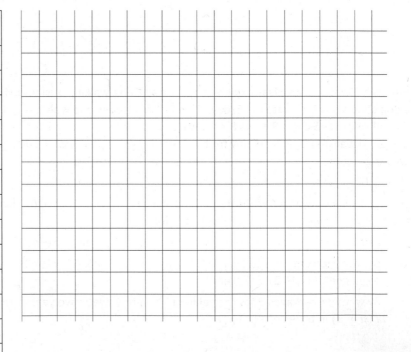

1. Complete the table by recording the total number of sightings for each year.

2. Examine the total number of sightings data. Which model appears to be a better fit for the data, linear or exponential? Explain your reasoning.

3. Make a scatterplot of the year versus the total number of sightings.

4. Based on the scatterplot, either revise your answer from Exercise 2 or explain how the scatterplot supports your answer from Exercise 2.

5. On the scatterplot, draw a smooth curve that best fits the data.

6. From your table, calculate the average rate of change in total number of sightings for each of the following time intervals.

   a. 1995–2000   b. 2000–2005   c. 2005–2010

7. How do the average rates of change help to support your argument of whether a linear or exponential model is better suited for the data?

8. Use the regression feature of a graphing calculator to find an equation that models the number of lionfish sightings each year.

9. Use your model to predict the total number of lionfish sightings by the end of 2013.

10. The actual number of sightings as of July 2013 was 3,776. Does it seem that your model produced an accurate prediction? Explain.

Problem Set

Another invasive species problem: kudzu

Kudzu, a perennial vine native to Southeast Asia, now covers a large area of the southern United States. Kudzu was promoted as a forage crop and an ornamental plant when it was introduced to the U.S. at the Philadelphia Centennial Exposition in 1876. Many southern farmers were encouraged to plant kudzu for erosion control from the mid 1930's to the mid 1950's. In 1953, kudzu was removed from the U.S. Department of Agriculture's list of permissible cover plants due to its recognition as an invasive species.

1. Look up information about kudzu in the United States on Wikipedia and write a short (1–2 pg.) report on the growth of kudzu since its introduction. In your report, choose a function (linear or exponential) to model and graph the growth of kudzu (in hectares) in the U.S. per year over the past half-century or so. Remember to cite your sources!

Lesson 23: Newton's Law of Cooling

Classwork

Opening Exercise

A detective is called to the scene of a crime where a dead body has just been found. He arrives at the scene and measures the temperature of the dead body at 9:30 p.m. After investigating the scene, he declares that the person died 10 hours prior at approximately 11:30 a.m. A crime scene investigator arrives a little later and declares that the detective is wrong. She says that the person died at approximately 6:00 a.m., 15.5 hours prior to the measurement of the body temperature. She claims she can prove it by using Newton's Law of Cooling:

$$T(t) = T_a + (T_0 - T_a) \cdot 2.718^{-kt},$$

where:

$T(t)$ is the temperature of the object after a time of t hours has elapsed,

T_a is the ambient temperature (the temperature of the surroundings), assumed to be constant, not impacted by the cooling process,

T_0 is the initial temperature of the object, and

k is the decay constant.

Using the data collected at the scene, decide who is correct: the detective or the crime scene investigator.

$T_a = 68°F$ (the temperature of the room)

$T_0 = 98.6°F$ (the initial temperature of the body)

$k = 0.1335$ (13.35 % per hour - calculated by the investigator from the data collected)

Temperature of the body at 9:30 p.m. is 72°F.

Mathematical Modeling Exercise

Allow students to work through the exercise in groups. Encourage students to use the language from previous lessons on transformations such as translate, stretch, and shrink. If students ask how k is determined, explain that finding k requires algebra that they will learn Algebra II (logarithms). So, for this exercise, k is given.

Two cups of coffee are poured from the same pot. The initial temperature of the coffee is 180°F and k is 0.2337 (for time in minutes).

1. Suppose both cups are poured at the same time. Cup 1 is left sitting in the room that is 75°F, and cup 2 is taken outside where it is 42°F.

    a. Use Newton's Law of Cooling to write equations for the temperature of each cup of coffee after t minutes has elapsed.

    b. Graph both on the same coordinate plane and compare and contrast the two graphs.

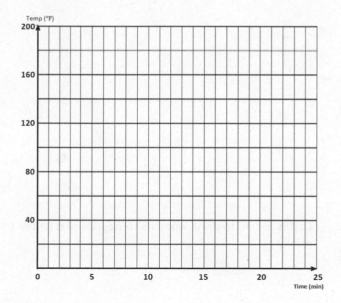

    c. Coffee is safe to drink when its temperature is below 140°F. Estimate how much time elapses before each cup is safe to drink.

2. Suppose both cups are poured at the same time, and both are left sitting in the room that is 75°F. But this time milk is immediately poured into cup 2 cooling it to an initial temperature of 162°F.

    a. Use Newton's Law of Cooling to write equations for the temperature of each cup of coffee after t minutes has elapsed.

    b. Graph both on the same coordinate plane and compare and contrast the two graphs.

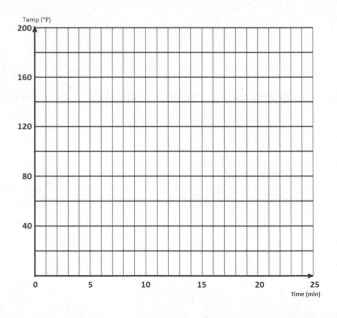

    c. Coffee is safe to drink when its temperature is below 140°F. How much time elapses before each cup is safe to drink?

3. Suppose cup 2 is poured 5 minutes after cup 1 (the pot of coffee is maintained at 180°F over the 5 minutes). Both are left sitting in the room that is 75°F.

    a. Use the equation for cup 1 found in Exercise 1 (a) to write an equation for cup 2.

    b. Graph both on the same coordinate plane and describe how to obtain the graph of cup 2 from the graph of cup 1.

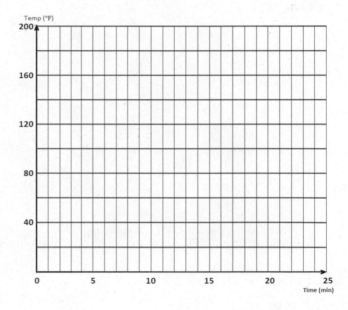

Problem Set

Use the Coffee Cooling demonstration on Wolfram Alpha to write a short report on the questions that follow.
http://demonstrations.wolfram.com/TheCoffeeCoolingProblem/

1. If you want your coffee to become drinkable as quickly as possible, should you add cream immediately after pouring or wait?

2. If you want your coffee to stay warm longer, should you add cream immediately after pouring or wait?

Use results from the demonstration to support your claim.

Lesson 24: Piecewise and Step Functions in Context

Classwork

Opening Exercise

Here are two different parking options in the city.

1-2-3 Parking	Blue Line Parking
$6 for the 1st hr (or part of an hr) $5 for the 2nd hr (or part of an hr) $4 for the each hr (or part of an hr) starting with the 3rd hr	$5 per hour up to 5 hr $4 per hr after that

The cost of a 2.75-hr stay at 1-2-3 Parking would be $6 + $5 + $4 = $15. The cost of a 2.75-hr stay at Blue Line Parking would be $5(2.75) = $13.75.

Which garage costs less for a 5.25-hr stay? Show your work to support your answer.

Exploratory Challenge

Helena works as a summer intern at the Albany International Airport. She is studying the parking rates and various parking options. Her department needs to raise parking revenues by 10% to help address increased operating costs. The parking rates as of 2008 are displayed below. Your class will write piecewise linear functions to model each type of rate and then use those functions to develop a plan to increase parking revenues.

Parking Rates (Effective October 28, 2008)

Short Term Rates
Located on first floor of parking garage and front of the terminal

First Half Hour:	FREE
Second Half Hour:	$2.00
Each Additional Half Hour:	$1.00
Maximum Daily Rate:	$24.00

Long Term Parking Rates
Located behind the parking garage

First Hour:	$2.00
Each Additional Hour:	$1.00
Maximum Daily Rate:	$9.00
Five Days:	$36.00
Seven Days:	$45.00

Garage Parking Rates
Located on floors two, three, four and five of the parking garage

First Hour:	$2.00
Each Additional Hour:	$2.00
Maximum Daily Rate:	$12.00
Five Consecutive Days:	$50.00
Seven Consecutive Days:	$64.00

Economy Remote Lot E - Shuttle to and from Terminal

First Hour:	$1.00
Hourly Rate:	$1.00
Maximum Daily Rate:	$5.00

1. Write a piecewise linear function using step functions that models your group's assigned parking rate. Note: Like in the opening exercise, assume that if the car is there for any part of the next time period, then that period is counted in full (i.e., 3.75 hours is counted as 4 hours, 3.5 days is counted as 4 days, etc.).

Helena collected all the parking tickets from one day during the summer to help her analyze ways to increase parking revenues, and used that data to create the table shown below. The table displays the number of tickets turned in for each time and cost category at the four different parking lots.

Parking Tickets Collected on a Summer Day at the Albany International Airport

Short Term			Long Term			Parking Garage			Economy Remote		
Time on Ticket (hours)	Parking Cost ($)	Number of Tickets	Time on Ticket (hours)	Parking Cost ($)	Number of Tickets	Time on Ticket (hours)	Parking Cost ($)	Number of Tickets	Time on Ticket (hours)	Parking Cost ($)	Number of Tickets
0.5	0	400	1	2	8	1	2	8	1	1	
1	2	600	2	3	20	2	4	12	2	2	
1.5	3	80	3	4	24	3	6	8	3	3	
2	4	64	4	5		4	8	4	4	4	
2.5	5	8	5	6		5	10	0	5	5	
3	6	24	6	7		6	12	16	5 to 24 hrs	5	84
3.5	7	4	7	8	60	6 to 24	12	156	2 days	10	112
4	8		8	9	92	2 days	24	96	3 days	15	64
4.5	9		8 to 24	9	260	3 days	36	40	4 days	20	60
5	10		2 days	18	164	4 days	48	12	5 days	25	72
5.5	11		3 days	27	12	5-6 days	50	8	6 days	30	24
6	12		4 days	36	8	7 days	64	4	7 days	35	76
6.5	13		5 days	36	20				8 days	40	28
7	14		6 days	36	36				9 days	45	8
7.5	15		7 days	45	32				10 days	50	4
8	16	4							14 days	70	8
8.5	17								18 days	90	4
9	18	8							21 days	105	4
9.5	19										
10	20										
10.5	21										
11	22										
11.5	23										
12 to 24	24	8									

For example, there were 600 short term 1-hr tickets charged $2 each. Total revenue for that type of ticket would be $1200.

2. Compute the total revenue generated by your assigned rate using the following parking ticket data.

3. The Albany International Airport wants to increase average daily parking revenue by 10%. Make a recommendation to management of one or more parking rates to change to increase daily parking revenue by 10%. Then use the data Helena collected to show that revenue would increase by 10% if they implement the recommended change.

Problem Set

1. Recall the parking problem from the opening exercise.

    a. Write a piecewise linear function P using step functions that models the cost of parking at 1-2-3 Parking for x hrs.

    b. Write a piecewise linear function B that models the cost of parking at Blue Line parking for x hrs.

    c. Evaluate each function at 2.75 and 5.25 hrs. Do your answers agree with the work in the opening? If not, refine your model.

    d. Is there a time where both models have the same parking cost? Support your reasoning with graphs and/or equations.

    e. Apply your knowledge of transformations to write a new function that would represent the result of a $2 across the board increase in hourly rates at 1-2-3 Parking. (Hint: Draw its graph first and then use the graph to help you determine the step functions and domains.)

2. There was no snow on the ground when it started falling at midnight at a constant rate of 1.5 inches per hour. At 4:00 a.m., it starting falling at a constant rate of 3 in. per hr. and then from 7:00 a.m. to 9:00 a.m., snow was falling at a constant rate of 2 in. per hr. It stopped snowing at 9:00 a.m. (Note—this problem models snow falling by a constant rate during each time period. In reality, the snowfall rate might be very close to constant but is unlikely to be perfectly uniform throughout any given time period.)

    a. Write a piecewise linear function that models the depth of snow as a function of time since midnight.

    b. Create a graph of the function.

    c. When was depth of the snow on the ground 8 inches deep?

    d. How deep was the snow at 9:00 a.m.?

3. If you earned up to $113,700 in 2013 from an employer, you Social Security tax rate was 6.2% of your income. If you earned over $113,700, you pay a fixed amount of $7,049.40.

    a. Write a piecewise linear function to represent the 2013 Social Security taxes for incomes between $0 and $500,000.

    b. How much Social Security tax would someone who made $50,000 owe?

    c. How much money would you have made if you paid $4000 in social security tax in 2013.

    d. What is the meaning of $f(150,000)$? What is the value of $f(150,000)$?

4. The function f gives the cost to ship x lbs. via Fed Ex Standard Overnight Rates to Zone 2 in 2013.

$$f(x) = \begin{cases} 21.50 & 0 < x \le 1 \\ 23.00 & 1 < x \le 2 \\ 24.70 & 2 < x \le 3 \\ 26.60 & 3 < x \le 4 \\ 27.05 & 4 < x \le 5 \\ 28.60 & 5 < x \le 6 \\ 29.50 & 6 < x \le 7 \\ 31.00 & 7 < x \le 8 \\ 32.25 & 8 < x \le 9 \end{cases}$$

   a. How much would it cost to ship a 3 lb. package?

   b. How much would it cost to ship a 7.25 lb. package.

   c. What is the domain and range of f?

   d. Could you use the ceiling function to write this function more concisely? Explain your reasoning.

5. Use the floor or ceiling function and your knowledge of transformations to write a piecewise linear function f whose graph is shown below.

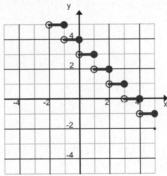

Copy Ready Materials

Name _____ Date_____

Lesson 1: Integer Sequences—Should You Believe in Patterns?

Exit Ticket

1. Consider the sequence given by a "plus 8" pattern: $2, 10, 18, 26, \ldots$. Shae says that the formula for the sequence is $f(n) = 8n + 2$. Marcus tells Shae that she is wrong because the formula for the sequence is $f(n) = 8n - 6$.

   a. Which formula generates the sequence by starting at $n = 1$? At $n = 0$?

   b. Find the 100th term in the sequence.

2. Write a formula for the sequence of cube numbers: $1, 8, 27, 64, \ldots$.

COMMON CORE™

Lesson 1: Integer Sequences—Should You Believe in Patterns?
Date: 9/11/13

© 2013 Common Core, Inc. All rights reserved. commoncore.org

Name _____   Date_____

Lesson 2: Recursive Formulas for Sequences

Exit Ticket

1. Consider the sequence following a "minus 8" pattern: $9, 1, -7, -15, \ldots$
    a. Write an explicit formula for the sequence.

    b. Write a recursive formula for the sequence.

    c. Find the 38th term of the sequence.

2. Consider the sequence given by the formula $a(n + 1) = 5a(n)$ and $a(1) = 2$ for $n \geq 1$.
    a. Explain what the formula means.

    b. List the first 5 terms of the sequence.

Name _____   Date_____

Lesson 3: Arithmetic and Geometric Sequences

Exit Ticket

1. Write the first 3 terms in the following sequences. Identify them as arithmetic or geometric.

    a. $A(n+1) = A(n) - 5$ for $n \geq 1$ and $A(1) = 9$.

    b. $A(n+1) = \frac{1}{2}A(n)$ for $n \geq 1$ and $A(1) = 4$.

    c. $A(n+1) = A(n) \div 10$ for $n \geq 1$ and $A(1) = 10$.

2. Identify each sequence as arithmetic or geometric. Explain your answer, and write an explicit formula for the sequence.

    a. $14, 11, 8, 5, \dots$

    b. $2, 10, 50, 250, \dots$

    c. $-\frac{1}{2}, -\frac{3}{2}, -\frac{5}{2}, -\frac{7}{2}, \dots$

Name _____   Date_____

Lesson 4: Why do Banks Pay YOU to Provide Their Services?

Exit Ticket

A youth group has a yard sale to raise money for a charity. The group earns $800 but decided to put its money in the bank for a while. Calculate the amount of money the group will have if:

a. Cool Bank pays simple interest at a rate of 4% and the youth group leaves the money in for 3 years.

b. Hot Bank pays compound interest at a rate of 3% and the youth group leaves the money in for 5 years.

c. If the youth group needs the money quickly, which is the better choice? Why?

Name _____   Date_____

Lesson 5: The Power of Exponential Growth

Exit Ticket

Chain emails are emails with a message suggesting you will have good luck if you forward the email on to others. Suppose a student started a chain email by sending the message to 3 friends and asking those friends to each send the same email to 3 more friends exactly 1 day after they received it.

    a.   Write an explicit formula for the sequence that models the number of people who will receive the email on the nth day. (Let the first day be the day the original email was sent.) Assume everyone who receives the email follows the directions.

    b.   Which day will be the first day that the number of people receiving the email exceeds 100?

Name _____   Date_____

Lesson 6: Exponential Growth—U.S. Population and World Population

Exit Ticket

Do the examples below require a linear or exponential growth model? State whether each example is linear or exponential, and write an explicit formula for the sequence that models the growth for each case. Include a description of the variables you use.

1.   A savings account accumulates no interest but receives a deposit of $825 per month.

2.   The value of a house increases by 1.5% per year.

3.   Every year, the alligator population is $\frac{9}{7}$ of the previous year's population.

4.   The temperature increases by 2° every 30 minutes from 8: 00 a.m. to 3: 30 p.m. each day for the month of July.

5.   Every 240 minutes, $\frac{1}{3}$ of the rodent population dies.

Name _____   Date_____

Lesson 7: Exponential Decay

Exit Ticket

A huge ping-pong tournament is held in Beijing, with 65,536 participants at the start of the tournament. Each round of the tournament eliminates half the participants.

    a.   If $p(r)$ represents the number of participants remaining after r rounds of play, write a formula to model the number of participants remaining.

    b.   Use your model to determine how many participants remain after 10 rounds of play.

    c.   How many rounds of play will it take to determine the champion ping-pong player?

Name _____   Date_____

Lesson 8: Why Stay With Whole Numbers?

Exit Ticket

Recall that an odd number is a number that is one more than or one less than twice an integer. Consider the sequence formed by the odd numbers $\{1, 3, 5, 7, \dots\}$.

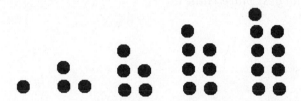

1.   Find a formula for $O(n)$, the nth odd number starting with $n = 1$?

2.   Write a convincing argument that 121 is an odd number.

3.   What is the meaning of $O(17)$?

COMMON CORE™

Lesson 8: Why Stay With Whole Numbers?
Date: 9/11/13

© 2013 Common Core, Inc. All rights reserved. commoncore.org

Name _____   Date_____

Lesson 9: Representing, Naming, and Evaluating Functions

Exit Ticket

1. Given f as described below.

$$f: \{whole\ numbers\} \rightarrow \{whole\ numbers\}$$
Assign each whole number to its largest place value digit.

For example, $f(4) = 4$, $f(14) = 4$, and $f(194) = 9$.

a. What is the domain and range of f?

b. What is $f(257)$?

c. What is $f(0)$?

d. What is $f(999)$?

e. Find a value of x that makes the equation $f(x) = 7$ a true statement.

2. Is the correspondence described below a function? Explain your reasoning.

$$M: \{women\} \rightarrow \{people\}$$
Assign each woman their child.

Name _____   Date_____

Lesson 10: Representing, Naming, and Evaluating Functions

Exit Ticket

1. Let $f(x) = 4(3)^x$. Complete the table shown below.

x	-1	0	1	2	3
$f(x)$					

2. Jenna knits scarves and then sells them on Etsy, an online marketplace. Let $C(x) = 4x + 20$ represent the cost C in dollars to produce from 0 to 6 scarves.

a.   Create a table to show the relationship between the number of scarves x and the cost C.

b.   What are the domain and range of C?

c.   What is the meaning of $C(3)$?

d.   What is the meaning of the solution to the equation $C(x) = 40$?

Name _____   Date_____

Lesson 11: The Graph of a Function

Exit Ticket

1. Perform the instructions for the following programming code as if *you were a computer and your paper was the computer screen*.

    ```
    Declare x integer
    Let f(x) = 2x + 1
    Initialize G as {}
    For all x from −3 to 2
            Append (x, f(x)) to G
    Next x
    Plot G
    ```

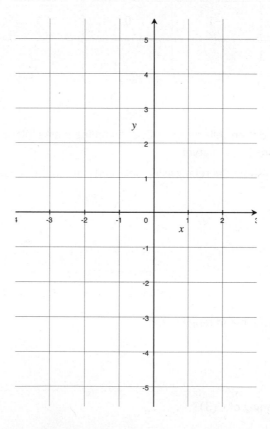

2. Write three or four sentences describing in words how the thought code works.

Name _____   Date_____

Lesson 12: The Graph of the Equation $y = f(x)$

Exit Ticket

1. Perform the instructions in the following programming code as if *you were a computer and your paper was the computer screen*:

```
Declare x integer
For all x from 2 to 7
    If x + 2 = 7 then
        Print True
    else
        Print False
    Endif
Next x
```

2. Let $f(x) = -\frac{1}{2}x + 2$ for x in the domain $0 \le x \le 2$.

   a. Write out in words the meaning of the set notation:

   $$\{(x, y) \mid 0 \le x \le 2 \text{ and } y = f(x)\}.$$

   b. Sketch the graph of $y = f(x)$.

   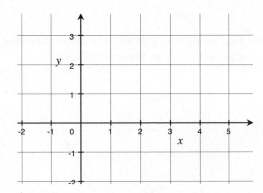

Name _____   Date_____

Lesson 13: Interpreting Graphs of Functions

Exit Ticket

1. Estimate the time intervals when mean energy use is decreasing on an average summer day. Why would power usage be decreasing during those time intervals?

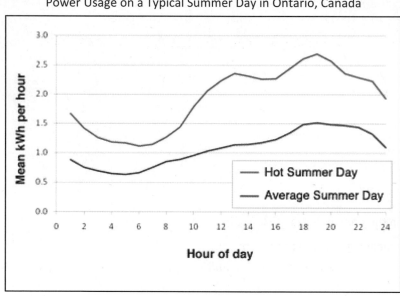

Source: National Resource Council Canada, 2011

2. The hot summer day energy use changes from decreasing to increasing and from increasing to decreasing more frequently than it does on an average summer day. Why do you think this occurs?

Name _____   Date_____

Lesson 14: Linear and Exponential Models—Comparing Growth Rates

Exit Ticket

A big company settles its new headquarters in a small city. The city council plans road construction based on traffic increasing at a linear rate, but based on the company's massive expansion, traffic is really increasing exponentially.

What will be the repercussions of the city council's current plans? Include what you know about linear and exponential growth in your discussion.

Name _____   Date _____

1. The diagram below shows how tables and chairs are arranged in the school cafeteria. One table can seat 4 people, and tables can be pushed together. When two tables are pushed together, 6 people can sit around the table.

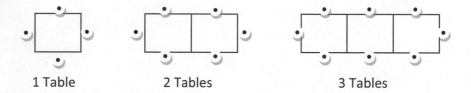

    1 Table   2 Tables   3 Tables

    a. Complete this table to show the relationship between the number of tables, n, and the number of students, S, that can be seated around the table.

n (tables)						
S (students)						

    b. If we made a sequence where the first term of the sequence was the number of students that can fit at 1 table, the 2nd term where the number that could fit at 2 tables, etc, would the sequence be arithmetic, geometric, or neither? Explain your reasoning.

    c. Create an explicit formula for a sequence that models this situation. Use $n = 1$ as the first term, representing how many students can sit at 1 table. How do the constants in your formula relate to the situation?

    d. Using this seating arrangement, how many students could fit around 15 tables pushed together in a row?

The cafeteria needs to provide seating for 189 students. They can fit up to 15 rows of tables in the cafeteria. Each row can contain at most 9 tables but could contain less than that. The tables on each row must be pushed together. Students will still be seated around the tables as described earlier.

e. If they use exactly 9 tables pushed together to make each row, how many rows will they need to seat 189 students, and how many tables will they have used to make those rows?

f. Is it possible to seat the 189 students with fewer total tables? If so, what is the fewest number of tables needed? How many tables would be used in each row? (Remember that the tables on each row must be pushed together.) Explain your thinking.

2. Sydney was studying the following functions:

$$f(x) = 2x + 4 \text{ and } g(x) = 2(2^x) + 4$$

She said that linear functions and exponential functions are basically the same. She made her statement based on plotting points at $x = 0$ and $x = 1$ and graphing the functions.

Help Sydney understand the difference between linear functions and exponential functions by comparing and constrasting f and g. Support your answer with a written explanation that includes use of the average rate of change and supporting tables and/or graphs of these functions.

3. Dots can be arranged in rectangular shapes like the one shown below.

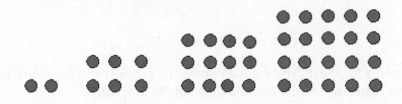

Shape 1   Shape 2   Shape 3   Shape 4 . . . . .

a. Assuming the trend continues, draw the next three shapes in this particular sequence of rectangles. How many dots are in each of the shapes you drew?

The numbers that represent the number of dots in this sequence of rectangular shapes are called rectangular numbers. For example, 2 is the first rectangular number and 6 is the 2nd rectangular number.

b. What is the 50th rectangular number? Explain how you arrived at your answer.

c. Write a recursive formula for the rectangular numbers.

d. Write an explicit formula for the rectangular numbers.

e. Could an explicit formula for the nth rectangular number be considered a function? Explain why or why not. If yes, what would be the domain and range of the function?

4. Stephen is assigning parts for the school musical.

a. Suppose there are 20 students participating, and he has 20 roles available. If each of the 20 students will be assigned to exactly one role in the play, and each role will be played by only one student, is the assignment of the roles to the students in this way certain to be an example of a function? Explain why or why not. If yes, state the domain and range of the function.

The school musical also has a pit orchestra.

b. Suppose there are 10 instrumental parts but only 7 musicians in the orchestra. The conductor assigns an instrumental part to each musician. Some musicians will have to cover two instrumental parts, but no two musicians will have the same instrumental part. If the instrumental parts are the domain and the musicians are the range, is the assignment of instrumental parts to musicians as described sure to be an example of a function? Explain why or why not. If so, what would be the meaning of $A(Piano) = Scott$?

c. Suppose there are 10 instrumental parts but 13 musicians in the orchestra. The conductor assigns an instrumental part to each musician. Some instrumental parts will have two musicians assigned so that all the musicians have instrumental parts. When two musicians are assigned to one part, they alternate who plays at each performance of the play. If the instrumental parts are the domain, and the musicians are the range, is the assignment of instrumental parts to musicians as described sure to be an example of a function? Explain why or why not. If so, what would be the meaning of $A(Piano) = Scott$?

5. The population of a remote island has been experiencing a decline since the year 1950. Scientists used census data from 1950 and 1970 to model the declining population. In 1950 the population was 2350. In 1962 the population was 1270. They chose an exponential decay model and arrived at the function: $p(x) = 2350(0.95)^x, x \geq 0$, where x is the number of years since 1950. The graph of this function is given below.

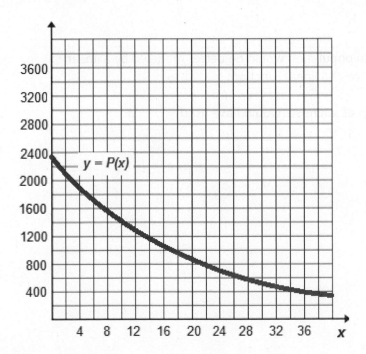

a. What is the y-intercept of the graph? Interpret its meaning in the context of the problem.

b. Over what intervals is the function increasing? What does your answer mean within the context of the problem?

c. Over what intervals is the function decreasing? What does your answer mean within the context of the problem?

Another group of scientists argues that the decline in population would be better modeled by a linear function. They use the same two data points to arrive at a linear function.

d. Write the linear function that this second group of scientists would have used.

e. What is an appropriate domain for the function? Explain your choice within the context of the problem.

f. Graph the function on the coordinate plane.

g. What is the x-intercept of the function? Interpret its meaning in the context of the problem.

Name _____   Date_____

Lesson 15: Piecewise Functions

Exit Ticket

Each graph shown below represents the solution set to a two-variable equation.

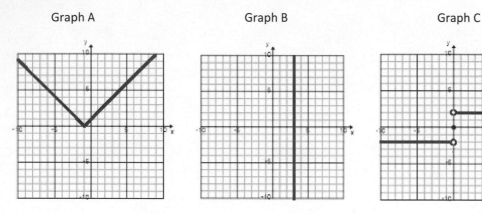

Graph A   Graph B   Graph C

1.   Which of these graphs could be represented by a function? Explain your reasoning.

2.   For each one that can be represented by a function, define a piecewise function whose graph would be identical to the solution set shown.

COMMON
CORE™

Lesson 15:
Date:

Piecewise Functions
9/12/13

Name _____   Date_____

Lesson 16: Graphs Can Solve Equations Too

Exit Ticket

1. How do intersection points of the graphs of two functions f and g relate of the solution to an equation in the form $f(x) = g(x)$?

2. What are some benefits of solving equations graphically? What are some limitations?

Name _____   Date_____

Lesson 17: Four Interesting Transformations of Functions

Exit Ticket

Let $p(x) = |x|$ for every real number x. The graph of $y = p(x)$ is shown below.

1.   Let $q(x) = -\frac{1}{2}|x|$ for every real number x. Describe how to obtain the graph of $y = q(x)$ from the graph of $y = p(x)$. Sketch the graph of $y = q(x)$ on the same set of axes as the graph of $y = p(x)$.

2.   Let $r(x) = |x| - 1$ for every real number x. Describe how to obtain the graph of $y = r(x)$ from the graph of $y = p(x)$. Sketch the graph of $y = r(x)$ on the same set of axes as the graphs of $y = p(x)$ and $y = q(x)$.

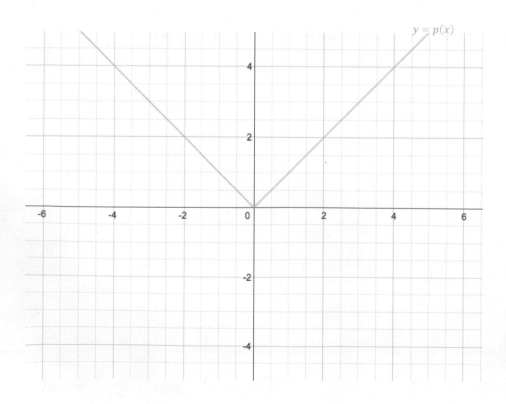

Name _____   Date_____

Lesson 18: Four Interesting Transformations of Functions

Exit Ticket

Write the formula for the functions depicted by the graphs below:

a. $f(x) =$ _____

b. $g(x) =$ _____

c. $h(x) =$ _____

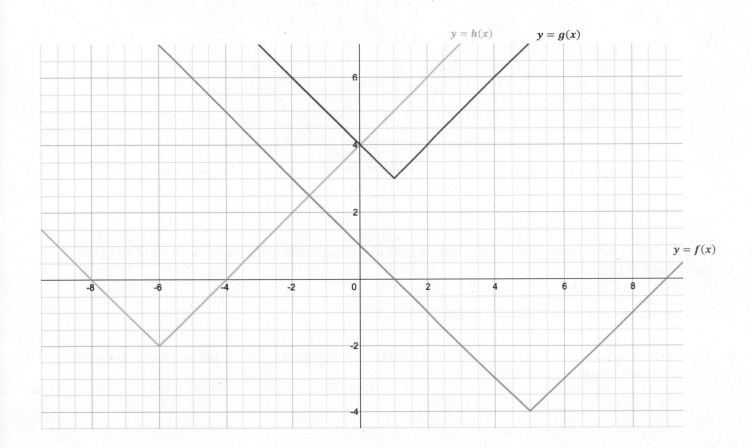

Name _____   Date_____

Lesson 19: Four Interesting Transformations of Functions

Exit Ticket

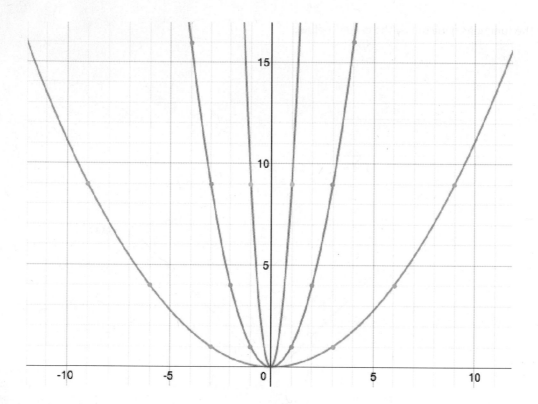

Let $f(x) = x^2$, $g(x) = (3x)^2$, and $h(x) = \left(\frac{1}{3}x\right)^2$, where x can be any real number. The graphs above are of $y = f(x)$, $y = g(x)$, and $y = h(x)$.

1. Label each graph with the appropriate equation.

2. Describe the transformation that takes the graph of $y = f(x)$ to the graph of $y = g(x)$. Use coordinates of each to illustrate an example of the correspondence.

3. Describe the transformation that takes the graph of $y = f(x)$ to the graph of $y = h(x)$. Use coordinates to illustrate an example of the correspondence.

Name _____   Date_____

Lesson 20: Four Interesting Transformations of Functions

Exit Ticket

The graph of a piecewise function f is shown below.

Let $p(x) = f(x - 2)$, $q(x) = \frac{1}{2}f(x - 2)$, and $r(x) = \frac{1}{2}f(x - 2) + 3$.

Graph $y = p(x)$, $y = q(x)$, and $y = r(x)$ on the same set of axes as the graph of $y = f(x)$.

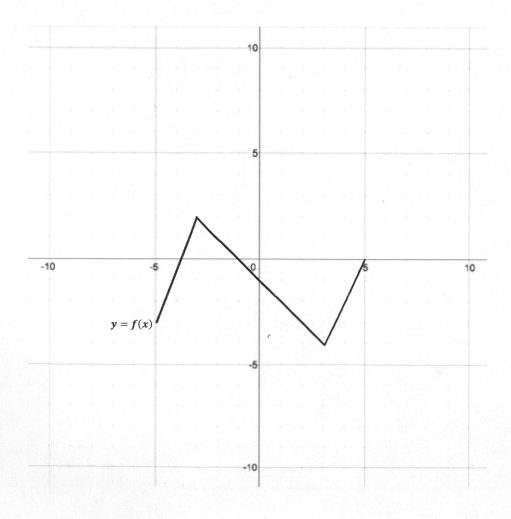

Name _____   Date_____

Lesson 21: Comparing Linear and Exponential Functions Again

Exit Ticket

Here is a classic riddle: Mr. Smith has an apple orchard. He hires his daughter, Lucy, to pick apples and offers her two payment options.

      Option A: $1.50 per bushel of apples picked.

      Option B: 1 *cent* for picking one bushel, 3 *cents* for picking two bushels, 9 *cents* for picking three bushels, and so on, with the amount of money tripling for each additional bushel picked.

a.   Write a function to model each option.

b.   If Lucy picks *six* bushels of apples, which option should she choose?

c.   If Lucy picks 12 bushels of apples, which option should she choose?

d.   How many bushels of apples does Lucy need to pick to make option B better for her than option A?

Name _____ Date_____

Lesson 22: Modeling an Invasive Species Population

Exit Ticket

1. For the equation found in Exercise 8, explain the parameters of the equation within the context of the problem.

2. Given each of the following, describe what features in the data or graph make it apparent that an exponential model would be more suitable than a linear model?

   a. The table of data.

   b. The scatterplot.

   c. The average rates of change found in question 6.

3. Use your equation from Exercise 8 to predict the number of lionfish sightings by year 2020. Is this prediction accurate? Explain.

Name _____   Date_____

Lesson 23: Newton's Law of Cooling

Shown below is the graph of cup 1 from the exercise completed in class. For each scenario, sketch a graph of cup 2 on the same coordinate plane.

1. Cup 2 is poured 10 minutes after cup 1 (the pot of coffee is maintained at 180°F over the 10 minutes).

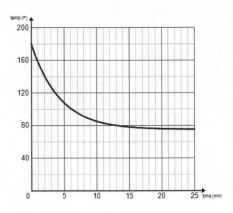

2. Cup 2 is immediately taken outside where the temperature is 90°F.

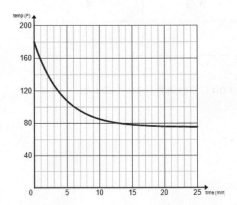

Name _____   Date_____

Lesson 24: Piecewise and Step Functions in Context

Exit Ticket

1.   Use the graph to complete the table.

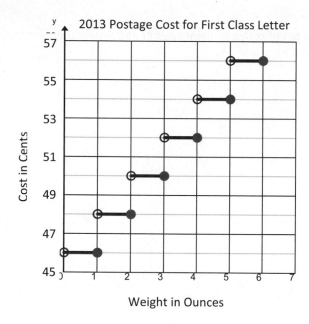

Weight in ounces, x	2	2.2	3	3.5	4
Cost of postage, $C(x)$					

2.   Write a formula involving step functions that represents the cost of postage based on the graph shown above.

3.   It cost Trina $0.54 to mail her letter, how many ounces did it weigh?

Name _____   Date _____

1. Given $h(x) = |x + 2| - 3$ and $g(x) = -|x| + 4$.

   a. Describe how to obtain the graph of g from the graph of $a(x) = |x|$ using transformations.

   b. Describe how to obtain the graph of h from the graph of $a(x) = |x|$ using transformations.

   c. Sketch the graphs of $h(x)$ and $g(x)$ on the same coordinate plane.

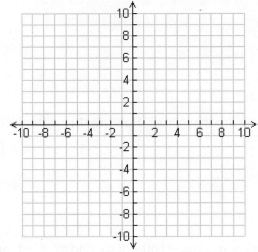

   d. Use your graphs to estimate the solutions to the equation:
   $$|x + 2| - 3 = -|x| + 4$$

   Explain how you got your answer.

   e. Were your estimations you made in part (d) correct? If yes, explain how you know. If not explain why not.

2. Let f and g be the functions given by $f(x) = x^2$ and $g(x) = x|x|$.

   a. Find $f\left(\frac{1}{3}\right)$, $g(4)$, and $g\left(-\sqrt{3}\right)$.

   b. What is the domain of f?

   c. What is the range of g?

   d. Evaluate $f(-67) + g(-67)$.

   e. Compare and contrast f and g. How are they alike? How are they different?

   f. Is there a value of x, such that $f(x) + g(x) = -100$? If so, find x. If not, explain why no such value exists.

   g. Is there a value of x such that $(x) + g(x) = 50$? If so, find x. If not, explain why no such value exists.

3. A boy bought 6 guppies at the beginning of the month. One month later the number of guppies in his tank had doubled. His guppy population continued to grow in this same manner. His sister bought some tetras at the same time. The table below shows the number of tetras, t, after n months have passed since they bought the fish.

n, months	0	1	2	3
t, tetras	8	16	24	32

a. Create a function g to model the growth of the boy's guppy population, where $g(n)$ is the number of guppies at the beginning of each month, and n is the number of months that have passed since he bought the 6 guppies. What is a reasonable domain for g in this situation?

b. How many guppies will there be one year after he bought the 6 guppies?

c. Create an equation that could be solved to determine how many months after he bought the guppies there will be 100 guppies.

d. Use graphs or tables to approximate a solution to the equation from part (c). Explain how you arrived at your estimate.

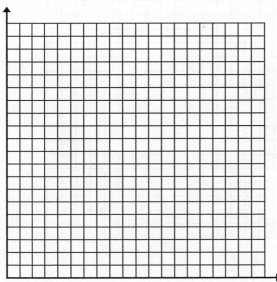

e. Create a function, t, to model the growth of the sister's tetra population, where $t(n)$ is the number of tetras after n months have passed since she bought the tetras.

f. Compare the growth of the sister's tetra population to the growth of the guppy population. Include a comparison of the average rate of change for the functions that model each population's growth over time.

g. Use graphs to estimate the number of months that will have passed when the population of guppies and tetras will be the same.

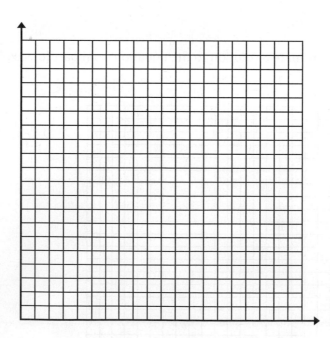

h. Use graphs or tables to explain why the guppy population will eventually exceed the tetra population even though there were more tetras to start with.

i. Write the function $g(n)$ in such a way that the percent increase in the number of fish per month can be identified. Circle or underline the expression representing percent increase in number of fish per month.

4. Regard the solid dark equilateral triangle as figure 0. Then, the first figure in this sequence is the one composed of three dark triangles, the second figure is the one composed of nine dark triangles, and so on.

Figure 0

Figure 1

Figure 2

Figure 3

Figure 4

a. How many dark triangles are in each figure? Make a table to show this data.

n (Figure Number)					
T (# of dark triangles)					

b. Describe in words how, given the number of dark triangles in a figure, to determine the number of dark triangles in the next figure.

c. Create a function that models this sequence. What is the domain of this function?

d. Suppose the area of the solid dark triangle in Figure 0 is 1 square meter. The areas of one dark triangle in each figure form a sequence. Create an explicit formula that gives the area of just one of the dark triangles in the nth figure in the sequence?

e. The sum of the areas of all the dark triangles in Figure 0 is 1 m^2; there is only one triangle in this case. The sum of the areas of <u>all</u> the dark triangles in Figure 1 is $\frac{3}{4}$ m^2. What is the sum of the areas of <u>all</u> the dark triangles in the nth figure in the sequence? Is this total area increasing or decreasing as n increases?

f. Let $P(n)$ be the sum of the perimeters of the <u>all</u> dark triangles in the nth figure in the sequence of figures. There is a real number k so that:

$$P(n+1) = kP(n)$$

is true for each positive whole number n. What is the value of k?

5. The graph of a piecewise function f is shown to the right. The domain of f is $-3 \leq x \leq 3$.

    a. Create an algebraic representation for f. Assume that the graph of f is composed of straight line segments.

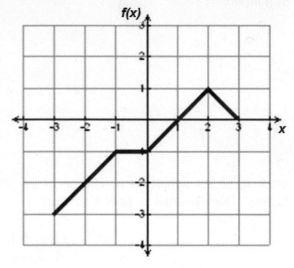

    b. Sketch the graph of $y = 2f(x)$ and state the domain and range.

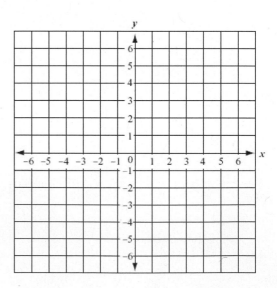

c.   Sketch the graph of $y = f(2x)$ and state the domain and range.

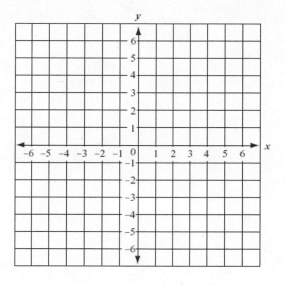

d.   How does the range of $y = f(x)$ compare to the range of $y = kf(x)$, where $k > 1$?

e.   How does the domain of $y = f(x)$ compare to the domain of $y = f(kx)$, where $k > 1$?